SCALE MODEL AIRCRAFT
FOR RADIO CONTROL

Argus Books Limited
Model & Allied Publications,
Wolsey House,
Wolsey Road,
Hemel Hempstead,
Hertfordshire, HP2 4SS
England

ISBN 0 85242 810 3

Phototypesetting by M & G Studios Ltd., London NW 10
Repro by Tenreck Ltd., London NW 10

Printed and bound by R. J. Acford, Chichester.

Scale
Model Aircraft
for
Radio Control

DAVID BODDINGTON

ARGUS BOOKS LIMITED

Contents

Preface

My first ever flying model project was a small rubber powered scale *Hurricane* – entirely the wrong subject and, needless to say, it didn't fly. Despite the lack of success it fired me with my lifelong enthusiasm for flying scale models. Although for many years the models were of the freeflight or control line type, the advent of radio control opened up the possibilities of controlling a model in a scale-like manner, and in all three dimensions. I derive great pleasure from all aspects of radio control flying – general sports models, pylon racing, flying boats, etc. etc. – but scale is an ever-recurring theme. Competition-standard scale models require a great deal of time, in addition to skill and practice, to achieve success and I seem always to have too many projects planned to spend overmuch time on one example. For me, the pleasure and satisfaction comes from designing, building and, hopefully, seeing the model fly in a similar fashion to its full size counterpart. To detail a model to the 'Nth' degree can be highly satisfying but, at the time that this should be done, I'm already, mentally, working on the next model. I am fortunate enough to have my hobby as my work – not only in writing articles and books, and manufacturing kits but also in designing models for filming. This latter 'work' is not only enjoyable, it is also highly demanding and rewarding.

In this book, I have tried to cover most aspects of radio control scale model designing, building and flying. It would be the height of arrogance for me to suggest that the thinking and methods are entirely from my own experiences. Most of it has come from talking to other modellers, looking at their models and reading about them. Few modellers are unwilling to share in their experiences and give away their 'secrets' – even the top competition modellers will assist their fellow competitors although they may lose a competition as a result of this aid. To those modellers from whom I have borrowed, whose brains I have picked, or from whom I have generally assimilated knowledge, knowingly or unknowingly, my sincere thanks. Some I have mentioned by name, but in cases where, through my faulty memory, I have forgotten the source I offer my apologies.

My thanks also to Model and Allied Publications for their assistance in producing the book, and to my wife, not only for suffering the hours and hours spent drawing, modelling and flying – not to mention the constant wood chippings, oil and glue on the carpet – but for understanding.

David Boddington
Wellingborough 1983

Chapter 1

Introduction

"The sky at 30,000 feet was deep azure blue and in the voiceless silence it seemed impossible that war could be raging below. My *Spitfire* seemed to be a part of me and I a natural extension of its controls; we were as one and moved in harmony. My reverie was broken as a brief bright flash reflected in my overhead rear view mirror. In the split second of this happening I was fully alert and the adrenalin had started to pump through my body. Without changing the attitude of my *Spitfire* my eyes stayed riveted on to the mirror and slowly the shape of an aircraft, still far away, came into focus. As it began to gain on me the rounded shape of the cowling and familiar square lines of the FockeWulfe 190 became all too obvious. Now was the time to stay cool: to break away now would offer an all too easy target for the adversary. With my mouth beginning to dry, and the cool sweat forming on my forehead and in my oxygen mask, I forced myself to hold on the same course and airspeed. Slowly – it seemed like hours – the F.W. loomed larger in the mirror, until, at the moment I anticipated the pilot would open fire, I pulled the *Spitfire* hard round to the left. As the turn tightened I felt myself being pushed hard into the seat and, pulling even tighter, my eyes began to dim with the greyness caused by too much 'G'. After a full turn I eased off slightly hoping to see the grey-green tones and black and white crosses of the German in front of me. A quick glance in the mirror proved to me that I was dealing with no trainee pilot but a skilled and formidable opponent. Before he was able to get more than a second's burst of his lethal cannons at me I screamed the *Spitfire* into another maximum rate turn, this time to the right. Holding the turn for 180° I then let the bank continue and then, with the aircraft on the opposite bank, pulled hard in the other direction. Only by trying every trick in the book, and a few more that I hadn't tried before, was I able, eventually, to get on the F.W's tail for a second or two. So we flew, like two gladiatorial air knights, aiming brief but ineffectual blows at one another, oblivious to all of mankind and they unregarding of us. As the altimeter unwound and the ground, seemingly, came up to meet us, it was time for me to break off the engagement; my *Spitfire* was no match for the 190 at low altitudes. I was thankful for the presence of some cumulus clouds and entered the welcoming folds with no small feelings of relief. In all, the combat had taken but a few minutes but it had been a lifetime of experience and I was thankful for the chance to live and fight another day".

Fanciful? Of course it is fanciful, but I

Opposite, top, the Spitfire in all its marks remains a firm favourite. This one is 'stand off scale'.
Opposite, bottom, Ross Woodcock in contemporary dress with a geared Webra 61 model of a Qantas Avro 504 (Dyak engine).

doubt that many scale model aircraft modellers do not have such dreams at one time or another. Perhaps the majority of scale modellers would prefer to be flying full-size aircraft but, because of lack of opportunity or finances, the goal is unattainable. For us it is the art of make-believe, the chance to simulate in miniature the actions and appearance of the full-size aircraft. We have thereby a tremendous advantage. Not only can we duplicate the existing, we can also choose to make replicas of totally extinct aircraft or examples that were designed and never built. Ours is the satisfaction of transposing the full size into model form and having the thrill of test flying our creations. Rewards and excitement in building and flying radio control scale model aircraft there certainly are, as can be understood from this quotation of 'purple prose', as published in 'Model Builder': "The eastern sky had lightened and the sombre black changed moment by moment with streaks of colour. The cirrus reflected the awakening sun about to climb the horizon. Blades of grass were bathed in pristine crystals of dew. Still air, freshened by a night of rest, and cooled by the preceding hours of darkness, felt delicious to the skin, but experience served notice that the full-blown day would climax in the same searing summer mood.

Muffled sounds of small creatures revealed the busy preparations for the new day's birth. Another sound began to fill the air as larger creatures made their presence known. Machines and humans worked their way into the scene, quietly working in preparation for another kind of day.

As the rays of gold fingered their way above the dark earth's line, they were caught, reflected from the white outlines of a magnificent craft posing majestically

in the vast open space. Fabric traced the gaunt outlines of framework, hanging loosened in wrinkled folds.

The senses combined the ingredients to form a composite that would fill the enthusiast with longing nostalgia.

The 'Jenny' was perfect. Wires welded the parts into one with the precision of a spider's home. Varnished layers tracing graceful arcs formed the propellor, and a myriad flickering fingers rested on the ancient engine. The 'Jenny' was beautiful and it fitted so wonderfully into this early morning scene. It could have been right out of a barnstormer's diary, or an early aviator's flight training. But it wasn't.

The scene occurred at Dayton, in the summer of 1976, during the 'Nats'. The 'Jenny' belonged to Charles Nelson, a gentleman with a love for the craft and the love was reflected in the perfect way the model was executed.

Several things make that event a memorable one. As that model sat in the dewy, damp environment, the fabric was lifeless and limp. As the sun warmed the air and burned the dampness from the grass, the fabric slowly tightened as if telling the many gathered about, "I'm ready!"

Imagine, standing around watching fabric shrink! But what we saw that day was the essence of scale modelling. It isn't a perfect model or any one thing. It's the sum total of many experiences. In the case of the 'Jenny', it was the perfection of the model, the love lavished by Charles, and many other things, not the least of which was the slow, elegant flight through which the pilot put the

A Japanese kit of the colourful Pitts aerobatic display aircraft, mostly ply and balsa with some vac-formed parts.

craft. That's scale modelling ... a feeling".

In radio control modelling there is no greater thrill than to be able to study, at close quarters, a scale model aircraft of the highest standards. The interior of the model will be detailed down to the smallest knob and switch, the instruments may operate as the full size and the control surfaces be linked to controls in the cockpit. Authenticity of the external finish and colour will be total, with every rivet and bolt accurately portrayed. Not being satisfied with that, the modeller will have taken the trouble to include the 'atmospherics' of the full size prototype – the full size subject is usually referred to as the prototype. He will have simulated the weathering of the aircraft with the scratches, smudges and dirt all faithfully reproduced. Then to witness the model being prepared for flight, the engine bursting into life followed by a take-off and scale-like flight, is indeed a minor miracle. It is small wonder that we can imagine ourselves sitting in the cockpit and actually flying in the aircraft,

because there in miniature is everything needed to operate it. No doubt some fellow beings would consider our hobby as playing with toy aeroplanes. They have the right to their opinions but it is their loss, for they do not have the imagination, or satisfaction, of being able to create, perhaps not a work of art – that may be putting it too high – but, at a minimum, a subject demanding many and diverse skills.

The object of this book is really twofold. One, to create the enthusiasm for the reader to want to build and fly scale radio control models and, secondly, to give him an insight into the methods used. If it succeeds in doing this, in some measure, the exercise will have been worthwhile.

In common with many hobbies and sports, the more that you put into the activity the greater are the rewards that will ensue. The ultimate must be designing your own model, building it – using as few commercial components as possible – and flying it. To this may be added, for some modellers at least, the

A different approach to the same subject, this kit has glass-fibre fuselage and cowl and veneered foam wings.

satisfaction of winning a competition with his creation. Not everyone is gifted with the skills necessary for the design of a model aircraft, although most modellers are capable if they work at it.

For some there will be ample satisfaction in building a model from a kit or plan and for others the flying of the model will be the most important feature of the activity. Now for the first word of warning. It is courting disaster to attempt to build and fly scale model aircraft before you have learned the basic skills required by starting with suitable training models. The temptation to commence building and flying with an unsuitable scale model is considerable, but the chances are that it will disenchant you rather than make you more enthusiastic. Just look at it logically. A scale model will take you longer to build and is likely to be more difficult to fly than a sports training model. To learn to fly a radio controlled model will inevitably lead to a number of crashes — it is all part of the learning leading to proficiency. Is it sensible to use a model that has consumed many

hours of patient construction to this end? No, whatever your aims and desires may eventually be, it is essential that you work towards them gradually and do not try to 'short circuit' the initial training stages. There are enough problems, and excitement, in learning to fly a standard training model without having the additional burdens of a scale design.

Assuming that you have acquired a reasonable standard of efficiency with sports models, including aerobatics, scale becomes a practical proposition. Even so, it is not advisable to go straight in on the more difficult subjects, time enough to start building *Flying Fortresses* and *Concordes*. Think in terms of a scale model that is not too far away from the proportions of a simple sports model initially. Models of the Piper *Cub*, Cessna and Auster type make a good starting point. They are neither too difficult to build or fly. If you are completely sold on building something a little more difficult, say an SE5A or Sopwith *Pup* biplane, build a semi-scale biplane first and learn to fly it before

11

attempting the true scale version. This will allow you to become competent with the flying of a biplane *and* will also give you the opportunity to try out some 'scale' finishes and details.

Whether you build from a plan or a kit will depend, to a large degree, on the satisfaction you obtain from building. To some the building and finishing is as much, or even more, satisfying than the flying of the model. For these modellers building from a plan will probably give the greater joy as they can vary the amount of detail they wish to incorporate into the model as building progresses. If you are the type that can't wait to get flying then a kit is the best answer — as prefabricated as you like, depending on the amount of time you intend spending on the constructions. Kits, and plans for that matter, vary according to the accuracy of scale and the degree of detailing; some are prepared to sacrifice a little of scale accuracy to improve 'flyability'. This is seldom justified with the use of modern proportional radio control equipment, as most prototypes that flew reasonably will fly in model form. Any scale 'fanatic' should study a plan or kit thoroughly before purchasing

to verify the scale authenticity. It can be most frustrating to find, at various building stages, scale discrepancies that were not initially obvious. Such errors can lead to endless modifications and, more likely, a loss of interest in the subject.

Not everyone will worry about minor scale inaccuracies and providing the model reasonably resembles the prototype in the air they will be well satisfied. There is certainly a wide selection of both kits and plans on the market covering many types of aircraft, but you are less likely to find kits of the more 'way out' type of model. The economics of kit manufacture dictate that fairly popular subjects must be chosen as lesser known aircraft will not create sufficient sales potential. That is not to say that the kits are not of a high scale standard. At least one World Champion produces kits of his winning model capable of being built up to the same championship standard. Unfortunately, some modellers make the elementary mistake of believing that providing they build from a kit of a championship-winning model, and use the same engine and radio equipment, they will also become champions. There is a great deal more to it than that! On

Author's quarter-scale 'Auster' used for some shots in the TV series 'Airline'

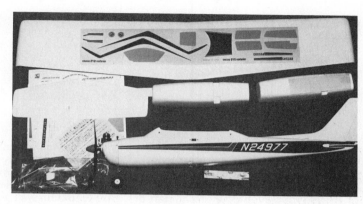

Almost-ready-to-fly (ARTF) kits tend to use foam for many components and are often scale-like rather than true scale.

balance, it is probably better to commence with building from a kit as there is less likelihood of becoming bored with the construction and one arrives at the interesting bits sooner. Once you know you are hooked on scale then you can start building the more complex designs from plans. To advance from this stage to designing your own model comes, if you wish it to come, when you have had experience of a number of different types of models. Again, start gently, using a known and tried design as your basis and taking the overall dimensions and wing sections as your guide.

In writing a book, even a specialised book, it is not so much a matter of what to include as what must be left out. The limits of space make it impossible to include all of the information that is available and some must be eliminated. For this reason, and because they are covered in other publications, the subject of rotary wing aircraft (helicopters and autogyros) has been omitted. No detailed information is included on flying boats or seaplanes, not because they are not worthy of consideration but because they are specialised subjects in their own right. It would be idle to think that everything apart from these subjects has been included in this book — there will be omissions by error and ignorance. However, there should be sufficient information to interest the novice to scale aircraft building and flying and possibly even some points helpful to the near expert. Those of you that have already entered into the subject will know what a fantastic challenge it is and, for the newcomer, one can safely claim that the rewards are equally satisfying. Flying a well-built scale model aircraft must be the pinnacle of ambition of most radio control modellers, and it really is good at the top!

Chapter 2

Choice of Subject

The scope of subject for scale R/C (radio control) model aircraft is limited only by the number of full size prototypes designed. Not only types, but variations of those types even down to aircraft of different colour schemes and markings. A list of possible models would run into many thousands, but the modeller can normally reduce this to a handful through personal preference and practicalities. Choosing the aircraft to be modelled can be an interesting part of the total project as it can involve the reading of books on aircraft, possibly visiting aircraft museums and collections and, often, having to do a bit of amateur detective work to find out some of the more obscure details of the subject. The more one can 'absorb' on the subject aircraft – from construction to flying characteristics – the more one is likely to achieve an accurate flying replica, in all respects. Are any subjects taboo? In the early days of radio control equipment, with its limited control capability, it was necessary to choose some of the more inherently stable prototypes for modelling purposes. Now that we can accurately and proportionally duplicate all of the principal functions of the full size counterpart these reservations no longer apply. Virtually any prototype can be satisfactorily modelled, but not all will be easy to fly. If during your research into the full size aircraft you find out that the prototype was something of a handful to fly, you can be fairly sure that the same will apply in the miniaturised version – and probably even more of a handful. You would be well advised to steer clear of these 'difficult' subjects unless, of course, you happen to be a masochist with an insatiable appetite for challenges! Of the prototypes that did meet their flight specifications and, within their specifications, flew well, there are a few that should be considered with a jaundiced eye. Aircraft with heavy wing loadings inevitably have high landing speeds – unless fitted with complex flap systems that may be difficult to incorporate in a model. Very fast models with high stalling speeds are not the most desirable features of an R/C model and it will need the utmost flying skill to land the model safely and regularly. Pure jet aircraft (as opposed to turbo jets) can present considerable problems. It is possible to 'cheat' and use a normal propellor and engine situated in the least obtrusive position but this would offend the purist. A resurgence of interest has been shown in the ducted fan units as a substitute for the real life jet engine. These, too, have limitations and require air inlets and outlets of generous size to give a good thrust from the unit. Model pulse jets are not very commonly used, although they have been in existence for many years. Earlier problems associated with this form of

14

propulsion, i.e. starting and fuel feed, have largely been overcome but the main environmental objection – that of noise – remains. Using a model jet engine also poses the danger of fire hazard. Should the model, using a jet engine, get out of control there must be the risk of the engine setting fire to crops or a building, a risk that is virtually non-existent with a normal i.c. model engine.

To give an example of an *unsuitable* scale subject for an R/C model the Lockheed 104 *Starfighter* could be cited. This aircraft, with its small wings and high wing loading, has performed successfully (well, almost!) over many years in a number of different air forces. In model form it would, however, be rather a disaster. The landing speed would be extremely high, the retractable landing gear difficult to copy and the fitting of a pulse jet engine somewhat taxing of your ingenuity. It is *just* feasible to build and fly one – perhaps someone, somewhere, has already done so – but why go to the extreme lengths of near impossibilities when there are so many easier subjects to model? It is gratifying when you make, and successfully fly, a model of a prototype that was previously considered 'impossible' but be sure in your own mind that this is the sort of challenge you are looking for.

There are many books by test pilots describing their experiences with a variety of aircraft. Not only do they make very entertaining reading but they will tell you a lot about the flying character-

Scale competitions have mushroomed enormously over the last few years. One of the biggest is the Aeromodeller Scale Meeting at Old Warden (home of the Shuttleworth Collection) where 300 models make official flights.

istics of the aircraft in question. If the consensus of opinion was that the proto-type was a 'pig' it should be enough to make the modeller wary. Not all aircraft flew well 'off the drawing board' and some only just managed to fly at all. Scaling down an aircraft does not normally improve the flying ability, rather the reverse, so aim for an original design that pilots approved of.

Before entering into the building of a scale model there are a number of questions that must be asked, and answered. The most important question relates to the standard of model with respect to its scale fidelity and standard of detailing. There are three basic classi-fications of scale models and they can be defined as follows:

A. Sports Scale Models.

These are the models that you will seen flown regularly by club members at their local flying fields at weekends. They will not be highly detailed, the external 'fine' detail would quickly be damaged in the hurly burly or normal club flying. The standard of finish, too, may not be immaculate but this is hardly surprising if they are to stand up to the rigours of

regular flying. Perhaps there will be some inaccuracies of scale outline or wing section in the interests of making the model simpler to construct. What is important, though, is that an aeroplane enthusiast should be able to see the model in the air and state "Look, there's a *Swordfish*", 'Messerschmitt 109', '*Tiger Moth*', or whatever it may be. The Sports Scale Model represents the largest group of scale models and the majority of kit designs are in this class. Practicality takes precedence over absolute scale accuracy and this is of importance to the greater number of modellers. An engine cylinder head and silencer sticking outside the fuselage would offend the scale purist, but to the average club member, it won't even be noticeable at twenty feet distance.

B. Stand-Off Scale Models for Competition

Stand-off Scale is so called because the static judging is carried out at a specified distance away from the model – usually about 3–4 metres. Because of this method of judging there is no need to detail the model minutely as fine detail will not be seen at the judging distance.

This 62in. Cessna Skylane kitted by Carl Goldberg Models is described as 'semi-scale' but is still recognisably a Skylane.

A sports model of semi-scale appearance probably best describes this machine, which shows S.E.5 influence.

The fact that many builders of Stand-off Scale models do go to the trouble of executing a high degree of detail, including cockpit detail, is purely for their own pleasure and satisfaction. Apart from accuracy of outline, colours and marking, the static effect that the modeller is striving for can only be described as 'atmosphere'. The model must give the impression of being made from the same materials as the original aircraft − even if it is not − and have a convincing appearance of 'weight'. An authentic finish is essential, neither too glossy nor too matt, with the markings looking like the 'real thing'. The 'sit' of the model on the ground should give the impression that it is the full-size aircraft and has just been wheeled out of the hangar in readiness for take-off. No model will achieve these effects unless it is built accurately to scale but then

Probably 'stand off scale' is reasonable for this Jemco Hellcat Kit, which is accurate in shape but lacks fine details.

17

comes the art of 'camouflaging' it with paint to give the illusion of a full-size aircraft.

C. Super Scale

Here there are no holds barred. The model must stand up to the closest of scrutiny. Every part, right down to the mechanic's dirty finger marks, must be faithfully reproduced. Scale accuracy, measured by the judges, is imperative and must be in accordance with the scale drawings and photographs of the proto-type supplied to authenticate the model. No amount of detailing is too great and the more 'working' features there are the higher the judges' mark is likely to be. Naturally, to build a model to this standard involves many hours of pain-staking research and modelling but, after all, it is the ultimate.

No mention has been made in the descriptions of the above three classes of flying the models. In the final analysis this is what R/C scale model aircraft are all about. If we wanted to build a super detailed model that did not have to fly we would be better advised to concentrate on plastic non-flying models. A scale model must be capable of flying well and flying with the scale characteristics of the prototype. It is completely farcical to see a one sixth model of, say, a Bleriot tearing around the sky at 50–60 mph. This may be an exaggeration but the 'scale-like' flying of a model is an essential part of its design.

Having decided on the style of model to be produced, i.e. sports scale, stand-off scale or super scale, we must then select a particular subject. It is impossible to recommend specific designs because there are simply too many possibilities. There are the obvious prototypes to model such as the *Spitfire, Mustang,* ME109, Piper *Cub, Tiger Moth,* SE5A, etc. etc. but there is no reason whatso-ever to stick to these somewhat 'hackneyed' designs. The alternatives are almost limitless and there are references

Inclusion of panel lines and a little wear and weathering transforms this Tempest V. No doubt a four-blade prop is used for static display.

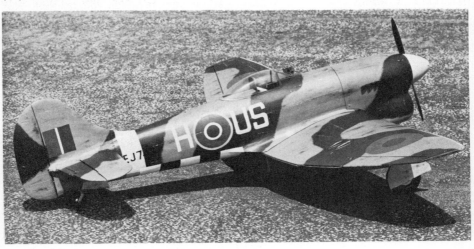

The Handley Page HP42 1930s airliner is an ambitious prototype but quite a number of successful radio models have been built in various scales.

available of the vast majority of aircraft – some may take a little more searching for. Although there can be no specific recommendations there are a number of guide lines that should be considered.

Firstly, and most importantly, the subject must be one that attracts you. Many modellers will have their 'dream' aircraft that they have wanted to model ever since they became interested in aeroplanes. If you haven't got such dictatorial views then a look through a few general aircraft books (the small pocket book series) will soon throw up a dozen or more prototypes that are worthy of copying. You will be working with a scale model for some time, and hopefully flying it for a long time also, so the choice of model as one that really appeals to you is very important.

Perhaps the large four engined bombers have always had a fascination for you? Before plunging into the construction of this complexity of model – feasible as it may be – we must decide whether it is within our capabilities of construction and flying. To aim a little higher with each successive model is laudable but to reach too far initially will result in frustration and disappointment.

Time limitations must be considered. Dedicated modellers would like nothing better than to be able to spend all of their spare time working at their favourite hobby but there *are* other factors. There *is* the lounge to paint and the garden to be done, and we must be realistic about the number of hours we can devote to the hobby. Allow, in your choice of model, for finishing the project within a reasonable time. What is a reasonable time? That will vary from modeller to modeller. To one a period of three months will be the maximum that he can sustain interest in a single subject but to another – particularly the super scale enthusiast – a year is quite in order.

Costs must also be borne in mind. A twin engine *Mosquito* with retracting undercarriage, flaps and bomb dropping facilities is not cheap to build and there is no point in breaking the bank just to achieve your dream. It won't bring happiness – more likely discord with your family. How will the model be transported? Bus conductors will not take kindly to an eight-foot wingspan model being carried on to a bus. Nor is it likely to fit in a Mini. Keep the dimensions of the model with the practical limitations of your transport and of your storage capacity at home.

When you arrive at the flying site with your model what are the ground conditions you will encounter? Many club flying fields are little more than rough pasture strips and these will obviously preclude the operation of models with delicate landing gear, retracting or fixed. A small mown strip will still limit the choice of design to a model with a fairly slow landing speed or otherwise the landing patch may be overflown. Large areas of short, mown, flat grass or hard paved runways are ideal. On these surfaces there should be no problems with take-offs and landings — apart from the operator's skills and the model's flying capabilities.

If your aim is to build a model for competition purposes then there is the further consideration of documentation. For Stand-off Scale the requirements are fairly minimal. A three-view dimensioned drawing plus an authentic colour scheme are often all that is required. You may, however, require rather more information, including photographs, if you intend to design the model from scratch. The more popular aircraft are very well documented and it is probably for this reason that there is a plethora of replicas of the more common designs to be seen at any scale competition. Designing a model to the Super Scale standards requires considerably more thought on the choice of subject. It must be extremely well documented, or offer the possibility of researching the prototype yourself, with complete knowledge of every visible part of the subject to be modelled. Because of the high standards required in detailing and finishing these models the builder will often select a relatively simple prototype, e.g. a modern light aircraft. Only in this way is

he able to include the wealth of detail and still finish with a model that is not excessively heavy and flies well. In other words, the design must have the potential to score well in both the static and flying sections of the competition.

Flying characteristics must figure highly on the list of desirable features of your model selection. It may be that with your super detailed competition model you will only fly it on three or four occasions in the year. When those times come, though, the model must be flying superbly to have any hopes of winning a competition. Gone are the days when a fabulously finished model could win a competition by putting in a 'token' flight. 'Flyability' is even more desirable for the sports scale model as this may be your only regular flying model at any one time. For these purposes we require a model that will put up a good performance in virtually all weather conditions and, in Britain, that covers a wide spectrum of weathers.

With the above considerations taken into account we will have further narrowed the field of selection of suitable prototypes and the size of the model.

SCALE REFERENCES

A visit to a specialised aviation bookshop (such as Beaumont's Aviation in London) will quickly dispel any fears that it may be difficult to find scale references for your project. The opposite is likely to be true and you will be overwhelmed by the quantity of publications that are available. From book reviews in aircraft magazines it is obvious that about a dozen books, specifically on aircraft, are published *every* month. Not all of them are of interest to the scale R/C enthusiast as they may deal with more mundane, to us, items such as aircraft registrations.

Allowing for the unsuitable books, the remainder of useful references would be sufficient to fill a very large library and keep the modeller in reading matter for the rest of his life.

In addition to the aviation books there are the specialised model magazines and these will have been publishing scale model plans, suitable for R/C, over the past twenty or thirty years. Back issues of magazines are often available, either through the distributors or from the specialised book shops. A very useful booklet is produced by the American magazine 'Radio Control Modeler' that collates and lists all of the three-view scale drawings published in the major English and American magazines over the last forty years. Details can be obtained from R.C.M., Box 487, Sierra Madre, California 91024, U.S.A.

R/C magazines are not the only ones to include three-view drawings of aircraft, the publications dealing with full-size aircraft, e.g. 'Aviation News', and other model magazines such as 'Scale

Models' include articles, frequently in considerable depth, on aircraft. The range of three-view line drawings, often with constructional details, produced by M.A.P. Ltd., (Wolsey House, Wolsey Road, Hemel Hempstead, Herts, England) is second to none and these, together with a fully illustrated list of their scale model plans, are included in their No. 1 and No. 5 Handbooks. Of the other useful books and magazines available it is probably best to subdivide the flying eras into separate periods for reference purposes.

The earliest period of flying, i.e. before 1914, is not well documented generally, although individual examples such as the Wright Flyer and Bleriot XI have had more than their fair share of attention. An invaluable book dealing with this period is 'British Aircraft 1809–1914' by Peter Lewis, published by Putnams. Small scale three-views of aircraft are included and these are backed up by basic dimensions and one or two photographs of each subject. For more

Pre-1914 aircraft can have their problems, since they are usually ultra-light and float around at low speeds. This Avro D is quarter scale, Webra T90 motor.

detailed information it will be necessary to refer to the 'Aeroplane' and 'Flight' magazines of that period. Although it is possible occasionally to purchase odd copies of these magazines – and very interesting reading they make – the best source of these reference books is through the major libraries. It may be possible to order one of the bound copies of these magazines, providing you know the dates of inclusion of the subject, but visiting one of the larger cities' reference libraries is to be preferred. Often the library will have photocopying facilities to enable you to copy the drawings from the magazines at a nominal charge.

Aircraft of the First World War (1914–1918) have been much better researched and documented. A good standard reference is J.M. Bruce's 'British Aeroplanes 1914–1918' (Putnam) and this will help you in your initial selection of model. For the more detailed examination of the selected aircraft it is possible to refer to the 'Profile' series of publications (they have many WWI examples) and these include excellent historical and operational descriptions with many photographs. The scale drawings are tonal, and in colour rather than line drawings. Although this is not so advantageous for enlarging into plan form, the colour schemes are especially useful. Harleyford Publications also cover this period extensively with books on fighters, bombers, reconnaissance and seaplanes. Some of these books may be out of print but it is usually possible to buy second hand examples. The 1918 to 1939 period is, again, less well covered in detailed information on aircraft. It would seem that the military aspect, in wartime, is of greater interest to the aviation historian – and perhaps to the modeller also. Sound information of

the '18–30' era is particularly hard to come by, possibly because flying was rather in the doldrums at this time. For specific detail it will pay dividends again to research the full size flying magazines of those years. Putnams publish an excellent series of books on individual manufacturers (e.g. Blackburn, Bristol, De Havillands etc.) and these include of course, aircraft produced in these and all other periods.

World War Two has had many millions of words written about the aircraft used, together with drawings showing the aircraft in actual combat conditions. There should be no problems in obtaining all the 'gen' that is needed to produce an accurate replica of these machines – except, perhaps the colour of the pilot's socks. The 'Profile' series covers the major examples of all air forces, and the occasional 'rara avis'. Line drawings are available from many sources, as plans and in magazine form (Koku-Fan, Mavu-Mechanic, Kookaburra etc.) but it is advisable to obtain a number of plans for cross-reference purposes to ensure accuracy. Aircraft built since 1945 have been adequately dealt with in contemporary magazines and the annual 'Janes's All the World's Aircraft' will act as a guide to selection. Many libraries auction off their copies of magazines at the end of the year and this can be a low cost way of increasing your collection of magazines on aircraft. Some of the titles worth collecting include:- 'Aeroplane Monthly', 'Flight International', 'Air Illustrated', 'Scale Models', 'Aviation News' and any of the magazines dealing directly with aeromodelling.

There are a number of organisations that deal entirely with aircraft and produce their own magazines with informative articles. Included in these are Cross and Cockade (exclusive to WWI aircraft),

World War I pushers such as the FE2 are attractive subjects though not the easiest.

Below, prototypes abound. This Blackburn Shark is an unusual choice for a '30s machine.

Air Britain and the American Association of Scale Aeromodellers. The British P.F.A. (Popular Flying Association) and American E.A.A. (Experimental Aircraft Association) look after the interests of persons wishing to build or own light and ultra-light aircraft. No doubt there are many other similar organisations scattered throughout the world.

We are fortunate in Britain in having one of the best collections of historic aircraft maintained in flying condition. The Shuttleworth Collection, at Old Warden in Bedfordshire, has aircraft, most of them original, dating from 1911 to the end of the Second World War. These aircraft are magnificently maintained and are flown regularly at their Air Days on the last Sunday of each month from March to October each year. Seeing these vintage and veteran aircraft flying gives a rare insight into the flight capabilities of the various type. Here, it is possible to study the length of take off, the angle of climb, the aerobatic potential (if any) and the overall impression of fly-

The Westland Lysander has always been a favourite scale subject with its high wing and generous tail areas.

Below, Spitfires are often based on a specific aircraft flown by an ace. Nose of this one appears slightly too thin.

ing. No more vital information is available than seeing the actual aircraft fly as our chief aim must be to achieve similar flight characteristics with our scale model. All too often a modeller will spend many hours making a superb replica of a certain type of aircraft only to ruin the illusion by flying it around the sky in a totally unscale manner at a scale speed that the prototype could never have reached.

Finding actual flying examples of

modern aircraft is a lot easier and it is possible to obtain books containing the registration of current aircraft and where they are based. Before you start poking about in hangars and measuring up aircraft do make sure you have the full permission of the owner and the airfield authorities. Most owners are only too willing to co-operate in allowing you to inspect their aircraft once they are assured that your intentions are serious. You may even be lucky enough to be offered a flight in the aircraft. For obtaining three-view general arrangement drawings and technical information, the manufacturers can be approached via their P.R.O. They will normally be able to supply a package of information that will prove to be extremely useful, but do offer to pay for any drawings and special photographs that you may require. It is advisable to explain your reasons for wanting the information or you may be visited by a salesman trying to sell you a full-size aircraft.

Museums, such as the RAF Museum at Hendon, Imperial War Museum, the Science Museum and the many smaller museums run by aircraft preservation societies, give the opportunity to inspect historic aircraft at close quarters. There is no substitute for viewing the original aircraft, although some of the museums may have exhibits that are almost better than the original examples. They have been so well restored that the faulty workmanship that could occur, on early aircraft in particular, has entirely been rectified.

Another opportunity to see full size aircraft in flight is at the many Air Displays organised throughout the summer months. The Displays are varied in their aircraft content, some dealing with only military aircraft (Duxford for historic military aircraft, Greenham Common for current military aircraft etc.). Very few of the Display organisers will allow you to inspect the aircraft at very close quarters as the dangers of accidental damage are too great, but it is usually possible to obtain some worthwhile photographs. For flying shots it is essential to use a telephoto lens to get acceptable results. A 135mm lens is a good compromise size as this will allow you to acquire flying shots, with the subject of a reasonable size on the negative, and a good detailed picture of the static aircraft. Whether you take black and white or colour photographs will depend on your intentions but the former definitely have their uses and are frequently easier to 'read' when used as references. Some museums and other private commercial organisations have a photographic service where you can order prints and slides of aircraft. It is doubtful, unless you are a very proficient photographer, that your results will equal theirs and, on the grounds of economy, it may well be sensible to use their services. Certainly where photographs of obsolete aircraft are required there is little option and we must be thankful that, for example, the Imperial War Museum have such a comprehensive stock of military aircraft photographs.

The availability, and number of sources, for obtaining scale documentation of your aircraft subject are, then, considerable. It can be an exciting investigation but there are real dangers of being sidetracked during your sleuthing. You may well commence with the intention of researching into a Sopwith *Camel* and finish up building a Westland *Whirlwind*. What is vitally important is to collect *all* of the information you require *before* commencing your project. It can be more than frustrating to be halfway through building a model only to find that some further information that has come to light proves that your previous work is incorrect.

Many modellers in the past have been frightened to build scale models for the fear that they would not be able to fly them. This fear is groundless providing a little care is taken in the selection and the normal commonsense applied. The usual advice of making haste slowly applies particularly to the building and flying of scale models, but there is a wide choice of prototypes to select from and you should be able to choose one that meets all of your selection criteria. There are even aircraft designed by modellers (e.g. Phil Krafts' *Superfli*) and many that look as though they have been enlarged from models. For the uninitiated here are a few features of the full-size aircraft to look for and *avoid*.

1. A design that will result in a model with an excessively high wing loading, i.e. small wing relative to fuselage size'.

2. Small tail surfaces. Where, for instance, the tailplane is less than 15% of the area of the wing. Look for 'model' proportions.

3. An aircraft featuring highly tapered wings. In model form the design is likely to produce tip stalling with its consequent control difficulties.

4. Aircraft using retractable under-carriages with complex retract mechanisms – unless you are a qualified engineer.

5. Older designs where the wheels are positioned close to the balance point of the model (say at 30% of the wing chord from the leading edge). The model will easily tip up on landing and take-off.

6. 'Odd ball' designs using asymmetric layouts, canards, double deltas and anything that looks strange and unconventional. When you have had plenty of experience by all means go ahead and try these 'weirdies'.

It still leaves an enormous choice!

A view of the model aircraft hall at a 1982 exhibition at Dortmund. Scale models of amazing variety on view.

Chapter 3

Aerodynamics

The study of aerodynamics is an essential part of the designing process of any full-size aircraft. Although it is a science, it is not an exact science; if it were, all aircraft would fly exactly as predicted from all the design calculations. Even today, with all of the computer design facilities, an aircraft seldom, if ever, performs precisely to the design specification. The good aircraft will exceed those specifications but more frequently the problem is to reach the design criteria laid down. Aerodynamics for *model* aircraft is an even less exact science and it is not made easier by the number of controversies that abound on the theoretical aspect of the subject. No doubt *some* of the authorities are right but it is not always easy to pick the winner. Very few modellers are trained aerodynamicists and this is probably to the good, otherwise the models would never get built, only calculated. The whole subject of aerodynamics *can* be very complex, when related to models, and it would take another book to cover all aspects. Indeed, there are such books on the market for those of you that would like to explore the subject further. One title is 'Model Aircraft Aerodynamics' by Martin Simons, published by Argus Books Ltd., Great Britain. Although an excellent publication it is possibly a little too technical for all but the advanced

designer, who can derive added data to incorporate in his model design. A more useful exercise for many scale modellers, new and experienced, may be the reading of full-size flying training manuals, such as 'Flight Briefing for Pilots 1' by N.H. Birch and A.E. Bramson, published by Pitman. This is the trainee full-size aircraft pilots' "bible" and there is a second part dealing with advanced exercises. As we are going to attempt to simulate the actions of the full-size aircraft it would seem to make sense to read the theory and practice of full-size flying. These books deal with the theory of flight, the effects of controls, exercises leading up to the first solo, take-offs, the circuit and landing and forced landings — all of which directly concern the scale modeller.

It is difficult, in one chapter, to deal with model aerodynamics at any sensible level and rather than proceed with all of the basics of flight and control it is more useful to concern ourselves with some of the specific aspects appertaining to scale model aircraft flying. Hopefully, you will have learned these basic facts during your R/C flight training; if you haven't, now is the time to do your homework, as this knowledge is essential when it comes to trimming out a model. No model flies well by accident. It flies well because the laws of physics have been correctly applied and these lessons must first be learned. It was stated earlier that the *total* subject of aerodynamics is complex. This is true but, fortunately, the basic rules are fairly simple and there are no excuses for failing to study them. Many modellers have learned the rules almost by accident – called experience or trial and error – but they may not be very successful in analysing their actions or putting their explanations into words. Experience can be a hard taskmaster and too many models are destroyed, unnecessarily, during the testing stages, when a little knowledge would have avoided the catastrophe. Whether you intend to go on to design your own models, or only build from established plans or kits, the understanding of the fundamentals of aerodynamics will allow you to improve your flying.

The disciplines involved in designing a scale model help with the initial drawing stages. The shape and areas of the complete model are dictated to us and the aerofoil section, within certain limits, will be similar to the full-size. Perhaps there will be slight adjustments to the wing and tail incidences – although the original settings may well be suitable – and the engine thrust lines may need modification. Apart from these minor modifications we are limited to the layout of the prototype. Why is it necessary to make any variations when scaling down from the full size? Simply because as the model is made smaller, it becomes less efficient. Were it feasible to maintain 100% scale efficiency it would be possible to construct, say, a 1/6th scale model of a typical modern light aircraft and for it to be capable of a *controllable* air speed range of 9–30 m.p.h.. This is impossible. There are no problems in achieving the higher speed scale range, the model's speed will probably be well

in excess of this, but the 9 m.p.h. stalling speed is virtually unattainable. Most R/C scale models are overpowered in comparison with the prototypes and this solves the problems of coping with the high speed range despite the increases of scale drag effect. Where we cannot improve our efficiency, without some cheating, is in the production of lift from the wing. Using the same wing section as the prototype will inevitably lead to a poorer scale lift coefficient and the degree of reduction of lift is related to the Reynolds Number. Modern aircraft use a semi-symmetrical wing section, with a high Reynolds Number, because of its good lift/drag ratio through a wide speed range, thus allowing the aircraft to fly at a high cruising speed but maintain a relatively low landing speed. These sections, when scaled down, do not give us the same benefits. Wing sections used on earlier, and slower, aircraft are more suitable for model purposes simply because they were designed for the aircraft to fly at the slower speeds, nearer to the speeds that our models will be flying at. There is still a loss of efficiency due to the 'scale effect' but it is less pronounced.

So what are Reynolds Numbers? They are a convenient series of numbers that help us to predict the behaviour of the airflow over the wing surface, and how and where the airflow changes. Assume that a model wing is mounted in a wind tunnel (there is no difference whether the wing is moving forward in the air, or the air passing rearwards over the static wing) the air molecules in immediate contact with the wing surface hardly move at all. The next layer of air molecules try to stick to the first but are moving faster. Consequent layers are moving faster still and so on until, at a very short distance from the wing

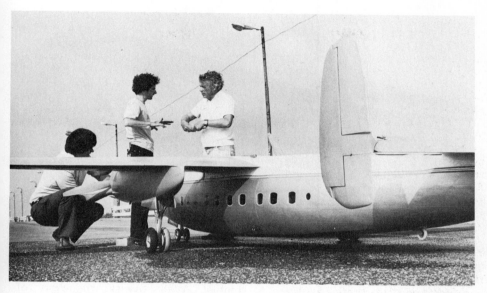

The maiden flight of a project such as this enormous Airspeed Ambassador is traumatic, but the sort of thing the author gets involved in occasionally.

surface, the air molecules are travelling at the same speed as the surrounding air. This thin total layer, where slippage takes place between the individual layers, is known as the Boundary Layer. Airflow on the Boundary Layer can either be Laminar or Turbulent. With Laminar airflow it passes along the wing surface in parallel and smooth lines, but a Turbulent airflow will cause eddies and swirls. Turbulence over the surface will cause additional skin friction and an increase in drag (parasitic drag). The Reynolds Number indicates whether the airflow is Laminar or Turbulent. It is relatively simple to calculate the Reynolds Number of any wing section but the vital part of the equation, for modellers, is the wing chord. Quite simply, if the wing chord is doubled so is the Reynolds Number. Reynolds Numbers, when quoted, normally refer

to the number at, or near, the trailing edge, i.e. the full width of the chord. Local Reynolds Numbers can be calculated at any point along the wing chord (the chord then becoming the distance from the leading edge to that point). It is at the Local Reynolds Number point, where the airflow changes from Laminar to Turbulent, that the Critical Reynolds Number is reached. Not many R/C models will reach this Critical Reynolds Number although a very fast or very small scale model may do so.

So why concern ourselves with Boundary Layers, Reynolds Numbers, Laminar Flow, Turbulent Flow, etc.? Because they can affect the type of wing section to be chosen for a particular style of flying that is required. Without going into too much technical detail, there are times during flight when we require Laminar Flow and other times when

Turbulent Flow would be more advantageous. In general terms, due to the considerations of pressure drag, a Turbulent Flow is more desirable for a model flying at a relatively high angle of attack. Although the drag is increased there is less likelihood of the airflow becoming separated from the wing surface (and consequent loss of lift) as would be the case with Laminar Flow. Therefore, a scale aerobatic model, flying tight manoeuvres, would benefit from a wing section designed for Turbulent Flow. A fast flying replica of a full size pylon racer would, except in tight pylon turns, preferably use a Laminar Flow wing section where drag is at a minimum and the model is flown at a low angle of attack.

There is much experimental work still to be done regarding wing sections for R/C model aircraft. Most of the information relating to wing sections is either concerned with full size aircraft or for model free flight competition models. However, it is important to remember that, with lower model Reynolds Numbers, the Coefficient of Lift will be lower and the Coefficient of Drag will be higher. With overall reduction of efficiency, compared with the prototype, the model will require a greater power to size ratio, but we cannot increase the lift requirement unless we artificially increase the area or use a more suitable wing section. Scale flying speeds will, therefore, be higher than the equivalent air speeds of the prototype, unless compensatory action is taken.

WEIGHT

Bearing in mind the reduction of lift efficiency, the only method of combating it, without affecting scale appearance, is to reduce the overall weight of the model. It also follows that as the aircraft becomes smaller in scale and efficiency is progressively affected, the wing loading must be correspondingly lowered to maintain equivalent flying characteristics. With these facts understood it becomes obvious why larger scale models tend to fly in a more realistic manner than the smaller versions. There

Contrast in styles between the WW1 0/400 bomber opposite and the modern Laser 200 (right) favoured for scale aerobatics etc.

are obvious limitations to the minimum weight that a model can be built to, the radio equipment remains a fixed weight factor and the engine weight does not decrease proportionally to its capacity. The other factor that remains at a fixed value, regardless of the scale of the model, is wind strength. A small, light model is bound to be more affected by wind gusts than larger models.

DRAG

There is not a lot that we are able to do with a scale model to influence the amount of total drag. We have set frontal areas, determined wing sections, scale wing/fuselage and tail surface/fuselage fillets, a surface finish to represent the full size aircraft, and the added details of rivets, pitot tubes, bracing wires, etc. etc., to give authenticity. Whether it is profile drag, interference drag, parasitic drag, pressure drag or any other type of drag, we have to live with it! For a model with a great deal of inherent drag, say a twin engine biplane with many struts

and bracing wires, it will be necessary to have a good reserve of power. As drag increases at, roughly, four times the rate of speed it should also be obvious that a high drag model will not fly fast unless very highly powered. The importance of a high drag coefficient becomes clear when the engine cuts; the model must be dived at a considerable angle to maintain airspeed and the *forward* speed of the aircraft will be small. A model exhibiting high drag and weight, and with minimal power, may have a very small differential in speed between stalling and maximum airspeed. Not the most desirable state of affairs for flying a scale model!

WASHOUT

Most wing designs allow for the root of the wing (i.e. inboard section) to stall before the tip. This is a highly desirable condition as the reverse effect will give us a dangerous condition, where the model will roll excessively towards the stalled wing tip. One of the main disadvantages of being unable to sit in the cockpit of our model is that we have no immediate indication of the impending stall. On a full-size aircraft there may be a stall warning device – audible, tactile or visual – to remind us that corrective action must be taken. Failing the inclusion of such automatic devices we will at least feel a buffeting – caused by the turbulent airflow from the near-stalled wing passing over the tail surfaces – before the stall occurs. With an R/C model our first indications are of the model rapidly changing to a nose-down attitude. This situation is bad enough but if it is also accompanied by a rolling motion we have further increased our problems of corrective action. To assist in preventing tip stalling, particu-larly with planform tapered wings, it is advisable to incorporate washout, as is done on many full size aircraft. Washout is a progressive change of wing incidence, to a more negative incidence (or less positive) at the wing tip. In making this incidence change we ensure that the wing root will stall first because of its greater angle of attack. There are

alternative methods of ensuring this, for example some aircraft (e.g. Piston *Provost*) have a piece of metal angle fixed to the upper surface of the wing, close to the fuselage, to reduce lift in this area. A gradual change of wing section towards the tip, with the thickness ratio increasing to provide extra lift, is another way of preventing tip stalling. There is no doubt that stalling the model, usually on take-off or landing, causes more accidents in models – and full-size air-craft – than any other pilot-induced error. The more we can incorporate into a model to make the stalling character-istics both docile and predictable, the safer the model will be to fly. Many factors, apart from washout, are involved in determining the stall characteristics, wing loading and wing section choice being the most important.

EFFECTS ON TAKE-OFF

As the take-offs, together with the land-ings, are the most critical aspects of fly-ing, it is important to understand the factors affecting the model from the point of commencing the take-off run to

David Vaughan's 'Mustang' takes to the air. The P51 has a tendency to swing on take-off in full-size and the characteristic can appear with models.

the time we are in straight and level flight. These factors can be subdivided as follows:-
1. The gyroscopic effect from the propellor,
2. The 'P' factor.
3. The spiralling slipstream,
4. The reaction to the rotating propellor.

The mass and rotation of the propellor causes it to act as a gyroscope and when we change the plane of a gyro it will cause a reaction at 90° to the force applied. When we lift the tail of a model during take-off (as for a tail wheel aircraft) it is the equivalent to applying a force to the top of the propellor arc. Viewed from the rear of the aircraft, this force causes, through 90° in the direction of rotation, a yaw of the model to the left (for engines with normal anti-clockwise rotation) which must be corrected by the application of right rudder. The model may be travelling quite slowly at the time of lifting the tail and quite large rudder movements may be required, initially, to correct the swing to port. In using a large or heavy (glass filled nylon) propellor the gyroscopic effect will be greater for any given engine speed. As the effect is transitory it is not possible to 'trim it out' on the model.

The so-called 'P' factor occurs when the model is pointing in one direction and moving in a slightly different one. This will happen when the model – again a tail dragger – is accelerating down the runway before lifting the tail. In this situation, the down-going blade of the propellor strikes the air at a higher angle of attack than the upgoing blade. With more thrust being produced on the right-hand side – viewed from behind – we shall again get a yaw to the left. The 'P' force disappears as soon as the model is flying straight and level, providing there are no excessive side and down thrusts used on the engine.

As the air leaves the propellor it does not stream rearwards in parallel lines but takes a spiral pattern path, due to the rotation of the propellor. At the rear of the fuselage the air impinges on the left-hand side of the fin and rudder (assuming a single, centrally positioned vertical tail surface) and yaws the nose to the left. This spiralling slipstream effect is obviously present at all times when the engine is running. It is possible to allow for the effect, at normal cruise speed, by offsetting the fin for a slight right turn and/or fitting side thrust to the engine. The practice of fin offsetting has been used in full size aircraft (e.g. Fokker D7 and other marks) as has the incorporation of side thrust.

For the action of the propellor rotating there must be an opposite reaction and this, in the case of our model, is for the aircraft to rotate to the left – from the pilot's take-off view. The rolling reaction to the left will apply a greater load to the left hand wheel on take-off, causing greater drag and, again, a ground yaw to the left. This force is also with us whilst the engine running but, because it is in the rolling plane, it can be cured by incorporating more washout on the right hand wing. Trimming, by this method, can only be a compromise and most modellers will be more likely, unconsciously, to trim out by adjusting the ailerons.

All very technical, but how much will it affect my take-off? With a tail dragger model – tricycle undercarriage models are much easier to take off – we must be careful to make our actions smooth and progressive. No sudden opening of the throttle or pushing the stick hard forward to raise the tail! You must learn the flying – and take-off – characteristics of the model as they all vary considerably;

some will need quite a lot of right rudder initially, gradually easing off as the model reaches take-off speed. The lift-off should be as smooth as possible and the climb out shallow – or the 'P' force will come into play again. "Smooth and gradual" is the answer for a straight scale-like take-off – only with considerable experience of the model can you afford to bang open the throttle and roar down the runway in a 'scramble'-like take-off.

required in a steeply banked turn is by increasing the speed or angle of attack but there is a limit to our airspeed capability and increasing the angle of attack will also increase the drag, requiring more power, which is not available. High speed stalls during tight turns are more likely with heavier loaded models, utilising low lift wing sections. With this type of model it is particularly important to avoid turning too soon after take-off before the airspeed has had a chance to

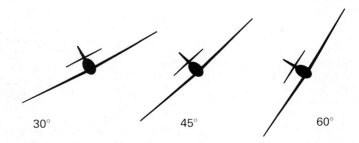

FIG. 3.1 'Safe' angles of bank should be memorised visually.

30°   45°   60°

EFFECTS IN TURNING

To sustain any banked turn, lift must be increased to compensate for the additional force required in turning the aircraft. This is not a serious matter in low rate turns but when continuous turns of 60° and above are attempted the additional loading on the model is very considerable. Taken to the limits, to sustain a 84¼° banked turn would exert a 10g loading on the model. Assuming that the model could cope with this structurally, the higher wing loading will also affect the stalling speed. As the loading on the aeroplane increases so does the stalling speed, with the wing at the same angle of attack. The only way we can produce the additional lift

build up; many pilots of full-size aircraft have come to grief in making this mistake. In some instances a high speed stall in a turn will develop into a spin – especially when rudder has also been used to balance the turn – and this can be embarrassing if the manoeuvre has been carried out close to the ground. The risks, and dangers, of unsolicited stalls are covered again in Chapter 21.

FLAPS

Flaps are frequently fitted to competition scale models but often, basically, as a method of gaining additional points as a 'working extra'. Do we need to fit flaps? That will depend on the type of model being constructed. A biplane with a high

A model of a well-known modeller's full-size aircraft design, the Kraft Super-Fli.

degree of 'built in' drag will certainly not require flaps for landing purposes, as the inherent drag will slow up the model sufficiently. Where flaps are of real assistance (as with the prototype) is with a model featuring low drag – a 'clean' modern monoplane – and high wing loading. In these circumstances the model, without flaps, will have to make its landing approach above its already high landing speed and, because of the low drag, will travel a long distance in losing the last few knots to the touch-down speed. This, naturally, makes it very difficult to judge the exact touch-down point and entails a long, low, approach to the landing – not the easiest to accomplish. By fitting flaps we have some degree of control over the lift/drag ratio, enabling us either to make a safe slower approach and touch-down, or increase our rate of descent by creating more drag than additional lift. The action of depressing the flaps will affect the longitudinal trim of the model but it is not possible to state categorically the degree of lateral trim change – or even the direction. Most models, contrary to most full-size aircraft, exhibit a distinct nose-up trim change that can verge on the excessive. The reason for the difference between full-size and model effect is probably related to the previously discussed Reynolds Number and/or the downwash effect on the tailplane. Providing the pitch change is not excessive, the model can be trimmed out to counteract the climbing – or diving –

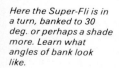

Here the Super-Fli is in a turn, banked to 30 deg. or perhaps a shade more. Learn what angles of bank look like.

attitude. Flap operation should be made gradually until the characteristics have been fully explored. Up to about 25° of flap will give a noticeable increase of lift but little extra drag – the reason why this amount of flap is used as a take-off setting, and also the reason why the flaps should not be retracted until the model is well airborne, as the model may sink slightly. Flap depressions increasing to 60° will progressively increase drag and limit the increase of lift. Over 60° (unusual in full-size aircraft) and there is only an increase in drag. It does, however, allow us to make a steeper descent with power on. The effect of the propellor slipstream over the rudder and elevator provides us with greater control at the critical low speeds during approach and landing.

ADVERSE YAW

The Yaw/Roll coupling causing the model to bank, when rudder is applied, is normally well understood, but less appreciated is the Roll/Yaw coupling encountered when operating ailerons. In most modern full-size aircraft, where ailerons are more sophisticated in design and manufacture, there is normally a rolling movement first followed by yaw. A model will not necessarily react in the same way and it is possible for the model first to yaw in the opposite direction to the aileron direction of turn due to aileron drag. This is known as adverse yaw. The reason for this occurrence is to be found by realising that the down-going aileron is not only producing more lift but also, because it is the high pressure area, creating a lot more drag. Amounts of

drag produced may be sufficient to yaw the model in the opposite direction and, in extreme cases, continue to turn the model in that direction. Biplanes, and high wing monoplanes using 'simple' ailerons are most likely to be affected in this way. By fitting differential ailerons or 'Frise' type ailerons it may be possible to overcome these problems and these types of ailerons will be discussed in a later chapter. With a completed model that shows signs of adverse yaw the solution may be to raise both ailerons (decreasing the amount of movement into the high pressure area) or coupling the rudder and elevator, mechanically or electronically.

Finally, in this chapter on aerodynamics, what if the model doesn't fly? There has to be a reason, assuming the prototype was capable of good flight. The laws of physics do not apply to one design and not to another so we must go back to basics. Checks must be made of incidences, for warps in the flying surfaces, of the balance point, the engine power, the wing loading, etc. etc.. Don't be scared of the problem, go systematically through the design and think out the problem logically. Of course, it may have been the radio equipment at fault, or could it just have been a case of pilot error? We have only skimmed the surface of aerodynamics, as previously intimated, but, fortunately, the chances are that our scale model *will* fly. How well it flies, and how to trim it to perfection, will depend on your knowledge and, as with a lot of full-size aircraft, a good deal of trial and error. We are, after all, amongst the last of the 'eyeball' designers.

Chapter 4

Designing your Scale Model

Having decided on the prototype aircraft you wish to model, you will also have researched it and compiled all the information, drawings and photographs that you can lay your hands on. If the subject has also been produced in a static, plastic kit form, so much the better. With the kit built up it will give a full three-dimensional representation of the aircraft and can also be used as a basis for experimenting with colour schemes.

Many modellers have previously failed to design their own scale model through fear and ignorance. Fear that the model may not fly, and ignorance of how to go about the drawing process. There are no secret barriers to cross and you do not have to be a Wright or an Einstein to design a scale R/C model – and there are many advantages in doing so. You are no longer limited in choice of subject by the availability of kits, or plans, and you can design the model to any size you require. Commonsense and a practical approach, as usual, are the most important ingredients in achieving successful design. Despite the advantages of complete flexibility of choice of size and prototype – building methods too – the greatest reward is, undoubtedly, in the satisfaction of creating your own scale model. To follow it through all of the stages of design, building and flying makes the additional efforts more than worthwhile.

Before we can put pencil to paper we must first decide on the size, and scale, of the projected model. There are many factors to consider – some of which were discussed in Chapter 2. Other determining factors concern the size of engine to be used and the type and weight of the radio equipment – assuming that you already own these. We have seen, from

Another Spitfire, this one the Mk.24 by Micro Mold. 350 sq.in. wing area.

the brief study of aerodynamics, that as a model decreases in size the wing loading should be reduced also. This fact holds good for any radio control model aircraft but is of greater relevance to scale models, because of requirement for them to fly at *scale* speeds. It does not matter unduly if a small '19' powered sports aerobatic model is flying at 50 m.p.h., but to see a similarly powered, $^1/_8$ scale, Piper *Comanche* flying at that speed would look ridiculous. The scale speed would represent about three times the fastest speed attainable by the proto-type. With ultra miniature radio control equipment, a light-weight engine and very careful selection of building materials, it is possible to construct small scale models *and* fly them realisti-

cally. The other proviso, or limitation, concerns our unpredictable weather. To have designed and built a small model, capable of flying well at an airspeed of 20 m.p.h., will have been a considerable achievement — at attempt to fly it in a wind of 15 m.p.h. will give ludicrous results. The ground speed into wind (the *apparent* forward speed) will only be 5 m.p.h. and, downwind, it will be travel-ling at an undignified 35 m.p.h. ground speed. Small scale models are therefore more limited by weather conditions from the point of view of realistic flying and for their greater susceptibility to gusts. Unless the idea of building small scale models particularly appeals to you, or the cost or physical size limitation dictate, the larger models will allow you

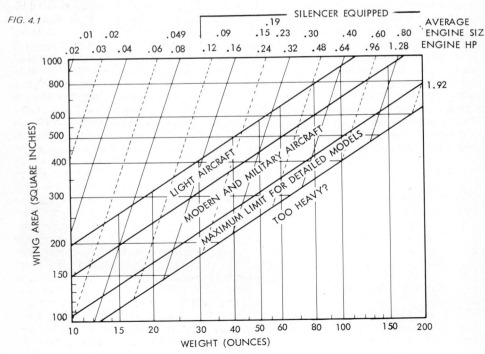

FIG. 4.1

a greater freedom in reaching sensible size/wing loading/power ratios.

Ted Off, from California, U.S.A., researched over a hundred typical radio control models to attempt to assess the 'Flyability' of the models relating to their wing area, weight and power. These researches were backed up by cross referring with many 'accepted' formulae to meet the same specifications. The final result was the production of the graph (Fig 4.1) showing these relationships in an easily understandable form. This graph is an excellent guide and basis for designing and building your scale R/C model, as it will give you the following information:

a. Approximate size of engine required for a particular size model.

b. Change of size of model to suit a different engine.

c. Design weight estimate within the type to be modelled, i.e. Light aircraft, WW2 Fighter, etc.

There are, of course, limitations to the generalisations inherent in a single graph. With high drag models the engine size may have to be increased slightly, and vice versa. Biplanes should be considered as having only 75% of their total wing area as being effective and with a slightly higher power requirement. Regarding engine sizes, providing that weight considerations are not of the utmost importance, there is no reason why a more powerful engine than theoretically required should not be fitted. Weight at the nose end of the model is rarely an embarrassment, as most models tend to be tail heavy. The extra power available from the engine does not have to be used in normal flying circumstances but it can be of use in certain 'emergency' situations. It can be likened to a reserve of power in a car, you may only use full throttle on very rare occasions but the few times that it is used may have saved you from an accident. Overpowered scale models are only unsuitable when full throttle is being used for normal flying.

To give a couple of examples of using the Graph Fig 4.1 let us first consider a scale Piper *Cub* which would put us in the 'Light Aircraft' area of the graph. We have calculated the wing area to be in the region of 580 square inches and, from the graph, we find that the weight should be around 50–75 ounces, with an engine giving .32–.5 h.p. (i.e. between a .23 cu ins–.35 cu ins capacity depending on the weight of the model). As the Piper *Cub* can be considered as having 'average' drag no further adjustment needs to be made. Secondly, we will investigate a highly detailed N.A. P51B *Mustang*. We know that, with all of the detail incorporated, and retracting undercarriage, the completed model will be very close to the maximum permitted competition weight. Because the model is quite 'clean', in its normal flying condition, we can afford to come down a little bit on engine power. Even so, it can be seen from the graph that we shall need a .60 cu ins of very high output to give us any reserve of power. A larger engine would be an advantage but that may not be permissible if the model is to be used competitively. Preferably, the model should have a total wing area of at least 800 sq. ins to give good flying characteristics. Whether you can achieve that wing area/weight combination will depend on the degree of careful construction detail you are prepared to go to. Remember, though, it is easy enough to add weight to a model but it is near impossible to take it off, once the basic construction is complete. Ted Off's graph has been retitled to correspond with scale model subjects but it can also be used for design considerations of other R/C model aircraft projects. The 'Light Aircraft' designation would become 'trainers' and the 'Modern and Military Aircraft' would refer to aerobatic and advanced sports models.

Armed with the general information of wing area, weight and engine capacity, we can begin to calculate the scale of the model to suit these criteria. In the past, designers have tended to design to a specific scale, i.e. $\frac{1}{8}$th, $\frac{1}{6}$th, $\frac{1}{4}$ etc. This is unnecessary as the methods of enlarging plans allows us infinite scale adjustment. The development of the pocket electronic calculator has been one of the greatest boons to the scale model designer as it eliminates all of the tiresome longhand calculations previously used. It requires only a few minutes' work to calculate roughly wing areas, for a variety of scales, until we reach a satisfactory scale. To find the wingspan, and chord, for a model of a specified wing area we must first find the aspect ratio of the wing, i.e. the span of the full size aircraft divided by the chord. With a parallel chord wing this presents little problem and only the wing tip shape need be 'averaged' out to give a mean span. As the aspect ratio of the model will be the same for the model as the prototype we can use the formula Span = $\sqrt{\text{Area} \times \text{Aspect ratio}}$ to find our model span and, hence, scale. For example, if the prototype has a mean span of 30'0'' and constant chord of 5'0'' width the aspect ratio is 6.0 and from consulting our graph we have decided on a model with a wing area of 600 square inches. The model span would therefore be

$$\sqrt{600 \times 6} = \sqrt{3600} = 60 \text{ inches span}$$

As the prototype had a span of 30'0'' our model scale will be 5'0'' to 30'0'' or 1 to 6

($\frac{1}{6}$th). Of course, the figures are most unlikely to work out to this simplicity but the calculator will not find the sums difficult. With a wing that has a tapered plan form we must take the average chord (not to be confused with the mean aerodynamic chord discussed later). For a straight taper we need only take the root and tip dimensions and divide by two to obtain the average chord; this is the measurement used to calculate the aspect ratio. For multi-tapered and elliptical wings the finding of the average chord is a little more complex but remember, at this stage in particular, we are not working to the last square inch or centimetre in our calculations.

Now that we have an approximate scale to work to, we can make a few preliminary skirmishes into the feasibility of the size of the model. For a 'passable' scale model we will not want the cylinder head of the working engine sticking obtrusively beyond the scale nose outline of the model. Rough out, on a piece of scrap paper, the nose area of the model, i.e. if we are working from a $\frac{1}{48}$th the scale drawing and the model is to $\frac{1}{6}$th scale, we will need to multiply the measurements from the scale drawing by a factor of eight. By enlarging a few scale dimensions we can soon sketch the front end of the model to see whether the proposed engine can be incorporated. For prototypes with relatively short noses it is worthwhile taking the sketch a little further to consider the siting of the fuel tank. O.K. so far? There may be other areas to consider, with smaller scale models at least, such as the installation of the radio equipment. As soon as you are reasonably satisfied that the scale selected will provide a model that is a practical proposition, i.e. all of the ancillary equipment can be fitted in without an impossible degree of 'tightness', you are ready to commence the drawing of the plan. What if the model is not turning out large enough to fit in the engine and/or the radio equipment? Then you must go up a scale and resketch the vital areas but, at the same time, you must not overlook the possibility of having to resort to a larger engine. Fortunately model aircraft engines do not abide by the scale factor and an engine producing 1.25 h.p. will not be five times as large as an engine capable of giving .25 h.p.

DRAWING THE OUTLINE

Included in our information pack on the prototype we should have at least one three-view drawing – if you haven't even a basic three-view of the aircraft, forget it, and select another prototype! The larger the scale of the three-view drawing the better the accuracy (assuming the original drawing to be correct) of our model drawing. Irrespective of the method of enlarging, the minimum degree of enlargement will allow us to reach a higher degree of accuracy, and will simplify the drawing process. Studying small scale drawings can be difficult and it is often impossible to decipher the exact intention of some aspects of the drawing. Ideally, one should use the manufacturer's working drawings as a reference, but this is not always possible or economic. Surprisingly, full sets of working drawings are available for some W.W.1 aircraft produced by government factories (B.E.2.c and S.E.5A for instance) and some private firms. The cost of a full set of working drawings will be prohibitive to most modellers and they are normally only purchased by persons intending to make full-size replicas of the aircraft. Strictly speaking, there is no such 'beast' as a semiscale model; scale

is definitive and anything less than a precise replica of the full-size aircraft is no longer scale. This may be a pedantic attitude but it should lead us into trying extra hard to get the design as accurate as humanly possible. Certainly, there are few excuses for 'cheating' with the design and the old days of increasing the dihedral a little and making the tail surfaces slightly larger, should be gone for ever for competition standard models. What degree of 'modification' you allow yourself is more a matter of personal philosophy, but it is most likely that any latitude allowed at the design stage will concern you when the model is completed. It is easier to get it right from the start. Problems will be encountered, seemingly insuperable and it may – through lack of facilities – be necessary to use certain commercial items that are not totally scale. Most problems can be overcome with ingenuity, even with basic modelling facilities, but if not, select the most suitable alternatives.

Although it is true that a scale model can be designed using only a roll of wallpaper, a pencil, a straight piece of wood and a ruler, it is not to be recommended. The full size prototype De Havilland 82 *Tiger Moth* was 'designed' with chalk on a hangar floor, but there *are* easier ways of designing aircraft. You will need a drafting machine or a drawing board and 'T'-square (the largest you can afford and store away), a ruler with millimetres and $1/_{10}$th of an inch marked on, compasses, french curves and a flexible curve, adjustable set square, pencils (HB and 3H) and a rubber. These items do not have to cost you a fortune – place a 'small ad' in the newspaper and it is quite likely that a retired draughtsman will have equipment for sale. A worthwhile investment is the purchase of some suit-

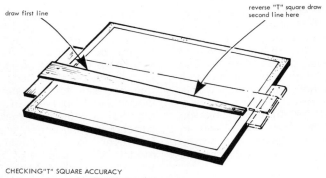

draw first line

reverse "T" square draw second line here

CHECKING "T" SQUARE ACCURACY

FIG. 4.2

draw line with "T" square in normal position – reverse "T" square,
draw second line – the two lines should be coincidental

able tracing paper to draw the design on. Not only is this paper much more pleasant to draw on, (mistakes can be rubbed out easier than on poorer quality paper) but when the drawing is completed, it is possible to have dyeline prints taken from it. The design may be so successful that other modellers will want to purchase copies of the plan and this is not possible with drawings on opaque papers! Cut yourself a piece of paper the full length of the fuselage – measure it, don't guess it – and stick it to the drawing board at the corners with masking or drafting tape. Try to visualise the approximate positions of the design on the drawing, i.e. fuselage side view at the top, plan view immediately under-

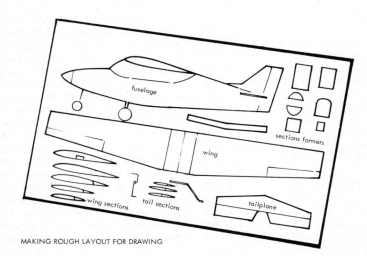

fuselage

sections formers

wing

wing sections

tail sections

tailplane

FIG. 4.3   MAKING ROUGH LAYOUT FOR DRAWING

neath, tail surfaces below this, etc.. It will probably be necessary to draw the wings, formers, etc., on separate sheet /s of paper. A further advantage of using tracing paper results in the need to draw only one wing half (assuming identical wing halves) and this can be printed in reverse for the opposite wing. Nearly all fuselage side views show a datum line; this may be related to the fuselage top longeron, to the engine crankshaft centre line or even to the tailplane incidence. The precise position is not important but the model should use the

as most electronic calculators have a 'constant' button incorporated and after we have made our first calculation we only have to 'punch in' the succeeding measurements to obtain the scale measurement. Direct scaling is probably the most accurate of all measuring methods.

2. Scale Ruler. We can make a proportional scale ruler to any scale we desire. Preferably, two rulers should be made, one for the three-view drawing and one for the model to be designed. Accurate drawing of the graduations is essential,

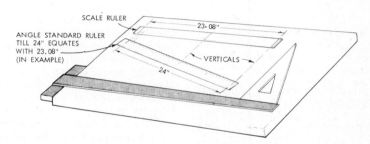

FIG. 4.4

same datum as that shown on the three-view drawing. If no datum line is indicated on the three-view drawing, indicate one down the length of the fuselage, parallel to the tailplane incidence; it is only a reference line. Draw an equivalent line on your tracing paper – you have started the design process. How you transfer the measurements from the three-view drawing to your larger scale drawing is a matter of choice; there are four basic methods – plus a few aids that will be described later.

1. Direct Scaling. This entails measuring off the three-view drawing, multiplying by the scale factor and using that measurement on your design drawing. It is not as tedious as may first be imagined

as everything will be based on the measurements taken from the rulers, and the method tends to be inaccurate for large enlargements (eight times and above). Most three-view drawings will have a small illustrated scale included and this can be used for preparation of your ruler, although it is more accurate to use the stated scale (if there is one) as the basis. Quite often the scale used for the three-view drawing will correspond to a scale on a draughtsman's ruler (e.g. $1/_{48}$th is the same as $\frac{1}{4}''$ to the foot) and that dispenses with the need to make a special ruler. For the prepared model ruler we must first take a known basic measurement that is between eighteen and twenty-four inches (for the ruler length) in model scale form. Let us

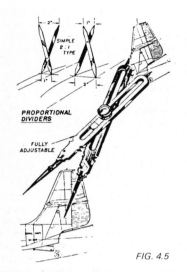

FIG. 4.5

say that our chosen scale is 1 to 5.2 then, if we measure off a line of 23.08″ we know that it will represent 10′0″ (120 inches) of the full size aircraft size. It is not easy to subdivide 23.08 inches into 10 feet markings and inches so we can do it more easily as shown in Fig. 4.4. Make the subdivisions of the feet (i.e. one inch or half inch divisions etc.) same for both scale rulers to avoid any misunderstanding when measuring on both sets of drawings. The rulers should be marked with neat, hard pencil lines,

on cartridge paper or thin card and affixed to a spare ruler or piece of straight thin metal, with clear cellulose tape. The tape should cover the marked areas to prevent them becoming dirty and unreadable. One added advantage of using this method is that the scale rulers will be required for scale verification by judges in competitions.

3. Proportional Dividers. Only high quality proportional dividers, obtainable from specialised retailers dealing in draughting equipment, are of use to us and, even then, only for enlargements up to a maximum of 5:1. It is all too easy to set the required enlargement inaccurately on the dividers and errors can soon creep in. Proportional dividers are at their most useful when dealing with smaller items, where a large number of measurements have to be taken, such as a canopy and its surrounds. They can also be of use in the initial roughing out stage, when we are checking to see whether the engine and radio equipment will fit into a model at a particular scale. Frequent checks should be made of the dividers during their use, to ensure that the enlargement ratio remains correct. Although proportional dividers have their uses they should be used in conjunction with basic line measurements fixed by Direct Scaling methods.

4. Pantograph. This device is somewhat antiquated and it may not be too easy to obtain them. As with the proportional dividers, it is essential to obtain a first class instrument, the types manufactured for children are too inaccurate for our purposes. A pantograph is a series of metal bars linked and pivoted in such a way as to allow for adjusting the degree of enlargement required. One end of the framework is firmly anchored on the drawing board and the centre point of the linkage is the pointer that is

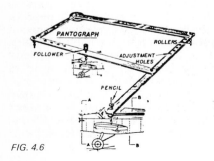

FIG. 4.6

moved to follow the lines of the three-view drawing. A pencil is fixed at the end of the 'free' arm of the pantograph and this faithfully follows, enlarged, the movements of the pointer. 'Faithfully' is perhaps too strong a word, as a considerable degree of skill is required before accurate following of the three-view drawing results in an equally accurate enlarged copy. A steady hand is needed and smooth operation, the greater the enlargement factor the more the inaccuracies of copying will show. The advantage of this method is really limited to the speed of the enlargement operation; it obviates the taking of many measurements and is particularly helpful when copying complex curves. You may have to use a very large drawing board to position successfully the panto-graph, the three-view drawing and the design drawing, for large items such as a fuselage. In general, it is probably advisable to limit the use of a pantograph to the drawing of fins, rudders, curved tail-planes etc. – always double checking that the enlargement is *precisely* to the same scale as the other method employed.

There can be little doubt that the Direct Scale method of measurement is employed by most scale model design-ers and has much to recommend it even though it is a little more tedious.

With our single datum line marked on the paper we can now, by our selected method, start to position some of the major features of the side view, i.e. wing chord position, tailplane, fuselage stern post etc. Following this, we can measure the fuselage heights, above and below the datum line, at regular intervals over the length of the fuselage. We are not interested, at this stage, with the con-struction of the model, only the basic outlines. Our next move will depend on whether the prototype's side view is a series of straight or curved lines. Straight lines present no problems and it is simply a matter of joining up the measured points with the straight edge of the 'T' square. Curves on a fuselage are normally fairly gentle except, possibly, around the nose area. It may be possible to reproduce these curves by using types of French curve known as Railway or Ships' curves; the names indicate the former were used for drawing the curves of railway lines on Ordnance maps and the latter were used for the design of ship hulls. We do not have to use these specialised items and can resort to either using a flexible curve (a lead cored plastic covered strip) or a

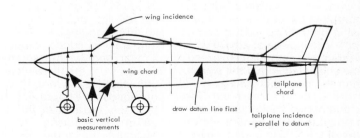

wing incidence

wing chord

tailplane chord

draw datum line first

basic vertical measurements

tailplane incidence – parallel to datum

FIG. 4.7   BASIC MEASUREMENTS DRAWN TO DATUM LINE

piece of spruce strip. By positioning pins at the measurement points a strip of spruce can be bent around the required curvature, and a line drawn along the edge of the strip. Sharper curves, when not part of a circle, should be drawn around a suitable French curve. Obviously, where rapid changes of directions take place it will be necessary to take considerably more measurements to obtain accuracy of outline. The amount of measurements is a matter of common-sense: a straight line of 30 inches in length only requires two measurements – one at each end – but a complicated curve may need a check measurement at quarter inch increments. Gradually, the fuselage will take shape until we start to reach some of the more difficult items. Some fuselage profiles, together with fins and rudders, are more tricky to copy than others. The time honoured system of dealing with these areas is by the 'squared' method with visual interpolation. Simply described, it is by putting a grid of squares on to the three-view drawing and putting the identically numbered and positioned squares, to the larger scale, on the design drawing. We can then see the points at which the lines 'cut' the squares on the three-view drawing and copy these on the design drawing. Use a soft pencil to rough the outlines and, when satisfied with the shape, complete the outline with a hard pencil using draughting aids to accomplish this. A small piece of advice when using the squared method of enlarging – look at the shape left within the squares rather than the lines themselves, it will give a more accurate assessment. Take time to stand back occasionally from the drawing board to take a general view of the outline of the design and compare it with the three-view. The eye, although

far from a perfect optical instrument, will quickly spot any errors – and it *is* possible to make dimensional errors.

After completing the general outline of the side view of the fuselage, undercarriage, fin and rudder we can think in terms of drawing in the wing and tailplane positions. First we must decide on the incidence angles i.e. the line joining the centre of the leading edge and the centre of the trailing edge. In all probability the incidence used on the prototype will suffice for the model too but, if you have any doubt, refer to published plans of similar types of aircraft for guidance. The same applies to the wing section but, overall, you should try to keep as far as possible to the scale section for authenticity. Before drawing the wing section on to the fuselage you may prefer to wait until the wing plan form is drawn. This enables you to slip the wing plan under the fuselage tracing and make sure that there is no discrepancy between the wing plan and the wing housing on the fuselage.

The datum line on the plan view of the fuselage is the centre line and, normally, the fuselage is identical on either side of the line. There are exceptions and, occasionally, cowlings may not have identical curvature. By positioning the plan view of the fuselage directly below the side view we can transfer the position of ends of cowlings, cockpits, wing chords etc. etc., by the use of a 90° set square. The angles of tailplane leading and trailing edges, canopy edges and similar angular measurements can be copied from the three-view by use of an adjustable set square. Three-views must be taped to the board with the datum line precisely parallel to the model design datum line (using the 'T' square). Measure the angle of the line being copied and transfer the set square to the design drawing. Lengths of lines must be ascertained by direct measurement. No allowance is normally made for the fact that the outside curvature measured on the plan view of the fuselage is slightly longer than the fuselage side drawing. In most cases the additional length is quite small but, with a bulbous fuselage using sheet or framework sides, it may be necessary to draw a separate projected side view at the constructional drawing stage.

Wings are not usually shown, on a three-view, with a datum line, so we must draw one. Where construction is indicated on the drawing the main spar will often prove to be a suitable datum line but we must check that the line is at right angles to the fuselage datum. A straight line drawn from identical positions on the wingtips will ensure that the two datums are at right angles. The same procedure is used for drawing the wing plan form and for the tailplane and elevator.

Highly curvaceous aeroplanes can be drawn by the methods described but the number of measurements taken and the accurate drawing of the curves becomes more difficult. There are other methods of obtaining the outlines we require; here are some of those methods.

A. Photostat enlargements. This is the easiest method for the designer *and* the most expensive. It involves taking the three-view to a commercial firm capable of making photostat enlargements, telling them the enlargement required and collecting the drawings, and bill, later. It is not a cheap way of obtaining enlargements and they will probably have to make the enlargements on a number of separate sheets. However, all of the work is done for you and, apart from the extra thick lines due to the enlargement, you can be sure of accuracy.

B. Opaque Projector or 'Epidiascope'. By using a projector of the type capable of handling images from books, papers etc., we can project our three-view on to a vertical surface at the degree of enlargement we require. This style of projector is frequently used in schools and colleges and you will want to use the highest quality available. Draw around the perimeter of the three-view drawing a scale, in inches or centimetres, for use to check the projected scale size and mount the drawing on stout card using 'Cow Gum' as the adhesive. Other adhesives may be used but take care not to stretch the three-view in the process. Tape your drawing paper on to a flat wall; if you are using tracing paper you will require a backing of thick white paper, such as decorators' lining paper. The projector must be positioned so that the centre of the lens is parallel to the centre of the paper and at 90° to it. Adjust the distance of the projector from the paper until the required degree of enlargement is achieved – by measuring the projected scale lines. Cross check that all of the scale lines are showing the same degree of enlargement i.e. there is no distortion. Once you are satisfied that the drawing projected is square, to the right size and the paper is flat to the wall you can commence drawing. Use a soft pencil and follow curves freehand, you will find it helpful to use a straight edge for the straight lines. A technique has to be established so that you do not mask the lines with your hand or body, as you prepare to draw them. Before removing the drawing from the wall, switch off the projector and study your drawing on the paper thoroughly to make certain that no

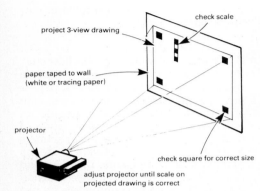

check scale

project 3-view drawing

paper taped to wall
(white or tracing paper)

projector

check square for correct size

adjust projector until scale on
projected drawing is correct

PROJECTING THREE-VIEW DRAWING ONTO PAPER   *FIG. 4.8*

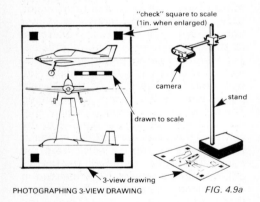

"check" square to scale
(1in. when enlarged)

camera

stand

drawn to scale

3-view drawing

PHOTOGRAPHING 3-VIEW DRAWING   *FIG. 4.9a*

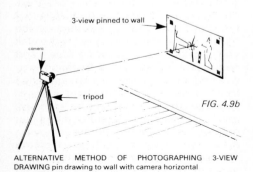

3-view pinned to wall

camera

tripod

FIG. 4.9b

ALTERNATIVE METHOD OF PHOTOGRAPHING 3-VIEW
DRAWING pin drawing to wall with camera horizontal

information has been missed. Once the equipment has been moved, the chance of reprojecting the three-view image in precisely the same position on the paper is extremely remote. With the drawing transferred to the drawing board the freehand lines can be more accurately marked in using the normal drawing instruments and dimensional checking.

C. Photographic. This process involves photographing the three-view drawing, mounting it into slide form and using a slide projector, or enlarger, to project the three-view image to the degree of enlargement required. There are professional photographers who will undertake this work but it is possible to do it yourself. Ideally, a plate camera should be used but not many modellers are likely to be in possession of this type of equipment. A 120 size (2¼ inch square negative) twin lens reflex, such as the Rolleicord or Rolleiflex, is also very suitable, having the advantage of a ground glass viewer to obtain good focusing. 35mm S.L.R. cameras can also be used but these do require a high quality lens if we are to obtain satisfactory results. Use a fine grain, black and white *negative* film; the speed of the film is not critical as we can vary the exposure times. Until you have determined the correct exposure settings experiment by taking various combinations of exposure time / aperture opening. Naturally, the small aperture setting and long exposure times are likely to be less critical to focus and will be an advantage when using 35mm cameras. Correct alignment of the camera with the three-view drawing is again essential to avoid distortion; the camera must be 'square on' to the drawing (complete with scale marks drawn on) in all respects. When setting up the camera avoid taking the image of the three-view to the extremities of the negative. If there is any distortion with the lens it will be most apparent at the edges. The use of a tripod, and remote shutter release, is recommended for the camera mounting. Having taken the photographs we must have them fine grain developed and transferred into slides, or a form suitable for projection by an enlarger. An enlarger, with a high quality lens, will probably give better results than a slide projector but, as always, it is important to use the highest standard of equipment available. The complexity of the equipment, or its modernity, is not the criterion, it is the lens quality that is the all-important factor.

Projecting the negative on to the paper follows the same process as described in item 2, but this time we have the advantage of using the negative film. With white lines on a black background it is easier to determine the lines that have already been overdrawn and those that have still to be filled in. Correct alignment of the projector or enlarger is, once again, vital – you know the degree of distortion that can occur when you are showing slides on a screen that is at an angle to the projector.

All of the three above methods can also be used for enlarging existing plans of radio control or free flight scale models if the designer feels that he does not wish to undertake the work of designing from 'scratch'. This system does have the advantage also, if the original form of construction is retained, of enlarging the ribs, former etc.. It should be remembered that a high degree of enlargement (it may be 12–15 times from small scale three view drawings) also enlarges the thickness of the lines of the drawing. A decision must

therefore be made to draw the design model lines on the same comparative position throughout the drawing, i.e. through the centre of the enlarged, projected lines.

CROSS SECTIONS

Now that our outline drawing is complete we must think about giving it shape and thickness. The cross sections of the fuselage must be plotted and the wing and tail aerofoils determined. This is also the time to consider the constructional aspects of the model, as it is pointless to draw a whole series of cross sections that do not correspond with former and rib stations. Methods of construction are dealt with in later chapters but we will continue with the process of how to draw the various sections needed. Suffice it to say at this stage that whatever the methods of construction employed, we must make due allowance for the installation of the engine, fuel tank, radio equipment *and* provide access for all of this equipment.

FUSELAGE CROSS SECTION

Prototypes using basic square box fuselages, with the addition of deckings and stringers, do not present too great a challenge to the designer. Many of the decking formers of old and new aircraft are based on the arc of a circle, or a combination of arcs of different radii, and these can be copied with the use of compasses. It is when we have to draw the cross sections of prototypes featuring monocoque fuselages that life becomes a little more exciting! With the fuselage side view taped to the drawing board, with the datum line parallel to the 'T' square, overlay the fuselage area with a piece of tracing paper. Draw in the datum line over the full length of the paper. At the former station of the first former to be drawn (choose one as close to the cross section shown on the three-view as possible) mark in a vertical line the full depth of the former. Using the plan view for total width measurement, and the small cross section drawing as a guide, plot out the shape of one vertical half of the former – or cross section as it is at this stage. The constructional elements of the former must now be drawn on to this cross section, i.e. box frame, stringers or sheeting thicknesses etc.. Only one half needs to be drawn because we now have the opportunity to draw the opposite half in one of two ways. We can obtain a photostat copy, from a standard photo-copying machine, or a dyeline print, of the *reverse* of our half former. This is then placed under the first half tracing and the remainder of the former drawn in, using the datum line and vertical line as references. Alternatively, we can retrace the first half, reverse it and line it up under the original tracing to allow the complete former to be drawn. Proceed in this manner for the remainder of the former positions; obviously, if a glass fibre fuselage is to be constructed, the cross sections will be used as external templates for the mould plug, and a half cross section will be adequate. Fuselages that feature subtle changes of section and shape require careful consideration and, in these situations, it is often preferable to superimpose the cross sections – excluding constructional details – so that we can obtain a clearer impression of the gradual change of section. In doing this, it is also easier to draw in sections not shown on the three-view drawing by visual interpolation. There are occasions when the number of cross sections indicated on the three-view are insufficient for our purposes and the 'unknown' areas impossible to assess from the drawing. Not wishing to guess at these sections we must make use of photographs to aid us in judging the cross sections. By taking a photograph – as large as possible – we can draw in the three dimensional datum line and 'vertical' lines at the stations to be considered. Known cross sections can then be sketched in to assist in getting the 'feel' of the shape of the fuselage. Using any convenient panel lines, obvious bulkheads etc., and cross referring to other photographs, it is possible to sketch in an isometric view of the cross section. This must then be translated onto the design drawing by interpolation, i.e. judging the shapes of the isometric view and relating them to the known dimensions of height and maximum width on the design drawing. Although this sounds a rather hit and miss affair it can, with experience, be surprisingly accurate.

AEROFOILS

For the scale modeller, intent on producing an accurate replica of the prototype, the selection of aerofoil and the incidence settings of the wing and tailplane are resolved – they will be as the fullsize aircraft. Following the fullsize example *may* produce a good flying model but this will not always be the case and it may be necessary to make some minor changes in sections, areas or incidence settings to achieve satisfactory flight. If this approach is unacceptable there is no alternative to abandoning the project and selecting a different prototype to model. There are no simple methods of ensuring that our model design will perform in a 'scale like' manner – and that must be the object of

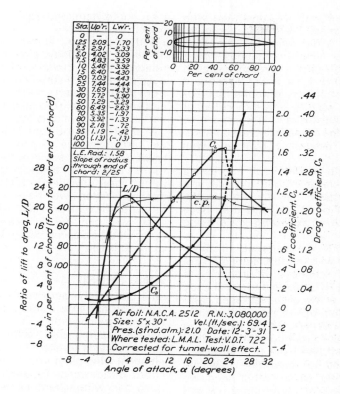

FIG. 4.10 Typical aerofoil information

the exercise – there are many factors involved that will influence the final flying characteristics.

Although the theory of aerodynamics remains the same for fullsize aircraft and models the practice is somewhat different. 'Scale effects' relating to aerofoils, wing loadings, drag coefficients, power / weight ratios, engine torque effects and slipstream patterns preclude the use of aerodynamic data as being directly proportional to the scale of the model. Little scientific work has been undertaken on models of the sizes that we are likely to

fly, and wind tunnel tests and aerofoil data are researched for fullsize aircraft, even though 'models' are used for these experiments. As "scale effects" (generally resulting in reductions of efficiency) increase as the size of the model decreases it follows that the larger our model construction the more efficiently it will fly and, probably, the nearer its flight characteristics will be to the prototype. For this reason, some subjects that are impractical as small models can be made to perform perfectly well when increased in size. Lower levels of efficiency are well demonstrated with scale sailplanes. We cannot hope to match the glide ratios of the high performance fullsize sailplanes where the glide angle (lift/drag ratio) may be in excess of 40 to 1, i.e. it will fly forward 40 feet whilst only sinking one foot. For model work we may only expect half of this figure but the ratio is improved as the scale of the model is increased – providing it is accurately built and well finished.

Large scale models look impressive not only because of their physical size but also because they fly more in the style of the prototype and they have more chance of achieving scale flying speeds.

Reduction in aerodynamic efficiency experienced with models is not going to improve our chances of producing a stable flying R/C model and we already suffer from a few disadvantages compared with the fullsize aircraft designer! Not for us the benefit of a test pilot sitting in the cockpit to monitor the behaviour of the aircraft, we have to rely on our visual senses to determine how the model is flying. On the other hand, we are not putting the pilot's life at risk and the worst that is likely to happen is that we shall return home with a large bag of bits, some damaged equipment and a dent in our pride!

Although the aerodynamic data obtained for fullsize aircraft may not relate directly to model work, it does give a guide to the results we may expect from the use of certain aerofoil sections and other factors in model design. This is particularly true of data obtained for full-size slow flying and light aircraft. Before we can make use of aerofoil data we must understand some of the technical terms and how these apply to the information provided in text books and articles. When we have learned to interpret the data provided with aerofoil tests we can further consider the associated influences determining flight characteristics.

WING CHORD

–the size of the aerofoil, i.e. the width from the extreme leading edge to the extreme trailing edge. For a wing with parallel leading and trailing edges the chord remains constant but tapered and elliptical wing planforms have changing chord dimensions. Tapered wings can have the wing chord expressed as a mean chord i.e. the average chord dimension of the planform (Fig. 4.11).

The chord of an aerofoil section may be expressed as a geometric chord or tangential chord, the former being introduced as symmetrical and semi-symmetrical sections were evolved. Examples of tangential and geometric chords are shown in Fig. 4.12. Note that these chord lines are identical for a fully flat bottom section without any raised or rounded leading and trailing edges. Because of the possibility of misinterpreting the two chord definitions the aerofoil data is related to its Angle of Attack (angle which the chord line makes

FIG. 4.11

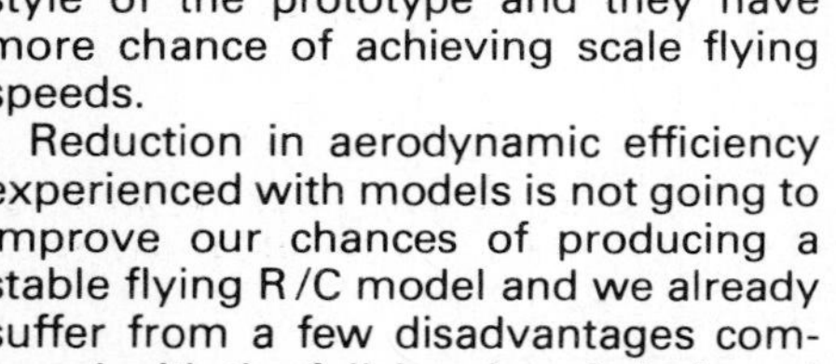

CONSTANT CHORD

TAPERED WING

MEAN CHORD POSITION

ELLIPTICAL WING

TAPERED WING - MEAN CHORD

with the airstream) and will depend on how the section was originally plotted. An example of this can be seen later when the RAF 28 section is considered.

Confusion of technical terms has always been a problem in model aerodynamics and some of the terms used are not to be found in the fullsize aircraft industry. One such misuse of a term is when 'Mean Chord' is referred to an aerofoil section instead of the 'Camberline' i.e. the mean curvature of the section — see Fig. 4.13. Early cambered wings were often designed in the sense of adding symmetrical fairings to a curved 'plate' aerofoil – the curved plate representing the camberline.

Increasing the camber (B) has the effect of increasing the amount of lift at low Angles of Attack but it also increases the Drag. The point of maximum camber (A – as a percentage of wing chord rearwards of the leading edge) also affects the characteristics of the aerofoil. A forward position will give a wider lifting range, i.e. from negative Angles of Attack. It is unusual to have model wing sections of this type in excess of 6% as the drag increases outweigh the additional lift.

ANGLE OF ATTACK (A/A)

As previously explained, the Angle of Attack is the actual angle of the aerofoil / relative to the oncoming air (see Fig. 4.14). This angle will vary according to wing and tailplane settings and the elevator position. With a low Angle of Attack the model will fly fast and, conversely, it will have a relatively low flying speed with a high Angle of Attack.

LIFT COEFFICIENT (CL)

–the lift value of an aerofoil section relative to the Angle of Attack.

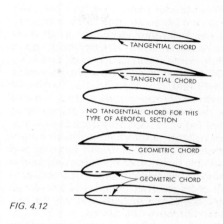

FIG. 4.12

DRAG COEFFICIENT (CD)

The Drag component value of the aerofoil, again relative to varying Angles of Attack.

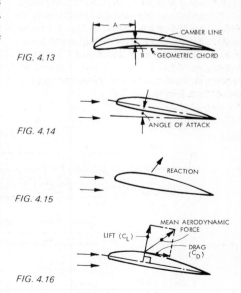

FIG. 4.13

FIG. 4.14

FIG. 4.15

FIG. 4.16

Wind tunnel tests allow the performance of a given aerofoil to be evaluated for set airstream velocities at set A/A. The aerodynamic reaction will be a single force inclined upwards and rearwards – see Fig. 4.15. However, it is more convenient to signify the vertically upwards component as a Lift force and the rearward component as a Drag Force – see Fig. 4.16. Not only does the magnitude of the aerodynamic reaction vary according to the airstream velocity and A/A, the position of the force (where the lifting force may be said to be focused) will change. This position is known as the Centre of Pressure and will be discussed in more detail later.

By taking individual measurements at specific A/A it is possible to plot, in the format of a curve, the CL against A/A. Similarly the CD can be plotted from the point of zero lift to the stall point. By combining this information a Lift/Drag (L/D) curve can be plotted to indicate the efficiency of the wing at A/A up to the stall. The fourth curve in standard aerofoil data tables concerns the Centre of Pressure (C.P.) movement measured from the leading edge as a percentage of the chord. (Fig 4.10)

A typical aerofoil section – the ubiquitous Clark Y – is shown in Fig. 4.17.

Aerofoils were initially developed as families, e.g. Clark X, Y, etc., RAF, Göttingen, etc.. Later developments of the NACA series resulted in four or five digits being added to impart more immediate information regarding the type of section involved. Four digit aerofoils were the first types and the first figure denoted the % camber, the second the maximum camber position in tenths of the chord from the leading edge and the final two digits the total thickness of the wing as a percentage of the chord. An early NACA aerofoil (2312) is shown in Fig. 4.18.

For fully symmetrical wing sections the first two digits are always 00 and the last two specify the thickness value, e.g. Fig. 4.19. Five figured numbers use the 2nd and 3rd digits to represent the position of maximum camber and numerically are twice the value of the distance i.e. 10 (5%) 20 (10%) 30 (15%) etc. Fig. 4.20. Later NACA and NASA designations became more complex but these, and other aerofoil families, can be understood once the basics are known.

Armed with the data we can, theoretic-

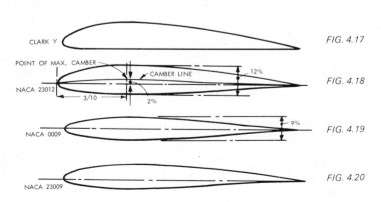

CLARK Y *FIG. 4.17*

POINT OF MAX. CAMBER CAMBER LINE 12%
NACA 23012 3/10 2% *FIG. 4.18*

NACA 0009 9% *FIG. 4.19*

NACA 23009 *FIG. 4.20*

ally, calculate many of the factors that will interest us when flying our model i.e. the airspeed to be flown (or stalling speed) for an aircraft of specified weight, wing area, A/A and air density to maintain level flight. The optimum Lift/Drag ratio will indicate the best gliding angle for a sailplane and we can find the minimum Angle of Attack required to maintain flight, important for fast flying models. All this we can do in theory, but, the scale effect is governed by the Reynolds Number of the aerofoil size to be used i.e. the product of the chord length and airspeed. Tests for fullsize aircraft aerofoils are based on high Reynolds Numbers (3,000,000 typically) whereas the model's aerofoil may only be 100,000 or less. Measurements are also based on an Aspect Ratio (Wing Span/Mean Chord ratio) of 6:1 and the data will be incorrect if there is a serious deviation from this ratio. In general, there is a degrading of the CL performance curves, due to earlier separation of the airflow over the wing for model aerofoils and a higher CD value at equivalent A/A. It follows, therefore, that the L/D curve is also degraded and the model will stall at lower A/A – i.e. at higher speeds. Sizes of models and wing chords are important when studying aerofoil data, 6–8 in. wing chords may have considerably different characteristics from the examples shown and, below 3–4 in. chord, a curved plate

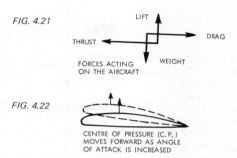

FIG. 4.21

FORCES ACTING ON THE AIRCRAFT

FIG. 4.22

CENTRE OF PRESSURE (C.P.) MOVES FORWARD AS ANGLE OF ATTACK IS INCREASED

section will give results as good as any aerofoil section employed.

CENTRE OF PRESSURE

Changes of C.P. will inevitably alter the balance of forces acting upon the aircraft and it is desirable to select an aerofoil with a minimum of C.P. movement, as the A/A varies. What happens when it moves? With an increase in the A/A the centre of lift (C.P.) moves forward, with the risk of a stall unless compensating elevator trim is introduced – see Fig. 4.22. Highly cambered aerofoils with a forward maximum camber are subject to considerable C.P. changes. The reverse situation can also be dangerous, i.e. a rearward movement of the C.P. will cause the model to pitch nose down and continue in this state unless 'up' elevator is introduced (Fig. 4.23). Most modellers know that a forward C of G is reckoned to be a safe, stable position for a model and is frequently employed in scale models

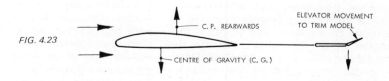

FIG. 4.23

C.P. REARWARDS

ELEVATOR MOVEMENT TO TRIM MODEL

CENTRE OF GRAVITY (C.G.)

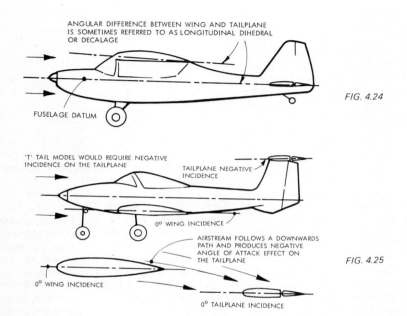

ANGULAR DIFFERENCE BETWEEN WING AND TAILPLANE
IS SOMETIMES REFERRED TO AS LONGITUDINAL DIHEDRAL
OR DECALAGE

FUSELAGE DATUM

FIG. 4.24

'T' TAIL MODEL WOULD REQUIRE NEGATIVE
INCIDENCE ON THE TAILPLANE

TAILPLANE NEGATIVE
INCIDENCE

0° WING INCIDENCE

AIRSTREAM FOLLOWS A DOWNWARDS
PATH AND PRODUCES NEGATIVE
ANGLE OF ATTACK EFFECT ON
THE TAILPLANE

FIG. 4.25

0° WING INCIDENCE

0° TAILPLANE INCIDENCE

where tailplane areas may be small and the tailplane moment short (distance from wing to tailplane measured in multiples of wing chord). There is no doubt that a forward C of G is generally safe but, in association with a rearward moving C.P. the forces on the tailplane and elevator may be sufficient to cause a structural failure. There is also the risk of having insufficient elevator control to prevent the nose down pitching moment when a combination of rearward C.P. and forward C of G are employed.

To digress for a moment, to cover another misunderstood and misused model term, the difference in incidence settings of the wing and tailplane (the angles of the aerofoils built into the model and related to the fuselage datum – which may also be the tailplane incidence) are variously referred to as

longitudinal dihedral and decalage. These terms have no scientific basis but they at least describe the angular difference of the incidence settings. What these settings do *not* do is to affect the stability of the model. Changes of wing or tailplane incidence – or elevator movement changes the *trim* of the model, normally to assist balancing out the forces to achieve straight and level flight. See Fig. 4.24. It might be assumed that an aircraft with no decalage i.e. 0° incidence on the wing and 0° incidence on the tail could not create lift to maintain flight unless 'up' elevator is introduced. Although this is true for models with high set tailplanes, where the tailplane and elevator are in clear air, it may not be true of an aircraft with a more commonly placed low position tailplane. The airstream from the wing does not flow straight back to the rear of the air-craft but takes a slightly downward path from the trailing edge of the wing and impinges on the tailplane to give an effective negative A/A. This effective angular difference between the airflow over the wing and tailplane may be sufficient to produce the lift required for level flight at normal speeds and with the elevator neutral. See fig. 4.25.

If you are left in any doubt about whether decalage affects stability consider the case of the flying wing. There are no tail surfaces to balance out change of trim conditions so, how is longitudinal stability achieved? By using a reflex wing aerofoil section having the properties of virtually nil C.P. movement over the A/A flying range. Incorporting a wing section with a reverse camber at the trailing edge (and elevons in the case of an R/C model) it is possible to obtain stable flight. If your conventional model is longitudinally unstable – as opposed to 'out of trim' – the answer will not lie with changing the decalage; moving the C of G forward may well be the correct remedial action.

PLOTTING AEROFOILS
(using RAF 28 section as a basis)
From the information supplied in the table or ordinates supplied, and the sketch of the aerofoil showing the datum line, we can plot a section with any chord line to suit the model to be built. Imperial or metric measurements may be used but millimetres are a convenient form of measurement. Using an electronic calculator will reduce the tedious mathematics to a minimum. The only other equipment we require is a rule, a pencil, a set square, some tracing paper, french curves and a small compass. You will notice from Table 4.27 that the chord of the aerofoil is subdivided into percent-

LITTLE, OR NO C.P. MOVEMENT – OBTAINED AT THE COST OF LESS EFFICIENCY – LESS LIFT, MORE DRAG

FIG. 4.26

REFLEX, OR REVERSE CAMBER AEROFOIL

ages – mostly 10% divisions but small increments at the leading and trailing edges i.e. 1¼%, 2½%, 5%, 7½% etc.. The smaller divisions are situated where the curvature of the section is at its greatest and allows more accurate plotting of the outline. Leading edge and trailing edge radii are often quoted on the data sheet, again as a percentage of the chord, and this further assists in the accurate plotting of the front and rear ends. These radii are not always stated and the leading and trailing edge shapes must then be copied by observation of the aerofoil shown on the data sheet.

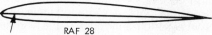

RAF 28

A/A IS TAKEN RELATIVE TO THIS LINE *FIG. 4.27*

RAF 28		
Distance from LE	Distance above datum line	Distance below datum line
0	0	0
0.0125	0.0137	0.0126
0.025	0.0217	0.0168
0.05	0.0314	0.0233
0.075	0.0385	0.0255
0.10	0.0444	0.0276
0.15	0.0538	0.0304
0.20	0.0600	0.0313
0.30	0.0664	0.0311
0.40	0.0670	0.0286
0.50	0.0627	0.0251
0.60	0.0540	0.0207
0.70	0.0428	0.0160
0.80	0.0302	0.0111
0.90	0.0163	0.0064
0.95	0.0091	0.0042
1.00	0	0

Assuming that we wish to draw an RAF 28 section with a chord of 300mm (approximately 12in.) we must multiply the ordinate measurements by a factor of 3 i.e. the height above the datum line at the 30% chord point will be 20.1mm, and below the datum line – 9.6mm. First draw the datum line 300mm long and sub-divide it at the 1¼% (3.75mm) 2½% (7.5mm) 5% (15mm) positions etc., etc.. Draw vertical lines at all of these points and mark the respective heights above and below the datum line (Figs. 4.28 and 29). Draw, with a springbow compass, the leading and trailing edge radii of 2.22mm and 0.66mm respectively. All of the plotted points are now joined together to form smooth curved lines representing the upper and lower surfaces of the wing section. Lightly rough in the curvature freehand and follow this with a more positive line drawn around french curves or a flexible

curve. Fig. 4.30 shows the final aerofoil section. It is not a difficult procedure to follow and you should then be able to convince the scale judges that you *have* done your homework.

GENERAL CHARACTERISTICS OF AEROFOILS

Bearing in mind the limitations in transposing the data intended for fullsize aircraft to models, we can learn the general characteristics of an aerofoil by studying the wind tunnel tests. We can deduce whether the section will have good lifting properties, whether the inverted performance will be reasonable, if the stall is likely to be sudden etc., etc.. Due to the scale effect regarding the test results much of the useful information regarding model sized aerofoils has been obtained by practical tests and observation. Empirical design (the art of 'feeling' that something is right and

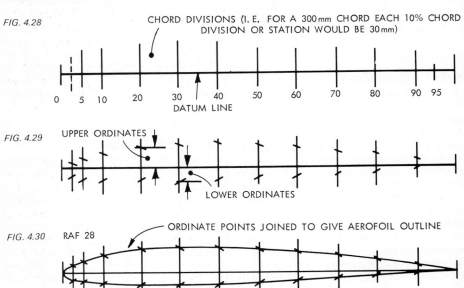

FIG. 4.28   CHORD DIVISIONS (I. E. FOR A 300mm CHORD EACH 10% CHORD DIVISION OR STATION WOULD BE 30mm)

0   5 10   20   30   40   50   60   70   80   90 95

DATUM LINE

FIG. 4.29   UPPER ORDINATES

LOWER ORDINATES

FIG. 4.30   RAF 28   ORDINATE POINTS JOINED TO GIVE AEROFOIL OUTLINE

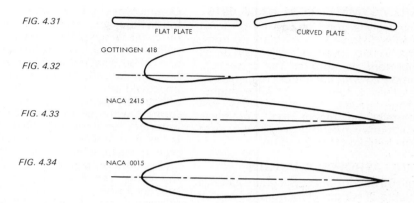

FIG. 4.31 FLAT PLATE   CURVED PLATE

FIG. 4.32 GOTTINGEN 418

FIG. 4.33 NACA 2415

FIG. 4.34 NACA 0015

proving it by trial and error) is nothing new in aeromodelling, nearly all of our knowledge has been gained in this way. However, having built up this fund of information we can predict the behaviour of certain wing aerofoils when applied to models. When we have to use specific sections, for scale authenticity, this knowledge will forewarn us of the flight characteristics to expect. Here are a few typical examples:

FLAT AND CURVED PLATE

A flat plate aerofoil is inefficient for wing sections but is quite suitable for tailplanes.

Curved plate aerofoils can be surprisingly efficient and are particularly good for small models. They have a reasonably good L/D ratio and are simple to construct. There are not many full size aircraft with this type of aerofoil!

CLARK Y

Efficient over a wide range of sizes, from 5in. chord upwards and the characteristics do not vary greatly over this range. The aerofoil offers good lift and a gentle stall but has poor inverted performance.

A fair C.P. change will call for elevator trim changes at differing model speeds — hence the 'ballooning' of non-elevator R/C models where no elevator compensation can be made.

FLAT BOTTOM, WELL CAMBERED, THICK AEROFOIL GÖTTINGEN 418

Excellent CL makes it suitable for heavily loaded models. Although CD is also increased it is outweighed by the high L/D values and should allow safe slow flying characteristics. The stall is more aggressive than would be experienced with, say, a Clark Y aerofoil and it is only suitable for normal upright flying.

SEMI SYMMETRICAL

(Typical example NACA 2415 – Fig. 4.33)
A semi-symmetrical aerofoil does not produce much greater lift than the equivalent symmetrical section but the stall will be gentler. 15% thickness is a good average figure for model work and increasing the thickness, say to 20%, may reduce the CL. Reducing the lift and increasing the drag may not be a disadvantage e.g. where the maximum speed of the model requires limiting.

FULLY SYMMETRICAL NACA 0015

Obviously a good section for a model needing to have a full aerobatic performance where inverted flight may be as important as upright. The lower CL, compared with flat bottom or cambered aerofoils, is compensated for by higher flying speeds. Stalling speeds will naturally be higher too, but these conditions can be improved by the use of flaps for take-off and landing.

WING AEROFOIL CHANGES

Fullsize aircraft wings will often feature a change of wing section from the root of the wing to the tip, probably to improve the stall characteristics. This makes the plotting of the aerofoil sections at the rib stations difficult and the simplest method of overcoming the problem is by making the ribs, or templates, by the 'sandwich' method. For this method to be accurate the ribs must be equidistant and any additional or non-standard ribs will have to be drawn by interpolation. As an alternative to changing the wing aerofoil throughout the span, a change of wing incidence may be introduced. The effect of reducing the incidence towards the tip (washout) will be to allow the inboard area of the wing to stall before the tip – a desirable effect producing a more controllable situation. *Excessive* use of washout (often seen on WW2 fighter models) should not be used as it is readily discernible on the completed model.

WING PLANFORM EFFECTS

The plan shape of the wing affects the stall characteristics and stability of the model and will, therefore, dictate the way in which we fly the model. Rectangular, parallel chord wings (or wings with only slight taper on the outboard panels e.g.

Cessna types) are not prone to tip stalling as they have consistent performance out to the wing tip. Similar shaped wings with sweepback have the further advantages of better spiral stability (sweepback has similar effects to dihedral) and improved pitch damping if the model is affected by gusts. High taper wing planforms, with small tip chords are notorious for producing a lift pattern that is likely to induce a vicious stall. Introducing washout into the wing panels, or stall generators on the inboard section of the wing (see Fig. 4.35) will help to prevent a violent and unpredictable stall. Elliptical shaped wings (Spitfire) are efficient at high speeds but may suffer from the same problems associated with highly tapered planform wings. Construction of curved planform wings is difficult as the aerofoil section must be separately plotted for each rib station (foam wings with large trailing and leading edge blocks will not result in a consistent aerofoil throughout the span of the wing).

Delta wings, with a leading edge sweepback of approximately 45°, have very stable characteristics and, with a suitable wing section, can be safely flown at high Angles of Attack and slow speeds without the fear of stalling. More often the Delta will 'mush' in a descent rather than stall and (surprisingly, with the heavy taper) tip stalling is not prevalent. High aspect ratio wings, as found on fullsize sailplanes, are only efficient on large models where the Reynolds Number (based on wing chord and speed) does not become impossibly low. Small models with high A/R wings are likely to exhibit tip stalling and poor spiral stability – we do not have the advantage of the precise and delicate control shown by fullsize contest sailplane pilots!

CONCLUSIONS

There is still much scientific work to be done in connection with aerofoils for R/C models and, until this is carried out, we must be satisfied with generalisations and empirical studies. If you intend to build a Class 1 scale model with an 'odd' wing section it would be worthwhile experimenting first with a sports model (built to the same dimensions, wing loading and incidences as the proposed scale model) and to investigate the characteristics of the wing aerofoil, balance points and incidence settings.

FINAL DRAFTING

In addition to drawing the basic outlines, formers, wing ribs and general construction, the drawing must include the position of all of the equipment (including supporting bearers, linkage runs, horns, bell cranks, etc.), plus all detailed

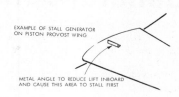

EXAMPLE OF STALL GENERATOR
ON PISTON PROVOST WING

METAL ANGLE TO REDUCE LIFT INBOARD
AND CAUSE THIS AREA TO STALL FIRST

FIG. 4.35

fitments. Suggested methods of carrying out some of these items are included later, but it should be understood that *all* of these factors must be considered and drawn *before* construction is commenced. To semi-complete the fuselage before thought is given to the placement of the control linkages, engine hatches, switch position, or whatever, is inviting trouble at a later stage.

FIG. 4.36. Callipers devised by Graham Smith for plotting full-size aerofoils.

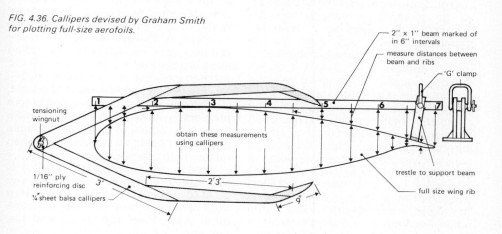

2″ x 1″ beam marked of in 6″ intervals

measure distances between beam and ribs

'G' clamp

tensioning wingnut

obtain these measurements using callipers

1/16″ ply reinforcing disc

¼″ sheet balsa callipers

trestle to support beam

full size wing rib

Chapter 5

General Construction

Radio control scale models often suffer from a malady that is all too common in human beings — overweight. As with humans, a model that is overweight will rarely perform well and every effort must be made to keep loadings to a minimum. A confirmed slimmer will watch every calorie of intake, so must we watch every gram and ounce that is added to the model. It is inevitable, or nearly so, that a scale model will weigh more than a sports model of equivalent size and power; the addition of the scale details, cockpit furnishings and the scale finish all go towards increasing the total weight. Small detailed items may not in themselves weigh very much but the sum total of all of the details incorporated may be sufficient to 'cripple' the model. Often a modeller has weighed his scale project in its uncovered state and been delighted with the result, only on completion of the model to be dismayed at the increase of weight that has, almost surreptitiously, taken place. It is only by constant vigilance that we are going to be within our target weight and any area where we can save even the smallest fraction of an ounce (providing it is not at the expense of strength) will be worthwhile. Even more frustrating is having a completed model that is within the total weight target, but considerably tail heavy. So we must watch the overall weight and the distribution of weight. Unless the prototype had a particularly

long nose moment we are far more likely to end up with a model that is tail heavy. This fact should not surprise us because the weight of a full size propulsion unit is much heavier in proportion than our model engine. Although it should not surprise us, we must be on our guard against it and make every effort to keep the tail area as light as possible. Tail heaviness is a particularly unfortunate state of affairs as to fly in this condition is almost certain to end in disaster — many have tried and failed. Equally, to counteract the weight imbalance requires a considerable amount of weight being fitted to the nose area due to the short nose moment. A forward Centre of Gravity position can be tolerated, providing there is adequate elevator movement to compensate, but a rearward C of G — NEVER. Weight, or the excess of weight, is probably the factor that causes more problems with flying R/C scale models than any other — with the possible exception of pilot error, and this is often related to the same problem.

How to construct your model? It is impossible to say that for a *Spitfire* you must construct by one method or, if it is a *Puss Moth* you must construct it some other way. There are many methods, and combinations of methods, used to construct model aircraft and no one way is 'better' than another. You will by now have built a number of models and may have developed a preference for a particular way of building, whether it be of the foam and fibreglass style, or the conventional balsa-wood method. Take time off to have a look at other examples of scale models, both 'in the flesh' and in magazines, to assist you in your choice of materials and construction. The next two chapters deal with the 'ancient and modern' prototype aircraft, and various methods of construction applicable to the period will be suggested. For this chapter we shall be considering some of the basics of construction and materials.

TOOLS

Books written on the subject of aero-modelling often used to commence with words to the effect that to build a model aircraft, you only needed a broken razor-blade, some pins, a pair of pliers, a tube of balsa cement and a kitchen table to build on. To build an R/C scale model, this is hardly true. It *is* possible to build with limited facilities and tools but where this is the situation, it would be advisable to build from a kit where much of the cutting, wire bending and mould-ing has been done for you. Modellers tend to build up their stocks of tools over a number of years and there is absolutely no doubt that the more good tools you possess the easier the job will be. If you can afford to buy electric drills, band-saws, sanders, fretsaws, wire benders, special pliers, belt sanders, grinders, vacuum formers, etc. etc., then do so because it will save you a lot of hard 'grafting'. That is, of course, assuming that you have a workshop to put them in. In general terms, your work load in modelling will be in proportion to the number and variety of useful tools you possess. Avoid 'gimmicky' tools – ones that promise you that they will do every-thing, saw, sand, drill and practically everything except eat your breakfast!

Geodetic structure used by Graham Smith in his 100 in. span under-5kg Miles Messenger to keep weight minimal

They rarely do, without spending an inordinate length of time converting them each time a different function is required. The two most useful electrical tools are a powered fretsaw and a pillar drill. Without these your work time is considerably increased – although not impossibly so. With regard to hand tools, you will probably have a reasonable variety of these already; add to them when you can and improvise when you are short.

MATERIALS

The same principle as with tools applies to materials for construction. Few materials deteriorate with age and the bigger the selection you have of balsa, ply, spruce, beech, ramin, glass fibre, plastics, piano wire etc. etc., the less you are likely to be frustrated at not having the particular item you need. It is not only the collecting of standard materials that is important, but storing a whole host of bits and pieces that may come in handy for some specific piece of detailing. Nuts and bolts, plastic tube, old watches, all sorts of fasteners, screwtops to tubes, used gas lighters – any of these may be useful in some part of the construction of the model. Because the majority of scale models built from plans are one-offs, the standard forms of construction, balsa and hardwood, tend to be used more than the materials that lend themselves to mass production. Timber selection is important, in the context of weight, and time should be taken at the suppliers to choose your balsa carefully. Avoid the heavyweight sheets of balsa – there are very few areas of construction where their extra strength is justified. Balsa strip is a different matter; it is necessary to use firm stock for some longerons and spars, and for

these areas we should select wood that is long grained, stringy even, and pliable. The very hard but short grained balsa strip will too easily snap across the grain and the extra weight will not have resulted in any gain of strength. Plywood comes not only in different thicknesses (always measured in millimetres i.e. 0.4mm, 0.8mm, 1.2mm, 1.5mm, 2.0mm, 3.0mm, 4.0mm, 5.0mm, 6.0mm, 6.5mm, etc.) but also in different woods. Some of the smaller specified thicknesses, i.e. 1.2mm and 2.0mm may be difficult to find and you may have to resort to laminating two thinner sheets to obtain the desired thickness (properly glued, this will result in a stronger ply). The most common ply used in modelling is made from Finnish or Russian birch; it is a light coloured 'clean' wood of good quality and ideal for most of our purposes. If we are looking for a strong thick ply, say for an engine bulkhead, mahogany marine ply is most suitable – boat builders will probably have a stock of offcuts that you can purchase. There are also lighter plywoods than birch, although these may be none too easy to come across. Larch and Parana pine are good examples of the softer, lighter, plywoods that can be used for formers that incorporate large cut out areas and are not highly stressed.

Most modellers contemplating building a scale R/C model will be fairly familiar with the basic constructional methods using wood but here are a few tips that may be of assistance in building your scale project.

A. Splicing Sheets. Larger scale models with sheeted wings and fuselages will almost certainly require the joining of sheets to obtain sufficient overall lengths of sheet. Butt joints are

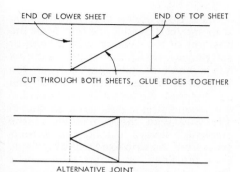

END OF LOWER SHEET   END OF TOP SHEET

CUT THROUGH BOTH SHEETS, GLUE EDGES TOGETHER

ALTERNATIVE JOINT

FIG 5.1 Splicing balsa sheets

is made simpler if the long edges of the balsa are first accurately trimmed with a sharp knife and metal *straight* edge. All woods, though well seasoned, are prone to warping and few sheets of balsa have a truly straight edge. Joining sheets where the edges are not absolutely straight will lead to the complete sheeted area 'cockling' and twisting. With the edges trimmed, position two edges together and run a piece of masking tape or Scotch tape over the dry joint. Continue this procedure until all the sheets are joined. The sheeted area is then turned over and the first joint opened by bending the first sheet back over the edge of the work bench. A bead of glue is run down the joint, the sheets closed together and the surplus glue wiped off. Continue in like manner for the remainder of the joints. When all joints are glued place the panel on a flat surface – a large sheet of glass is perfect – and weight down until thoroughly set. Afterwards, the tape may be removed. The use of the correct adhesive is important. P.V.A. glue is too 'rubbery' for this purpose and when sanding at a later stage is likely to leave ridges of adhesive. Aliphatic glues are more suitable because of their improved 'sandability' and balsa cement is good for the same reason. Select a 'thin' balsa cement to give you adequate time in making the joint before the cement dries.

not recommended because of the risk of weakness inherent in this method of joining. A tapered (scarf) joint will increase the gluing area and result in greater strength and examples are shown in Fig 5.1. Overlap the sheets by the length of the joint and cut through both sheets at the same time – this will ensure a close fit of the joint.

B. Edge to Edge joining of sheets. When you are fully sheeting for instance, a wing, the balsa sheets should be joined *before* the sheeting is commenced. To attempt to edge-join one sheet to another that is already fixed to the wing rib will result in a 'wavy' join unless it coincides with a spar. Joining a number of sheets together (sufficient to cover the whole of one side of one panel of a wing)

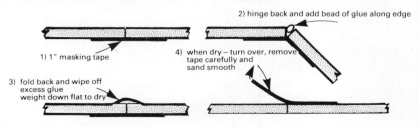

2) hinge back and add bead of glue along edge

1) 1" masking tape

4) when dry – turn over, remove tape carefully and sand smooth

3) fold back and wipe off excess glue weight down flat to dry

FIG 5.2 Butt-joining balsa sheet

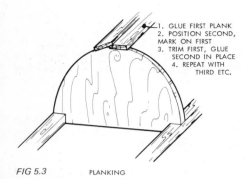

1. GLUE FIRST PLANK
2. POSITION SECOND, MARK ON FIRST
3. TRIM FIRST, GLUE SECOND IN PLACE
4. REPEAT WITH THIRD ETC.

FIG 5.3   PLANKING

C. Planking. Curved and tapered decking can often be constructed only by planking with strips of balsa. The width of strip you can use will depend on the curvature to be followed but the wider the strip you can conveniently use the quicker the job will be. Inevitably, the strips will have to be tapered towards the narrow end of the decking and we must aim for close fitting joints. Gaps between the planking will have to be filled, and fillers equate with weight. The normal method of tapering the strips is to start with parallel strips until it is necessary to trim the following strip to fit. This is a tedious and 'hit and miss' method and the following way is quicker and more accurate. With one strip glued in position

– use a slow drying glue – fit the next strip and let it overlap the first. Mark the position of the overlap with a knife or soft pencil – not a ballpoint pen as the ink has a habit of 'bleeding' through the finishes at a later stage. Trim off the surplus from the *first* strip and then glue the second strip in position. Continue in this way with the remainder of the planking, always cutting the surplus away from the strip fixed to the fuselage. Even the final, top centre, strip can be fitted without difficulty by marking the strips on either side. Naturally, the decking should be constructed working from both sides of the fuselage and meeting in the middle.

D. Tapered Wing Ribs. The time-honoured method of cutting and sanding wing ribs for constant chord or tapered wings is by the 'blocking' method using templates and balsa sheet pieces sandwiched between. Some modellers come unstuck with this method, on tapered wings especially, because of a failure to appreciate all of the implications and limitations of this method. The first essential is that all ribs on the wing must be equi-spaced along the span of the wing, otherwise some of the ribs will not be of the desired chord

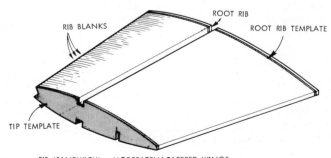

ROOT RIB
RIB BLANKS
ROOT RIB TEMPLATE
TIP TEMPLATE

FIG 5.4   RIB 'SANDWICH' – MODERATELY TAPERED WINGS

or thickness. Frequently the centre section of the wing features closer rib spacing than the remainder of the wing and intermediate ribs, or the root rib, will have to be drawn and cut separately in this instance. Secondly, the plan form or thickness will require two sets of templates and 'sandwiches' to be made. The third point concerns the positioning of the templates. Although the tip rib template, positioned on the outside of the block, will provide a tip rib that is large enough after the leading and trailing edges have been trimmed, the same is not true of the root rib. If we place the template on the outside of the ribs the root rib is bound to finish a little undersize and we must, therefore, position the template in the penultimate position of the rib blanks. A small point, perhaps, but one that can save a lot of annoyance and packing out of ribs. The method is shown in Fig. 5.4. A highly tapered wing may cause an excessive degree of slope on the edges of the ribs and to lessen this, a 'dummy' blank should be positioned between each normal rib blank. The thickness of balsa (or dense polyurethane foam can be used) will depend on the extent of the wing taper. (See Fig. 5.5.) By far the most suitable method of holding the whole sandwich assembly together is by using metal studding (threaded rod), washers and nuts. These can be obtained from good engineering and tool stockists. On larger models three lengths of studding (2 or 3mm.) should be used, but even so there is a tendency for the thin trailing edge to move around disconcertingly. To prevent this happening 'spot' glue the rib blanks at the trailing edge when assembling the sandwich – they can easily be separated afterwards. Slots for spars can be carefully cut with a razor

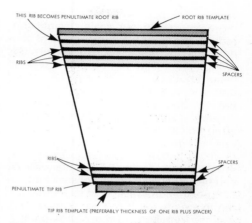

FIG.5.5 Sandwich method for high tapers

saw and filed clean using square files, with cutting surfaces on two sides only.

E. Doublers and Wing Dihedral Braces
Ply and balsa doublers and braces are used at positions of high stress and for giving structural continuity of a joint. All too often they extend to an arbitrary position and then stop dead, the same width and thickness as they started. This is bad structural practice and wasteful in

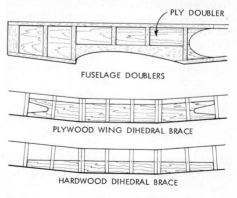

FIG 5.6   DOUBLER AND BRACE DESIGN

weight. We must try to introduce a little more finesse in our scale design and reduce the strengthening effect of the doublers and braces more gradually. By doing so we shall not only save a little weight but achieve a *stronger* construction than with the cruder methods – for the stresses to be confronted with a *sudden* change of constructional strength can *lead* to failure. We are only talking about a gentle tapering of the doublers and braces and some examples are illustrated in Fig. 5.6. Similar effects can be achieved in wing construction by composite construction of spars (reducing in area towards the tip) or by reducing the frequency of the webbing used between the top and bottom spars.

F. Photocopy Transfers. Copying parts from a plan and transferring them to the material are usually carried out by a, Tracing. b, Carbon paper under the plan. c, 'Pinning' through the plan to the material (if it is soft enough) or d, Cutting the part out and gluing it to the material. All methods are fairly time consuming and the accuracy, apart from 'd'. will depend on the skill of the modeller. It is now possible to make redundant these methods for a wide variety of materials for parts up to the size of a sheet of foolscap paper. Photocopiers, on plain paper, produce an image that can be transferred to our work material by the application of heat and pressure. The method will work on balsa, ply, plastic laminate and most sheet metals, providing they have been thoroughly degreased. All we have to do is to obtain a photocopy (Xerox or similar – your local library will probably have one on hire) of the parts to be cut out, e.g. fuselage formers, bulkheads, ribs etc.. Apply the photocopy face down to the material and apply a steady pressure to the paper

with the iron you normally use to apply 'Coverite', 'Monocote', 'Solarfilm' etc.. Balsa and ply should be sanded smooth first, blowing away the residual dust. The iron must be pressed firmly on to the paper allowing time for the heat to soften the ink before moving steadily along the image. Take care not to miss any parts – the position of the paper on the material can be defined by four pin pricks at the corners, in case the paper has to be replaced. The image on the material, although not as dark as the original, is better than any previously used methods. It is, of course, a reverse image but that is normally irrelevant as most formers can be reversed without problems. Some machines do produce a copy that is marginally enlarged, but this is normally so small an increase that it is negligible for average sized components. Dyeline prints are in themselves unstable to temperature and humidity and you should always check the accuracy of the part to the plan, regardless of the means of marking and cutting. A few minutes experimenting with this transfer method will be sufficient to assure you of its potential for quicker and more accurate construction.

JIGS

A model can be constructed absolutely truly without the use of a jig but it *is* possible to build twisted wings and fuselages even with a straight flat building board. Using a jig *almost* eliminates the risk of obtaining twists in components. Building a jig is not too difficult but there are commercially available units should you prefer not to attempt to do it yourself. The model must, to some extent, be designed around the jig so it is important to have the jig before you commence designing or building. Allowance will have to be made for holes in

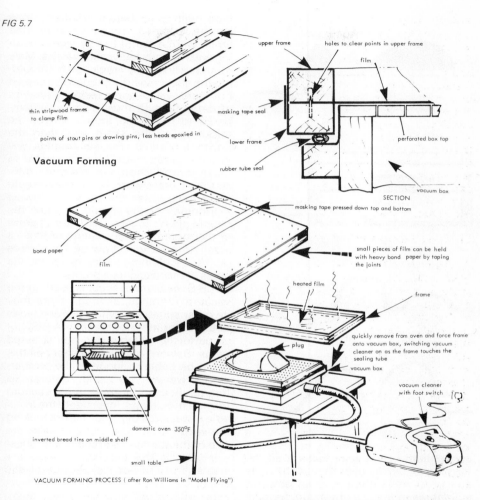

FIG 5.7

upper frame
holes to clear points in upper frame
film
thin stripwood frames to clamp film
masking tape seal
points of stout pins or drawing pins, less heads epoxied in
lower frame
perforated box top

Vacuum Forming

rubber tube seal
vacuum box
SECTION

masking tape pressed down top and bottom

bond paper
small pieces of film can be held with heavy bond paper by taping the joints
film

heated film
frame

quickly remove from oven and force frame onto vacuum box, switching vacuum cleaner on as the frame touches the sealing tube

plug
vacuum box

vacuum cleaner with foot switch

domestic oven 350°F

inverted bread tins on middle shelf

small table

VACUUM FORMING PROCESS (after Ron Williams in "Model Flying")

ribs and formers for some jigs. Surprisingly, few modellers use building jigs; they can be rather 'fiddly' until you are used to them but once familiar with the practice they can give many advantages. Depending on the type of jig used, it may be possible to work on both surfaces of a wing without removing it from the jig,

and for the full 360° of the fuselage side to be free for sheeting and planking.

VACUUM FORMING

For many items on a model such as canopies, wheel spats, air scoops, blisters, exhaust stacks, etc. etc., vacuum forming represents an alternative to

69

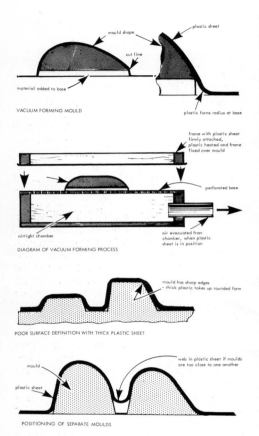

FIG 5.8

conventional carving of balsawood, or forming of plastic over moulds by heat and pressure. Lightness is an obvious advantage in the use of vacuum formed items, as is the ability to reproduce any number of identical items from the same mould. To produce vacuum formed parts we will need the vacuum forming unit (see Fig. 5.7), heat (normally a domestic oven) and a source of suction (although a domestic vacuum cleaner with hose and nozzle can be used, the industrial

type will give better results). Draw depths of up to 3″ are quite feasible; the limits will be found out by experimenting with various heats and plastics. Male moulds are usually employed for moulding the sheet *over* the shape to be copied but there will be some lack of definition of detail lines. It must also be remembered to make the mould almost the thickness of the sheet *less* than the finished product. Female moulds will provide greater fidelity, with regard to detail reproduction, but are more difficult to operate with. The female mould must have holes drilled in the lowest extremities of the mould to allow the heated plastic to be sucked into all areas of the mould. At the position of these a small 'pimple' will show on the surface of the mouldings so try to locate the holes at inconspicuous points.

A.B.S. or Styrene sheet is used for the vacuum formings, although there may be other suitable plastics. Styrene tends to be rather more brittle than A.B.S. but is perfectly suitable for non-stressed items. Beware of cellulose sheet as this could be liable to ignite at the temperatures we will be using; butyrate is frequently used for transparent vacuum formed mouldings. Investigate the available sheet sizes of plastic before making the vacuum forming unit and tailor the size of the frame to suit the plastic sheet – or half of it. This will avoid unnecessary wastage of the not inexpensive plastic sheet.

As with most new ventures, techniques must be developed and it may take a while before you are getting consistently good results. The oven temperature is reasonably critical but it is impossible to give precise settings as domestic oven thermostats are somewhat variable (ask your wife!). Start with a setting of 250°F and if this does not give sufficient heat to allow the plastic to 'droop' increase the temperature gradually until satisfactory results are obtained. Unless you have a glass door to the oven it is suggested that you do not close the oven door as the final part of the softening operation is fairly rapid. Transfer of the frame and plastic from the oven to the vacuum chamber must be quickly carried out to prevent excessive cooling. The use of oven gloves or stout leather gloves is strongly recommended for this operation as burnt fingers do not assist the operation one little bit! Having an assistant to turn on the vacuum machine and assist generally, will be found useful. The vacuum cleaner must be switched on immediately the frame is secured to the chamber. A heat proof glue must be used for construction of the frame for the joints to withstand the heat of the oven. Firm gripping of the plastic to the frame is essential or the plastic will pull away and produce a faulty moulding. It is feasible to mould smaller items by using a blanking plate in the frame (with a square hole in the centre) and taping the smaller piece of plastic to the plate – the results are a little inconsistent. No undercuts are permissible on moulds, otherwise it will be impossible to remove the mould from the sheet after moulding. When moulding more than one part at a time the individual moulds must not be positioned too close or a web of plastic will form between the two moulds.

For moulds in excess of a 3 inch draw it would be advisable to take the mould to a commercial organisation, with a higher capacity machine for vacuum forming. The moulds themselves can be made from balsa, softwood, plaster, in fact almost anything that will not burn or melt at temperatures up to 250°F, but mouldings will only be as good as the mould finish.

SILICONE MOULDS

For relatively small moulded items where additional strength is required, the use of glass fibre has distinct advantages. The methods of producing glass fibre mouldings are fairly well known but they usually involve the use of glass fibre moulds also. Moulding glass fibre over male moulds is not suitable for most work as the external surface of the moulding will be rough and require an exorbitant amount of effort to obtain a smooth surface. As an alternative to a glass fibre female mould, for items such as cowls and wheel spats, silicone can be utilised, and with advantage. Some of the bonuses of using silicone are a, No highly polished male plug required and no burnishing of the interior of the female mould. b, No release agent required. c, Flexibility of mould for easy release of moulding. The only disadvantage is that care must be taken not to cut the mould when trimming a moulding whilst it is still in the mould.

To make the female mould we must first secure the male mould to a piece of Formica with a three inch overlap around the mould. It is not necessary to have a glass-like finish to the mould but the final moulding will only be as good as the smoothness of the original. Three or four coats of thick dope should be sufficient sealing for a balsa plug. No further preparation is needed as the silicone will not adhere to the plug. Form a dam around the mould high enough to give about half an inch cover to the top and two inches or so around the mould. The dam can be from Plasticine, or wood that is held in place with tape. Lightly grease the Formica base with petroleum jelly

71

(Vaseline) and spray the mould with a dry silicone lubricant. The spray will dry very rapidly and after fifteen minutes the white silicone (as supplied for bathroom sealants, e.g. Clam etc.) can be applied over the mould to a depth of approximately $3/16''$. Smooth out the silicone with a damp finger and leave to dry for a period of two to three hours. Mix sufficient plaster of paris to fill the dammed area and pour on to the mould, tapping and shaking the assembly to eliminate air bubbles.

When the plaster has set the dam can be removed and the base-board and mould removed from the plaster. The silicone mould may also be lifted out from the plaster — it will not adhere to it — and the mould inspected. When glass fibre mouldings are made in the silicone mould no release agent is required; the mould should be repositioned in the plaster to give it rigidity and the mass of the plaster will stabilise the mould during the laying up operation. Once the glass fibre moulding has cured the silicone mould is removed from the plaster and peeled off the glass fibre. The process of producing a silicone mould involves considerably less work than a comparable glass fibre mould.

ADHESIVES

The range of specialised adhesives is growing daily and there are on the market, including industrial applications, thousands of different adhesives specifically formulated to bond virtually every type of material. Unless we have a very unusual gluing application we can narrow the field down to about six types.

1. Balsa cement.
2. P.V.A. white glue and aliphatic glues.
3. Epoxy adhesives.
4. General contact adhesives (where two surfaces are coated and the adhesive allowed to dry before mating).
5. Styrofoam contact adhesives.
6. Cyanoacrylates.

Balsa cement, one of the original adhesives specially developed for balsa, is faster drying than most other glues. It does not have the strength of P.V.A.s and epoxies but the strength of the joint can be improved by precementing (coating the two surfaces, allowing to dry and recementing before making the joint). The slight gap filling qualities and easy sanding make it suitable for planking. It is not suitable for plywood, hardwood or wood to metal joints.

P.V.A. is an excellent general purpose adhesive for balsa, plywood and hardwoods, providing an accurate close joint is made — it has no gap filling qualities. Being a water based adhesive it should not be used in any area where water is likely to be present, e.g. seaplanes. The slow drying of the P.V.A. glue makes it ideal for attaching large areas of balsa sheet but the poor 'sandability' makes it less ideal for surface areas where considerable sanding has to be undertaken. As the glue requires air for drying purposes it may take many hours to dry completely in large areas in confined space. For this reason it is not good for sticking large doublers in position.

Epoxies, although in many forms, are of two types for general modelling purposes, the quick setting (often called 5 minute epoxy) and the standard (or 24 hour) variety. Although the former type is very useful for field repairs the standard epoxy should be used wherever possible due to its greater strength and the additional time it has to soak into the fibres of materials. Epoxy is reasonably fuel proof and has applications for fitting engine bearers to firewalls, etc., where its gap filling properties may also be useful. However, the strongest joint will result – in common with all adhesives – where a thin film of adhesive and close fitting joint is used.

Contact adhesives should be limited in use to the joining of large area doublers involving balsa and ply. It may have a few other minor applications, e.g. used in a thinned down form for fixing canopies, but it is not suitable for the majority of modelling purposes.

Styrofoam adhesives have been developed because most of the other available glues will dissolve polystyrene foam when applied to it. Being a contact adhesive, the two glued surfaces must be allowed to become completely touch dry before the surfaces are joined – when an immediate bond takes place.

One of the growing range of 'miracle' adhesives is the type known as cyanoacrylates. This is a one part adhesive which relies on water being present in the material, or the air, to achieve its set. Used correctly, it will make an extremely strong joint, often in excess of the materials being joined. It can be used to strengthen thin, vulnerable edges of balsa and adds very little extra weight. The bond is made within seconds of introducing the adhesive and maximum strength is achieved quite rapidly. It has many uses for tack-gluing parts together that are being permanently glued with a different adhesive – almost a 'pinning' operation. Probably its greatest value is in being able to glue a wide variety of dissimilar materials together, many of them in the 'difficult' class. These include nylon, rubber, silicone, PTFE, metals etc. Not all proprietary cyanoacrylate adhesives are to the same formulation and they will not all have the same properties. It may take some experimenting to find the most suitable variety for some

of the more 'exotic' materials. Slower drying and thicker cyanoacrylates are on the market and these allow more 'positioning' time (usually about thirty seconds).

When you are unsure of the suitability of an adhesive for a particular purpose the best answer is to make a simple practical test, using scrap materials. Some adhesives have potential dangers when used in confined spaces, or when in contact with the skin. Abide by the instructions and warnings!

METALWORK

Although the average modeller can cope with the woodworking aspects of making scale models, many find difficulties when tackling metalwork. This may be through a lack of correct tools, or a knowledge of how to use them correctly. It may also be as a result of being unfamiliar with the metals and alloys we are likely to use. Most scale models will feature a reasonably high degree of metal fittings and it is, therefore, important to be able to work with various 'modelling' metals.

The first essential is to have sufficient tools. In addition to the basic tools mentioned earlier we shall need:-

1. A pair of soft jaws for the bench vice. These can be formed from copper or aluminium.
2. A hand vice. To hold metal when being drilled with a bench drill.
3. An engineers square. 4 inch or 6 inch.
4. A variety of second cut files – complete with handles.
5. A pair of dividers for scribing circles.
6. A scriber – can be made from a piece of piano wire.
7. A centre punch – can be made from a piece of piano wire.

FIG 5.9

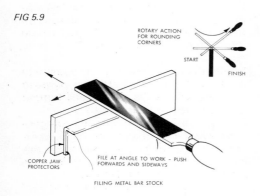

FILING METAL BAR STOCK

8. Drill bits to correspond with clearance holes for piano wire and bolts—See table.
9. Abrafiles and adapter for hacksaw.
10. A pair of tin snips.
A large selection of pliers will assist in forming metals and high speed hacksaw blades will speed up the cutting of hard metals.

MATERIALS

You will probably have collected a quantity of 'scrap' aluminium brass and tin plate sheet, tubing and piano wire; most of these items are available from your model shop or metal dealers. A selection of steel rod (welding rods come in diameters from $^1/_{16}$'' to $^3/_{16}$''). Larger sizes of dural and brass tubing and steel strip and bar will also be useful. Never pass the chance of collecting odd pieces of metals from any source. It is normally fairly easy to identify the metal, although aluminium alloys and steels may vary considerably in composition. Aluminium is, of course, much softer than aluminium alloy and will readily bend—the alloy will give a much sharper 'ring' when struck with another piece of metal.

Unlike the marking of wood, metal is marked direct — with a scribe and dividers — by direct measurement. Carry out any drilling operations before cutting the outline of the part as this will give a larger area to hold and with less likelihood of damage. Centre punching is a 'must' before drilling or the drill point will simply wander over the surface of the metal. For any drilling or tapping operation the metal should be well lubricated to prevent the breaking of drills and taps. Use paraffin for aluminium based metals, 3 in 1 oil for steel and tallow for brass. Using lubricants when cutting metals makes life a lot easier but is frequently over-looked by modellers.

Thin sheet metals can be cut with tin snips, although it will often cause the metal to curl slightly. Forming the rounded areas, and accurate finishing, is undertaken with files but thin sheet material must be supported by clamping between two pieces of wood. There are correct and incorrect ways to use files, as with all tools, but in all cases the metal must be firmly fixed in the vice. For filing straight edges use the action shown in Fig. 5.9 but for convex curves the file

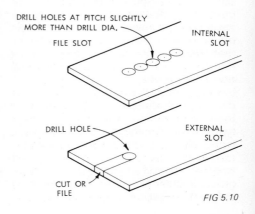

FIG 5.10

should be rotated in a motion as also indicated in Fig. 5.9. To make an internal slot the material must first be drilled with a series of holes, at a pitch larger than the drill diameter, and then the slot filed out. Use a drill slightly smaller than the finished slot width to allow for filing out any slight inaccuracies and don't try to drill the holes too close together – the drill will only slip into the previous hole. External slots are easily formed by drilling a hole at the extremity of the slot and cutting to it with a saw, abrafile or tin snips, see Fig. 5.10.

Bending sheet metal will be undertaken with more confidence if the nature of the various metals is understood. Most metals have a property of 'work hardening' which means the metal becomes progressively harder and more brittle as it is hammered and bent. To overcome this natural disadvantage the metal must be softened (annealed) during the forming process. Non-ferrous metals, i.e. copper and brass, will need probably only one annealing process but steel and particularly aluminium alloy must be frequently softened. Table 5.11 gives the methods of annealing different metals. Aluminium alloys vary considerably in their composition and their ease of working, and the biggest problems the modeller is likely to encounter will be with the use of Dural. This metal has a very high tensile strength and for this reason is used for areas where there is likely to be high stresses, e.g. undercarriages. Dural does not take kindly to being 'cold' bent, where a simple bend may cause serious weakening along the bend line. Conversely, annealing will soften the dural to an unacceptable level requiring retempering to achieve the original strength. Unfortunately, from the modeller's point of view, the temperatures for annealing and hardening are fairly critical and considerable experiment may be necessary to achieve good results. The technical data for heat treating dural is as follows:-

a. Anneal at 400°C.
b. Heat treat for hardness by heating to between 450°C and 550°C then quench in clean cold water (Metal will harden over a period of 1–2 weeks).
c. To speed up the hardening process the dural can be reheated to 200°C.

For the modellers, prepared to experiment, the following procedure is recommended for hardening:-
1. Coat the area of dural to be treated with soap.
2. Heat until soap blackens (400°C) and continue to heat for a further 20% of the total time to obtain a temperature in excess of 450°C.
3. Plunge into clean cold water and stir vigorously.

FIG 5.11 Annealing Metals

Aluminium and Aluminium Alloy, including Dural*. Heat to 350-400 deg. C. Quench in cold water. Use soap rubbed on to metal to indicate temperature – it will blacken at 400 deg. C.

Brass. Heat to dull red and allow to cool slowly to avoid fractures. Pickle in vinegar.

Copper. Heat to dull red, quench in cold water, pickle in vinegar.

Steel. Heat to cherry red, allow to cool naturally.

Stainless Steel. Scour surface, heat to dull red, quench in clean cold water.

* Re-tempering of Dural is difficult, re-heat to 500°C, quench in cold water, leave to harden for two weeks.

4. Leave for two weeks to harden or heat to 200°C in a domestic oven to accelerate the hardening process.

Piano wire is probably the most common metal used by aeromodellers because of its high strength/weight ratio and its ability to 'spring' without breaking. These desirable characteristics come as a result of using a high quality carbon steel and a critical method of tempering. The modeller cannot hope to re-enact the tempering process used by the manufacturer and he must avoid, as far as practical, any annealing process that will inevitably soften and weaken the wire. Soft soldering piano wire will not detemper the wire but hard soldering (silver soldering) requires temperatures that will affect its strength. For this reason, any silver soldering of stressed structural items should be confined locally to the joint. As most of the bending of piano wire will be carried out 'cold' it is important to limit the radius of the bend to a reasonable minimum to avoid fatiguing the wire where it is stretched. The radius of the bend will depend on the gauge of piano wire being used (thin gauges may be bent with tight radii) and to some extent, the type of piano wire. The 'bendability' and brittleness of wire will vary from one manufacturer to another, and will even vary in the same batch of material. If you are having difficulties in achieving the radius of bend dictated by the design, it may be worth while sorting around for an alternative supply.

Where a complex and symmetrical shape is to be formed, the wire must first be accurately marked out – leaving ample material beyond the last bend. Markings should be made with a felt pen or chinagraph pencil – never with a file as this will weaken the wire – and then protected with Scotch tape. Bending of heavy gauge wire ($\frac{1}{16}$" (1.5mm) and thicker) can only be done in a satisfactory manner by holding the wire in a vice, using plain jaws with a radiused top edge. The bend itself should be made by pushing the wire with a hardwood block to ensure that the 'free' end of the wire remains straight. Always work symmetrically from the centre of the item to be bent, bending lefthand and righthand angles in turn. The marks on the piano wire should be placed in the vice in the same relative positions.

Sheet metal bending, except for single bends, can be more troublesome and it is often necessary to make special wooden blocks to the internal dimen-

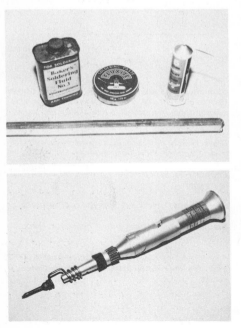

Baker's Fluid, Fluxite, cored and tinman's solder cover most soft soldering jobs. Bottom, small portable butane-heated iron.

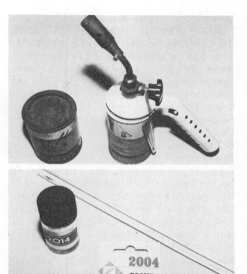

A gas blowlamp and special flux for silver soldering; centre, aluminium can be soldered. Bottom, midget blowtorch for intense local heat.

sions, to form the metal around. To achieve a neat regular bend in sheet metal (typically tinplate) the metal must be clamped between two pieces of timber at least the full length of the bend. Thin gauges of softer metals can be bent by pushing with a hardwood block but more stubborn examples will have to be encouraged by hitting the block with a hammer. Avoid hitting the metal direct with a hammer as this will distort and work harden it more rapidly.

It is to be hoped that the prospective scale modeller has already had experience in soft soldering from his previous modelling attempts. Should there still be problems in making good solder joints these are the main considerations for a sound joint.

1. Cleanliness – the metal parts must be thoroughly cleaned.

2. Tinning – where possible the parts to be joined should be tinned with a *thin* coat of solder.

3. Heat – your iron must have sufficient heat to raise the temperature of the metal to give a good 'flow' of the solder.

4. Close joint – the parts to be joined must be in *close* proximity and bound with tinned wire if possible. Solder should not be used as a gap filler as it has little inherent strength for this purpose.

5. Solder – use cored acid flux solder (or tinmans solder and acid flux) for all but electrical joints. For the latter a resin cored solder must be used to avoid risk of attack by the residual flux.

6. Heat transference – use heat sinks to avoid heat reaching unwanted areas, but use insulators where you want to retain heat, e.g. wooden blocks in a vice to prevent the heat being lost from the parts to be soldered to the metal jaws of the vice.

Silver soldering (so called because of the silver/copper composition of the solder) may be employed where a joint of increased strength is required. Typical areas where this form of hard soldering should be used includes undercarriage wire joints on large models, cabane strut joints, elevator horn joints, metal wheel spokes etc. With the solder having a melting point of between 600°C–800°C the ordinary soldering iron is obviously going to be useless. We must resort to a form of blowlamp to reach these temperatures and a variety of these are available commercially. They range from methylated spirit blowlamps to butane and propane torches and the more complex oxy-butane soldering equipment. The disadvantage with the former devices is that with their limited heat output they may take a long time to bring the parts to be silver soldered up to the required temperature. This will have the effect of annealing the metal, as described previously, and this could be detrimental for metals such as piano wire. Oxy-butane units provide a much higher *concentrated* temperature allowing the immediate parts to be soldered to be brought up to temperature in a short period of time. Safety precautions *must* be observed when using oxy-butane equipment and full instructions are included with each unit – read them and obey them.

Low temperature silver solder is adequate for most of our needs, although the higher temperature variety may be used with an oxy-butane flame. Clean the areas to be joined and treat with the Borax-based flux. Limit the flux to the precise area to be silver soldered or you will find the solder flowing beyond the area involved. Retaining the metal parts in position during the soldering operation can be achieved by binding with copper wire or by clamping. The silver solder (it's available in thin rods or small section strip) may be pre-positioned by placing short lengths of the solder adjacent to the joint. Alternatively, the metal can be heated to the desired temperature and then the solder stick applied. When you have

reached the appropriate temperature of the metal the solder should flow smoothly around the joint. Once the joint is made the work may be quenched in cold water and the surplus flux removed. Piano wire should be left to cool naturally for a short period before quenching to avoid it becoming too brittle.

Soldering aluminium is possible, but specialised, as is the jointing of stainless steel, and this work is best left to the expert or by reading up books on the subject and being prepared to experiment for long periods.

It is, of couse, possible to join metal parts by other means than soldering. Riveting and the use of specialised adhesives immediately come to mind. Epoxy resin glues are particularly suitable for joining dissimilar metals where it may be impossible to use soldering techniques. Attention must be paid here to keying the surfaces to be joined and thoroughly degreasing (carbon tetrachloride will act as a cleaning agent). A slow setting epoxy is preferable to the quickset variety as it gives more time to ensure that the surfaces are closely mated before clamping together. Only a thin covering of epoxy is required as the joint will weaken in proportion to the gap filled by the epoxy. Cyanoacrylate adhesives may also be used for joining metals but remember that these have limited gap filling properties. It should also be remembered that although the tensile, shear and impact strengths are good to reasonable, the 'peel' resistance is poor.

NUTS, BOLTS AND WASHERS

Screws and bolts (bolts have only part of the shank threaded) are available in a wide variety of sizes and head shapes. Try to use the type of head applicable to its purpose – functional, or for appear-

*Simple basic trad-
itional structure used by
the author on a ⅛ scale
(48in) Fokker Eindekker*

ances sake when representing the full size equivalent. For example, a countersunk bolt is not suitable for fixing an engine to a metal motor mount, a hexagonal or cheese head bolt is far more applicable. However, it is unlikely that a cheese head bolt would be used on the external surface of a full size aircraft and a countersunk screw would be more appropriate to use on a model in this situation. Standard steel screws, bolts and nuts – or brass where a 'weak' link is required – are suitable for most modelling purposes but high tensile steel bolts should be used for such items as wheel axle bolts. For additional security the addition of spring or locking washers to the nuts is advisable and to the same end, stiff nuts are an advantage. Maximum security is obtained by using lock nuts, i.e. half nuts tightly secured on to the standard nut, for positions such as engine retaining bolts. Loctite and similar proprietary brands of sealant may be used for security nuts, but remember that these may need the application of heat to remove them at a later date.

Some situations preclude the use of nuts and bolts and we must turn to taps and dies to obtain our fixing requirements. The principal requirements for obtaining good threads are in the use of the correct size holes for taps and the correct diameter rod for threading. Although metric sizes are becoming more widely used the U.N.C. sizes are likely to be the most common for modellers for some years to come in the States.

Chapter 6

Construction of 1903 – 1939 Aircraft

Although this chapter and chapter seven deal with aircraft of two separate periods, for the sake of convenience there is inevitably an overlap of prototypes between the two periods. The intention is to divide the forms of construction used, in the first instance, to the open framework aircraft, and in the following chapter, aircraft using wooden or metal monocoque construction. Indeed, many aircraft in the thirties and later used a combination of the earlier and later forms of construction. It must be the scale modeller's intention to simulate whatever type of construction and finish was employed on the prototype to the best of his ability. Not that we have to look too far underneath the skin; there is little point in reproducing the complex internal structures of aircraft that will be *completely* hidden by sheeting. Our time will be more rewardingly spent in providing adequate internal structure and concentrating on the surface detailing and finishing. The *knowledge* of the prototype's construction will, however, be of value as this can give clues to the positioning of formers etc., and the choice of materials to be used.

At this point it might be as well to dispose of one controversy that has been much discussed in the past. When radio control equipment was less reliable than it is today it was often argued that models should be designed with a certain degree of 'crashability' built into them. In other words, it was thought desirable to incorporate such features as wings that would easily knock off and the same with tailplanes. Nowadays this view is no longer acceptable, with the possible exception of small sports scale models. The use of external rubber bands to hold wings in position, or even tongue and box devices at too obvious positions, deviates excessively from the scale appearance. Full-size aircraft have never incorporated such methods and neither should we. Of course, there will always be crashes, that is part of the frustration and challenge of this hobby, but we must learn to accept this philosophically – if we cannot, then scale R/C modelling is the wrong pursuit for us.

The earliest aircraft were mostly very 'minimum' in their construction. Surfaces that provided lift were covered, sometimes only on the top surface, and the remainder was simply an open braced structure. Occasionally there was a small token gesture to the creature comforts of the pilot in the form of rudimentary covering around the cockpit area, but he was frequently totally exposed to the elements. One of the most limiting factors facing the early designers was the poor power/weight ratio of the engines available, and the limited *maximum* power produced by any suitable engine. It was only later, spurred on by the necessities of war, that more suitable power plants were developed. The knowledge of aerodynamics was not always lacking by the pioneers, although some designed by imagination rather than experience; had they possessed first rate engines, their aircraft would have been designed differently. One only has to look closely at some of the surviving aircraft from the second decade of the twentieth century to realise that their standards of construction could be very high indeed. Individual craftsmanship was not the dying art that mass production has now brought about, and there was an abundance of men capable of first rate joinery and producing excellent metal fittings. The idea of the aircraft being sticks of wood held together with string and sealing wax is far from the truth!

Fuselages were constructed from a variety of timbers, thoughtfully selected for their purpose and qualities. Ash was frequently used for longerons and spruce for the upright and cross pieces, taking the compression stresses. Other timbers were used (there was a greater selection available then) including mahogany and bamboo. In order to save weight – yes, they had this perennial problem too – the strut members would often be shaped to taper at the ends in accordance with sound structural principles. Cross bracing took the form of piano wire, although standard steel cable was also used, sometimes with tensioning adjustment by turnbuckles and sometimes with the ends looped and bound. Examination of photographs, contemporary magazines, or the actual examples will clarify these points. The use of turnbuckles on a fuselage, following the examples of boats, was to assist the truing up and tensioning during assembly.

Wing construction, by today's standards, was very flimsy with very thin wing sections and usually multi-spar construction. The rigidity of the wings was achieved almost entirely by internal bracing and the wire rigging from the wings to cabane struts above and below the fuselage. Some early aircraft followed boat practices to a considerable degree, an example being the *Antoinette* which used a mast, protruding through and below the boat-like fuselage, for attaching the wing rigging wires. Bleached linen or calico was the standard covering until doped Irish linen became the standard accepted practice by 1914. Some of the early attempts at 'air proofing' the fabrics were quite interesting. A rubberised fabric was

Bristol Boxkite at 86in. span, 11lb weight by Richard Hawke uses a Fox Eagle 60. A nightmare to trim!

This large scale Demoiselle by J. Vogesang (Germany) weighs 19kg and flies at about 35k.p.h. with a Husqvarna engine. On display at Dortmund.

developed and proved reasonably efficacious and some experimenters tried coating the linen with a mixture of thin gruel (Scots porridge) — not to be recommended on a scale model with the vagaries of our weather!

Tail structures too were of very light construction, using wood or light metal tubing for the outlines and some fins were no more than a canvas 'sail', devoid of any structure apart from stiffening of the fabric edges.

No standard form of undercarriage was employed and many types, often extremely complex, were tried. Skids, projecting in front of the aircraft, were commonly included to prevent the aircraft tipping nose over on take-off and landing. It must be remembered that there was little dual training in those days and straight 'hops' were the only way of getting the 'feel' of the aircraft. Regrettably, we seldom fly from a 'scale' take-off and landing surface and the

landing attitude must be absolutely right to prevent these skids, on a scale model replica, from tripping the model nose over.

Exposed engines, particularly the rotary types, will tax the ingenuity of the modeller contemplating the building of an R/C scale model of an early 'bird'. This is one area where the lack of complete scale fidelity might be excused, as the exposed engine, in conjunction with open fuselage construction, leaves little opportunity to include remote drive devices and the such like. There will be enough problems in trying to hide away the radio equipment and it may be necessary to use the dummy pilot for this purpose.

In construction of an R/C model of the early examples of flying machines, it is totally essential to think in terms of working structural rigging. Without the rigidity and strength supplied by the structural rigging the general construc-

An unusual choice of prototype is the Caudron GIII of 1913, used at one time by the R.F.C. This model has twin Graupner Wankel engines, also unusual!

tion would have to be 'beefed up' to the extent that the model would be a mockery of the prototype. Without the light, fragile – almost gossamer – appearance that the full size aircraft displayed the model will just not look right. With larger scale models, say ⅕th or ¼ scale, it may be possible to use scale sections for the longerons if spruce, or preferably ash (in the unlikely event of it being available) is used. On a quarter scale model we are talking in terms of not more than ¼ inch square longerons, for most models, with a fuselage length of possibly six feet – not very much of a safety margin. Our problems are compounded by the full-size use of often cleverly designed metal fittings that are difficult to reproduce. You will have to decide whether to go to the extremes of making a multitude of metal fittings, that can be bolted to the structure or glued in place, or opt for a simpler method of bracing the fuselage

structure, Fig. 6.1 shows examples. Scale wing sections are viable using balsa ribs and, where necessary because of the thinness of the aerofoil section, spruce spars. Your strip stock for longerons and spars *must* be straight grained and true. Strips may well become warped during storage and these can be straightened by steaming them, placing them on a flat surface and weighting them down until *thoroughly* dry. It is not necessary to include the lateral crossbracing in the internal wing structure as we have a greater strength / weight scale wing structure than did the prototypes. Our covering methods also add to the strength of the wing structure in a way that was absent from the full-size aircraft. Allowances must be made for the rigging points on the wing and they must be securely affixed to the stronger areas of the wing structure. If you follow the general construction of the prototype this should not present too

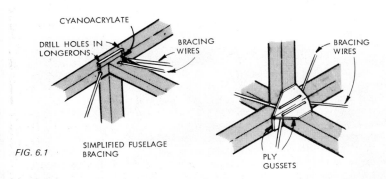

FIG. 6.1   SIMPLIFIED FUSELAGE BRACING

many problems as they were faced with the same complications! Tail surfaces can be built up in a variety of ways, always trying to duplicate the lightness of the structure. Methods of construction to be described for aircraft of a slightly later period will largely apply to these pre-1914 examples, but the important factor to bear in mind is the virtually 'transparent' effect of these models in flight.

Leading up to W.W.1, and from then on, fuselages became fully covered in either linen or plywood. Gradually the aircraft became more sophisticated with more attention being paid to streamlining, speed and, with the advent of the war, manoeuvrability. Prior to the war there were individual examples showing quite advanced design for speed, notably the Deperdussin 'Racer', but most of the aircraft maintained a simple box fuselage structure. Initially, monoplanes were quite common but with the increasing importance of strength and manoeuvrability, the biplane – and to a lesser extent the triplane – found favour. It was found easier to brace the wings of biplanes, with the interplane rigging wires, to withstand the loads experienced in combat. Wing sections, although still undercambered, became a little thicker and undercarriages were simplified, normally using 'V' struts with bungee springing for the axles.

With the relatively small cross-sections of longerons still being used, both wood and tubular metal, there is still a modelling problem in using an unreinforced box framework. With the fuselages being covered and painted this problem can be overcome. We have a choice of making sheet fuselage sides and superimposing the correct size longerons and cross members, or we can introduce an additional internal longeron to reinforce the structure. See Fig. 6.2. Where rounded tube was used for the basic fuselage structure this can be duplicated by using ramin, birch or balsa dowel, or by sanding off the external edges of the square section longerons. The former method will give

FIG. 6.2

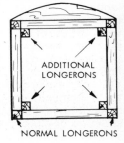

ADDITIONAL LONGERONS

NORMAL LONGERONS

the better scale effect as the covering will only touch the structure in the same relative positions as the prototype. Incidentally, where linen came into contact with steel tubing the latter was often wrapped with strips of linen before the covering was applied – the purist may wish to include this. Balsa dowel may be perfectly adequate for construction of the rear half of the fuselage (weight saving again) but would not have sufficient strength for the higher stressed front end. We can either change to birch or ramin dowel at the front – the joint between the balsa and stronger dowel does present some difficulties – or we can go to a welded metal tube structure using lightweight steel or aluminium alloy tube. Perhaps silver soldered tubular structure would be more accurate, for this is the method of joining the most modellers prefer. It is described in more detail in Chapter 7. There are always exceptions to the rule and the W.W.1 period produced a number of aircraft that used different layouts or constructional techniques. For some time in the early part of the war, the Allies used a pusher layout for their fighters. This was dictated to them due to the lack of an efficient interrupter gear

for the machine gun/s, and the only alternative was to fire the machine gun outside the arc of the propeller. By situating the engine behind the pilot the gun could be mounted to be 'sight fired' by the pilot, thus allowing a greater degree of accuracy. With the engine behind it also involved the design of twin open booms to support the tail surfaces and avoid the propeller. The pusher configuration presents two main problems to the modeller, 1. The design and construction of the booms and 2. The weight distribution – with the engine mounted behind the C. of G.

To overcome the first, and not aggravate the second, thick wall aluminium tube should be used for the booms with the vertical supports from spruce or beech. This will not only give a very scale appearance, but when properly braced will be more than sufficiently strong. Fittings between the booms and wing and tail surface require careful planning, as do the control cable runs to the elevator and rudder. You can do no better than to follow the routes used on the prototype. Almost certainly the completed model will require some weight in the nose to obtain the correct balance so there is no point in skimping

The German firm of Junkers developed corrugated metal skinning as a means of reinforcement. This D.I 'Tin Donkey' model is by Arthur Searle; a fine model.

on weight at the front of the cockpit. A heavy glass fibre moulding for the engineless front of the fuselage will give weight where it is necessary and give more protection for less-than-perfect landings. Examples of British pusher designs include the D.H.2., F.E.2. and F.E.8.

The German firm of Junkers developed unbraced monoplanes towards the end of W.W.1, and as part of the solution for additional strength, used corrugated metal covering to the aircraft. It was a system which worked well and they employed it for the next twenty years. Corrugated cardboard can be used to simulate the corrugations, provided the pitch of the corrugations are commensurate to the scale, but it suffers from being too soft to withstand knocks and handling. Arthur Searle of Liverpool, England, an avid scale modeller of early prototype aircraft, has developed a system of preforming corrugated lightweight metal sheets ideal for such subjects as the Junkers range and the Ford Trimotor aircraft. The system for producing the panels is by a 'mangling' process using intermeshing rollers of the required pitch and depth. Scale measurements must be made of the prototype to calculate the pitch of the corrugations and the width of sheet used. With a template of the undulations for guidance, rollers are turned from a hard but workable nylon on a lathe. Accuracy is important as the volutes must complement each other. The rollers are fixed to spindles, with winding handles at one end, and set in a rigid metal framework. An adjustable top roller, to vary the gap between the rollers, is advisable, to allow for experiment. Handles should be fixed to both rollers as the material must be passed through in a single smooth

action. Litho printing plates, about four thousandths of an inch thick, can be used for the panels and they should be cut a little wider than the scale width to allow for width reduction caused by forming the corrugations. Several passes are required through the rollers (adjusting the top roller as necessary) and the plate must be frequently annealed to prevent work hardening. That the system works is amply demonstrated by Arthur's excellent model of the Junkers D.1. with the corrugated metal panels correct in scale and material.

The open structure wings of the period had, at the most, plywood sheet covering limited to the top wing centre section and the immediate area behind the leading edge. The model wing, where the full size construction is followed, will be flexible and prone to warping unless care is taken at all stages. For sports scale models with 'thickish' wing sections, foam construction can be employed to produce a quite acceptable imitation of a full size ribbed and under cambered wing. The method follows the traditional pattern but includes additional spars and capping strips fitted at the positions of the ribs. Cut the foam core $^1/_8$in. smaller in depth than the finished depth of the wing — it may be necessary to cheat slightly by making the wing thicker — it will depend on the prototype. Cut slots in the foam for $^1/_8$in. thick spruce spars, $^3/_{16}$in. wide for average size models, two top and two bottom. The leading and trailing edges are from balsa and are glued to the foam with P.V.A. glue followed by the $^1/_8$in. square 'ribs'. Wing tips can be formed from thin sheet balsa with thin plywood reinforcement. Attachment areas for cabane strut fixing bolts are reinforced with 3mm ply and aluminium tubing, the full depth of the wing, is glued in position

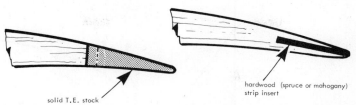

hardwood (spruce or mahogany)
strip insert

solid T.E. stock

FIG. 6.3   METHOD OF FORMING WOODEN TRAILING EDGES

for interplane struts and rigging points. The danger of the dope being applied to the covering attacking the foam should be appreciated and foam areas likely to be affected should be rubbed with a wax candle. Water shrinking the covering and spraying on the clear dope is to be preferred for this form of foam wings. Wings made by this method are strong, less prone to warping and 'undetectable' providing they are painted on both surfaces.

Standard construction wings, of thin section and open framework, rely for their rigidity on the wing bracing – rigging wires – and substantial depth spars as used on the original aircraft. Spars near to the full depth of the wing section are required for maximum strength but we must be careful not to interrupt the natural form of the covering with the edges of the spars. There is always a tendency for the covering to sag slightly between the rib stations and, therefore, the spars must be kept at least $^1/_8$in.

below the surface of the rib. At the doping of the covering stage there is still the risk of the covering attaching itself to the spars and the ways of overcoming these problems are dealt with in Chapter 15. Because of the higher camber of the upper surface of the wing, and greater area, there is a natural tendency for the wing to assume an elliptical dihedral during doping and it may be prudent to fit an additional top spar at the central chord position. This does not have to be to the same dimensions as the main spars but it must be set below the surface of the rib, and the between-rib gap unfilled, to avoid the covering touching. Leading edges can be from dowel (ramin is available in lengths of up to two metres) or strip set into the leading edge of the rib, diagonal fashion. Trailing edges of these thin sectioned wings can present greater difficulties and the standard tapered trailing edge stock is not really suitable, as it becomes too obvious on the top surface. Very small

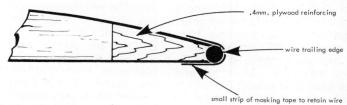

.4mm. plywood reinforcing

wire trailing edge

small strip of masking tape to retain wire

FIG. 6.4   WIRE TRAILING EDGE

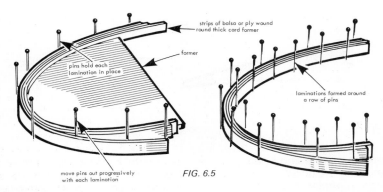

strips of balsa or ply wound round thick card former

former

pins hold each lamination in place

laminations formed around a row of pins

move pins out progressively with each lamination

FIG. 6.5

trailing edge sections (wood, metal tube or piano wire) were used on early aircraft and it is difficult to reproduce these on a model and maintain structural integrity. For the straight edged trailing edge the insertion of a 0.8mm ply strip is as aesthetically satisfying as any method and it provides adequate strength. Cut the slots into the trailing edge of the rib with a hacksaw blade; it is difficult to cut these slots in a 'sandwich' of ribs. An alternative system is to use a hard balsa strip insert of about $^1/_{16}$in. and edge this top and bottom with strips of $^1/_{16}$in. × $^3/_{16}$in. balsa. For simulation of the wire trailing edge there is no alternative, for authenticity, to using a wire trailing edge on the model wing. This is not as difficult as it may sound, but the end of the rib must be strengthened to take the pressure of the wire pushing on to it. Cyanoacrylate adhesive applied to the end of the balsa rib will toughen it considerably, and a small length of 0.4mm ply can be glued to the end of the rib. Stainless steel stranded wire, as used by fishermen, is used for the trailing edge. It must be anchored at the tip end, pulled tight, and bound and glued at the root rib position. With the covering applied the tautening process will pull the wire inwards to

produce the scallops reminiscent of the prototype aircraft.

Wing tip construction will depend on the shape to be followed but most tips are cambered to follow the under camber curvature of the wing section. If a laminated tip, consisting of 0.8mm ply/balsa construction, it must either be moulded to follow this curvature or made to sufficient depth to allow trimming to the curvature. As the original aircraft nearly always used metal tube outlines to the tips it makes sense to use aluminium tubing for our purposes. It is available from aluminium stockists in $^1/_8$in., $^3/_{16}$in. and $^1/_4$in. outside diameters at any length we may require. Bending the tubing is not difficult as it has a reasonable wall thickness and it can be formed in the hand, or round wooden formers. Don't be too worried if the curvature is not quite as smooth as you would wish, the tautening of the covering will take care of this – just avoid any 'kinks'. Flatten the tube where it meets the trailing edge, filing if needed, and glue and bind it at a convenient point of the wood structure. You will notice that many of the prototypes had small diagonal struts from the spars out to the tubular tip. These should not be omitted as they support the tip and reduce the unsupported length.

Ailerons were normally of the simple type, i.e. centre hinged, and should be constructed in a similar fashion to the wing. With inset ailerons there should not be any difficulties but ailerons extending to the tip must have the hinge (vertical) centre line coincidental with the centre of the tip. Many German biplanes featured ailerons with washout built into them, giving a characteristic upwards curvature of the tip at the trailing edge. Before commencing the building of the wing the method of aileron operation must be planned. A closed loop system is to be favoured, although this may add too much friction to the control linkage unless genuine pulley systems are incorporated. The standard pushrod and bellcrank method can be used, aiming to make the control horn as scale-like as possible and fitting a dummy horn on the opposite side of the wing. A third alternative is to use a torque rod method; this is particularly applicable to some biplanes (e.g. Nieuports) as this was the method used on the prototypes.

Transport of large scale biplanes can be problematic and demountable wings are a distinct advantage. The 'split' lines of the wings should coincide with those of the prototype – they had to be derigged for transportation too. Where an aircraft had inverted 'V' centre section struts, with a two piece top wing, this should be copied for the model (e.g. Albatros CI–V). On the majority of W.W.1 biplanes there was a separate centre section to the upper wing with wing panels each side. This is ideal for model purposes as the centre section can be a permanent fixture to the centre section struts and fuselage, with the outer wing panels plugging into it. Bottom wings normally bolted on to the fuselage sides.

The simplest method of attaching the wing panels is by installing tube in the wings and fuselage and using piano wire joiners. It is not necessary to use large diameters, or great lengths, as they only have to locate and take care of a certain degree of shear stress; the main loadings are taken care of by the rigging. Wing root ribs have a tendency to bow in when the covering tightens, causing unsightly gaps between the wing panels and/or fuselage. Strengthening the root rib by reinforcement of a ply outer rib (1.5mm) and diagonal internal bracing should help to avoid this.

Stresses on the tail surfaces of the early, slow aircraft were not great and the light structures used were wire braced between the fin, the tailplane and the fuselage. To achieve comparative strength/weight ratios our tail surfaces must also be structurally braced, or there will be a danger of tail flutter and the tailplane breaking up in flight. Numerous methods may be used for the construction of the tail surfaces including:-
1. Balsa strip, with strengthening gussets, for simple shapes of tailplane.
2. Aluminium tube bent to the outline with dowel crosspieces and plywood reinforcing. Provision must be made with this form of construction for attachment to the fuselage and of the fin to the tailplane. Inspection of the

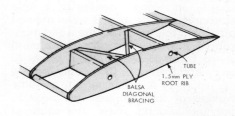

TUBE

1.5mm PLY
ROOT RIB

BALSA
DIAGONAL
BRACING

FIG. 6.6

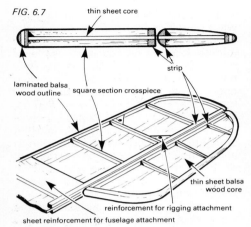

FIG. 6.7

thin sheet core

strip

laminated balsa wood outline

square section crosspiece

thin sheet balsa wood core

reinforcement for rigging attachment

sheet reinforcement for fuselage attachment

TYPICAL CONSTRUCTION OF TAILPLANE AND ELEVATOR USING SHEET CENTRE CORE

methods used on the prototype will probably suggest ways of doing this; metal clips and brackets were used a great deal.

3. Laminated wood, using alternative strips of balsa and thin ply, results in a very strong light outline. An inside or outside former, cut from hardboard, ply or balsa is used as the template. Commence with a strip of $^1/_{32}$in. or $^1/_{16}$in. balsa (depending on the size of the model) slightly wider than the thickness of the tail outline shape. Where bends with a tight radius are to be negotiated the strips of wood are first soaked in water containing a little ammonia and the surplus water drained off. Doing this will make the wood more supple and easier to negotiate around sharp corners. The alternate layers of balsa and 0.4mm or 0.8mm ply are laid up, using P.V.A. adhesive, with a candle waxing of the template and base to prevent sticking. Pins are used to position each layer and these are repositioned with each succeeding layer.

Leave the outline for at least 24 hours to harden thoroughly before removing from the template. Further stiffening of the laminated outline can be achieved by applying cyanocrylate adhesive to the assembly. When set, the laminations can be sanded to a rounded section and the remainder of the construction added.

4. A sheet outline of the tail surface ($^1/_{16}$in. or $^3/_{32}$in.) can be stiffened by the addition of strips round the outline and at cross member positions, on both sides of the sheet. This method produces a reasonably light structure, with good anti-warp qualities, and is valuable to reproduce tailplanes and fins using a double cambered section.

Thought should be given, before construction, to the hingeing of the elevator and rudder and the methods used will influence to some extent the constructional materials used. Where metal tube is used for the hinged members the type of hinge should resemble the full size component; normal hinges may be used for fixing into balsa.

CENTRE SECTION STRUTS AND CABANE STRUTS

Spruce struts with metal end fittings, oval sectioned metal tube, or round tube with spruce fairings, were the normal methods of producing centre section and cabane structures. These would be cross braced with stranded steel cable using turnbuckles for tensioning. On some of the very early aircraft a simple rounded tube was used for the cabane struts. Metal fittings were quite complex, highly engineered and often relieved with cut-outs for lightness. It is these metal fittings that provide the modeller with his biggest challenges – and headaches. Few modellers have sufficient facilities or skills to reproduce accurately each and every fitting used on, say, a Sopwith *Camel*. It has been known for world class champions to do just this, but most of us will be looking for ways of portraying the fittings without them actually being functional. Most common of the methods used is to make up the basic structure from piano wire and to fair in the struts with spruce, if a natural finish is required, or balsa covered with nylon for strength where a painted finish is used. There are alternative methods that can be employed by using dural strip faired on both sides, or welded – or bolted – tube construction. As the accuracy of wing rigging depends on the rigidity of cabane and centre section struts, the cross bracing, and any additional bracing employed on the

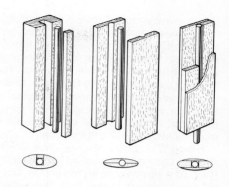

FIG. 6.8

prototype, should not be omitted. A variety of methods of fairing piano wire struts is shown in Fig. 6.8.

Epoxy adhesive is the most suitable glue to use for securing the fairings; the

FIG. 6.9

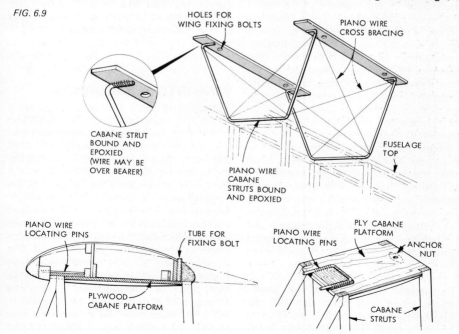

piano wire should be well cleaned and roughened before the fairings are applied. Certain metal fittings where the structural rigging lines for bracing the wings are attached are essential but these are not difficult to fabricate. Metal fittings used on the prototype for strut to fuselage, and wing, fixings can be simulated for non-structural elements from plastic card or postcard material.

Fixing the centre section structure to the top centre wing section can be in the form of a removable wing section, but it is advisable to make it a permanent fixture. It is virtually impossible to produce an undetectable removable centre wing section as the fixing points will be seen and unless these take the form of scale size bolts into metal fittings, the result will be less than scale in appearance. If, for reasons of transport or radio equipment access, it is essential to have a removable top wing centre section, two of the possible methods are illustrated in Fig. 6.9. Admittedly, the underside of the wing centre section is not the most conspicuous area of the model and if the fittings are painted in to the background colour they will not be too noticeable. Prototypes that used inverted 'V' centre section struts are not, as might be imagined, too difficult to reproduce. The important consideration is that the rigging wires are responsible for holding the wings in their correct positions and to the prescribed dihedrals, and not the tubes and rods joining the wings. Because of the high stresses and loadings that may be experienced on the centre section the piano wire/brass centre rib joints should be silver soldered.

Permanent securing of the centre section struts and wing can be best achieved by binding and epoxying the piano wire cross members to spruce or ply. It is a moot point whether the strut fairings should be fitted to the piano wire before the wing section is secured. A sensible compromise is to 'offer up' the wing section to the piano wire structure and when you are satisfied that the fit is correct it can be removed – first marking the limits of the strut fairings. The fairings can now be fitted and shaped prior to the binding and gluing of the wing section. Use a strong terylene thread for binding, clean and roughen up the piano wire, rub the epoxy in well with your finger and you need have no fears of the wing section coming adrift. Strut fairings inevitably come into close proximity to the fuselage and it will prove fruitful to finish shaping the strut fairings before adding any fuselage top decking. To sand the fairing around the decking is very tricky and it is simpler to trim the decking to fit around the strut – as performed with the full size aircraft.

WING INTERPLANE STRUTS

Spruce and oval shaped tubing were again the materials used for interplane struts in biplanes. Their primary purpose is to take a compressive load, i.e. to hold the wings apart. For this reason, the fixing at the wings needs only to be in the form of location with the tension of the rigging wires holding them in position. To prevent the wings moving fore and aft the front and rear interplane struts were cross braced using rigging wire, or were in the form of an 'N' strut. The incorporation of this structural design feature is equally important in the model. Methods of reproducing interplane struts, and the bracing, are shown in Fig 6.10. including one system that allows for adjusting the length of the

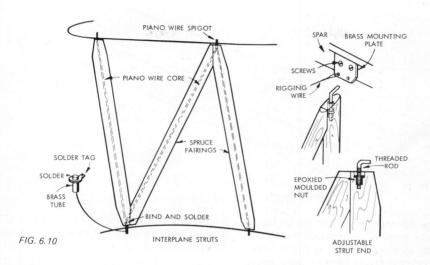

FIG. 6.10

struts. In theory this should not be necessary as the lengths of the struts should be accurately cut and the model rigged correctly. In practice, however, the adjustment may be of value for trimming purposes.

RIGGING

What are the main essentials for rigging? That the rigging material should be strong enough to withstand the stresses applied to it. That the material should not be too difficult to work. That the fittings can be securely attached to the wing structure. That the completed rigging system is scale-like in appearance. That it is capable of being removable – at least in part – and that individual components can be replaced. Of course, it is possible to follow the full size practice totally, especially for very large scale models, and to use scale metal fittings, stranded metal cable rigging wires and turn-buckles to every rigging wire. If you are an expert at metal fabrication in miniature and you are building a large

scale model, this is undoubtedly the ultimate aim. Considering that turn-buckles on the prototypes were only about a ¼ inch in diameter, or less, it does pose problems for the average modeller constructing, say, a ¹/₆th scale model. In these instances if may well be prudent to tension the rigging wires by eye, secure them, and fit dummy turnbuckles. First let us consider the alternatives for simulating stranded cable rigging wires.

1. Piano wire. Certainly strong enough but difficult to form for the attachment points.

2. Control-line stranded wire. Again, no problems with strength, but it is difficult material to work with as it 'kinks' very easily. Because of the inflexibility inherent in control-line cable the process of tensioning, by pulling through a hole in a metal fitting, is hard to control precisely. Soldered joints must be made to secure all loops.

3. Stainless steel flexible cable – the fisherman's variety. Excellent in all

93

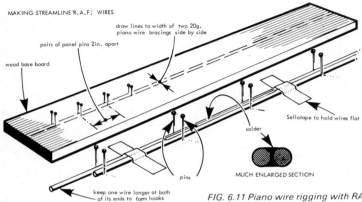

MAKING STREAMLINE R.A.F. WIRES

draw lines to width of two 20g.
piano wire bracings side by side

pairs of panel pins 2in. apart

wood base board

Sellotape to hold wires flat

solder

MUCH ENLARGED SECTION

pins

keep one wire longer at both
of its ends to form hooks

FIG. 6.11 Piano wire rigging with RAF wires

respects except for the problem of securing – it won't solder and the use of crimping pieces is not entirely satisfactory as the crimp cannot 'bite' on to the wire. Possibly there are suitable ferrous stranded cables that are pliable and would be suitable for our purposes. The ends could be soldered and the wire painted to prevent rusting – unfortunately such wire cable is not readily available.

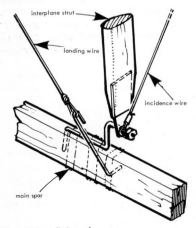

interplane strut

landing wire

incidence wire

main spar

FIG. 6.12 Lug fixing of
struts and simplified rigging

Linen or Terylene Thread Unsuitable, except for the smallest models, due to the lack of strength and elasticity.

Nylon covered trace line This nylon coated stranded metal cable is available from fishing tackle retailers (those that deal with sea angling, at least) and offers the best potential for our purposes. Being nylon covered it can be dyed to any colour and it is available in a wide range of breaking strains from 10 lbs up to, if you required it, hundreds of pounds strength. It does stretch slightly, towards the maximum strain of the line, but this can be an advantage as it will stretch, or break, the rigging line rather than break the model structure. No doubt an aerodynamicist, in the stress field, could calculate the likely stress limits in every rigging wire but we need only to take an intelligent guess at the strains and use the appropriate trace line strength. The flying wires, i.e. those preventing the wings from taking on excessive dihedral, take the highest strains (this is the reason that they are sometimes duplicated on full size aircraft).

Initial rigging of the model should be carried out with the model in the uncovered state as the flexibility of the wing structure in this state does not resist the tensioning. With the thin section wings there is always the danger, even when extreme care is taken, for the wings to warp after covering and doping. Rigging after covering entails pulling out these warps to give correct alignment. Conversely, once the model has been correctly rigged it will remain that way, when reassembled, even though the surfaces have twisted. Rigging a model is made easier if you have a good 'eye' for it. Although it is possible to use straight edges, incidence boards and other aids to rigging, a model can be completely rigged by 'eye' and is certainly less time consuming this way.

The degree of fidelity of the metal fittings is up to you and how much time you have available for filing and shaping! For monoplanes, with their wings rigged to cabane struts and / or the undercarriage structure, the rigging pick-up points of the landing and flying wires are usually in the same relative position above and below the wing. A single nut and bolt, housed in an aluminium tube through the wing depth, can be used for the attachment points

above and below the wing. See Fig 6.13. Should the nut and bolt size be objectionable, from a scale standpoint, miniature split pins can be used instead as shown in Fig 6.14. Wing warping was used for lateral control on early aircraft and this can be included as a working feature on R/C models. It is very much a case of precisely following the methods used on the prototype as these were both logical and effective in operation. Pulleys can be made to scale (but check that the warping wire cannot come adrift) and gather the warping wires from the wing together as the prototype, often terminating with a metal ring. Some adjustment should be included for varying the amount of warp on each wing and this can be included in the pushrod to the 'rocker' arm or in the single warp wires adjacent to the top pulley. Fishing trace line is again suitable for all warp wires. The power required for operating the wing warping will vary from model to model, depending on the degree of rigidity of the wings. It is suggested that a servo of the extra powerful type be used for this function. Fortunately, for the less ambitious modeller, most of these early aircraft featured wing dihedral and turned quite

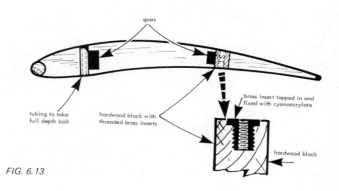

spars

tubing to take
full depth bolt

hardwood block with
threaded brass inserts

brass insert tapped in and
fixed with cyanoacrylate

hardwood block

FIG. 6.13

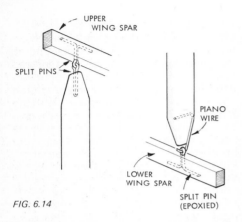

FIG. 6.14

may have thirty or more to be fitted. Genuine turnbuckles use left hand and right hand threads at the ends of the turnbuckle body and this allows adjustment without twisting the wires. Left and right hand threads for very small taps and dies do not appear to be available — or very hard to come by — and we have to find ways of avoiding their use. Examples of turnbuckles which will work, although not in the same sense as the original, are shown in Fig 6.16. Note that, with one method, a small fishing swivel must be used at the opposite end to prevent the twisting of the rigging wire.

well on rudder control and without the use of wing warping. Indeed, a balanced turn, by the use of wing warping only, was just about impossible.

For the purist, the thought of using operating turnbuckles may appeal and it is possible to purchase them, or make them. Unfortunately, the commercially available types are often too large in scale and some are not the correct style — they also come expensive when you

A simpler method is, undoubtedly, in rigging the model with trace line, as previously described, and the fitting of dummy turnbuckles for scale effect. Not too much ingenuity is required to fake a turnbuckle by the use of small lengths of tubing and nuts.

Later aircraft using rigging wires (e.g. Ryan and Stearman) did not have round stranded wires but, produced to specific lengths, streamline wires known as RAF

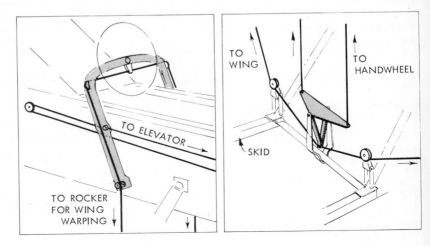

FIG. 6.15

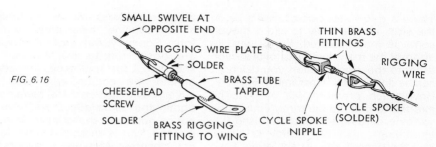

FIG. 6.16

SMALL SWIVEL AT OPPOSITE END

RIGGING WIRE PLATE

SOLDER

CHEESEHEAD SCREW

SOLDER

BRASS RIGGING FITTING TO WING

BRASS TUBE TAPPED

CYCLE SPOKE NIPPLE

THIN BRASS FITTINGS

RIGGING WIRE

CYCLE SPOKE (SOLDER)

wires. These streamline wires were made for their specific location and the end rods were threaded with a left hand thread at one end and right hand thread at the opposite end. Duplication of these streamline wires is not so simple (one method is shown in Fig 6.11) and fabricating them identically to the originals is beyond the means of most modellers. It is possible to use small diameter aluminium tube – slip through the tube a piece of piano wire, put the tube in a wood vice (with the jaws extended to the length of the tube) and gently squeeze the tube until it is oval in shape. Where it is not possible to get sufficient pressure

over the whole length of the tube you can try instead rolling the tube – with a rolling pin – until flat. Naturally, the oval aluminium must be cut to length (allowing for the turnbuckles) and the rigging wire slipped through before the rigging wire is made up. You will notice that prototypes, using RAF wires, have lengths of dowel fitted between the front and rear wing rigging wires to hold the wires in the correct plane i.e. with the streamline section facing forwards. These should be incorporated on the model for the same reason.

Oval section tube can present problems due to its lack of availability.

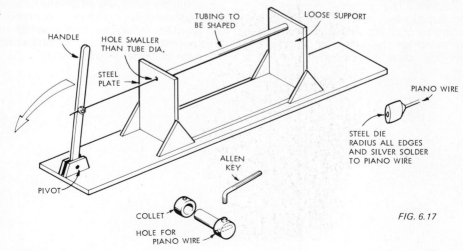

HANDLE

HOLE SMALLER THAN TUBE DIA.

STEEL PLATE

TUBING TO BE SHAPED

LOOSE SUPPORT

PIANO WIRE

STEEL DIE RADIUS ALL EDGES AND SILVER SOLDER TO PIANO WIRE

ALLEN KEY

PIVOT

COLLET

HOLE FOR PIANO WIRE

FIG. 6.17

There are few stockists of oval tube, in the sizes we are likely to use, although some is manufactured. If you wish to attempt the manufacture of oval section tube, to the cross section you desire, it can be done and is illustrated in Fig 6.17. How much pressure will need to be exerted to pull the die through the tube varies according to the metal used (i.e. aluminium, aluminium alloy or brass) and the overall size. In any event keep the die well lubricated. The size of the tube used must be sufficiently small to allow the die completely to fill the internal circumference of the tube with a slight degree of stretching. It should also be possible to roll round tube into an oval section, and a device similar to that described for producing corrugated aluminium sheet may be suitable. Construction of interplane struts etc. is both feasible and scale-like when brass tubing is used and the parts soldered together.

From the end of W.W.1 onwards, more exotic shapes of fuselages were designed although many of these were still based on the basic box girder structure. The external shapes were produced by adding formers and stringers or sheeting. Plywood was used for most of the sheeting and as this material does not readily form compound curvatures, we have no problems in reproducing these areas in model form. Similarly, with the stringers, these are positioned to the numbers and stations of the prototype. Immediately behind the engine area was often covered with beaten metal panels and to obtain the same effect, we have little option but to use the same material and method. This is described in the following chapter. Metallised papers and 'sticky back' thin metal sheet can be used for simple areas, but not for any panels with double curvatures.

Looking at photographs of early aircraft, some of the W.W.1 aircraft particularly look very 'scruffily' built. The somewhat desperate appearance of many of them can be almost totally explained by the poor application of the covering, some of it being laced-up over considerable areas. The wrinkles in the covering hide a sound under-structure; many of the subcontractors were quite used to high quality joinery and the use of metal fittings, but were less 'at home' with covering methods. By all means include some of the covering flaws in your model (most of them look too well finished for this period) but it must *not* be an excuse for poor workmanship beneath.

Chapter 7

Construction of Aircraft from 1939 Onwards

One of the delights of designing and building scale models is the scope it gives for experimentation in new techniques. With sports or aerobatic R/C models, particularly when built from kits or plans, the opportunities for attempting something different are strictly limited. With scale models we are constantly coming up against problems of how to reproduce a certain part of the full size, and a solution must be found. There will not always be an obvious solution to hand that has been used before on a model, and the challenge of

devising a suitable answer to the problem is all part of the excitement. No two modellers, set a specific modelling problem, will come up with identical solutions, and it should never be assumed that someone else's answer is automatically the best one. New methods of construction are constantly being found, and the room for experiment in the area of modern aircraft is unlimited.

Modern aircraft, in the main, feature stressed skin metal structures and few incorporate any open structures covered

This D.H. Mosquito by Brian Taylor is uncanny in closely following the swing pattern in take-off of the full-size, due mostly to the single rudder not biting early.

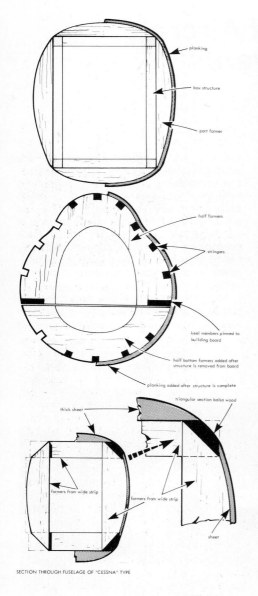

planking

box structure

part former

half formers

stringers

keel members pinned to building board

half bottom formers added after structure is removed from board

planking added after structure is complete

triangular section balsa wood

thick sheet

formers from wide strip

formers from wide strip

sheet

SECTION THROUGH FUSELAGE OF "CESSNA" TYPE

FIG. 7.1

in linen, or its modern equivalents. Some specialist light aircraft, e.g. Pitts *Special,* do still use fabric covered construction, as do some of the home built ultra-light aircraft, but the majority feature a smooth finish of 'solid' appearance. Metal clad aircraft do not have the same maintenance problems inherent in the wood and fabric designs and they are more serviceable for general operation. It is interesting to note the increasing use of 'modelling' materials in the world of full-size aircraft. Many of the more advanced ultra-light aircraft now being designed in the U.S.A. feature liberal use of foam and glass fibre techniques. This is probably an instance of the full-size aircraft designer imitating the modeller, rather than the opposite. In any case, it gives us some marvellous opportunities to build a truly scale structure. For the reproduction of most of the other aircraft it will be a matter of using balsa sheeting and planking, or glass-fibre shell fuselages, and sheeted foam wings or built-up construction, sheet covered. As usual there are some model builders who swear by one particular method and others who swear at it! To some extent, your choice will depend on your 'feel' for a particular method and the materials used. There are some more basic advantages and disadvantages with the two methods — glass fibre and foam techniques are grouped under one heading.

A. CONVENTIONAL CONSTRUCTION i.e. BALSA, PLY, etc.

Own design, and models built from plans, tend to be 'one off' creations and having completed and flown the model, the builder is ready to move on to construction of a different model. Conven-

David Vaughan's P51 Mustang again. To reproduce a metal-clad aircraft convincingly in wood is something of an art, but one which can be learned.

tional techniques meet these requirements quite well as they are very adaptable and give the designer/builder full freedom in choice of prototype. Using a combination of balsa planking, thin ply sheeting, or block, on a formered and ribbed undersurface, any shapes and curvatures of fuselages can be copied. The substructure can take the form of:-

1. A basic box structure with part formers added:
2. Forming an outline crutch and gluing to this half formers:
3. A jig assembled fuselage using full formers – although the interiors of these formers may be removed at a later stage of construction to lighten the structure.

Balsa covering is then glued to the substructure, in sheet form where the curvature is slight, or planking for complex areas. Ply or aluminium sheeting is sometimes substituted for balsa where this was a feature of the full size aircraft.

A very necessary consideration, before commencing building the fuselage, is the positioning of hatches for access to equipment. These should be designed so that they match up with convenient panel lines, where they will be less obtrusive, and the fixing of the hatches should be arranged to make the catches, springs etc., as secret – or scale-like – as possible. To have unscale bolts, dowels and rubber bands, screw heads etc., totally mars the scale effect of the model. Fuselage formers can be from ply (highly relieved for lightness) balsa, or a combination of the two. A disadvantage in using tough ply is sometimes found where the shape and size of the former is not exactly correct. This is more apparent at the pre-sheeting stage, where one can look down the sides of the fuselage, longitudinally, and immediately notice any formers that are obviously proud. David Vaughan, in the construction of his magnificent P51B *Mustang*, overcomes the problems of sanding down

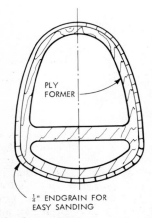

PLY
FORMER

¼" ENDGRAIN FOR
EASY SANDING

FIG.7.2

ply formers that are too large, in the following way. The ply formers are cut slightly less than a ¼ in. undersize and ¼ in. cross-grain balsa strips are glued around the perimeter of the former. This allows you to sand the edges to fit the 'flow' of the balsa skin. Before sanding is commenced the centre and horizontal points of the formers must be marked so that the sanding takes place on the correct fuselage line. A normal sanding block is completely inadequate for the longitudinal sanding of a fuselage structure, or for wings. An aluminium 'T' section bar is ideal as the basis of a long sander as the vertical web gives rigidity to the bar, and a means of gripping the sander. Garnet paper can be purchased by the roll — for making up into belt sanders etc. — and should be cut to the

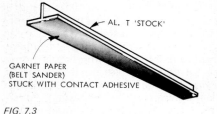

AL. T 'STOCK'

GARNET PAPER
(BELT SANDER)
STUCK WITH CONTACT ADHESIVE

FIG. 7.3

required length and width; the edges are contact glued to the rear flanges of the crosspiece of the 'T' section. Medium soft balsa, thicker than the finished design thickness, is used for the sheeting and planking and energetic final sanding removes any further irregularities. Sanding should be undertaken with enthusiasm at this point as it will be the final opportunity to remove any major areas of depression — and it is surprising how a sunken area of less than $^1/_{64}$in. maximum depth will show up on the finished model. Small gaps between sheeting and planking can be filled at a later date but wide indentations are not possible to treat with fillers. A wide spacing of formers, or ribs, and the use of thin hard sheeting will often result in a 'sagging' of the sheet between the supports; use a thick, soft and lightweight balsa skin in preference to a hard thin one.

Once a wing structure is fully sheeted there is no further opportunity of removing any warps or twists — the whole structure is too rigid. Open structure wings may, after they are covered and doped, be straightened by steaming and twisting in the opposite direction to the warp. No such remedial action can be taken with fully sheeted wings and it is imperative for them to be truly built in the first instance. Aids to true building include the use of jigs and jig pieces, purposely left on the underside of the wing ribs to position the ribs on the building board. It may be that the wing aerofoil section has a straight portion to the bottom rear surface and the wing can then be built directly on to the building board. There are many methods of assisting in the alignment of the ribs during construction, including false leading and trailing edges and jigging the ribs by using the 'cut off' area of the rib to act as a cradle. One aid that is often overlooked is the marking of a centre line down the length of the rib. This will give a visual reference and 'sighting' the centre lines will usually show if one rib is misplaced. It is impossible to discuss all of the methods of basic wing construction as they are so varied in the numbers and types of spar construction etc. A glance through the plan reproductions of the many scale models introduced by radio control model magazines will give you plenty of food for thought if you are designing your own model. Just remember such important factors as wing fixings, undercarriage positions, aileron linkages, servo position and aileron construction.

Ailerons can be constructed as part of the wing or built separately. The former method has the advantage of ensuring that the aileron follows through as part of the wing aerofoil, but can present difficulties in the cutting away and adding of aileron leading edge stage. You "pays your money and takes your choice". Spars should never be made a tight push fit into ribs or they are likely to 'bow' the rib by slightly opening up the rib slot. Where a spar is reluctant to enter the slot cut out in the rib, take a file, or very sharp knife, and enlarge the slot until it is an 'interference' fit. Wing tip construction will depend on the shape of the wing tip and where balsa block is used it should be hollowed out for lightness. Aerodynamically, heavy weights at the wing tip will make the model laterally less stable and, structurally, we can afford to reduce the strength of the wing towards the tip where the loads are less. Reduction of spar strength towards the tip should, as previously discussed, be incorporated if possible, but as a progressive reduction.

How strong should the construction of a conventionally built structure be?

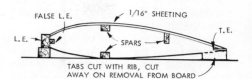

FIG. 7.4

Another impossible question to answer, particularly as there are two schools of thought on the question. One group of scale modellers will maintain that the model should only be built strong enough to withstand the normal flight loads and the stresses of reasonable landings. The other school are in favour of a structure, and finish, capable of withstanding a fair degree of 'rough and tumble' and the occasional 'arrival'. As

Formers for a large fuselage cut from laminated balsa. Tail end parts shown.

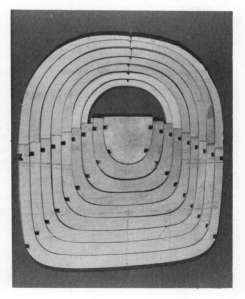

can be imagined, the former opinion comes mainly from serious competition modellers, and the latter more often from the sports scale enthusiast.

With regard to the tail surfaces, the oft repeated plea for minimum weight is in order again here. Avoid the use of thick solid sheet tail surfaces, but when sheet is used on smaller models, balsa that is both soft and light must be used. The danger of using this category of balsa is that the leading edge may be 'dinged' during flying operations. This risk can be reduced by gluing a small ($^1/_{16}$ or $^3/_{32}$ in.) square spruce section to the leading edge. When sanded into the aerofoil section of the tailplane, or fin, the weight penalty is minimal but it will toughen up the leading edge considerably. Spar and rib construction is certainly to be favoured for general tail surface construction wherever this is practical.

B. GLASS FIBRE TECHNIQUES

For a 'one off' model the work involved in producing a glass fibre complete fuselage is considerable. Where more than one model of the same prototype is to be produced, e.g. a club or group project or a commercial application, the use of glass fibre mouldings becomes an attractive proposition. Providing the male mould plug is accurately finished, with panel line, rivet, hatches and other detail included, all mouldings produced should be to the same high finish. Glass fibre mouldings can be made to allow for different strength requirements throughout the length of the fuselage by using more or less layers of glass fibre mat or cloth, or the use of carbon fibres. There is not the same degree of flexibility in this respect as with the use of conventional structures, and it is at the rear end of the fuselage that the problems usually occur. There is a limit to the thinness of resin and mat/cloth we can use to maintain strength and rigidity and the materials we use are *relatively* heavy. For a prototype with a long tail moment, compared with the nose moment, we are going to be very pushed to finish with a model that is not tail heavy. So, if glass fibre construction appeals to you, try to select

Conventional built up structure for a Hart variant, probably a Demon or Audax. Such airframes are light and easy to repair.

Marcus Norman with one of his famous ducted fan models. Structure is basically simple and light, an essential in early ducted fan experiments.

a prototype with a long nose moment or. short tail moment. The basic techniques of glass fibre moulding are generally well known but here is a method that applies well to scale models.

To produce a good standard of glass fibre fuselage moulding six steps are required.

1. Preparation of master plug:
2. Detailing and finishing of male mould:
3. Laying up of female mould halves:
4. Finishing and preparation of female mould:
5. Laminating the fuselage moulding halves:
6. Joining the fuselage halves.

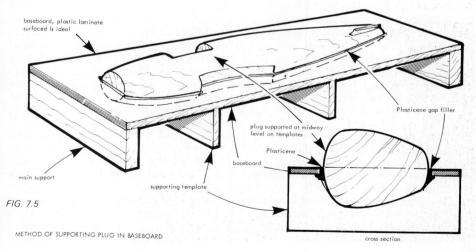

baseboard, plastic laminate surfaced is ideal

plug supported at midway level on templates

Plasticene gap filler

main support

Plasticene

baseboard

supporting template

FIG. 7.5

METHOD OF SUPPORTING PLUG IN BASEBOARD

cross section

Materials required include the resins, glass cloth and mat, resin thinner, aluminium or waxed cup containers, stiff cheap brushes, small roller with extended handles, wet and dry abrasive paper in various grits from 130 up to 1200, acetone for cleaning brushes, hard mould polishing wax, P.V.A. release agent, cutting paste, Plasticine, beeswax, barrier cream and wood for the master plug. These items are listed to indicate that making a glass fibre mould for a single fuselage is far from cheap and the basic glass fibre materials for the female moulds, plus one moulding, can involve a considerable outlay. Costs, and time saving, only become competitive when reasonable numbers of fuselages are produced. Glass fibre moulding should be carried out in warm, dry conditions with adequate ventilation – the last point being the more important when epoxy resins are used. The male plug is carved to the full finished size of the fuselage and provision must naturally be made for fitting the wing and tail surfaces. Whether the fin is moulded in, as part of the fuselage, will depend on the size and section of the fin. With a resonably thick fin, and a rounded leading edge, it can be integral with the fuselage, but a narrow section fin will give joining problems. Reverse tapers and undercuts must be excluded on the plug, which will be divided along the vertical centre line, as these will prevent the plug or moulding being released from the mould. Careful consideration must be given to the wing fillets as a deep narrow cavity will not mould in a satisfactory manner, it being impossible to fit the glass cloth in position. Thought must be given to the access in the mould for joining the moulding halves when the female moulds are clamped together. The wing seating area is the most

obvious access but it must be possible to reach all positions of the joint with the extended brushes and rollers.

Balsa can be used for the master plug but this is both expensive and requires a lot of filling and preparation. Columbian pine is an excellent wood for the modeller to use as it is straight grained, easy to carve in both grain directions and takes a good finish; Jelutong is equally suitable for carving. It is unlikely that you will find a piece of sufficient cross section for the plug, and it will be necessary to laminate pieces of the timber to obtain the size required. Good mating of the edges of the blocks is important and the laminations must be clamped together during the gluing process. Use a good wood working adhesive such as Aerolite or Cascamite. If a large cross section fuselage is to be attempted there will be many laminations; take them a few at a time, clamping each section until the adhesive has set. Carving the block to shape is a case of using every suitable tool at your disposal, plus a lot of elbow grease. There is no rapid method of carving the mould but cut the side view and planform shapes as accurately as possible to keep the amount of subsequent carving to a minimum. The use of a commercial band saw will be of great assistance for this operation; cut the side view first and then temporarily replace the offcuts to aid in cutting the plan view. Marking the centre lines of all surfaces, with the plug in the 'squared' state, is helpful. Hack and carve the plug with chisels, spokeshaves and knives until you are very close to the required shape, using external templates to check the cross sections. Final shaping is undertaken using, initially, 130 grit abrasive paper and working down to No. 340 grit for the final sanding. Try never to carve or sand away too much of the plug as

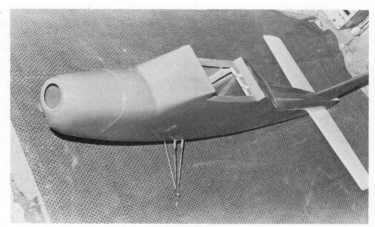

Glass fibre fuselage for a relatively simple high wing design, with separate cowl moulding, by Ian Peacock.

filling large areas is difficult.

With the basic shape completed we must consider the detailing of panel lines, rivets, hatch positions, prominences, etc. Glass fibre moulding, correctly carried out, will faithfully reproduce every marking of the original mould and it is worth while taking trouble to include all

of the detail required on the male plug. Conversely, glass fibre is a hard material and it will be difficult to inscribe the detail on the finished moulding at a later stage. Scoring the panel lines, impressing the rivet detail etc., is carried out in a similar fashion to preparing a conventional model and the methods are

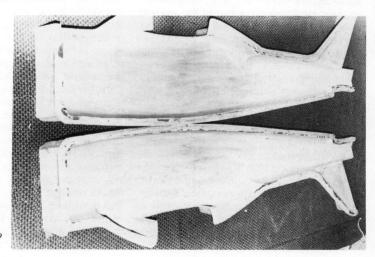

The two-piece mould for the basic fuselage above. Separate cowling eases access to interior joints.

107

described in Chapter 18. Protuberances can be formed with wood, soundly glued to the plug, or G.R.P. filler type materials. The latter material can also be used for filling any small nicks or flaws. A high degree of finish of the male master is essential as, with the applied detail, there will be less opportunity to polish the interior of the female moulds than would be the case with a smooth, non-scale subject. Apply special finishing varnish, or similar filler that is compatible with the resin to be used, sand thoroughly and continue the process until you are completely satisfied that the finish is absolutely smooth, and no grain is showing. Final hard wax polishing completes the preparation of the male master.

Cut out a ply plate, with the centre fretted out about $1/16$ to $3/32$ in. larger all round than the side view of the male master. The ply, or similar laminated board, should be rigid enough not to bow in the centre under its own weight and battens may be tacked to the underside to stiffen the plate. Support the male master into the cut out until the vertical centre line is coincidental with the top surface of the plywood plate. Fill the gap between the plate and the master with Plasticine – the addition of a little beeswax will help the Plasticine to harden and to obtain a smoother finish. Leave for a day or two to harden and then trim the Plasticine flush with the plate and up to the master, making a smooth precise joint. Apply thoroughly a P.V.A. liquid release agent to the top half of the master and to the Plasticine and plywood surround. It should be mentioned here that it is feasible to use a conventional, and proven, model fuselage as the male master. There are risks that there will be some damage to it and areas around the tail surfaces, engine

cowling and cockpit canopy must be very carefully considered.

When you are satisfied that the release agent has covered every part, the lay-up of the first half of the female mould can commence. Brush on a generous layer of tooling grade gel coat, checking that no bubbles occur. As the gel coat has thixotropic characteristics it will remain on the vertical surfaces. Leave this initial coat to cure to the stage of being touch dry (2–4 hours) before applying the first layer of glass fibre cloth. A six ounce per square metre weight of cloth is suitable for both the female and final mouldings although glass fibre chopped strand mat can be used for the female moulds if desired, for cost saving. It would also be advantageous to use different resins for the female moulds and the finished moulding, to minimise the risk of accidental fusion during the laminating of the moulding, i.e. polyester resin for the moulds, epoxy resin for the mouldings.

Continue to build up the female mould half until a thickness of about $1/8$ in. has been achieved. *Thoroughly* tamp all of the glass fibre layers into place with a stiff brush to avoid air bubbles and delamination of the mould at a later stage. A flange of $3/4$–1 in. is incorporated at all edges, for the purposes of joining the mould halves. Allow the mould to cure for two days and then remove the plate and the Plasticine, but leaving the male master in the mould half. Drill locating holes at six inch intervals along the flanges using the tip only of a $3/8$ in. drill bit. Hard wax polish the flange area and coat the whole of the second half of the master, and the flange, with P.V.A. liquid release agent. The second half of the female mould can now be laid up to match the first half. Leave for a further two days and then remove the second female half and the male master. There

The one-piece mould and finished nose for the model in the preceding photos.

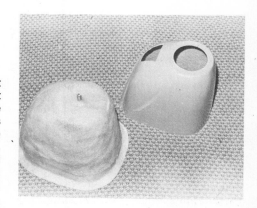

may be small areas where the gel coat has pulled away with the master but these can be attended to later. Patience is now required as the mould halves must be left for a further two weeks to completely cure and stabilise. When, and only when, this period has passed the halves can be joined by drilling ¼ in. diameter holes at three or four inch pitch around the flange to receive short ¼ in. bolts and nuts. The precise location is looked after by the recesses and dimples formed by the previous low relief drilling of the flanges. Minor repairs to blemishes are made by filling with gel coat resin and cutting back with wet and dry paper. Polishing the interior surface of the mould must be carried out with care. Do not round off the edges of the mould, or a ridge will form on the final moulding, and do not be too aggressive on the detail lines. Work down from a No. 400 grit to a No. 1200 grit wet and dry paper – used wet – and lubricated with the addition of a little washing-up liquid in the water. A cutting paste (of the 'T-cut' variety) is the final operation before waxing the surfaces with six to eight coats of mould polish, rubbing energetically with a lambs-wool pad between each coat.

At last we come to the rewarding phase of the operation when we can commence the lamination of the actual fuselage mouldings. The use of glass fibre woven cloth (6 oz. per sq. metre) and fresh resin is recommended, the number of layers, amount of reinforcement etc., will vary with the size of moulding being produced and some experiment may be needed. The first moulding will probably be too heavy.

Check that the glue size used on the cloth – if any – is compatible with the type of resin you are using. Cut the cloth oversize to allow for fitting into the concave surface and cut to shape any additional layers and reinforcement that will be required. Apply a coat of laminating resin gel coat to the mould and leave to 'touch dry' cure before positioning the first layer of glass fibre cloth. Stipple the cloth into position with resin, being punctilious in forcing the cloth into the more 'difficult' areas and avoiding air bubbles. Continue the process until the required thickness and reinforcement has been achieved. Trim the edges of the mouldings, level with the glass fibre mould flange, with a *very* sharp Stanley blade knife – pulling the knife blade towards the outside of the mould during the cutting action. Before the mouldings have cured, bolt the mould halves together and commence the joining of the halves. It is important to do this before complete curing of the halves otherwise a satisfactory bond may not be obtained and cracking of the joint may occur when stressed. When the mould halves are tightly joined, with no excess material in the joint, apply resin to the joint area and follow this with the glass fibre joining tape; it must be pulled through from the wing opening to the tail and nose ends. Work the tape down until you are satisfied the joint is straight and secure. When the assembly is fully cured the mould can be opened and the fuselage released. If all has gone well you will have an absolute replica of the original male master, although there will probably be a few holes to fill and the joint to smooth out. Automobile G.R.P. filler can be used to fill the small irregularities which are then smoothed with wet and dry paper. It may be necessary to 'cut back' a hole in the moulding, to get a reasonable fixing for the filler – clean the hole thoroughly before applying the filler.

Paint is best applied with a spray gun, and the fuselage should first be painted with a primer, followed by one or two white undercoats. Rub down the first coats, right back to the glass fibre, so that only the slight scratches and marks remained filled. The final coat should be lightly sanded with No. 500 grit paper; clean down and the fuselage is ready for final painting.

FOAM AND VENEER CONSTRUCTION

The use of foam with veneer covering is well known for wing construction; it can also be used for some fuselage decking. Many prototype aircraft use a thick aerofoil which if copied as a standard polystyrene veneered wing will be too heavy. Where this is likely to occur the foam core should be hollowed out leaving vertical webs of foam to retain strength. This can be done as follows:- (See Fig. 7.6).

1. Make a jig to hold the wing vertically with guides for the 10g piano wire 'holemaker':

2. Mount the wing core in the jig and check with the 'plumb bob' that the wire will fall vertically:

3. Heat the wire (10g) with a gas blow torch until it is hot enough to melt the polystyrene:

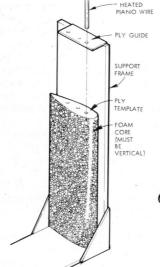

HEATED PIANO WIRE

PLY GUIDE

SUPPORT FRAME

PLY TEMPLATE

FOAM CORE (MUST BE VERTICAL)

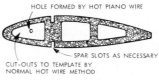

HOLE FORMED BY HOT PIANO WIRE

SPAR SLOTS AS NECESSARY

CUT-OUTS TO TEMPLATE BY NORMAL HOT WIRE METHOD

FIG. 7.6

4. Drop the wire through the foam core and remove it:

5. Attach the ply templates to the cores:

6. Pass the cutting wire of the hot wire cutter through the hole and reconnect it to the end of the cutter bow:

7. Using the internal lines of the templates cut the centre from the core.

Balsa sheet, for covering foam cores, has the advantage of being light and easy to sand. It can be applied in one thickness greater than needed as a final thickness so that it can be sanded down to remove any surface distortions. Obeche veneer is only a little heavier but it can only be slightly sanded due to the limited thickness, and surface variations may be visible. It is not only the weight of the veneer that has to be watched. Polystyrene foam of approximately one pound per cubic foot is most suitable for modelling purposes, with a small 'bead' size for smooth cutting. Foam should be stored in a warm dry atmosphere where it can be left for a time to dry out totally before it is used — the weight reduction may be considerable. Adhesives must be spread evenly and thinly on the foam and veneer skinning and allowed to dry thoroughly before covering is attempted. Using too heavy an application of contact adhesive, and not allowing the adhesive to dry fully, can add unnecessary weight. The same applies to the centre section joining with glass fibre tape and resin; one all too often sees a great thickness of resin on the tape that is just not necessary. Take care with the distance of the tape and resin from the wing centre. If it protrudes beyond the fuselage or fairing it will be almost impossible to treat, to obtain a smooth transition between the glass fibre and the skinning. With the hardness of the glass fibre and the softness of the balsa, the joint

FIG. 7.7

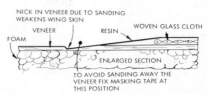

NICK IN VENEER DUE TO SANDING WEAKENS WING SKIN
VENEER   RESIN   WOVEN GLASS CLOTH
FOAM
ENLARGED SECTION
TO AVOID SANDING AWAY THE VENEER FIX MASKING TAPE AT THIS POSITION

between the end of the resin and the balsa sheeting should be treated very circumspectly (see Fig. 7.7).

Foam techniques can also be used in making fuselage formers. The outline of the former, less approximately $1/8$ inch for the edging, is cut from polystyrene sheet — such as a ceiling tile. Glue the edging balsa with P.V.A. glue and, when dried, the former is veneered on both sides. The principle of veneering the polystyrene on *both* sides is an important one to balance the structure. To attempt to cover only one side of a foam structure will certainly result in warping. Light and strong decking can be made from foam and veneer where a straight taper, side view and plan view is involved. Cut the inside shape, using templates, as shown in Fig 7.8, followed by the external outline. Replace the decking into the block from which it was cut and veneer the inside surface. Remove from the block and veneer the outside.

FIG. 7.8

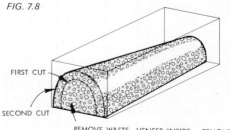

FIRST CUT

SECOND CUT

REMOVE WASTE, VENEER INSIDE. REMOVE FROM BLOCK AND VENEER OUTSIDE

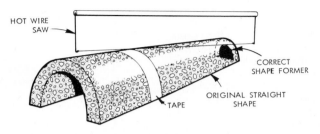

HOT WIRE SAW

CORRECT SHAPE FORMER

ORIGINAL STRAIGHT SHAPE

TAPE

SEVERAL INTERMEDIATE CUTS FOLLOWED BY
LIGHT SANDING MAY BE NECESSARY

FIG. 7.9

The result is a very strong construction that is comparable in weight with conventional methods. Curved decking can be formed from foam but it does require more hand finishing. A method of cutting the foam and skimming the shape is shown in Fig 7.9. A number of cuts may have to be made with the hot wire before finally sanding to shape.

WING FAIRINGS

Wing to fuselage fairings are not only a problem to the modeller, but a close inspection of prototypes will show they have caused more than a few headaches to many full size designers. They have the problem of reducing the interference drag at the wing/fuselage junction and overcome it as best they can – usually with metal panel sections beaten to shape. On slower aircraft, where the increase in drag is minimal, fairings are not used, much to the delight of the modeller! With small fairings, the modeller can use triangular balsa fillets to form the fairing, sanding them to an inside radius after they have been glued in place. The triangular balsa stock must be applied in short lengths, or saw cut part the way through, so that the curvature of the fillet can be followed. To obtain the final smooth contour of the fillet the balsa can be covered with a filler

(Contour or similar car filler) or a mix of resin and microballoons. The latter must be sanded before it completely cures or it will be too hard. Larger wing fillets, for aircraft such as the *Spitfire,* should be built up from sheet, or plywood for strength, with the bending of the sheet being assisted by applying water on the outer curve and dope on the inner curve. Occasionally, a fillet will have a compound curve that cannot be reproduced by bending sheet ply or balsa and we must use a moulded section for this area, preferably vacuum formed. It may be possible to follow the full size practice and panel beat the fairing from thin gauge aluminium, although it would take considerable skill to do so.

Most R/C scale models feature demountable wings for the convenience of transportation and for equipment access – the full size aircraft designers have an advantage there, they rarely have to allow for rapid wing removal. The wing/fuselage fairing is the obvious position for the 'split' line and the top fairing (for a low wing aircraft) becomes the wing seating. This, however, poses a further problem. Where the wing sits on to the fairing the edge of the fairing becomes proud of the wing surface – it will be out of scale even when sanded to the structural limitations of the fairing

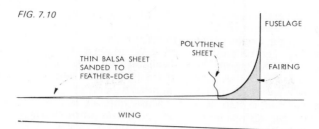

FIG. 7.10

THIN BALSA SHEET
SANDED TO
FEATHER-EDGE

POLYTHENE
SHEET

FUSELAGE

FAIRING

WING

material. To overcome this unsightly projection we must slightly build up the wing thickness adjacent to the fairing. Fit the wing in position with thin polythene sheeting between the wing centre section and the fuselage wing seating area. Tighten up the wing retaining bolts, as for flying, and fold back the free edges of the polythene sheet and tape them to the fuselage sides. Glue with an aliphatic or similar sandable adhesive, sheets of balsa about six to nine inches long to the top of the wing adjacent to the edge of the fairing. The balsa sheet should have the grain running span wise and needs to be slightly in excess of the thickness of the fairing at its edge. Carefully sand the sheeting to conform with the fairing at the root and tapering to a feather edge at the opposite end. We are only talking about a total thickness of $1/32$ in. or so and the tapered section leading to the fillet will not be noticeable — it could be allowed for in the initial design. The appearance of finishing off a wing to fuselage fillet with this method is far superior to the normal style, and it also helps to position the wing seating.

COMBINATIONS OF CONSTRUCTIONAL METHODS

Of course, we are not restricted to any specific methods for construction on a model. A scale model of a *Harvard* may, for instance, feature a foam cored wing with built up balsa tail surfaces, conventional rear structure fuselage and glass fibre cowl area. The combinations will be used as giving the best answer, in the view of the designer, to the practical considerations applying. Some designers will do a certain amount of research work before commencing the project to evaluate the practicability of using different constructional techniques. They may build a sports R/C model to test out a new design theory or build a 'rough' scale model before starting the super scale version. The expert's 'rough' model will often turn out to be better than the average modellers' 'good' scale model! Other scale designers will gradually introduce new techniques over a series of designs, so that models built over a four or five year separation period may have gone through a nearly total change of constructional methods. Always, the quest will be to find the material that lends itself most suitably to reproducing the full size component and be efficient in the strength/weight ratio.

WING FIXINGS

Simplest, and still the most practical, of wing fixings, is the tongue and slot (or dowels in holes) and bolts system. The front fixing, with tongue or dowels, locates and holds and the bolts — normally nylon — screw into captive nuts in the fuselage and hold the rear of the wing in position. Automatically, the front fixing is invisible externally but we have to find a way of hiding the heads of the rear securing bolts. This can be done by having a removable fairing under (or over) the wing, but this in turn has to be fixed in position. On some aircraft a centre section aerodynamic flap was used and this can be conveniently adapted to hide the bolts underneath. The flap can be spring loaded, even if it is a working flap, and sprung back into position after the bolts are secured. For models of prototypes without this facility it is a matter of using your ingenuity and closely inspecting drawings and photographs of the original, to see whether any panels or hatches exist that can cover the position of the bolt fixings.

AILERONS

With a fast flying radio control model we are likely to run into difficulties with aileron balance. There are, in fact, two forms of balance. a. Aerodynamic balance: b. Mass balance. We cannot do much about the former as, with a scale model, it will be dictated to us by the shape and hingeing of the aileron. This also applies to the other control surfaces.

The purpose of aerodynamic balance is to reduce the loads required to operate the control surface and is of practical use to us when we have limited servo power available for the size of the control surface (e.g. for a large, fast model using 'standard' servos).

Mass balance is the mechanical balancing of the control surface and is most useful to us in relation to aileron flutter. The technical reason for aileron flutter is somewhat complex and involves the oscillatory frequencies on the aerodynamic forces. What is more important to understand is when the flutter is likely to happen and how we can avoid it. Flutter occurs at low angles of attack and at high speed, i.e. when you are doing a low fast run in front of the judges. It can be most disconcerting! How can we avoid it? By paying cognisance to the following:-

1. The aileron must be structurally stiff and have low weight:
2. By having a minimum gap between the wing and aileron. A wide gap will not necessarily induce flutter but it will certainly reduce the effectiveness of the control:
3. By keeping the control linkages stiff and free from 'slop':
4. By using a servo with a good resolution (no backlash), mounting it securely and using a rigid output arm:
5. By mass balancing the control surfaces.

The cross section shape of the aileron is also important but this is, or should be, according to the full size section. However, avoid having an aileron section with convex curvatures or rounded trailing edges.

Rudders often combine mass and aerodynamic balancing by weighting the top area projecting forward of the hinges.

One of the simplest mass aileron balances is the forward extension of the aileron tip plate on the Volksplane.

Having realised that mass balance is exclusively for the elimination of flutter, and that aerodynamic balance has no effect on flutter, should we mass balance the ailerons? The majority of modern aircraft have the mass balance of the aileron as part of the internal structure but some earlier aircraft (1930s biplanes etc.) used external mass balance weights secured to rods above and below the aileron. A few ultra-light aircraft use simple external mass weights, e.g. *Volksplane* where the weight is fixed into an extension of the aileron tip rib. There is certainly no disadvantage in fitting mass balance weights, except for the additional work involved, and their use is recommended for scale models of fast flying prototypes and where the balances were visible externally. Flutter is likely to be initiated at the point furthest away from the control horn connection – usually inboard on the aileron – and the balance should be situated towards the free end. It is not necessary to fit weights above *and* below the aileron (with an internal balance weight this is not possible) and the weight should be just sufficient to counterbalance the weight of the aileron. Knowing that the amount of weight required for balancing will depend on the distance from the hinge line, there is a tendency to mount the weight on a lengthy piece of piano wire.

Below, aileron mass balance on a large jet. Note also flaps and 'droop-snoot'. Bottom, large cantilevered mass balance weight on Junkers Ju52.

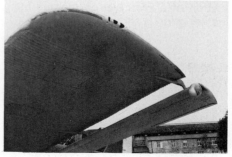

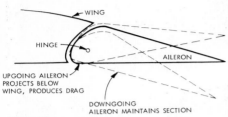

FIG. 7.11

This wire must be stiff or a vibration could be set up whereby the wire will flex unduly! Fitting mass balances is not easy once the model is completed and consideration should be given to installation at the design stage. Examples of mass balance installations are shown in the photographs.

FRIZE AILERONS

We discussed in Chapter 3 the development of differential and Frize ailerons and, as many modern aircraft use the latter form of aileron, we must incorporate them on our scale models. How effective they are on an average size scale R/C model for their designed purpose is open to doubt. The 'scale effect' of the model must reduce their efficiency, but as with mass balanced ailerons, there will be nothing lost and scale appearance gained. A typical section of a Frize aileron (named after the designer) is shown in Fig 7.11.

FLAPS

Three basic types of flaps are used at the trailing edge of the aircraft wings. There are many additional forms of slots, slats, leading edge flaps, boundary layer blowing and other devices for augmenting lift, or 'dumping' lift and increasing drag.

The three fundamental types cover the large proportion of prototypes and these are:-

1. Simple Flap:
2. Split Flap:
3. Fowler Flap.

The purpose and effect of the flaps has been previously considered but we must also consider the construction and operation. No problems should be encountered with the simple flap – it can be treated as an aileron (except that both flaps must go up and down together, of course). With the split flap the construction is rather more tricky as we are dividing an existing structural problem area. Due to the thin cross section of the flap the construction must be from a rigid material that will not twist – this also applies to the trailing edge of the wing above the flap, where some plywood reinforcing will be needed. Sheet aluminium can be used for the flap, with the edges seamed, or ply with carbon fibre and resin reinforcement on the top surface. Similar problems occur with the Fowler flap system, although the aerofoil section of the flap gives a little more 'meat' for the flap construction.

TRIM TABS

With the electronic trim facility, and mechanical adjustment of the linkage, it is seldom necessary to use operating trim tabs on a model. The trim tabs fitted on full-size aircraft are operated by a trim level, or wheel, to adjust the control stick forces for changes of weight distribution and throttle settings. The former we can ignore and the latter can be coped with by the transmitter trim adjustments.

There are aircraft that incorporate anti-balance tabs, or balance tabs, linked to the elevators and operating in conjunc-

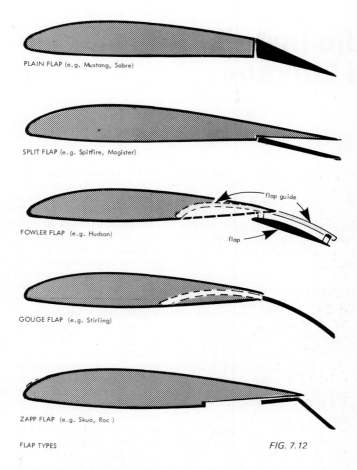

PLAIN FLAP (e.g. Mustang, Sabre)

SPLIT FLAP (e.g. Spitfire, Magister)

FOWLER FLAP (e.g. Hudson)

flap guide

flap

GOUGE FLAP (e.g. Stirling)

ZAPP FLAP (e.g. Skua, Roc)

FLAP TYPES

FIG. 7.12

tion with them. Anti-balance tabs move in the same direction as the elevator and are fitted to 'all-flying' tailplanes. Balance tabs are fitted to conventional elevators and operate in the reverse direction to the elevator. On larger aircraft there may also be trimming devices on the rudder and ailerons. Whether these devices are included on your scale model will depend on the degree of scale complexity you wish to encompass – they will be incorporated by some modellers for the purpose of accuracy, rather than operating effectiveness.

Chapter 8

Radio Installation and Linkages

The correct installation of the radio control equipment, and the efficient operation of the linkages and control surfaces, is of prime concern in any radio controlled model. It has an even greater priority when we are dealing with scale radio models. More time and effort has been spent on producing our masterpiece and it would be irrational to put this effort at risk through a second-rate control system. No radio control equipment is totally immune to failure and if this basic fact cannot be accepted, we would be more suited to building boats or cars, where the consequences of a radio failure are less disastrous. Superb scale models have been 'written off' through a servo failure and it is a sickening sight – it is also a possibility that we must be able to accept with a degree of equanimity. What *is* in our power is to purchase the most reliable radio equipment available, install it correctly, ensure that the linkages operate properly and maintain it efficiently. Surely we owe ourselves that much!

All of the normal precautions of shock absorbing, servo mounting, plug retention, battery protection, switch actuation etc. etc., must be observed in a scale model, but within the limited confines available. Certainly in a Class 1 scale model, and in many Class 2 scale models, none of the radio gear or linkages must be visible externally, or through the cockpit area. In many cases this means that the 'obvious' position for the servos and receiver cannot be used otherwise they would be visible in the cockpit area. The same applies, to a lesser degree, to the control linkages and they will probably have to be routed through the limited space below the cockpit floor, or the servos positioned behind the cockpit, where access may be problematic. Planning of the equipment installation and linkage routes, at the design stage, is imperative. The position of every component, and access to it, must be accurately plotted on the drawings, allowing sufficient space for leads, battery removal and protective padding. You must decide on the types of linkage to be incorporated and work out the method of fitting them *and* determine the stage of construction that they must be fitted. It can be an embarrassment to have pushrod ends projecting through the fuselage and wings during the preparation and finishing stages, but it may be unavoidable. This is one aspect where the study of the prototype, apart from earlier designs using partially external closed loop systems, may be of little value to us. It will show us the position of exiting of the pushrods and the size and location of control horns, but the linkages internally are primarily a modelling problem. Closed loop systems have the great advantage of flexibility of routing of the linkage. With the control command always being in the pull mode it does not matter that the path of the control wire, via nylon tube, is not in a direct line between the servo and control surface horn. Obviously, the fewer bends we incorporate the better the linkage as the friction losses are reduced. Using nylon covered fishing trace line in nylon tube (or similar plastic) does not introduce too much friction and a few bends can be tolerated without overloading the servo.

The same is not necessarily true with the tube and rod, tube and tube or bowden cable type systems of linkage. Not only does the amount of friction increase considerably with tight radius bends but so does the 'lost movement' of the linkage. Any tube and inner tube, rod or stranded metal cable system of pushrod (sometimes referred to as 'snakes') has to have a working clearance between the inner and outer components. When changes of direction are introduced in the linkage the amount of freedom of movement of the inner within the outer is increased – without a corresponding operation of the control surface. This 'slop' cannot be tolerated for control of a sensitive scale aircraft but

may be acceptable for a slow flying design where large surface movements are used. In general, the use of flexible pushrods should be limited to reasonably straight runs.

Rigid pushrods may be used if it is feasible to instal these; abide by the standard practices involved. That is, the rods must have a low inertia but high rigidity and have limited offsets at the connection to the control horn. 'Blow back' of control surfaces of large and fast models is a very real concern and the pushrod must be stiff enough, and restrained laterally, not to bow under the air pressures exerted on the control surfaces. The primary control surface suffering from 'blow-back' is the elevator and if it can be arranged for the pushrod to 'pull' for up elevator this is advisable. Flattening of the elevator is most likely to take place in a fast, full power, dive and to be able to 'pull' in the up elevator will be more effective than pushing and increasing the risk of bowing the elevator push rod. Adjustments for the lengths of the control linkages will normally be situated at the servo end, as the standard threaded rods and devices are hardly going to look scale on control surfaces. Ample space to make

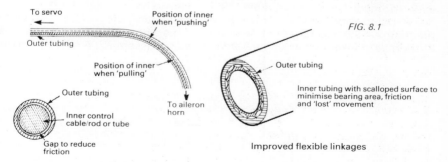

To servo

Position of inner when 'pushing'

Outer tubing

Position of inner when 'pulling'

To aileron horn

Outer tubing

Inner control cable/rod or tube

Gap to reduce friction

Lost movement in flexible linkage

FIG. 8.1

Outer tubing

Inner tubing with scalloped surface to minimise bearing area, friction and 'lost' movement

Improved flexible linkages

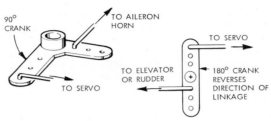

FIG. 8.2   REDUCING CONTROL MOVEMENT

these all important adjustments must be allowed for when considering access. Modern aircraft, where they use external control horns, use horns that are much smaller than comparable fittings on non-scale R/C models. Because of the short distance between the control horn/linkage attachment point, and the centre line of the control surface hinge, we will obtain more movement of the surface than normal – or needed. Even with the control linkage attached to the inner-most hole of the servo output arm, control surface movement may be excessive, and for these situations, a reducing crank may have to be intro-duced in the linkage chain to limit the movement. For ailerons, this can be achieved by using the bell crank as the movement reducing element but for elevators and rudders it will be neces-sary to incorporate a separate 180° crank. Using short control horns puts a premium on the accuracy of fit between the horn and linkage connection. A small

amount of free play of the rod in the hole will allow an excessive 'free' movement of the control surface.

Whatever hinge is used, commercial or home made, the basic requirements remain constant. The hinge must have freedom of movement, with no binding, and the control surface to wing/fin/tailplane fit should have a minimum gap. Prototype methods of control surface hingeing will dictate also the methods used on the model. For straight line hinges we can use commercial leaf and pin hinges and it will probably be con-venient to secure the control surfaces at, or after, the finishing stages. Where off-set hinges have to be duplicated more thought will have to be given to the con-struction of the hinge and the method of retaining the control surface. As it is probable that the control surface will have to be installed before final painting takes place, the surfaces adjacent to the hinge should be finished and painted before assembly. A slightly darker tone

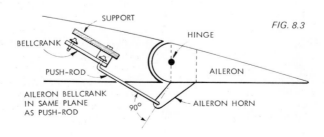

of the adjacent colour is in order as these areas inevitably become dirtier than the surrounding surface – it also helps to give 'depth' to the joint. A fear of many modellers is of the hinge coming adrift in flight. This has been known to happen when using nylon leaf and pin hinges but is invariably through incorrect fitting. Where the hinge is fitted before the model is prepared for finishing there is no excuse for failure, as the leaves of the hinge can be glued and pegged. With hinges fitted after completion of the decoration, we must take a little more care to obtain a secure hinge fixing. The first essential before fitting is to do a 'dry run' to check that the hinges fit and there is full and free movement of the control surface. When you are satisfied that this is so, the hinges can be glued permanently in position. All of the commercial hinges have some method of keying the hinge into the surface, and providing the hole or slot for the hinge leaf, or spigot, is not too enlarged, the glue, combined with the keying, will adequately hold the hinge. Rub petroleum jelly on the hinge axis portion only and fit the first half of the hinge into the prepared surface, using slow drying epoxy. The 24 hours type of epoxy is used as this gives ample time for readjustment and for the adhesive to penetrate the wood and holes/barbs of the hinge. After setting, fit the control surface similarly, but slipping small pieces of thin polythene sheet (backing material to plastic coverings) over the hinge part. Leave to dry completely, and with a sharp pointed knife trim away the surplus epoxy squeezed into the hinge gap. The use of petroleum jelly and the polythene should allow it to be removed easily. By all means check the security of the control surface by pulling hard on it, but properly installed there should be little chance of it coming

out unless it has a very hard knock. Some of the hinge leaves have a smooth shiny surface and these should be roughened up with coarse glasspaper before fitting. One of the biggest problems in connecting to hinged surfaces comes with the use of swept-back tail surfaces. If we consider, for instance, the elevators of a Mig 15 or 17 jet we have a compounded problem because both elevators sweep back in opposite directions, and the tailplane is mounted midway up the fin. We know, from basic geometry, that we cannot connect the elevators with a standard horn and connector and yet we have insufficient room in the fin area to fit horns and ball links. Ball links solve most of the problems encountered with swept-back control surfaces but they can hardly be considered scale, and if used the aim must be to hide them from view. The Mig 15 elevator problem is virtually impossible (until somebody succeeds in doing it) without some form of cheating and this could take the form of using only one elevator or making it into an all flying tailplane – the original used conventional elevators. Few linkage and control surface problems are insoluble but some will take considerable ingenuity and working out from basic principles. The more complex the linkage the more insistent we must be that each change of direction is as 'slop'-free as possible, and if to be inaccessible on completion of the model, is absolutely secure with nuts sealed and bearings greased.

Although we have previously discussed the advantage of differential movement of ailerons it is all too easy to finish up with unwanted differential movement – usually in the wrong direction. To avoid this we must understand the geometry of the linkage between the bellcrank and the aileron horn – assuming that no differential

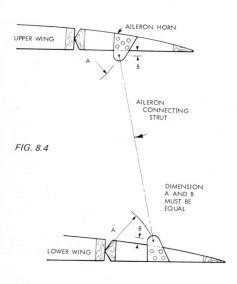

FIG. 8.4

along, or inside the leading edges of the bottom wing, round a pulley to an aileron horn on the lower surface. The two ailerons were linked by an adjustable tension wire and from an aileron horn on the top surface, the control wire continued round a pulley back along the leading edge of the top wing, via another pulley back to the fuselage. This total closed loop allowed only a single wire, in tension, to be used between top and bottom ailerons. If we use the standard pushrod method for aileron linkage, on the bottom wing, we must use some form of pushrod (i.e. stiff wire) to actuate the top aileron from the bottom aileron. Inevitably this will have to be thicker than the scale equivalent and serious thought should be given to adopting the closed loop system — the disconnection of the control cables for demounting the wings being the hardest obstacle to overcome. Not all biplanes used a wire interconnection for the ailerons, some used a wooden, or metal strut. To simulate this form of connection we must fit horns to the bottom of the top aileron, and top of the bottom aileron, and instal the strut with pivots at the horn positions. To avoid any unwanted differential movement between the sets of ailerons the horns must be centred at the same radius from the hinge line on the top and bottom ailerons. See Fig. 8.4.

Concealed aileron and flap linkages, i.e. where no external horns are visible, must be fabricated with the use of very small internal horns or 'skew rod' actuation. Both systems, to operate precisely, have to be well engineered as any excess movement on the fit of rods in horns, or bellcranks, will be magnified at the control surface. With internal linkages it is impossible to provide for any adjustment, except at the servo, and provision should be made here for adjustment of

effect is emanating from the servo connection. It is not only essential to have the hole in the control horn at right angles to the control connection axis (passing through the hinge line) but to have the bell crank operating in that plane. See Fig. 8.3. The bellcrank must also be set at 90° to the control horn, in the neutral position, to avoid differential. Where we positively require differential movement, or reduction of movement, there are numerous ways that this can be achieved and all of them have been adequately covered in other publications.

Biplanes, with ailerons on top and bottom wings, will require the ailerons to be interconnected. The mechanical methods of connecting them will vary according to the linkage systems adopted. Full size aircraft often used a closed loop system, leading out from either side of the bottom of the fuselage,

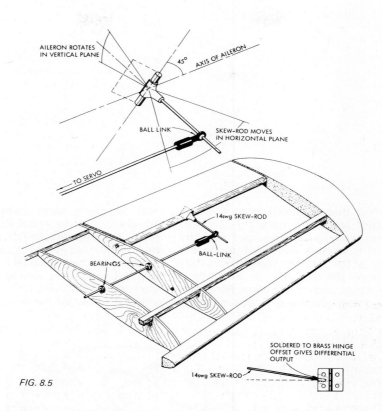

AILERON ROTATES
IN VERTICAL PLANE

45° AXIS OF AILERON

BALL LINK

SKEW-ROD MOVES
IN HORIZONTAL PLANE

TO SERVO

14swg SKEW-ROD

BALL-LINK

BEARINGS

SOLDERED TO BRASS HINGE
OFFSET GIVES DIFFERENTIAL
OUTPUT

14swg SKEW-ROD

FIG. 8.5

linkage lengths *and* throw. Fig. 8.5 illustrates the internal linkage systems.

All moving, high set tailplanes are used on numerous modern light aircraft, particularly sailplanes. The standard method of actuation is by a system of bellcranks and pushrods to a control horn. It is also possible to operate the all-moving tailplane by the closed loop system and this method is illustrated in Fig. 8.6.

Coupled ailerons and rudders have advantages on certain aircraft – notably high wing cabin type models and over-stable biplanes. Mechanical coupling of the aileron and rudder is not normally difficult but the use of separate servos and 'Y' lead, connecting to the aileron socket on the receiver is a simpler way of achieving the coupling. Simpler still is the use of a transmitter with an electronic rudder/aileron coupling switch incorporated. This gives you the best of both worlds and you can decouple the rudder when this is needed as a separate function i.e. for a stall turn or during take-

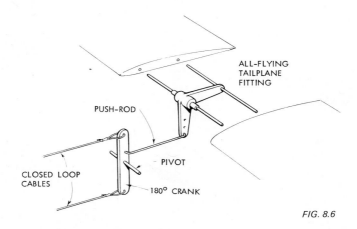

ALL-FLYING
TAILPLANE
FITTING

PUSH-ROD

PIVOT

CLOSED LOOP
CABLES

180° CRANK

FIG. 8.6

off. Not that the latter manoeuvre is difficult with permanently coupled aileron and rudder *provided* that the model is headed into wind during the whole of the take-off. Transmitters may also have the dual rate control function for ailerons and/or elevators. For sports flying these 'additional' functions of dual rates, coupling, servo mode reversal, etc., are far from essential. Flying a scale model can, however, be rather trickier in the trimming out stages and the benefits of paying for the additional functions are fully justified. To be able to increase or decrease the throws of the control surfaces, or change the centring position

C.A.R. System retaining separate rudder control

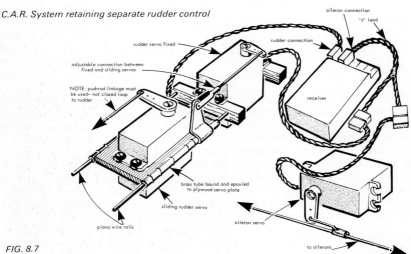

aileron connection

'Y' lead

rudder servo fixed

rudder connection

adjustable connection between
fixed and sliding servos

NOTE: pushrod linkage must
be used- not closed loop
to rudder

receiver

brass tube bound and epoxied
to plywood servo plate

sliding rudder servo

piano wire rails

aileron servo

to ailerons

FIG. 8.7

FIG. 8.8

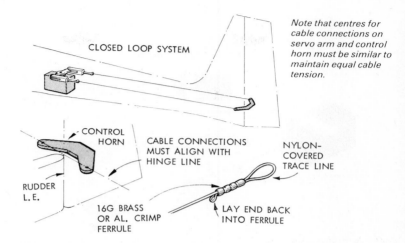

CLOSED LOOP SYSTEM

Note that centres for cable connections on servo arm and control horn must be similar to maintain equal cable tension.

CONTROL HORN

CABLE CONNECTIONS MUST ALIGN WITH HINGE LINE

NYLON-COVERED TRACE LINE

RUDDER L.E.

16G BRASS OR AL. CRIMP FERRULE

LAY END BACK INTO FERRULE

of a servo, without having to dismantle the model can be a real bonus during those critical early flights.

Charger socket and switch actuation locations can be within the cockpit area (hidden from view) or reached via a spring loaded hatch in a scale position. Routing the receiver aerial is only perplexing when the aerial length is in excess of the fuselage length and this is only likely to happen with small scale models. There are electronic methods of reducing the physical length of the aerial but these would probably invalidate any warranty of the radio equipment and, in any case, should only be carried out by a qualified electronics engineer. An uncomplicated method of dealing with the receiver aerial is to instal a rigid lightweight plastic tube down the length of the fuselage, from the radio compartment to the tail, exiting at an

inconspicuous position, and to feed the aerial into this. Bind and cyanoacrylate a length of cotton to the end of the aerial and tape the cotton to a piece of thin piano wire. Feed the piano wire through the tube, secure the cotton to the end of the tube with a spot of cyanoacrylate and cut off the surplus cotton and piano wire.

Never be satisfied with second best when it comes to the operation of any control function. If the flap is not quite

A modern transmitter with control mixers, rate adjusters. pre-programming, servo reversers and other sophistications.

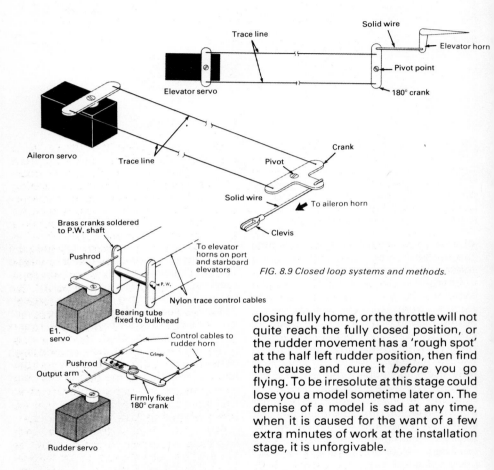

FIG. 8.9 Closed loop systems and methods.

closing fully home, or the throttle will not quite reach the fully closed position, or the rudder movement has a 'rough spot' at the half left rudder position, then find the cause and cure it *before* you go flying. To be irresolute at this stage could lose you a model sometime later on. The demise of a model is sad at any time, when it is caused for the want of a few extra minutes of work at the installation stage, it is unforgivable.

Chapter 9

Engine Installations, Ducted Fan Units and Jets

Watch an R/C scale competition for any length of time and one fact will soon become obvious; some of the scale models will be 'wallowing' around with barely any reserve of flying speed. They give the appearance of "an accident looking for somewhere to happen" and flit from one semi-stalled condition to another. Usually the inevitable happens, and during a turn, a wing will drop and the model will reach terra-firma with a thump, accompanied by a wisp of smoke from the engine. The causes of this condition can be ascribed to over-weight, under-power and, possibly a rearward C of G to aggravate the situation. Once the aircraft is finished there is little we can do about the total weight condition but the location of the correct C of G is all-important. That only leaves us with the engine to overcome this ever-dangerous situation of minimum performance, or to be more correct, the engine, propeller, fuel, glowplug, fuel system and engine cooling combinations. It is, perhaps, not surprising that the scale modeller, in his quest to complete his scale masterpiece, tends to overlook the power source of the model. With all the hours employed in construction, finishing and detailing the model there is insufficient time to give the new engine more than a few perfunctory runs on the test bench. After all, the standards of R/C engines are very

good these days and they rarely fail to operate. Factual as this may be, there is a vast difference between simply operating and for the engine to be operating at maximum efficiency. We may need, in difficult flying situations, to use every bit of power available and it is imperative that power is on hand precisely when it is required. To have a totally reliable and controllable engine that will operate smoothly throughout its full speed range is not just desirable — it is essential. To achieve this we must know the engine, run it in *thoroughly*, adjust the carburettor and find the most suitable fuel/plug/propeller combination. It is to be assumed that the rudimentary workings of the engine and carburettor are understood, if not, it is suggested that the proposed engine for the scale model be first fitted to a sports model until you are thoroughly conversant with its operation.

Rigid mounting of the engine, with substantial bearers, engine plate, or mount is a must to reduce vibrational effects. Ideally, provision should be made for engine thrust adjustments to be made for flight trimming. In practice this is less easy to accomplish, particularly when representing inline engines, complete with close fitting spinners. Cowled radial and rotary engines offer a little more scope in this direction but even this arrangement does not allow for an easy form of thrust adjustment.

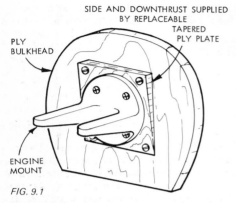

SIDE AND DOWNTHRUST SUPPLIED
BY REPLACEABLE
TAPERED
PLY PLATE

PLY
BULKHEAD

ENGINE
MOUNT

FIG. 9.1

Sometimes an aluminium mount can be mounted on a ply square (itself fixed to the engine bulkhead) that is sanded to incorporate side and down thrust. Should thrust adjustments be necessary, the ply square can be substituted with one incorporating the adjustments. For the majority of models, however, it will be a matter of making sensible speculation of the amount of down and side thrust to be used and being stuck

with them. The use of nylon, or nylon filled engine mounts, should be confined to small scale models; the vibration levels can be excessive with larger engine sizes. Aluminium engine mounts should be carefully drilled and tapped to receive the engine, checking that the mounting flanges are flat, smooth and parallel. Use cap head screws for mounting the engine, with the addition of lock washers; it is much easier to use an Allen key for securing the bolts than a standard or crosspoint screwdriver. When using an engine plate, i.e. breakaway plate, Tufnol of adequate thickness ($^3/_{16}$ or ¼ in. for larger engines) should be used – this method also allows for thrust line adjustments. Beech, maple, or similar hardwood engine bearers are quite acceptable and they can be strengthened by coating with glass fibre resin. Better still is the surfacing of the top and bottom faces of the hardwood with thin steel sheet; this will prevent any indentation of the surface as the engine mounting bolts are tightened. The securing nuts can be permanently silver

Installation of one of the two Webra 91 four-strokes on a large Curtiss Condor. Note toothed-belt valve drive on this motor.

128

soldered to the underside steel strip. Stiff nuts are not of great value in engine mounting unless they are renewed every time the engine is removed; lock nuts, together with locking washers, will give more secure fixing.

Over the past few years there have been a number of attempts to produce flexible, vibration-reducing engine mounts. These have met with very limited success as the isolation of the engine vibration requires the use of flexible materials that do not stand up well to the operating conditions. Full size aircraft engines do, of course, have anti-vibration mountings, but these engines are far less vibratory than the single cylinder two-stroke engines we employ. It is not unknown, with light aircraft, for a 100 h.p. engine to be directly mounted on to ⁷/₈in. square *hardwood* engine bearers! To attempt the scale equivalent of that, in a model, would be disastrous. The other problem in having an anti-vibration mount, assuming the technical problems of materials can be overcome, is the flexibility. This will allow the engine to move to quite a high degree, particularly with torque effect, and it will become impossible to use a close fitting spinner without encountering inter-ference between the spinner and the nose cowl.

SILENCERS

It is rare that the manufacturers' stan-dard engine silencer can be fitted to a scale model — it will normally extend beyond the fuselage outline. Fortunately, a number of specialist manufacturers produce silencers that are more suited for scale purposes. These may be in the form of 'dumpy' silencers or remote ones specifically designed for scale subjects. In the event of no suitable

commercial silencer being available you will have to resort to fabricating it your-self. Before construction of the silencer begins take some R.P.M. readings from the engine, with the standard silencer fitted, so that you have a target to aim for when the special silencer arrangement is fitted. The silencer does not have to be fitted directly to the exhaust outlet — this is often difficult to achieve with a scale design. Fitting an exhaust manifold with flexible silicone tube to a remote silencer is the more normal way of coping with the limited space available inside a scale cowl. When designing the silencer arrangement, aim, if it is possible, to have the exhaust outlet from the silencer in a scale position. For instance, many modern light aircraft feature exhaust pipes that terminate at the bottom rear of the cowl and this can easily be adopted for our model set-up. Silencer boxes can be purchased, or fabricated from sheet brass, silver soldered together. The more tortuous the exhaust route from the engine the greater the power loss there will be from the engine. Keep bends in the silicone tube to the maximum possible radius and minimum overall length. Security of the flexible silicone tube to the exhaust manifold

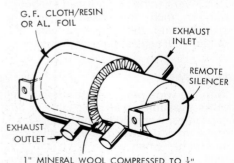

G.F. CLOTH/RESIN OR AL. FOIL

EXHAUST INLET

REMOTE SILENCER

EXHAUST OUTLET

1" MINERAL WOOL COMPRESSED TO ¼"

FIG. 9.2

and silencer box is important. Fit the tubing when the metal is thoroughly clean and dry (use dope thinners, or carbon tetrachloride, to remove all traces of oil) and secure with metal clips or nylon ties. Only use the highest quality of silicone tube, of ample internal diameter and wall thickness, as the tubing has to withstand considerable temperatures.

There will probably be some conflict between the degree of silencing you will obtain and the engine power loss as a result of attaching that silencer. For a scale model of a low powered light aircraft to fly with the engine giving out a throaty roar may look right but it certainly will not sound right. Compromise will most likely be the answer, but remember that the larger the volume of the silencer the better the silencing qualities – without added power loss. Back pressure caused by the silencing arrangement will, if excessive, seriously affect the power output and, probably, cause the engine to run hot. Silencing by the use of expansion chambers is not the only effective answer. A reasonable degree of sound deadening can be achieved by applying mineral wool (loft insulation) to the silencer box. A one inch layer can be compressed to about a quarter inch thickness around the silencer and then covered with aluminium foil or glass fibre cloth and resin.

FUEL TANKS

With the wide range of commercial fuel tanks available, in all sizes, shapes and capacities, it should not be necessary to make up your own. The important consideration when assembling the fuel tank is to be absolutely sure that it is airtight and leakproof. This is especially critical when using pressurised fuel

systems and a pressure test should be applied to the tank, under water, before the tank is fitted. High pressure fuel systems do create considerable fuel tank pressures and for these conditions it is expedient to wrap polythene rectangular tanks with self adhesive cloth tape, to assist them to withstand the pressures involved. Check that the silicone fuel feed tube is securely anchored to the clunk weight and brass tube. A tight fit tube should be used; the narrow internal bore will be perfectly adequate, and fitting of the tube can be made easier by first soaking the end of the tube with acetone. This will cause the tube to swell, allow it to be fitted to the brass and clunk weight and then shrink as the acetone evaporates. At least, it works with most types of tubing!

FILTERS

Even with the highest quality of fuel, and filtering from the fuel supply bottle, it is possible to have small foreign bodies pumped into the model's fuel tank. The introduction of a fuel filter between the fuel tank and the engine carburettor should take care of any remaining minute particles in the fuel. No full size engine fitter would dream of omitting a fuel filter to the fuel system – despite the greater clearances of the fuel metering needles – and yet the modeller often overlooks this basic precaution. The dismantlable type of filter is not recommended for scale purposes as there is the risk after cleaning of not obtaining an absolute seal in the filter, and allowing air to get into the system. Air leaks, through minute pin holes in the fuel tubing, the tank, the filter or loose bolts on the engine, can be the bane of a modeller's life. They will cause erratic running of the engine and extreme frus-

Crankcase-mounted fuel pressure pump (right) with associated carburettor allow mounting of fuel tank conveniently.

tration because the engine will not always quit, sometimes go lean for a period, run O.K. again and then finally stop altogether. If you have erratic running of the engine in flight and have to set the needle valve differently from normal, you should first suspect the plumbing. Following that inspection, if you do not find the cause, start looking for other reasons, e.g. loose carburettor or engine back plate, glowplug, fuel.

Filters should not be fitted and forgotten, they must be maintained by back flushing the accumulated dirt from the filter. In theory, it is advisable to clean the filter after each flying session but it is normally sufficient, when using clean fuel, to clean them after every three or four outings. Certainly, the filter should be back flushed clean when the model has been stored for any length of time, and the whole of the plumbing should be checked also. As some filters have identical ends, one end should be marked clearly so there is no risk of replacing the filter into the fuel line in the reverse direction. This could allow some of the residual dirt to be sucked into the engine carburettor causing a blockage. Engine metering systems work to very fine tolerances and the smallest particle of dirt is enough to cause fuel starvation.

PRESSURISATION SYSTEMS

On scale R/C models it is not always practicable to situate the fuel tank in the ideal position relative to the engine i.e. close to it and with the horizontal centre line of the tank on the same level as the carburettor needle valve centre. To overcome this problem in varying degrees, we can use a pressurised fuel system, although it should be stressed that achieving the correct positioning of the fuel tank is the ideal solution. Pressurisation can take three forms:—

1. Low pressure – taken from a tapping in the silencer:

2. High pressure – normally taken from the crankcase but sometimes from the crankshaft area;

3. Regulated high pressure – using the crankcase pressure and regulating it for fuel supply.

All that is required for the low pressure system is a nipple to be fitted to the silencer chamber (a nipple is normally fitted to the standard silencer) and connected to the fuel filter pipe on the tank. On completion of filling the tank, the vent must be sealed off – this applies to any pressurised system. The low pressure system is only suitable for slight tank head variations, but is simple to instal and effective.

High pressure is usually taken from a tapping in the rear of the crankcase. Many engines can be adapted for a high pressure 'bleed' by replacing one of the rear crankcase backplate bolts with a nipple of suitable thread. The bolt to replace is the top one adjacent to the inlet port (a bulge on the side of the upper crankcase) where the bolt hole is drilled through to the interior of the crankcase. Alternatively, a hole can be drilled and tapped in the backplate, and a nipple inserted, but the screwed end of the nipple must be cleaned off flush with the interior surface, to avoid obstruction of the crankshaft pin. The advantages of variations of fuel tank position can be outweighed by the lack of flexibility of engine control that the pressurisation may cause. Needle valve settings become more critical; check the engine on normal suction first and if the needle valve movement from rich to a 'lean' cut is less than a half turn it is unlikely that high pressure fuel feed system is likely to be suitable. The idle and intermediate engine range may also be affected.

To overcome the shortcomings of the simple high pressure system, regulated high pressure devices came on to the modelling market. Instead of a direct system that is influenced by engine speed and other factors, regulators (sometimes with diaphragm pumps) were introduced to govern the amount of fuel to the engine at a constant rate. The regulators vary in their method of operation but most are adjustable for the fuel delivery rate and provide the advantage of allowing the use of larger bore carburettors – and more realisable power. A boon to modellers of scale aircraft, with difficult tank positions, are the engines with integral fuel pumps and regulators. These simplify the plumbing arrangements and allow the fuel tank to be situated almost anywhere in the model. With any pressure system more consideration must be given to the fixing of the connecting tubing and the use of wire ties or clips will help to prevent the tubing accidentally coming adrift; regular plumbing checks are essential for consistent engine operation.

CRANKSHAFT EXTENSIONS

For scale appearance reasons, or for attempting to obtain a better balance

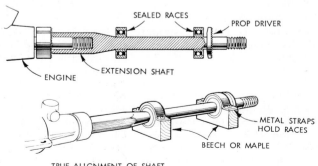

SEALED RACES

PROP DRIVER

EXTENSION SHAFT

ENGINE

METAL STRAPS
HOLD RACES

BEECH OR MAPLE

TRUE ALIGNMENT OF SHAFT
AND RACES VITAL

FIG. 9.3

position with pusher designs, the use of a crankshaft extension may be desired. Where the extension is small a short 'spacing' extender can be used, such as the items produced by Fox Manufacturing Co. Models requiring a longer extension involve more of an engineering solution, with shaft extensions. A rigid shaft extension, housed in a ball race at the prop-driver end, relies on a very firm mounting of the engine and a similarly rigid mounting of the ball race, plus perfect alignment. Engineering facilities are necessary for this type of project, and the extension arrangement should be bench tested for reliablity before fitting to the model.

As an alternative to the rigid extensions it should be worthwhile experimenting with the flexible couplings used for boat propeller drives. Although the engine and front prop-drive housing must still be rigidly fixed and supported, the alignment between them is not critical.

The reasons for fitting extension shafts to pusher aircraft (of the early open boom type) are to hide the working engine and to position it nearer to the C of G, thus reducing the tail heavy situation. It should also be realised that many of the larger capacity engines can be obtained in a reverse direction of operation i.e. clockwise viewed from the front. This enables standard tractor propellers – of which there is a great variety – to be used for pusher operation.

COOLING

At the beginning of the chapter it was stated that many have been the crashes of scale models through a lack of useful power from the engine. An important contributory factor to the limit of realisable power is inadequate, or inefficient, cooling air to the engine. A typical flight

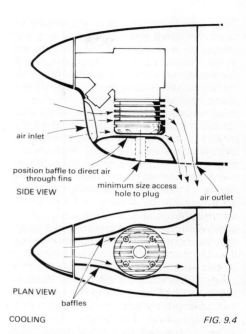

air inlet

position baffle to direct air through fins

SIDE VIEW

minimum size access hole to plug

air outlet

PLAN VIEW

baffles

COOLING

FIG. 9.4

pattern of a poorly cooled engine model will be for the engine to operate happily on the ground at low speed and take off satisfactorily but, with a minimum power/weight ratio, the model only makes headway and height very slowly. With this situation the engine must be kept at full throttle to prevent stalling and the engine begins to overheat. The overheating/full throttle situation becomes a vicious circle and as the cylinder head temperature increases, the power reduces until the inevitable happens. Scale models of prototypes using air cooled engines do not present too many difficulties but those using inline liquid cooled power plants are a different proposition entirely. Until someone perfects a liquid cooling system for model engines, in scale model aircraft, we are bound by the air flow cooling methods.

Unless air is passing over the engine in flight we shall not obtain any cooling effect, so it is essential to provide air inlets and outlets. As the air passing over the engine is heated it also expands and, therefore, we require larger outlets than inlets. Air will always take the line of least resistance and unless we take some action, it will flow directly from the inlet to the outlet, possibly bypassing the engine on the way. To avoid this happening, and to route the air to the cylinder head (the hottest operational area of the engine), it may be necessary to direct the air physically by means of baffles and fairings. Modellers do not always realise why, with the engine situated in a large diameter cowl, an engine still overheats. It is *not* the amount of free air inlet area, or the outlet area, that is at fault in this case, but *where* the air flows. Restrictions and baffles to route the air to the critical engine areas are not difficult and examples of possible arrangements are shown in Fig. 9.4. No hard and fast rules can be laid down with regard to free air areas (i.e. allowing for grille material etc.) for inlets and outlets but, typically, a .60 powered model will require 1–1¼ sq.ins. inlet and 2–2¼ sq.ins. outlet. It is appreciated that this is none too easy to incorporate on something like a *Hurricane* but it is *essential* to provide this cooling air – even with a well run-in engine. How it is achieved will depend on the ingenuity of the designer. Cooling flaps, that open during flight, can be incorporated and the use of fine metal mesh to cover some of the forward parts will preserve the outline of the model and allow additional air to be taken in, or extracted. If there is *no* alternative to going out of scale to provide adequate cooling then it is preferable to lose a few static scale points rather than finish up with virtually no flying points in a competition. Suppos-

ing the model is complete, the cooling problem is evident despite the engine being run in and air diverters fitted – external modifications are not possible – is there anything we can do? One action that can be taken is to use a higher nitro content fuel. This will give us more power at a lower throttle setting, the engine will run a little cooler and it may provide the difference between failure and success. We should also experiment with combinations of plugs and propeller sizes.

IN FLIGHT PLUG BOOSTER

Scale models, in competitions, have to perform for much of their time at idle and low engine speeds. Typically, a model will be started, the judges' readiness awaited, then it is taxied out and held before take-off. It is often, at this critical point, that the engine is opened up, there is a splutter, and the engine quits. This is due to the engine 'loading-up' and, with a surge of fresh fuel as the throttle is opened, the glow of the plug is doused. Even if we get past this obstacle the competition rules may require an extended slow flypast. With a model of a prototype with a slow cruising speed this will take some considerable time and, to gain good scale points, will have to be flown at a low throttle setting. As we open up the engine the same problem is likely to recur. The safe idle speed of the engine, and the pick-up from idle to full speed, can be made infinitely more assured by the use of a permanently connected nickel cadmium cell to the glowplug. Having emphasised the risks of scale models ending up tail heavy, the extra weight of single battery cell in the nose area is not likely to be an embarrassment. The size of the nicad will depend on the weight restrictions of the model and the length of time of operation.

Ideally, a 4a.H battery should be fitted (weighing about 6 oz.) as this will give you in excess of thirty minutes strong glow to the plug, when permanently connected. Alternatively a 1 or 2a.H cell (1.2 nominal volt) can be used in conjunction with a microswitch operating the cell *only* at the lower throttle settings. It is possible to use the in-flight battery to start the engine but this is not recommended as it will increase the battery drain and may not readily start the engine with a 2 volt plug fitted. Experimenting with plugs is important when using the plug booster, to find the most suitable voltage and type of plug. Switches and charging sockets for the battery must be situated to suit the scale requirements of the model. If you are suspicious of the value of this plug boosting device, try the following experiment. Start your engine, with the normal external plug battery, disconnect the battery, set the engine for the minimum safe idle speed. Leave the engine at idle for thirty seconds or so and rapidly open the throttle. Repeat the operation but keep the plug battery connected and notice the difference!

IN-FLIGHT ELECTRIC ENGINE STARTER

For the modeller who has everything, why not buy him an in-flight starter? Actually 'in-flight' is not the complete description because the starter can be used for starting on the ground as well as in the air. As the name suggests, the starter is an electro-mechanical device consisting of batteries, electric motor,

Gear reduction to the propeller and "in-flight" starters are two comparatively recent innovations made desirable by increasing model size.

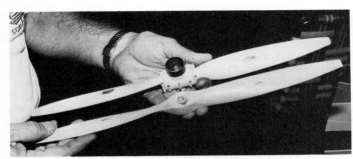

Some experts still carve props to suit specific models. Foreground is low pitch flying prop with scale equivalent behind.

gears and belt drive, to the crankshaft of the engine, with a clutch arrangement. It is quite uncanny to see the R/C pilot, standing some way from the model with his transmitter, control the starting of the engine, check the controls and taxi out to the take-off point. The only drawback to this piece of 'one-upmanship' is the cost of the equipment and the weight penalty. It probably has a greater application on 'large' scale models and while it may not oust the standard 'external' starter it certainly has fascination.

PROPELLERS

Manufacturers of engines usually recommend certain propeller sizes for their various engines. This should only be taken as a guide to propeller selection and is more likely to be related to sports or aerobatic models than heavier scale models. The selection of suitable propeller sizes and types of scale models tends to be a hit and miss affair, partly because of conflicting requirements. Although an engine (say a typical .60 Schnuerle ported engine) may reach its maximum output at 18,000 R.P.M. — suggesting the use of a 11 in. × 7 in. propeller—this may not accord with our propeller selection. A seventy inch wing span biplane weighing 10½ pounds may fly much better with a 14 in. × 5 in. propeller but, at the same time, could increase the work load

on the engine. The engine having more work to do will, compared with a lighter aerobatic model, run hotter — not the most desirable feature in a scale model. Selecting suitable propellers is not made easier by the fact that the stated pitch of the propeller is rarely the *actual* pitch. Manufacturers of wooden propellers vary considerably in the degree of accuracy of their products, but there can be very wide variations, even of the pitch of an 'identical' batch of propellers. We can only select the most suitable propeller by experiment, in flight, and hope that we can replace that propeller when it becomes necessary, with a very similar one. It is possible to check the propeller pitch by the use of a pitch gauge and it is *imperative* to balance every propeller correctly before use.

Wooden propellers should be used for all models with large engines, not merely for their scale appearance and greater efficiency, but also because of their greater safety compared with nylon or glass filled nylon propellers. These latter propellers, although strong and quite efficient, are very much heavier than equivalent wooden types. This will increase the gyro effect of the propeller and compound the take-off swing problems mentioned earlier. Most scale models, being heavy and with relatively high drag, will require a larger diameter propeller than for a sports design, and propeller design becomes an important factor. Wider bladed propellers, in theory at least, are more efficient because of the Reynolds Number effect, as are large diameter propellers turning at low speeds. Perhaps, before selecting the propeller, we should first be concerned with selecting the engine, bearing in mind the need to swing a large propeller. Inspect the performance figures of the range of engines in the capacity to be used and select the engine that will swing the larger sizes of propeller at the highest R.P.M. Consulting the torque graphs will give you similar information, and these facts can be elicited by reading the Engine Test articles in modelling magazines. From the scale modeller's point of view it would be helpful if engine manufacturers went back to the longer stroke, smaller bore format of engine design. One thing to watch when you are setting up an engine with a large propeller, after being used to a smaller propeller, is engine note. You may assume, from the exhaust note, that the engine is not putting out full power and be tempted to 'tweak' the needle valve. Don't! It will almost certainly lead you into a lean engine run and the engine 'cooking'. A notch or two rich is a much safer proposition.

Before leaving our comments on the two-stroke internal combustion engine for models the importance of the correct setting up of the carburettor must be emphasised. Full instructions for adjusting the carburettor are included with the engine – they will vary with the type of carburettor used – and these must be faithfully followed. There is no point in trying to adjust the carburettor finely during the running-in period of the engine but, then, the engine should not be installed in the model at that stage.

Once the carburettor has been accurately adjusted it should require little further adjustment unless there is a change of propeller, fuel or plug, or widely differing climatic conditions.

DUCTED FAN UNITS

There has been much nonsense talked about ducted fan units with claims ranging from the complete decrying of them as useless, to exaggerated claims of the thrust to be expected from the units. The truth lies somewhere in between and commercial units and fans have been developed to a stage where the ducted fan scale model is a practical proposition.

In the nineteen fifties both centrifugal and axial fans were experimented with for the propulsion of scale free flight and control line models, although the former type had little following. The centrifugal fan unit was mounted horizontally and herein lay its main scale disadvantage. Although scale jet outlets could be used, the inlet had to be on the top of the fuselage leaving an unsightly large opening. Axial fans for free flight models were largely pioneered in Britain by the late P.E. Norman and he eventually developed fans with sufficient thrust to fly single channel scale radio control models successfully. Other experiments produced some very promising ducted fan units but these were never put into quantity manufacture. To machine accurately, or hand finish, single units to work efficiently is one thing, to obtain the same results in mass production creates greater problems. Little more progress was made in radio control ducted fan scale models until the mid seventies. Over the intervening period there had been two major advances. Engines were developing about twice the output, per c.c., of their predecessors and advanced

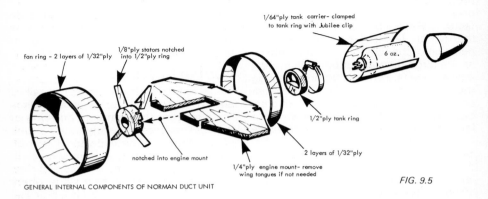

1/64"ply tank carrier- clamped to tank ring with Jubilee clip

6 oz.

1/8"ply stators notched into 1/2"ply ring

fan ring - 2 layers of 1/32"ply

1/2"ply tank ring

notched into engine mount

2 layers of 1/32"ply

1/4"ply engine mount- remove wing tongues if not needed

GENERAL INTERNAL COMPONENTS OF NORMAN DUCT UNIT

FIG. 9.5

techniques in moulding new forms of plastic had been established. The increased performance of the engines, in particular, opened the door to achieving thrust levels that made the building of a four function radio control scale jet not only possible but possessing reasonably scale flying characteristics.

Much of the development in America has been undertaken by Robert Kress, who has produced his 'Axiflo' units in a range of sizes, and Marcus Norman, son of P.E. Norman, was the first to demonstrate the potential of ducted fan R/C models in Britain. The approach to the problems of these two innovators could hardly be more different. Robert Kress designed his units from a very scientific view, with minor practical adjustments, whereas Marcus Norman's approach was more empirical. It is interesting to note that the theory and practice match very closely. For successful ducted fan flying it is vital to pay great attention to details. Duct sizes, shapes, finishes and the contours of the inlet and outlet are critical. Rotor blade shape, section and pitch must be right, as must the balance of the fan unit. Tolerances of the gap

between the perimeter of the fan and the shroud do not leave room for error. The engine installation must be precise, and rigid, with the engine giving absolutely maximum power. Ducted fan units will *never* compare in performance with a standard propeller – in their 'single stage' development at least – and we must extract every available ounce of thrust from the unit/engine combination that we are using. This is why the experts are seen to be achieving good results and the 'average' modeller seems to struggle; the expert is taking more care with the important details giving him the extra ounces of thrust needed to achieve convincing flight.

To make your own fan unit is possible, providing you have reasonable engineering skills and are prepared to spend many hours in experimenting with fan blade sections, pitches, numbers of blades, diameters, etc. With the commercial units now available it is very doubtful whether all of this labour is justified and the time saved would more profitably be put towards the design and construction of the model. At least the rotor and the shroud should be purchased as the basis of a ducted fan unit. Most of the commercially available units are capable of being transferred from one model to another, the unit forming part of the main duct. If we are working with only the rotor and the shroud the latter will be a permanent fixture in the fuselage, the duct being an integral part of the fuselage.

Assuming that we are using a commercial unit, what are the factors governing the successful operation of the unit?

1. The unit must be assembled precisely:
2. The rotor unit must be accurately balanced, and trimmed if necessary:
3. The engine/rotor unit must be precisely mounted in the unit duct to give the stated clearance between rotor and shroud:
4. The engine must be well run in, free and capable of producing the R.P.M.

quoted by the manufacturers of the fan unit. It may be necessary to use high nitro content fuels to achieve these speeds:

5. The fitting of a silencer, mandatory for many flying locations, can present difficulties due to the limited space available in the duct. One answer is to use a rear exhaust outlet engine and fit a tuned pipe. This keeps the free air area of the duct to a maximum — an important consideration as obstructions in the duct cause loss of efficiency.

Factors affecting the design of the model are rather more limiting when considering the selection of the scale model. Compared with a jet engine, the size of the air inlets and outlets are larger for ducted fan units and to reduce the areas below the design minimum criteria will result in a *serious* loss of performance. Both the size and the shape of inlets (which should not be less than 82%

FIG. 9.6

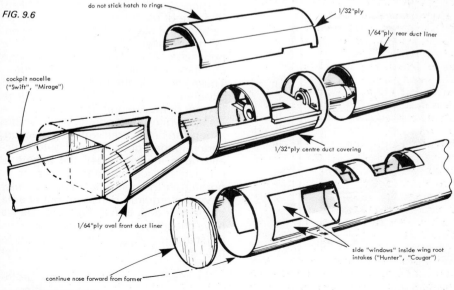

do not stick hatch to rings

1/32"ply

1/64"ply rear duct liner

cockpit nacelle ("Swift", "Mirage")

1/32"ply centre duct covering

1/64"ply oval front duct liner

side "windows" inside wing root intakes ("Hunter", "Cougar")

continue nose forward from former

INLET DUCT ARRANGEMENTS

of the fan duct area) are all-important and must be carefully considered at the design stage. (Bell mouth inlet sections were found to be important in the early days of full-size jet aircraft design when the performance of the Gloster *Meteor* was considerably improved by the re-design of the air intakes to the engines.) The outlet area can be reduced to 80% of the main duct area but this does not represent very much divergence of the duct towards the rear. Lengths of duct will also affect efficiency, the longer the duct the greater the friction drag. The internal surface of the duct should be smooth and any changes of direction, or section, gradual.

We have a fixed diameter of the fan unit duct and this will establish the minimum cross sectional area (allowing for fuselage construction) of the scale model. Using this as a basis of working out the scale of the model will almost

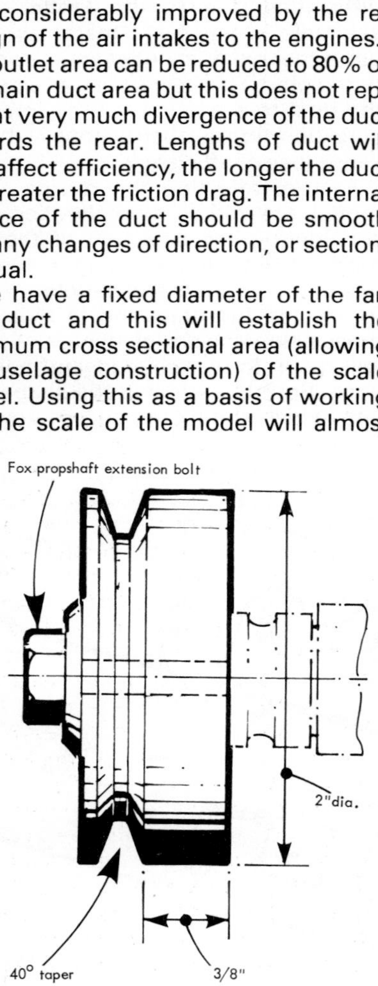

Fox propshaft extension bolt

2"dia.

40° taper   3/8"

FIG. 9.7. Starting pulley

certainly result in the scale inlet and outlet areas being too small. Working the other way round, and using the areas of the air inlets and outlets of the prototype, will equally probably result in a model that will be too large and heavy for good scale flying. An insoluble problem? Not entirely, but it does call for very considered selection of prototypes to be scaled and, possibly, cheating a little. Until more thrust becomes available from ducted fan units, or the full-size jet aircraft designers change their attitudes towards air inlets and outlets, we have a permanent problem to resolve. Some of the earlier jet designs (e.g. Mig 15, He 162) were not too parsimonious with inlet and outlet sizes and the occasional modern jet (e.g. *Mirage*) is just about acceptable without major modification. The vast amount of modern jets, however, use relative minute intake areas and are totally unsuitable for ducted fan purposes unless some action is taken. The size of the inlets, on the model, can be enlarged beyond the scale limits and, in many instances, this will not be too noticeable. Alternatively we can arrange auxiliary air inlets to feed the rotor. These can be in the form of 'air scoops' situated in the underside of the fuselage in front of the fan unit. They need not be visible when the model is static as the scoop can be covered with a light action, spring-loaded door that will automatically open inwards when the engine is running. No such cheating can be incorporated in the outlet duct and we *must* have the required minimum outlet area at the rear end. Either the prototype we have chosen will give us that area or we must increase it by making the model to a larger scale, or enlarging the outlet beyond scale.

Because the fuselage of some prototypes (e.g. N.A. *Sabre*) is in effect a

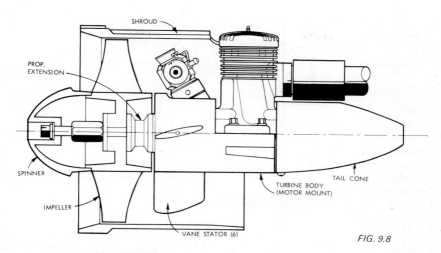

SHROUD

PROP.
EXTENSION

SPINNER

IMPELLER

VANE STATOR (6)

TURBINE BODY
(MOTOR MOUNT)

TAIL CONE

FIG. 9.8

straight through duct, problems are presented with regard to the positioning of the radio equipment. There may be sufficient room in the cockpit area but it is more likely that the radio equipment will have to be fitted in the wings. Even with aircraft using side inlets (D.H. *Vampire*, A4D *Skyhawk* – a 'natural' for ducted fan), where the radio equipment can be fitted in the nose area, we still have the problem of routing the control linkages, including the ailerons. Swept control surfaces do not help our linkage problem either! Despite this rather gloomy prognosis, the problems can be overcome and scale models of jets are feasible using ducted fan units – it just takes rather more care and ingenuity to achieve success.

Construction of ducted fan scale models can, as with propeller driven models, be from traditional materials or with glass fibre and polystyrene techniques. At first glance it would seem that glass fibre moulding is an obvious method to use for the fuselage, with its ability to be moulded to any rounded shapes. In addition to a well finished exterior we need, with a ducted fan unit, a smooth interior of specific contours that may not be identical with the external shape. Where glass fibre is used for the fuselage a separate internal duct should be fabricated and fitted for maximum efficiency. It may well be that polystyrene foam (or similar equivalents), in moulded or cut form, will give the best results for ducted fan fuselages. With this material it is possible to contour the external shape of the fuselage and the internal duct shape separately. The thickness of the body shell should allow for the mounting of the engine, or the unit, and the structure of the fuselage will absorb some of the engine noise. Starting the engine, unless a very short inlet duct is involved, will have to be performed by pulley and cord, or pulley and a belt connected to an electric starter, car fashion. The hatch allowing access for starting must be a good fit to the main duct and have a quick and positive locking arrangement. When a ducted fan engine is screaming away at 20,000

141

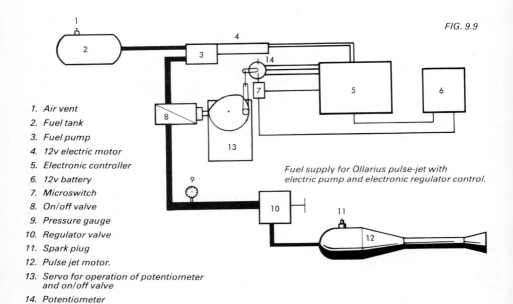

FIG. 9.9

1. Air vent
2. Fuel tank
3. Fuel pump
4. 12v electric motor
5. Electronic controller
6. 12v battery
7. Microswitch
8. On/off valve
9. Pressure gauge
10. Regulator valve
11. Spark plug
12. Pulse jet motor.
13. Servo for operation of potentiometer and on/off valve
14. Potentiometer

Fuel supply for Ollarius pulse-jet with electric pump and electronic regulator control.

R.P.M. plus there seems to be a natural urgency to get the model ready and in the air!

Undercarriages can be another problem area with models of jets – they certainly do not look right flying around at speed with the undercarriage down. Retractable undercarriages can be fitted where the prototype method can be copied, and the wing is thick enough. For smaller ducted fan models a compromise solution is to use a take-off 'dolly' and to belly land the model on grass. Ducted fan powered models have a much lower rate of acceleration than propeller driven designs and this must be borne in mind for take-off areas, or for hand launches. No doubt the number of ducted fan powered scale models will increase over the years – it is the most under-modelled facet of aircraft history.

PULSE JET MOTORS

Commonsense suggests that if we want to build flying model replicas of jet powered aircraft, the obvious propulsion unit to use would be a model jet engine. Indeed, such motors have been available for over twenty-five years. Unfortunately they have one major draw back – NOISE. With the increasing interest, and legislation, in controlling noise pollution the model pulse jet can only be described as anti-social. Whether it will ever be possible to quieten a pulse jet to a normally acceptable level is doubtful and, therefore, they can only have limited appeal. Also on the debit side is the fire hazard, should a model land, with the engine operating, in a cornfield or somewhere similar. The use of pulse jet engines is not banned in all countries, but their use is discouraged.

Early model jet motors were used

exclusively for control line models and because of the nature of their flight pattern, the problems of fuel feed were limited. A model pulse jet motor fitted in an R/C model must be equipped with a very sophisticated and efficient fuel feed system, which under relatively high pressure can continuously regulate the fuel injection. A break through in overcoming these technical problems has been made in recent years and the model pulse jet is a viable proposition – as has been demonstrated by the Ollarius Team flying their very fast jet motor equipped models. Heinz Ollarius has been perfecting this form of propulsion, and the complex pressurised fuel feed system, for over twenty years. The significant improvement came with the development of an efficient fuel supply system having an electrically driven fuel pump and associated electronics. This allowed the fuel pressure to be varied according to the speed and power required from the motor. Various fuels have been tried and the one that gives

good thrust values, with minimum aggressive effect on the supply system, consists of:–

50% Kerosene (Paraffin) 40% Cleaning Benzene and 10% Gasoline (Petrol)

Scale models for pulse jet motors must be built to rigorous specifications because of the high speeds and loadings that can be anticipated with these types of aircraft. Semi-scale models are already achieving speeds in excess of 240 km/hr (150 m.p.h.) and although the speed of a true scale model will be rather less, the implications must be obvious. A pulse jet powered R/C aircraft is extremely exciting – it is also potentially very dangerous and should only be operated by the most competent of pilots under ideal conditions. Whether model pure jet engines become popular will depend on the designers' and manufacturers' ability to produce motors that are acceptable from an environmental point of view. Until then, they are only likely to be seen in most countries as demonstration items.

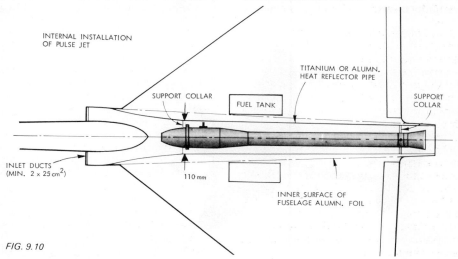

INTERNAL INSTALLATION OF PULSE JET

TITANIUM OR ALUMN. HEAT REFLECTOR PIPE

SUPPORT COLLAR

FUEL TANK

SUPPORT COLLAR

INLET DUCTS (MIN. 2 x 25 cm^2)

110 mm

INNER SURFACE OF FUSELAGE ALUMN. FOIL

FIG. 9.10

Chapter 10

Multi-engined Models

There can be no doubt that one of the most stirring sights in R/C flying is a multi-engined scale model flying past with the sound of the engines in synchronous beat. There is something indefinable that sets the multi-engined model apart; it has an appeal that is not to be found on the single-engined aircraft, no matter how good that model may be. It is all the more surprising, therefore, that more multi-engined designs are not built. With the advent of reliable proportional radio equipment it did appear that the number of twin- and four-engined models would increase rapidly. That this did not happen can probably be attributed to fear on the part of the modeller, fear created by the unknown factors involved (what if one engine stops?) and fear through stories of disasters with multi-engined models. The fact that many of the disasters were caused by the pilot's ignorance of the problems, poor preparation, or plain lack of flying skills, did not seem to be appreciated. It *can* be more difficult to fly a twin-engined model and we *must* have first rate preparation and reliability for a four-engined design, but is that so different from any worthwhile scale model? The chances of one engine stopping suddenly in flight are fairly remote, if the preparation has been good, and even then, the situation would only be

Stand-off scale D. H. Mosquito. Retracting under-carriage would do wonders for in-flight appearance.

Slow-flying but stable Handley Page 'Heyford' by Martin Fardell has won stand-off scale events.

really dangerous at a few critical moments – e.g. turning out after take-off. For the most part, the flying of a multi-engined scale model is no more difficult than flying a single-engined design – just more pleasurable.

The choice of subject is more critical than the selection of a single-engined prototype but there are very many designs that are well suited to scale R/C modelling. Look for the following characteristics in the prototype.

1. Engines close in to the fuselage – to minimise the adverse yaw effects of one engine stopping in flight:

2. Parallel chord, or slightly tapering, wing plan form – the chances of tip stalling are increased during single-engine performance of a twin:

3. Large rudder area – this is more important when there is a single fin and rudder, where the slipstream effect over the rudder is non-existent. Rudder is the primary control used to correct asymmetric engine power:

4. Engines that are fairly well forward on the wing – to ease the balance problems of the model without having to add large amounts of nose weight.

We are not restricted to conventional twin- and four-engined designs. There are push/pull prototypes (Cessna *Skymaster*) where we can fit a larger motor at the front and a smaller one at the rear position. Three-engined prototypes (Junkers 52 and Ford *Trimotor*) can be built, and to lessen the asymmetric power problems the centre engine can be the most powerful and the two outboard engines of smaller capacities. Models of four-engined prototypes can have the inboard engines only working, and the outboard engines merely dummies – in flight this will hardly be noticeable. With a little thought and imagination the range of suitable multi-engined designs can be extended for scale R/C requirements.

It should be obvious that the reliable operation of the engines is of prime importance on a scale multi-engined model. The model may fly well with one engine stopped, or slow, but it will inevitably fly better with all engines performing properly. Not only must the engines run reliably but they must be adjusted so that pick-up is smooth and equal on all engines. When one engine

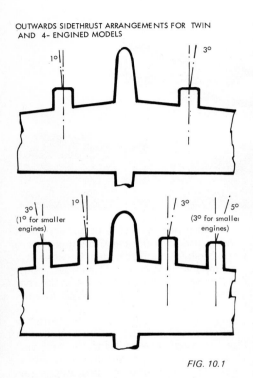

OUTWARDS SIDETHRUST ARRANGEMENTS FOR TWIN AND 4- ENGINED MODELS

FIG. 10.1

shown should be taken as a guide only; you may prefer to ignore the incorporation of sidethrust, for scale reasons, and rely on the reliability of your engines and skill of your piloting. Some full-size designs used engine sidethrusts to allow for better asymmetric flying characteristics, notable examples being the Short *Sunderland* and the Blackburn *Seagrave.* A more acceptable answer to the asymmetric engine problems is to fit one engine, for a twin, with opposite rotation. As previously mentioned many R/C motors can be obtained with modified crankshafts to allow reverse rotation operation. With other R/C engines it may be possible to achieve the same results by simply rotating the front crankshaft housing (including the carburettor) through 90°. Check with your engine instructions first. The engine/s using the opposite rotation should be fitted to the starboard wing so that the torque effect helps to counteract the asymmetric effect. With the opposite rotation engine, acting in the tractor mode, reverse pitch propellers will be required. These should be carefully matched to the standard propellers used on the port engines.

Downthrust may, or may not, be required according to the thrust line of the engines in relation to the wing position and total drag line. For high mounted engines, as frequently found on flying boats, a reasonable degree of *up*thrust will probably be needed to balance the aerodynamic forces acting on the aircraft. Fortunately, the prototypes usually incorporated this very feature. For low wing multi-engined designs a small amount of downthrust should be incorporated (unless the engine thrust lines are above the wing) but most midwing models will be happy with a 0° thrust line setting.

Avoid mounting the engines in a 'side

does quit the effect will depend on the position of that engine. If a starboard engine cuts we have the asymmetric effect of the port engine/s turning the model to the right, but the torque from these engines having some corrective turning effect to the left. With a port engine flame out we have all of the turning effects to the left. To overcome these asymmetric engine problems we can incorporate sidethrust to the engines as shown in Fig 10.1. Precise figures of engine sidethrust cannot be quoted as the amounts will depend on many factors — moment of engine from the fuselage, thrust from the engine, propellers used etc. The sidethrust measurements winder' mode (i.e. with the cylinders horizontal) as this will cause unsympathetic vibrations and the overall vibration levels will be increased. Upright mounting, or, even better, at 45°, will cure the problem to a great extent. Another means of reducing vibration levels is to position the propeller (two-bladed) in the top dead centre attitude and remove approximately a quarter inch from the tip of the propeller on the cylinder side; this will assist in the static balancing of the engine. Three-bladed propellers are frequently used with multi-engined models for scale appearance and propeller clearance reasons. There is no objection to this, providing efficient three-bladed propellers can be found, but there is a disadvantage in asymmetric power flying. The three-bladed propeller creates comparatively more drag than a two-bladed propeller, thus compounding the drag effect of asymmetric flight. On a full-size multi-engined prop-driven aircraft the first action, on failure of an engine, is to feather the propeller blades. There are controllable variable pitch propellers now on the market and the facility to feather the propeller blades (two, three of four) makes them a very attractive proposition for multis.

For the fuel system you can opt to have individual fuel tanks for the engines or a centralised fuel tank with engines using pump pressurised, and metered, fuel supply. The latter method has a number of advantages. The fuel tank can be situated in the fuselage at the most convenient position from a balance point of view and, theoretically, if you make the mistake of running out of fuel both engines will cut at the same time! This will avoid any asymmetric power problems but it is, of course, a cardinal error to run out of fuel and a careful check on flying time should be observed

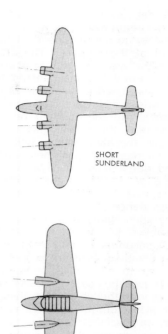

SHORT
SUNDERLAND

BLACKBURN
SEAGRAVE

FIG. 10.2

on all flights. For a single fuel tank installation, using a common fuel feed pick up in the tank, bench testing should first be carried out simulating actual tank and engine positions. Test the one-engine-off situations, it may be necessary to incorporate a non-return valve in the feed to each engine – much will depend on the type of pressurisation being used. Where no fuel pumping and metering system is being used (apart from low pressure from the silencer) the fuel tank must be positioned in the standard manner with the tank as close to the engine as possible and with its

147

horizontal centre line coincidental with the carburettor needle valve.

Whether to use independent throttle control of the engines? The problem here is the lack of thumbs to operate all of the controls on the transmitter! On take-off we need to have full control of the rudder, elevator, ailerons *and* engine/s. With the standard transmitter arrangement this poses difficulties if we have two throttle controls – with a four-engined model the engines would be paired, port and starboard pairs. The full sized pilot has none of these difficulties as he can use his hands *and* feet, or have the assistance of a co-pilot. For a really large multi-engined model it is probably advisable to follow the latter system and use a secondary control box for the engines with an assistant to operate the throttles. Good coordination and understanding will be needed in these circumstances with the 'chief' pilot giving firm and precise commands to his assistant. It may be possible to modify a transmitter to include two throttle controls that can be operated on each side of the case,

but they must come naturally to the hands and be comfortable to operate – not easy! Although there are advantages in having independent operation of the throttles the best compromise is to have the throttle control of all engines from a single transmitter control for take-off and landing, with a switching arrangement to allow decoupling in the air. This will allow you to experiment and practise with asymmetric power during flight, at a safe height, but allow you to concentrate on full coordination of all controls during the critical take-off and landing manoeuvres.

Preparation for flying should be methodical and any uncertainty in engine operation, or radio operation, is an automatic reason for postponement of flight, until the problems are resolved. A good general principle for engine starting, for a twin, is as follows:- Fill up both fuel tanks and check the radio operation, setting the throttles at near idle. Start the starboard engine, open up briefly and then cut the engine by reducing to idle plus full idle trim – the engines

North American B25 Mitchell, a good choice for a scale twin with good proportions and simple shapes.

should be adjusted to cut at this transmitter position. Open the throttle trim and start the port engine, open up to check the top speed range. Reduce engine to idle and restart the starboard engine – it should start easily because it is now warm. If there has been any undue delay in starting the engines the fuel tanks should be topped up. With both engines running get an assistant to hold the model until it is pointing vertically upwards. Open up the engines until they are both running at full speed and keep the model in the vertical position for at least ten seconds; there should be no sign of the engines leaning out. Return the model to the ground and check the 'pick-up' through the full range of throttle movement to ensure that the engines are at comparable speeds throughout the range. Adjust the carburettors if this is not the case. It is always safer to have the needle valve set one notch more open than is considered absolutely necessary – an engine flame out on take-off *is* dangerous – it may also prevent the engine from overheating

during the flight. When you know your multi-engined model really well, and its single-engined performance, you can start to tune to finer limits.

With a multi-engined model fitted with a tricycle undercarriage you can commence tests with fast taxi runs, getting the feel of the model and controls before reaching take-off speed. Keep some extra down trim on the elevator to prevent premature take-off so that you can build up reasonable speeds on the taxi trials. When you are satisfied with the control responses (it also gives you an opportunity to check the engines' operation) you can remove the down elevator trim and proceed to the take-off situation. The model should lift off itself, or with slight up elevator in calm conditions; any excessive degree of elevator control should suggest to you that the trim of the model is incorrect. Check the balance and the incidences; if the model is rather nose heavy it is acceptable to apply a little more up trim for take-off.

With a 'tail dragger' model taxi trials are of less value. By all means taxi the

The Avro Lancaster, a surprisingly popular subject for multi-engined scale, in sizes from about 5 to 24 feet.

One of the 11ft. Dakotas built for the 'Airline' series, a typical 'tail dragger'

model slowly around to get the feel of the controls, and build up your confidence, but don't attempt fast taxi runs. The danger with a fast run is that you will permit the model to leave the ground prematurely and that is the last thing that is required. When you are satisfied that the model is responding well under slow taxi conditions bring the model back, hold the tail end firmly and open the throttles fully to clear the engines. An engine may cut on opening up through excessive running at near idle conditions, and better now than during take-off. Head the model directly into wind, or straight down the runway (but not with too much cross-wind) and open up the throttles gently and progressively. A little down elevator can be given to get the tail up. If the model seems reluctant to do this automatically, this is better than taking off in a 'three point' attitude ('P' effect, extra drag et al). Let the model lift off in its own time, but if it is obviously not going to break ground, introduce a little up elevator. If the model still persists in staying groundborne abort the take off, return the model, retrim, fill up the fuel tanks and try again. The amount of rudder correction required will vary from model to model but it should become progressively less throughout the take-off run. With the model taking off straight into the prevailing wind you should not be needing a 'bootfull' of rudder as you reach take-off

Modern machine with fixed trike undercarriage is the Partenavia 'Victor'. Front wheel is normally spatted, as main ones.

speed. When this *is* the situation, abort and retrim the model before attempting the take-off. With the model safely airborne carry out a *shallow* climb out — there is a temptation to make for the comparative safety of height as quickly as possible but this will put you in a very difficult situation if one engine did fail. Keep the speed up and, at a safe height, commence a turn to starboard — many modellers find starboard turns and circuits more difficult simply because they practise them less; you must be competent in turning with equal facility in either direction before progressing on to multi-engined models. From now on it is a matter of learning the flying characteristics of the model at all throttle settings and at all speeds. Although few multi models come into the aerobatic category it is wise, at a very safe height, to check the aircraft for stalling. It is important to note the behaviour of the model before and during the stall, i.e. does it drop one wing excessively — if it does, try to correct it by retrimming the ailerons. Until you are thoroughly familiar with the model's characteristics here are a few 'don'ts'.

1. Don't let the model slow down too much if one engine cuts, it will reduce the effectiveness of the control surfaces:

2. If you have *any* doubt about the behaviour of the model with one engine out 'chop' the other engine completely and carry out a standard 'dead stick' glide landing:

3. Never turn towards a dead engine. In turning in to a dead engine, and losing speed, you have the ideal conditions for stalling off the turn and going into a spin. On the initial flights you may be 'nursing' the model round in the turns and, consequently, making very wide circles. If the engine quits at a long range it may be difficult to tell immediately which

engine has cut. An observer with powerful binoculars is of great assistance to follow the *whole* of the flight and give you immediate notification of an engine failure. In these circumstances it is still advisable, if you have reasonable height, to 'chop' the other engine and glide back for the landing — at least it should prevent you from turning towards the stopped engine.

4. Don't attempt low, slow flypasts. An engine failure can be embarrassing in these circumstances, as it can be on an overshoot when the engines have been at idle for some time. An occasional 'warming up' of the engines on the landing descent is good practice, but don't give an aggressive burst or it may upset your approach angle.

How much you can experiment with asymmetric power will depend on whether you have fitted independent throttles. With no independent control, begin, after you have had plenty of proving flights, by only half filling the starboard fuel tank. Fly the model at a good safe height, overhead, until the starboard engine cuts. Throttle back *slightly* on the port engine, keep the nose down a little and note how much rudder is needed to correct the turn. If the amount of rudder required is not excessive open up the port engine to full revolutions and note again the amount of rudder trim, and possibly aileron trim, to regain straight and level (or slightly diving) flight. Whether you can maintain straight and level or climbing flight on one engine will depend on the power/weight ratio etc. of the model. When you are satisfied that the model is stable in this configuration try the flying characteristics and attitudes throughout the throttle range of the engine. For the first experimental 'one engine' flight it is safer to carry out a 'dead stick' landing —

you will probably be feeling rather tensed up anyway! Similar experiments can be undertaken with the port engine stopped, but remember that this is the more dangerous asymmetric power condition. When you know and understand the 'single engine' conditions it should be possible to undertake approach and landings on 'one' but keep a few extra knots on the approach for safety and never use the throttle too coarsely.

It will obviously be easier to experiment with asymmetric power flight with independently controlled throttles as it is not necessary, initially, to stop one engine totally. You can be more progressive in checking out the effects knowing that, in an emergency, you can always open up the slow engine. Opening up the idling engine may not, automatically, be the correct remedial action. If you have got the model into a very awkward position, say an incipient spin, forget the fact that you have got two, or more, engines. Close *both* engines and concentrate only on getting the model back into a straight and level, unstalled, condition. Trying to include too many control movements may slow down the recovery action. Experimenting with asymmetric power conditions may seem rather fraught – it is not, but it should be learned methodically *before* it happens accidentally.

Starting twin-engine models can be made easier and more reliable if we have a special model box designed for the purpose. A field box of this type has been developed and includes all the desirable features required for starting twins, plus the facility for a single-engined model. The unit includes the following advantages:

1. The port and starboard plug leads are independently switched:

2. 2.5 volt lens end warning light bulbs glow bright enough to be seen in sunlight conditions:

3. The plug lead can be left connected to the started engine whilst it is at idle during the starting process of the other engine preventing the engine at idle from 'loading up' during this process:

4. Both engines can be left connected to the plug lead until the time for the take-off to be commenced:

5. Alternative 1.5 volt or 2.0 volt selection can be useful where particular engines perform better on a specific make of 1.5 volt plugs:

6. A meter is fitted on the positive line, giving a constant reading when plugs are connected and giving an indication of how many plugs are operating. Being of the centre zero, moving iron type it will also give a reading in the opposite direction when the accumulator is being charged.

A heavy duty accumulator should be used (particularly important if it is also used for the electric starter supply) and heavy duty wire used for the internal wiring.

No experienced scale R/C modellers should miss the 'kick' of flying a multi-engined model: the thrills and sense of power that you experience makes the additional work involved more than doubly rewarding. Ask any scale modeller, with multi experience, and ask him to relate his flying experiences with a two- or four-engined models – it is unlikely to be less than rapturous.

Chapter 11

Large Scale Models

We should start off any discourse on large scale models by defining the term 'Large'. We *should* do this but it is extremely difficult because large is a comparative term and not an absolute. At one time a six foot wingspan radio model was large and then nine or ten foot span became the norm for large models. Now, with models of eighteen foot wingspans and more, what is large? The only criteria we have to define the maximum weights, dimensions, wing loadings and power of a 'model' are the regulations enforced by the country's governing body of aeromodelling and / or the F.A.I. (Federation Aeronautique Internationale). Definitions of models and, therefore, a 'large model' or unmanned light aircraft, will vary considerably, but the limits and controls must be understood and regulations adhered to. We can take these model maxima as a start-

ing point and assume that anything above this figure is classed as a 'Large Model'. Not that large models are anything new, as some of the prewar free flight models were real giants – although not necessarily heavy. Also, the very early radio controlled models were often very big; they had to be to carry the heavy load of spark ignition motors, plus batteries and coils, and the valve operated superregen. radio equipment with its attendant high tension and low tension batteries. It is, however, with the introduction of belt driven engine reduction units and the re-introduction of large spark ignition engines that the true birth of the large scale model has taken place. With the increased power available from the larger engines the 'Big is Beautiful' movement has really taken off. That there is a worldwide interest in the larger models cannot be doubted and

One-third (at least!) scale model of a Pitts S2 with fully enclosed cockpit and modified fuselage.

the sight of quarter, one third and even half scale models is becoming a common one at the flying fields.

In some ways it is ironic that with the advent of sub-miniature radio control equipment, there should now be a swing to far from miniature airframes. Interest in the 'super' model is, however, fact and we should consider the reasons for the interest, the construction of the models, whether they are safe to fly and what are the legal implicatons.

We have stated before the need for a model to fly at a scale speed if it is going to look convincing. The model, to look right, must give the illusion of the full-size aircraft in flight, in all aspects. There is no doubt that this is easier to achieve with a large model as the lighter wing loadings allow slower flight *and* the scale factor is in our favour. It is not only the scale flight speeds that give the illusion of full-size flight, there is an ambience with the larger creations that comes from the sheer size of them and the wider sweep of the manoeuvres. They are not affected by gusts of wind to the same degree as a small model, as they cut imperiously through the air. Fast, close fly-bys are not necessary with a large model for impressive flying; the size of the model, in relation to its surroundings, makes a normal flypast, at safe height and speed, exciting enough. It is not easy to express in words the majesty of the large model, but it certainly exists. Nor is the visual aspect the only consideration, sound is another factor. This has been proved to the author with experiences of flying radio control scale models for film and television projects. With the sound of a two-stroke model glow engine accompanying the visual image the impression is of a model. Dub on the sound of the prototype engine and the illusion of reality on the screen is increased by at least 50%. Incidentally, where smaller R/C scale models are used, the camera is overcranked so that the speed of the model on the screen is slower than reality – all helping to add to the realism. The large petrol engines have a more authentic sound amplitude and pitch for scale work compared with the higher revving glow motors. Flying large models is more akin to flying a full-size aircraft and, as a result, the throttle control is used regularly – another factor aiding scale fidelity, particularly if the engine is 'blipped' on the approach as was the case with early full-size aircraft. A further bonus of the petrol engine is the lack of excessive oily smoke from the exhaust so noticeable with glow engines. Full-size aircraft can emit a certain amount of exhaust products but not to the extent of the unburnt castor oil products of the average two-stroke glow motor.

Among the most satisfying of all R/C flying manoeuvres are the take-off and landing. Equally, nothing is more frustrating than performing a beautiful touchdown only to have the model tip up on to its nose at the end of the landing run. The larger the model, the less the risk of this happening, as the scale effect of the landing surface is reduced and the more precisely, and slowly, the model can be positioned. Delightful, truly stalled, three-point landings can regularly be attained whereas, with smaller models, the ratio of success to failure is very much reduced. Control during the taxi out to take-off can be performed in a more scale-like manner, including the weaving along the taxi strip, so common with many prototypes for reasons of limited forward visibility. Smooth take-offs and slow climbouts are all easier to perform with larger models, as are side-slipping approaches and 'fish-

13ft. span, 44cc. Tartan Twin powered 'Eindekker' by the late Keith Hearne, Australia, flown by Geoff Tuck.

tailing' prior to landing. The control responses *are* slower and the manoeuvres have to be positively planned but the size and speed of the model make this possible. For demonstration purposes the large model is certainly more impressive to the modelling and general public alike; it is much easier to see, and appreciate, than fast small models.

So much for the credit side but what of the disadvantages? The first, and by far the most important consideration, is that of SAFETY. There is no argument that a ten kilo model flying at 120 k.p.h. is potentially more dangerous than a model weighing four kilos and flying at a speed of 80 k.p.h. But that is not the 'be all and end all' of safety, as many large models will have less kinetic energy than, say, a fast flying, overweight medium scale R/C model of a N.A. *Mustang*. Not only would the *Mustang* be potentially more dangerous, it is likely to be *actually* more dangerous because of the poor flying characteristics caused by the high wing loading. Nevertheless, the larger models must be given more consideration during all of the stages of design, construction and flying. Despite the fact

that, overall, they are easier to fly than small R/C models they are *different* to fly and the techniques must be learned — and learned safely. Distance perception may be an initial problem with a larger than normal model, and it is easy to overfly the landing area during the landing approach. Because of the size of the model, and initial hesitancy in giving too much control, the model may be flown at a greater distance away from the operator. This, in radio equipment range terms, is particularly critical on long low approaches where the radio signal is at its weakest. Radio control equipment manufacturers have been quick to respond to the requirements of the 'super scale' enthusiast and have produced heavier duty servos and accessories, but the transmitters have the same signal strength output. Range checks should be frequently undertaken when flying large models and maintenance and tuning considered of the utmost importance. Transport too can present problems for the large scale model enthusiast. A ten foot wing span model of a *Hurricane* into a Mini just does not go — especially when there is a family to consider — and you

SCALE MODEL AIRCRAFT

One-third scale 'Jungmeister' by Peter Griggs uses a Tartan Twin engine.

will have to devise other methods of transporting your monster (the 'plane, not the wife!). Trailers and roof racks are ways of overcoming the transportation problems, or simply get a second mortgage on the house and buy a larger car or van. New constructional methods will have to be explored as structural integrity must be of a high order to maintain safety.

At the top of the debit column must come the fear, and the consequences, of a large model crashing into a group of people, modellers or the general public. It may be that the larger model will do no more damage or harm than a smaller model – it will almost certainly make larger headlines in the news media. It can be likened to the results of a crash of a full-size aircraft – always guaranteed to

Large prototypes make large models. Propellers and motors on this vast 747 are unnoticeable in flight.

make front page news – the fact that many hundreds of people are 'slaughtered' on the roads every week seems of little relevance as they no longer make national news. One can almost read the headlines now, "Giant radio controlled aircraft scythes through crowd at public demonstration"; it is a possibility we have to live with and may one day become fact. The resulting publicity will undoubtedly be bad for our hobby but it is impossible to control the news media. We can only remain philosophical about the dangers of radio control flying *and* take every possible precaution against *any* accident happening. If we want to eliminate all risks in radio control model flying, regardless of the size and type of model, then we must cease flying entirely. All sports and hobbies have risks: fishermen have drowned or lost the sight of an eye from the hook, golfers have been killed by being struck by a golf ball, or lightning, and potholing, mountain climbing, motor racing, swimming and sailing, all have obvious dangers. Where we must be particularly vigilant is in relation to the general public during demonstrations. To involve yourself, and colleagues of a like mind is one thing, but to put third parties at unnecessary risk is totally different. They are not fully aware of the potential dangers of the radio controlled models – large or small!

DESIGN AND CONSTRUCTION

It is hoped that any trend towards bigger models will be in the field of scale and semi-scale aircraft. The thought of enlarged, fast aerobatic models carving through the air does not inspire me and they can hardly be considered as suitable club type models. Designing R/C models becomes more critical, structurally, with an increase in size and/or

speed of a model. It is very rare that you see a small R/C model break up in the air – even when flying fast – but many of us have probably seen larger models 'clapping' wings following a sharp pull-out from a dive. This occurrence often results from an overweight and repaired model. No-one is going to pretend that even large models are scientifically designed, for the tremendous variations of balsa strength would make this difficult. Empirical design can only be based on experience and the design of very large models should, therefore, be undertaken gradually. It is not simply a case of doubling up the sizes of materials of a 60-inch wing span model to make it into a well designed 120-inch span model. A ¼ in. wing rib on a smaller model would not need to be increased to ½ in. on its larger brother, and $^3/_{32}$ in. balsa wing sheeting does not have to be substituted with $^3/_{16}$ in. thick balsa. There is a danger of oversizing on non-structural areas *but* it must also be remembered that doubling the wing span results in an *area* four times greater. Overall weight is still our enemy and the heavier the model the faster it must fly to achieve sufficient lift for controlled flight – all other factors being equal.

FUSELAGE

Fuselages are not prone to failure in flight, although occasionally on a hard landing. It is important to concentrate the strength on highly stressed areas, i.e. engine bulkhead, wing position, undercarriage and fittings. An open structure, covered with nylon, well cross-braced can give an entirely adequate fuselage. The strength of this type of structure also includes a flexibility that allows it to 'give' on a hard landing. A fully sheeted fuselage may tend to split open in a similar situation. Formers may be built up from strip balsa or a sandwich of thin ply/balsa/thin ply with lightening holes cut in them. Local reinforcement can be achieved by using plywood webs and hardwoods such as spruce and beech. Caution must be observed when using hardwoods: a 5-inch crossmember of $^3/_8$ in. sq. beech in a small model is quite acceptable, but a 10-inch length of $^3/_4$ in. sq. beech is too much of a weight penalty. The engine bulkhead must be substantial, at least $^3/_8$ in. thick ply for one of the large petrol engines, and it must be well fixed to the fuselage sides with gussets or fillets. With a fabric covered full-size aircraft the covering is not considered to add to the overall strength of the structure. With a model it is a rather different proposition and the covering can add to both the structural strength and to its surface 'toughness'. For these reasons the use of nylon covering or fabric materials is virtually a must if you want the model to survive for any length of time. Plastic films are satisfactory for small models but are out of place on the 'big birds'.

WINGS

I suppose the ideal wing rib for a model with a large chord (in excess of 20 inches) is one that is built up from strip in a similar manner to full-size practice for light and ultra-light aircraft. Method of making built up ribs is shown in Fig. 11.1. The only function of the ribs is to keep the spars in position and to provide the aerofoil shape for affixing the covering sheet or material. However, it is something of a chore to construct each rib separately and sheet balsa is an easier material to work with and light enough for our purposes. With thick section wings (e.g. scale *Hurricane* or Fokker D7) lightening holes can be cut in the ribs. Scale models of modern aircraft featuring metal covered, or fully ply covered, wings will be best simulated by fully skinning the airframe with balsa sheet. Keep the rib spacing close enough to prevent sagging of the sheeting when the final covering is applied. Foam cores covered with obeche veneer or Mirralite ply are obvious alternatives, but large wings will probably require the addition of spars to increase the strength, and lightening holes cut in the foam to reduce weight – particularly towards the tips. For models of the Piper *Cub* type the formation of a 'D' box leading edge (leading edge, leading sheet top and bottom and full depth main spar) will add considerably to the rigidity of the wing. Similarly, a triangulated trailing edge with sheet top and bottom and vertical webbing will help to give longitudinal rigidity of the trailing edge. Models resembling earlier types of aircraft will lose authenticity if this technique is used and the lack of sheeting must be compensated for by having main spars of adequate strength and positioned relatively closer to the leading and trailing edges. There would be some advantage in installing cross-bracing wires, and compression struts between the spars, to improve the torsional strength of the wings. Such members are certainly an essential part of the strength of many full-size open structure wings. The larger scale the model becomes the more essential it is to follow full-size practice. We may not have the facilities to form 'I' section spars by spindle moulding away the centres from a solid piece of spruce, but at least we should apply vertical webbing between the top and bottom spars to achieve a similar result.

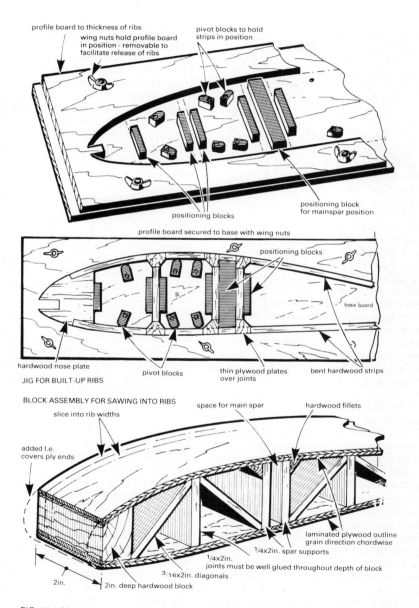

profile board to thickness of ribs

wing nuts hold profile board in position - removable to facilitate release of ribs

pivot blocks to hold strips in position

positioning blocks

positioning block for mainspar position

profile board secured to base with wing nuts

positioning blocks

base board

hardwood nose plate

JIG FOR BUILT-UP RIBS

pivot blocks

thin plywood plates over joints

bent hardwood strips

BLOCK ASSEMBLY FOR SAWING INTO RIBS

slice into rib widths

space for main spar

hardwood fillets

added l.e. covers ply ends

laminated plywood outline grain direction chordwise

$1/4$x2in. spar supports

$1/4$x2in. joints must be well glued throughout depth of block

$3/16$x2in. diagonals

2in.

2in. deep hardwood block

FIG. 11.1 Methods of producing large wing ribs.

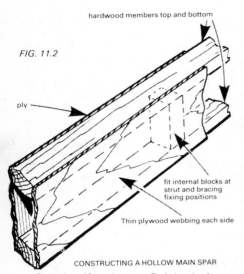

FIG. 11.2

hardwood members top and bottom

ply

fit internal blocks at strut and bracing fixing positions

Thin plywood webbing each side

CONSTRUCTING A HOLLOW MAIN SPAR

So what if we have a finished wing and are unsure of the completed strength? We can always resort to the time-honoured method of static testing the wing by loading it with weights. With a braced or strutted wing the model must be assembled first, but with a one-piece wing it can be tested separately. The wing must be supported at the wing tips (the last rib) and the top surface of the wing loaded evenly over the span plus an allowance for the remainder of the model if this is not fitted. Polythene bags of sand can be used as weights. How much to load the wings? Unless you are the type who would prefer to load it to breaking point for scientific research, I would suggest the following. For slow flying, high drag, non-aerobatic models a 2–3g loading (i.e. two or three times the total weight of the model) should be adequate. With an aerobatic model there is obviously a greater risk of pulling higher 'G' loads on to the model and an increased safety factor should be applied

– full size aerobatic aircraft such as the Pitts *Special* are stressed to 9g! Our finished model may weigh as much as 20 lbs which means that an aerobatically stressed load could be as high as a hundredweight – makes you stop and think, doesn't it!! Biplane wings should be individually loaded in proportion to the percentage of lift they are providing. This will vary with the areas of the wings, the incidence and the gap between the wings.

WING FIXINGS

With modern types of aircraft (fighters, low-wing light aircraft, etc.) it is advisable to have a one-piece wing fixed in the conventional way with dowels and/or bolts into anchor nuts. Nylon bolts are satisfactory as they have ample tensile strength and are only likely to fail in shear, i.e. in a crash, which can be an advantage. Most important is the installation of the fixing points on the fuselage and the spreading of the load around the bolts and dowels in the wing. Plywood plates and gussets plus good workmanship will take care of this. For wings with struts (Piper *Cubs,* Cessnas, etc.) the anchor points must be secure and the load spread to a substantial point of the airframe. The same applies to the rigging points for wire-braced monoplanes and biplanes. Tube and dowel, or rod, may be used for locating braced wings to the fuselage and centre section.

TAIL SURFACES

As usual, there is no point in building strong and heavy tail surfaces if these have to be compensated for by adding a few pounds of lead to the nose of the model to obtain the correct balance point. The tail end of most models has to be kept relatively light so we must be care-

This Fokker Triplane is 'only' quarter scale but stands hip high. By Ian Whiting.

ful in our selection of materials and efficient in their use. Braced tail surfaces make the modeller's life a little easier by allowing the bracing to strengthen an otherwise 'flimsy' structure. Simple cantilevered tailplanes should be permanently fixed to the fuselage if transportation of the model will allow this – if not, the fixing to the fuselage must be very positive.

UNDERCARRIAGES

It is preferable to incorporate some form of springing in the undercarriage assemblies of large models. Whether this is in the form of compression springs in oleo type legs or 'bungee' springing to axles is immaterial. With a scale model try to simulate the original method and geometry as near as possible. One advantage with a large model is the tendency to be able to land it more gently than the smaller versions. There seems to be more time to line up for a good approach and to flare out for the landing. Retractable undercarriages for large models are an engineering problem and should be left to engineers.

CONTROL LINKAGES

With greater control surface areas, weights and aerodynamic loads the servos are going to be working harder than normal. It is, therefore, even more important that the linkages should be operating as efficiently as possible with minimum friction. More thought should be given to aerodynamic and mass balancing of the control surfaces – the heavier and faster the model the more important are these considerations.

Closed loop control systems are ideal for the large models. Their positive action, with one side always pulling, help to prevent 'blow back' of control surfaces. If you have to use push-rods make sure they are rigid *and* light. Glass fibre tube, of the fishing rod type, is O.K., but beware of carbon fibre reinforced material as this may adversely affect radio signal reception. Any push-rod should be adequately supported over its full length to prevent bowing when a compression load is applied.

Standard adjustable clevises are suitable for most large models, although you may wish to consider alternatives

161

for fast, heavy models. The limiting factor would appear to be the output of the servo (say 6lbs thrust) and it is unlikely that standard clevises and horns will fail under these conditions. It *is* important to ensure that the clevises are a free – but not sloppy – fit in the horns; a twisting action on the clevis pin is not good. Do not use torque rod actuation of ailerons unless the rods are in the form of substantial diameter alloy tubes. Conventional push-rods and aileron cranks will give a better control system, but it may be necessary to build up the push-rods rather than using simple piano wire connections. Where piano wire *is* used it must be supported at each rib station with a nylon or ply guide. Nylon tube and rod, or cable, will allow a certain degree of 'lost' movement over a large arc and hence slack movement around the neutral position of the aileron. Preference would again be for a closed loop system with the cables routed in nylon tubes.

RADIO INSTALLATION

There is, of course, ample room to instal the radio gear in large models but, ironically, this does not automatically make the installation easier. The radio equipment may be positioned deep in the bowels of the fuselage with insufficient space to get your hands in to work on it. Keep the radio as far away as possible from petrol engines to minimise the risk of interference and plan the routes of linkages to be direct to the control horns. Fitting the elevator and rudder servos at the rear end, with extension leads, will simplify the routing of the linkages. (Avoid following the run of the extension leads with the receiver aerial.) Mounting the receiver, battery, switch and servos on a ply board assists the fitting and

removability of the basic radio equipment. Although standard servos can be used in quite large models I prefer to fit the more powerful servos for their extra power and heavier duty gear trains. One item where a little extra weight *is* justified is in the fitting of a more powerful nicad battery. A 1000 mAH battery will give safer reserve for the extra load taken by the servos.

The C.A.A. requirements for 'oversize' models include the fitting of a fail-safe device. It is possible to obtain fail-safe devices (*World Engines, Reftac*) that fit between the servo and the receiver and operate on a delay principle. If no signal is received for a set period – say one to two seconds – the servo automatically goes into failsafe. The most important operation is to stop the engine and this can be achieved with a petrol engine by shorting out the ignition via a micro-switch fitted to the throttle servo. A glow engine must have the throttle set to ensure an engine cut with the trans-mitter throttle and trim fully closed. There are doubts about the value of any other control surface 'failsafe' setting, such as up elevator, as this could aggra-vate some situations rather than improve them. Naturally, if the signal is regained the model can be landed in the normal way. It is feasible to fit a safety parachute to a sports model, but this is hardly practical in the case of most scale models.

ENGINE

Large petrol engines (Quadra, Evra) are delightful to operate – no starting batteries, clean, etc., but they do give one disadvantage – vibration. Vibration is a killer as far as radio equipment is concerned, hence another reason for keeping the radio well away from the

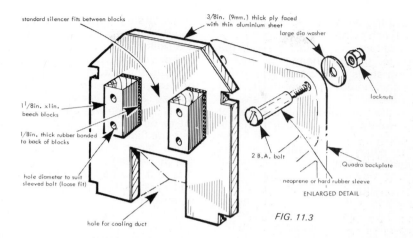

standard silencer fits between blocks

3/8in. (9mm.) thick ply faced with thin aluminium sheet

large dia washer

locknuts

1^1/8in. x1in. beech blocks

1/8in. thick rubber bonded to back of blocks

hole diameter to suit sleeved bolt (loose fit)

hole for cooling duct

2 B.A. bolt

neoprene or hard rubber sleeve

ENLARGED DETAIL

Quadra backplate

FIG. 11.3

engine and for mounting it with a maximum of insulation. The first essential in reducing the problem is to keep the inherent vibration as low as possible. Assuming we do not have the facilities, or knowledge, to rework the engine, the main item to check is the propeller. All propellers should be balanced and also checked for correct tracking when fitted to the engine. The latter can be simply done by propping up the fuselage until the propeller is vertical and placing a wooden block immediately adjacent to the tip of the bottom blade of the propeller. Hold the block in position and rotate the propeller through 180° and the other propeller blade should now be in the same relative position as the first. Multiple bolt propeller fixings are the best as they allow simple adjustment of tracking, but propellers with a single fixing nut can be shimmed out to obtain the same effect. Try different propeller settings, relative to top dead centre, to see if there is any improvement in vibration

levels. Remember, too, that any spinners fitted should also be carefully balanced and fitted.

In mounting the engine, the object is to prevent the vibration from being trans-

Thulin 1917 fighter from Sweden has an 18cc. Damo engine and nice detail.

mitted to the airframe. How successful we are in achieving this will depend on a number of factors. It is possible to fit the engine to the bulkhead via rubber mounting studs – threaded metal studs at each end and moulded to a central block of hard rubber. This method certainly reduces the transmitted vibration but it also allows the engine to rock from side to side quite substantially at the lower speeds – where the vibration level is at its highest. The amount of movement of the engine may well be unacceptable in a cowled-in engine of a scale model. A compromise is to mount the engine on beech blocks which are isolated from the bulkhead by hard rubber strips – the fixing bolts should also be housed in rubber or neoprene tube to reduce the transmitted vibration.

FLYING

Test flying a large model is little different from the first flights on any scale R/C model. Being a larger model it may be psychologically more intimidating and may build up the pressure on the nervous sytem. Rather than getting into

a total 'state' about the maiden flight it would be sensible to obtain the services of a skilled and trusted colleague to do the honours for you. There is no disgrace in taking this action – whoever heard of the designer or builder of a commercial full-size aircraft carrying out the test flights? In some ways it is an advantage not to be flying the model as you can view the flight more objectively. You will notice flight characteristics, and trim change needed, that you may well have missed if you had been totally committed to just getting the aeroplanes safely up and down. Time enough to fly the model when the tension of the first trimming flights has passed and the adrenalin has reverted to a normal level.

Treat the test flights as a method of *gradually* finding out about the model. Progressively increase the rates of turn and diving and don't be in a hurry to go into even mild aerobatics. This is probably the area of greatest difference with flying large models; with a standard sports or aerobatic model we know pretty well what the model is capable of before we take off. Test flying the big

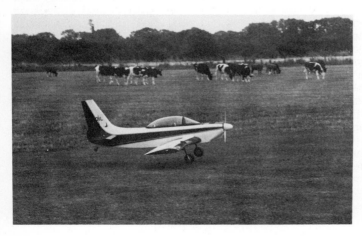

Flying with cows in the field may not be a good idea, though ex-world Champion Mick Charles' one-third Sirocco is safe enough.

ones concerns the gradual evaluation of its flight capabilities and limitations. Only when the full flight characteristics are understood should we begin to fly the model near its limits – but always with a good safety margin. In the interests of safety, and quiet concentration, pick a time for test flights when your local flying area will be relatively deserted – early morning is an excellent time as modellers are noticeably absent during that period! Check and double check the equipment, and the radio range, and off you go. You will be pleasantly surprised how easy, and infinitely exciting it is. Just watch the turns into finals, don't take it too far out, or too low down, and be careful you don't make too wide a final turn – there is a tendency, initially, to underrate the radius of the final turn.

LEGAL REQUIREMENTS

What are the rules and regulations governing large models, who makes them and how do they affect us? First it should be understood that ignorance is no defence in law and even though we may not agree with the regulations, we must abide by them, or pay the penalty. In common with definitions of model aircraft there will be a wide divergence in the regulations and restrictions governing the flying of large radio controlled scale model aircraft – some countries will have quite strict and limiting regulations, others may have few controls, apart from those relating to full-size air-

craft. When you consider that full-size aircraft may be flying down to height of only 160 metres above ground level – lower in some conditions – the need for some model flying discipline is quite obvious. From the full-size pilot's point the model, even a large one, is only noticed at a relatively short distance, and with closing speeds measured in 100s of k.p.h., the time for taking evasive action is short. Where no specific legislation applies it becomes the responsibility of the *modeller* to fly at a sensible height and distance and to keep a continuous look-out for any full-size aircraft in the vicinity.

Correct insurance cover is another essential when flying any form of R/C model aircraft – even more important when flying one of the larger scale models. Check that your insurance does cover the size and type of model you are proposing to fly. Make sure that you comply with all of the legal and insurance regulations in good time for that first flight – thinking about it the day before flying will only cause delays.

Finally, a reiteration that no form of legislation can make a radio control model safe to fly; ultimately it depends on how you fly your model and how well it is maintained. We have all seen examples of stupidly dangerous flying, and possibly been guilty ourselves, but how often have we been prepared to take action against it? Safety, regardless of the size of model, begins at the grassroot level.

Chapter 12

Sailplanes

On most occasions when we are flying a scale model the thought of being without engine power is rather off-putting. Not so with sailplanes, as these are efficiently designed to make the most of thermals (rising currents of warm air) and/or standing waves (areas of lift radiating from the slope of hill, when the wind is blowing on to the slope). The idea of silent flight appeals to many modellers in the same way that sailing dinghies or yachts appeal more than powerboats to some of the boating fraternity. It offers a different form of scale flying and one that can be followed to the exclusion of other types or in addition to it. Scale model sailplanes are not new, since there were many fine examples of free flight designs, but it is only since the early 1970's that there has been any considerable growth of interest in this branch of the hobby. The reason for this can again be traced back to the introduction of reliable proportional radio control equipment. A scale R/C sailplane, to fly efficiently, should have rudder, elevator and aileron control and coordination of the controls must be precise and delicate. The older reed outfits (non-proportional) and single channel, rudder-only radio control systems did not meet the control requirements. Because of the extremely aerodynamically clean configuration of scale sailplanes the use of air brakes, for

precision landings, is almost mandatory. The renaissance of scale model sailplanes, now fitted with reliable and accurate radio equipment, has resulted in the organisation of a large number of competitions and a considerable increase in the number of non-competitive flyers.

So why do enthusiasts build scale model sailplanes in preference to powered scale designs? Here are some of the reasons:-

1. Cost – no engine to purchase, or fuel systems, fuel, starter batteries, electric starters, etc. Although, in fairness, it is possible to spend upwards of £200 for a de luxe sailplane kit, if one so desires:

2. Cleanliness – a lack of fuel, exhaust residue and the other contaminations of power flying:

3. Quietness – the complete absence of noise, except for the slight 'whistle' as the model passes you on a fast run. There is a lot to be said for silence in these days of seemingly ever-increasing noise levels:

4. Beauty of flying sites – certainly true for slope soarers where the flying site is often on top of a hill with superb views all around. This can be used to great advantage by the family man where the wife and children can often be enticed out to a beauty spot where there 'just happens' to be a slope soaring site. Of course, the weather is not always perfect, either for flying or picnicking,

One-fifth model of the 19m. span 'Reiher 2', considered the ultimate in 1937, by Klaus Nietzer. Weight 4¹/₂lbs.

but we have to learn to take the rough with the smooth!

5. Aesthetic appeal of scale sailplanes – it cannot be denied that many of the full-size have tremendous grace and beauty in the lines of the aircraft and their appearance in the air. Beauty, it is said, is in the eye of the beholder, but few would deny that this quality is more evident in scale sailplanes than virtually any other type of scale model.

Much that is written in this book will apply equally to sailplanes and power model designs. Considerations of aerodynamics are the same for sailplanes except we shall be using the force of gravity rather than engine thrust. Constructional methods can be traditional, although there is a much greater use of glass fibre fuselages with scale R/C sailplanes. The subtle curves and slender shapes of the sailplane fuselage lend themselves ideally to GRP construction, for the models and the full-size aircraft. Glass fibre cloth and resin covering to wing surfaces are increasingly being used, the rigidity and ultra smooth surface making for improved efficiency – the most important single factor of a sailplane. We can get away to some extent with a loss of lift on a powered model, but to achieve good results the sailplane must maintain an efficient section throughout the wingspan and have a high standard of finish. Finishing techniques will obviously vary according to the method used on the prototype, but modern full-size sailplanes leave nothing to be desired in that respect. Only the earlier designs feature 'open' wing construction with fabric covering, although

these can be equally beautiful in their own way.

Scale R/C sailplanes have comparatively larger wingspans than their powered brothers. The reasons for this are not difficult to assess. Without the complications of engine, fuel supply and undercarriages the weight saved can be incorporated into a larger structure. Nearly all high efficiency sailplane prototypes use high aspect ratio wings which work very well on the full-size aircraft but can be less effective on models. The narrow chord, when scaled down for R/C model purposes, becomes so small that the efficiency (Reynolds Number effect) drops away seriously. To overcome this disadvantage the scale of the models should not be less than ¹/₅ th, and ¼ and ¹/₃ rd scale sailplanes are not uncommon these days, with wingspans of 20 feet and more. This may sound like an alarming size of model aircraft but the *apparent* size of the sailplane is less than a powered model of the same span. With a shorter fuselage, in comparison to the wing span, and high aspect wings with relatively small areas, the visual effect of the sailplane is to be smaller than it actually is. Smaller scale sailplanes will fly reasonably in stronger winds – for slope soaring – but their flying speed is too fast for scale.

The majority of scale R/C sailplanes are of the slope soaring variety but there are also many models flown from flat areas (thermal soaring). Not everyone is within easy reach of a suitable slope and there is then no alternative but to find some other method of getting the sailplane airborne. These alternative methods can include hand towing, pulley system launches, bungee launches, power winches, aerial towing, piggyback launch (from a powered model) or power-assisted flight. The last two methods would probably be frowned upon by the purist as they have no basis in full-size flying – unless the power-assisted sailplane is of a scale prototype such as the Moto Falke or Fournier F4. Hand towing and power winch methods

are well proven, and adequate, but aerial towing can be exciting and worthy of experiment.

AERIAL TOWING

Glider towing by 'tug' aircraft is an accepted method for full-size aircraft and is used increasingly, compared with powered winch tows. It is true though that aerial towing with full-size aircraft has certain advantages over radio controlled models. The sailplane pilot can position himself exactly where he wants to be relative to the tug aircraft. This is more difficult to achieve with a model as there is always one 'dimension' that is difficult to assess, depending on the position of the models relative to the transmitter operators. The full-size sailplane pilot will keep slightly lower than the tug aircraft to allow the tug pilot to adjust for the most efficient rate of climb. To fly the sailplane above the tug, full-size or model, can be dangerous as it will tend to lift the tail end of the tug and force it into a dive – an unhappy situation near the ground.

Scale R/C sailplanes, of modern prototypes, will be fitted with air brakes and these can be useful to prevent the towline from becoming slack by reducing

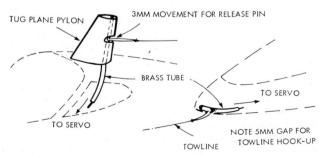

TUG PLANE PYLON

3MM MOVEMENT FOR RELEASE PIN

BRASS TUBE

TO SERVO

TO SERVO

NOTE 5MM GAP FOR TOWLINE HOOK-UP

TOWLINE

FIG. 12.1

the speed of the sailplane with the judicious use of the brakes. Aerial towing is great fun but does require good coordination between the tug and sailplane pilots and a little practice. It is suggested that the first experiments are carried out with a sports sailplane R/C model rather than risk your highly prized scale model. Towing aircraft and sailplane release mechanisms are shown in Fig. 12.1. The ideal attachment point for the tug model is undoubtedly as near to the C of G position as possible. With the towline attachment at, or near, the C of G the position of the sailplane relative to the tug is not critical, but you must ensure that the towline will not foul the tug's tail surfaces if the sailplane gets seriously out of position. Some model tug aircraft feature a pylon fitted above the fuselage, with the release mechanism on top of the pylon, to keep the towline well clear of the tailplane. The requirements and techniques of aerial towing can be summarised as follows:-

1. Compatibility of models. It is difficult to be dictatorial with regard to the suitability of models and some experiment will be necessary. The tug aircraft should have ample power and have a good speed range, i.e. differential between stalling speed and maximum speed. A fairly large model (not less than 72 inch wingspan) possessing reasonable 'hands off' stability is called for in the design of the sailplane. Air brakes with progressive movement, not simply in or out, are an advantage. Colours and decoration of the models are unimportant, as at the higher altitudes they will only appear as dark silhouettes.

2. Compatibility of radio control equipment of the two aircraft. Ground test the radio control outfits together carefully before committing to flight. Remember that the two pilots will be standing close together during the towing flight.

3. Check the operation of the release mechanisms thoroughly, both with and without tension applied to the towline.

4. A towline length of 100–150 feet will be satisfactory for most combinations. Tie a brightly coloured piece of nylon cloth to the sailplane end of the tow rope so that it is easily visible in the event of an emergency release. 'Non-stretch' twine or cord is preferable to monofilament fishing line for the tow rope.

5. Make sure that the models are correctly trimmed before attempting an aerial tow. A take-off with the tug aircraft and hand release with the sailplane is possible although, if you have a hard paved take-off area, the sailplane can also be allowed to rise off ground. The sailplane will be airborne first and should not be allowed to climb excessively. As soon as the aircraft are at a safe height the sailplane pilot should move up to the tug pilot so that normal conversation is possible.

6. Do not over-control with either model; if you do get into a position where a gross amount of control is essential for recovery it is probably better to release the sailplane and have a relaunch. Have a working understanding between the pilots, of control instructions and emergency procedures *before* you start flying. The tug pilot will, in normal circumstances, be the command pilot, but the sailplane will always retain the option of performing an emergency release.

7. Fly steady left or right hand circuits and if the sailplane is sufficiently stable, leave it to fly itself. You are more likely to get into difficult positions through excessive control action than through leaving it alone. Try to avoid a slack towline but be prepared for the 'snatch' when a slack towline becomes taut again.

8. The glider is normally released first, warning the tug pilot beforehand, but in an emergency situation either plane can release – quick reactions may be necessary. It is not recommended that the tug aircraft is landed with the towline attached in case the line snags on some obstruction during the landing approach.

'PIGGY BACK' LAUNCHING

Although it is not a scale method of launching (the only composite arrangements featured two powered aircraft) it is an efficient and simple way to get a sailplane to height. For the carrier model you require a large, stable, preferably high wing design with good load-carrying characteristics. A model of about 80–90 inches wingspan of the typical cabin sports high wing design is ideal, powered by a high performance 0.60 cu.in. capacity engine, or larger. The sailplane is mounted with its balance point over the balance point of the carrier aircraft. Stabilising assemblies will be needed to support the wings of the sailplane and, possibly, the rear of the fuselage. These need only take the form of bent wire cages that are banded to the wings and fuselage of the carrier model. Release of the sailplane is actuated from the 'mother' aircraft using a separate servo and auxiliary transmitter function. It is not difficult to devise a simple release mechanism, although the commercially available sailplane tow hook releases can be modified to suit our needs. Mount the sailplane with its wing incidence to coincide with that of the carrier model. Flying the carrier aircraft with the sailplane is not at all difficult but

you may find the rudder control less effective and the throw of the rudder should be increased. Do remember to switch on the radio of the sailplane on before you take off and do check the compatibility of the radios! All of the controlling of the combination is normally done from the carrier model but it is possible to give a 'tweak' of rudder on the glider to increase a rate of turn – this action should only be taken if the rear end of the sailplane is securely supported. During the run-up to the release the carrier model should be throttled back, the pilot of the sailplane warned, and the model released. It is not necessary for the carrier model to be dived, or the sailplane given up elevator, which would only put more stress on the release mechanism. The more efficient lifting properties of the sailplane will ensure a clean lift-off from the carrier model.

Despite the fact that the thermal soaring scale R/C sailplane is less popular than slope soaring versions, long and satisfying flights can be made in the right weather conditions. To 'hook' on to a thermal with a scale R/C sailplane is very exciting and the skill required in keeping in the invisible rising bubble of air is not to be underestimated. The tell-tale slight rocking of the wings that indicates the presence of the thermal, and the tight turn to keep the sailplane within the confines of the thermal, plus the consequent increasing of height of the model, are all very rewarding features of thermal soaring. It is true scale flying, only we do not, as yet, have the vertical speed indicators – or physical evidence – of the presence of thermals as do full-size pilots. No doubt the number of scale competitions for scale R/C thermal soaring events will increase as it has done in slope soaring.

SLOPE SOARING SCALE COMPETITIONS

Sailplanes are in many respects ideal as scale R/C subjects. They are not overly complicated in external detail, their cockpit interiors are sparse in comparison with powered aircraft – although becoming more comprehensive all the time – and the wing loadings used allow the inclusion of all the scale detail without fear of ending up with an overloaded model. Wing loading requirements vary according to the strength of the wind at the slope – the higher the wind speed the higher the wing loading to produce a faster model capable of making headway against the wind. Most scale sailplanes will incorporate a method of ballasting so that the model can be accurately flown in a variety of wind conditions. The only disadvantages with loading up a sailplane are connected with ground speed and structural considerations. Obviously, the model must be capable of withstanding the higher wing loadings imposed by weight ballasting, and there is a limit to every model's 'G' loading before failure occurs.

To make headway in a 30 m.p.h. wind will mean that the downwind *ground* speed is going to be well in excess of 60 m.p.h. and this will not appear to the ground observer to be very scale. Fortunately most of our flying will be taking place heading out from the slope, into wind, or tacking up and down parallel to the slope.

Test flights with sailplanes can be attempted on a 'nursery' slope, e.g. not at the top of the hill but further down, providing there is a suitable landing area into wind. With a smaller model a test glide may be made over level ground. None of the competitions are too demanding with regard to performance and this is generally restricted to loops and stall turns. Few of the sailplane prototypes are capable of advanced aerobatics, sailplane scale flight is more concerned with smooth elegant manoeuvres, accuracy of flying and the approach and landing. Although competition rules vary a typical set of rules is shown below. It will be noted that the balance between static and flying marks is fairly even, giving the model builder every encouragement to create an

Scale model of a Polish power-launched sailplane, this 'Ogar' is from a Robbe kit. Span 11ft.6in., powered by an O.S.40.

accurate, well finished model. The 'K' factor also encourages the modeller to design his own scale R/C sailplane, thus increasing the variety of designs likely to be entered in competitions. One potential drawback with scale sailplane events is the risk of the models being 'much of a muchness'.

SCALE COMPETITION RULES

STATIC JUDGING   *K Factor*

Built from substantially ready-made kit	K = 1
Built from kit of parts but with a substantial amount of work by the entrant, i.e. ready-made fibreglass fuselage and built-up wings	K = 1.1
Built from scratch to other person's plans	K = 1.2
Built from scratch to own design	K = 1.3

STATIC JUDGING POINTS
ALLOCATION   *Points*

Accuracy (simple measurements)	25
Complexity of type	15
Accuracy of structure	10
Complexity of fittings	10
Cockpit detail	10
Accuracy of finish (fuselage)	10
Accuracy of finish (wings and tail)	10
Colour and markings	10

SUPPORTING DOCUMENTATION

1. Entrant's declaration as to the builder and the K factor classification of the model.
2. A 3-view drawing with dimensions.
3. Colour photographs, or other way of identifying accuracy of markings and general appearance (i.e. authoritative or published text).

FLIGHT JUDGING

Builders are expected to fly the model but in the event of proxy-flying judging will cease.

PROVING FLIGHT   *Points*

1. 360° Turn	10
2. Straight stall and recovery	10
3. Approach and landing	10
4. Continuity	10

SCALE FLIGHT   *Points*

1. Two thermal turns	10
2. Straight and level along the slope	10
3. Dive and climb	10
4. Nominated manoeuvre	10
5. Approach and landing	10
6. Continuity and realism	10

Chapter 13

Undercarriage Assemblies and Wheels

The construction of undercarriages can present some of the greatest difficulties the scale R/C modeller is likely to encounter. Most of the problems arise because it is impossible, or nearly so, to reproduce in miniature the complexities of metal castings, oleos, plates and fixings used in the complex geometry of many undercarriage systems. This applies particularly to some of the retracting undercarriages where the designer of the prototype probably had innumerable problems to overcome in producing a system that was strong, and yet avoided structural airframe members when fully retracted. To achieve this, within the limited space available, often resulted in an intricate assemblage of pivots, gearing, sliding shafts, etc. For the modeller to duplicate, in miniature, some of the more perplexing of these arrangements would call for the highest degree of draughting and engineering skills. The full-size aircraft designer also has the advantage of being able to specify materials with strengths and qualities to suit each particular purpose. Modellers have only limited materials at hand and the one that is nearest to suiting the purpose must be used. Not for us the high strength steels or dural casting; we have to be satisfied with piano wire and simulated casting built up from wood and plastic, unless you happen to have full engineering facilities. Before

contemplating the design and construction of a scale model, where the prototype features a complex retracting undercarriage, the modeller should seriously consider whether he has the skills and facilities to produce a scale facsimile of the original.

Not all prototypes have fiendishly difficult undercarriages and many can be copied in scale form, whether fixed or retracting. The construction of the original should be closely studied, from plans and photographs, as well as the method of retraction, where appropriate. Of assistance here is the study of a plastic model kit, if one has been issued of your prototype; most plastic kits are extremely accurate and the draughtsmen have spent hundreds of hours pondering plans and preparing the model. Seeing the structural parts of the undercarriage in three dimensions, which may include a working retraction, will help to get a clearer picture of the complete unit.

One further disadvantage we have with model undercarriages concerns the landing loads. On average, the finesse shown in touching down a full-size aircraft is much greater than the landings experienced with R/C models. It is far more difficult to land a model precisely as we have no horizon, as a full-size aircraft pilot has, to use to determine height – and no positive speed information. Admittedly, the pilot of the full-size air-

Typical V-strut undercarriage which evolved for World War I aircraft. This is an Albatros C1 by the author for the 'Wings' TV series.

craft will occasionally make a total 'hash' of the landing (sometimes with structural damage) but the undercarriage of the model must be capable of taking a more severe hammering. How we go about reproducing the prototype's structure will depend whether we opt to reproduce it in the same constructional materials and methods or whether we 'cheat' and use more conventional modelling methods.

UNDERCARRIAGES OF EARLY AIRCRAFT

The early aircraft (pre 1914) mostly used a combination of wood struts, metal plate fittings and stranded wire or piano wire cross bracing. Ash, beech and bamboo were the most common woods used and the latter is the most difficult to represent. We can use cane, the type sold at art and crafts shops, but this lacks the 'knobbly' pieces so much a feature of bamboo. Bending actual bamboo, even small diameters, is very difficult, although they apparently managed it on some of the prototypes. It is feasible to

construct the ash and beech structures *a la* full-size but the nut and bolt sizes start to get down to the smallest dimensions for the metal fittings. These sizes are not readily obtainable, but you may find that suppliers to model engineering enthusiasts (steam locomotives and ships) may stock them. Where the wood members are curved, e.g. the fronts of the skids, the wood must be bent by steaming and binding to a hardwood former or by sawing narrow slots down the length of the grain. The slots will allow easier bending of the wood but will also reduce the amount of 'meat' left. Unless the section of the wood member reduces at this point the slots must be filled with thin strips of plywood. Use a slow drying wood glue for the laminating process. To obtain the necessary rigidity and strength of the assembly the cross bracing must be structural, as on the prototype. Stranded metal wire, flexible is obtainable, can be used or piano wire silver soldered to the metal fittings. Turnbuckles are best simulated, rather than working, on the undercarriages as we are looking for a better strength/weight ratio on the model. Fuselage connections must be made to hardwood members on the fuselage and these should be reinforced where necessary with ply.

An alternative to faithfully reproducing the construction of the full-size structures is to use a framework of piano wire, silver soldered, and fair this with hardwood to match the original. This method will give a much stronger basic construction at the expense of a little scale fidelity. The fixing of the piano wire crosspieces to the fuselage must be designed so that they are not visible beyond the struts and fittings. Cross bracing, in piano wire, may not coincide with the fitting of the original's connecting points unless a 'dog leg' is bent into the wire before it is soldered to the frame. This has the effect of reducing the tensional strength of the bracing – all bracing wires operate in tension, the struts in compression. Metal plate fittings can be simulated by the use of thin ply or plastic card and bolt heads from small lengths of hexagonal wood or plastic glued to the dummy plates or struts. Although some metal leaf springing was used on some of the early prototypes the most common type of shock absorbing was by 'bungee' cord springing. It is possible to purchase bungee cord down to $1/8$ inch diameter from yacht fitters and ship's chandlers, but smaller sizes are not easy to come by. (Proctor Enterprises stock a $3/32$ in. diameter bungee.) The method of locating the axle to the horizontal undercarriage member varied but was often in the form of a hardwood 'stopblock'. Study the prototype for this information and wind the bungee cord to suit.

The larger the scale of your R/C model of this period the more practical it

becomes to follow the original construction. Not only do the metal fittings, nuts and bracing become easier to produce but the landings can be more accurately judged and, with the lighter wing loadings, are softer.

W.W.1 AIRCRAFT

Metal tube construction became more widely used during the first great war but many aircraft continued to use wooden undercarriage struts. Simpler structures were evolved, culminating in the 'V' struts of many fighter undercarriages; the front skids were only retained on training aircraft and some bombers. The wooden struts were often wrapped in linen, doped and painted, to give a more serviceable finish, but, again, others retained the natural wood and varnished finish. The varnish used on early aircraft had the effect of darkening the wood considerably so that spruce, ash and beech were darker in tone and warmer in colour than one might expect. Structural bracing of the undercarriage is of equal importance to the earlier versions and the lateral cross bracing must be capable of taking the heavy loads sustained in a crosswind landing. Rigid, single piece axles were used on most aircraft, with suspension supplied by bungee cord bound round the ends of the axle. More sophisticated axle arrangements were adopted by some manufacturers, including the British Sopwith Company. They patented a split axle device where the axle was hinged at the centre position allowing the axle halves to spring independently from the hinge point. This gave the wheels the typical cant (sloping inwards at the top) of Sopwith aircraft at rest on the ground. In the air, however, the axle, without the load of the aircraft, took up a near straight line position. As this was such a distinctive feature it should be simulated in the model. One of the problems with take-offs of these narrow tracked W.W.1 models is their propensity for ground looping – swinging uncontrollably on the take-off run. Careful application of power and rudder control will reduce this danger but it is possible to further reduce it by using a common axle for the wheels. Instead of having the wheels freely revolving on the axle they should be permanently fixed at each end. The axle is then housed in short brass tube bearings fixed to each undercarriage strut. Admittedly, this precludes the use of axle springing, but with both wheels travelling at the same speed, it helps to keep the model straight on the take-off and landing runs.

Tailskids on early aircraft were often of the non-steerable variety and utilised bungee springing, accessible through a hole in the bottom of the fuselage, or a simple tension spring. These methods are straightforward to duplicate on models and work well on take-offs from grass strips. They are less suitable (and this also applies to full-size aircraft such as the *Tiger Moth*) for taxying and taking off from tarmac strips. Longitudinal control at slow speeds is severely lacking. To overcome this lack of control we can do one of two things:- (a) fit a small wheel in the thickness of the tailskid – not exactly scale but distinctly helpful, or (b) fit a hard rubber shoe to the underside of the skid. The rubber will cause more friction between the skid and the take-off surface, requiring more power to move the aircraft on the ground. Because of the slipstream effect of the propeller over the tail surfaces the model will be more controllable at the slow ground speeds.

INTER WAR PERIOD

The period between the two world wars saw many innovations in undercarriage designs, ranging from developments of the earlier compression springing (e.g. Avro 504) to the retractable undercarriages of the first generation of fighters used in the second world war. Many types and combinations were used including the use of bungee, solid rubber shock absorbers, compression spring oleo types, hydraulic and pneumatic. It is not possible, because of the wide range employed, to cite examples of each type and it may not be necessary to duplicate the method of suspension on our scale model. The geometry of the prototype's undercarriage must be studied, however, to determine which struts were fixed, which pivoted, which took compressive loads, which tensile loads and which were simply acting as radius struts. If it is at all possible to incorporate the same *structural* design of the undercarriage it should be done. This is especially important with wire braced aircraft where the transference of landing loads is often directed to structurally important locations on the airframe. It cannot be overstressed that, with the earlier generations of aircraft, the more we can keep to the prototype's methods of constructional and structural design the fewer will be our problems. The prototype designers' problems were, in effect, the same as ours.

One of the most used forms of undercarriage suspension in the thirties was the oleo strut, either as a single leg (e.g. Boeing, Stearman) or as part of a more complex undercarriage structure (e.g. Fokker F7). These shock absorbing sprung struts can be produced in model form to give excellent appearance and functionability. The basic system involves an inner metal tube having a sliding fit in an outer metal tube with a compression spring housed in the top of the outer

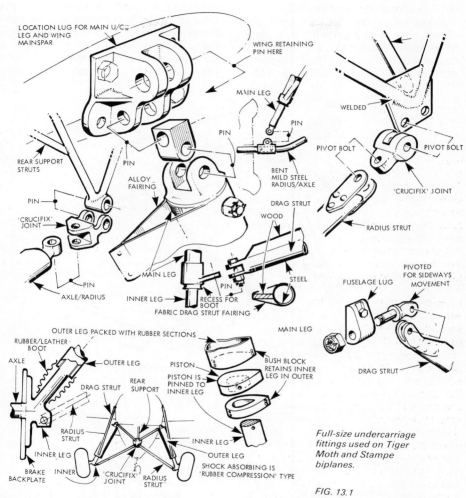

LOCATION LUG FOR MAIN U/C
LEG AND WING
MAINSPAR

WING RETAINING
PIN HERE

MAIN LEG

PIN

PIN

PIN

WELDED

PIVOT BOLT

PIVOT BOLT

REAR SUPPORT
STRUTS

PIN

ALLOY
FAIRING

BENT
MILD STEEL
RADIUS/AXLE

'CRUCIFIX' JOINT

PIN

DRAG STRUT

'CRUCIFIX'
JOINT

WOOD

RADIUS STRUT

MAIN LEG

PIN

STEEL

PIVOTED
FOR SIDEWAYS
MOVEMENT

PIN

AXLE/RADIUS

INNER LEG

RECESS FOR
BOOT

FABRIC DRAG STRUT FAIRING

MAIN LEG

FUSELAGE LUG

DRAG STRUT

OUTER LEG PACKED WITH RUBBER SECTIONS

RUBBER/LEATHER
BOOT

AXLE

OUTER LEG

PISTON

BUSH BLOCK
RETAINS INNER
LEG IN OUTER

DRAG STRUT

REAR
SUPPORT

PISTON IS
PINNED TO
INNER LEG

RADIUS
STRUT

INNER LEG

INNER LEG

OUTER LEG

BRAKE
BACKPLATE

INNER

'CRUCIFIX'
JOINT

RADIUS
STRUT

SHOCK ABSORBING IS
'RUBBER COMPRESSION' TYPE

*Full-size undercarriage
fittings used on Tiger
Moth and Stampe
biplanes.*

FIG. 13.1

tube. A method must be devised for preventing the inner from falling clear and also to prevent it from turning within its housing. This can be achieved by fixing a rod through the inner metal tube to project, at each end, into slots formed in the outer metal tube; the rod will also retain the compression spring. By varying the slot length the travel of the lower sprung leg tube can be limited. Most outer tubes will require strengthening to withstand the horizontal landing loads, and a further tube can be sleeved on to the top area and this will conveniently

177

hide the slot area. See Fig. 13.4.

Brass tubing is available from good non-ferrous metal stockists in a variety of outside diameters and wall thicknesses but it may be difficult to obtain all sizes in small quantities. The wall thick-ness required will have to be such that a 'telescopic' fit is obtained and be commensurate with the strength required. It really comes down to a matter of commonsense with the selection of tube sizes, and the understanding of a

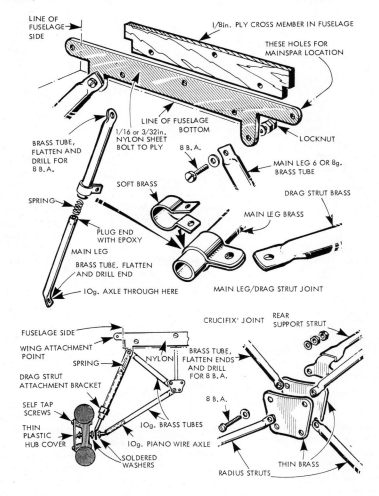

FIGS 13.2 & 13.3 Fabricating a model undercarriage on full-size principles.

sympathetic salesman at the stockists. Brass is a relatively easy material to work with, it solders well but care must be taken in drilling to prevent the drill 'snatching' in the material – lubricate well. Aluminium and copper tube have few uses in undercarriage structures as they are too soft and easily bent. Aluminium alloys (Dural for instance) are better from the strength point of view but can only be used where machined connections are to be made – solder joints with aluminium and its alloys are notoriously difficult. Steel tube and Bundy tube are far more useful and the latter is very simple to fabricate. It has a double wall thickness, being spiral wound in a similar method to a Damascus gun barrel, is copper coated on the inside and tinned on the outside. With the excellent working characteristics, and ductability, it has numerous model aircraft uses apart from undercarriages. Exposed tubular metal framework, e.g. the cockpit area of a Fieseler *Storch* or *Lysander* can be fabricated with Bundy tube, using silver solder techniques and simple jigs. Wall thicknesses of the tube are approximately 22g, with O.D.s of $1/8$, $5/32$, $3/16$, $1/4$, $5/16$, $3/8$ and $1/2$ inch, making many of the adjacent sizes a tolerable sliding fit.

For the axle of an oleo it is usually possible to adapt part of a commercial undercarriage leg to fit, via metal sleeves, the oleo tube. Alternatively the axle can be fabricated by fitting a hardened steel bolt to a prepared dural shank, or to use a preformed piano wire axle fitting into the lower tube. The strength of the compression spring is not terribly critical but you will probably need a tougher spring than you would expect – 10 lbs of model putting down at two or three 'Gs', sometimes on one wheel only, gives the springs a fair pounding. There is no doubt that this form of undercarriage

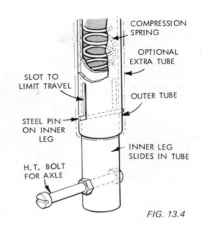

COMPRESSION SPRING

OPTIONAL EXTRA TUBE

SLOT TO LIMIT TRAVEL

OUTER TUBE

STEEL PIN ON INNER LEG

INNER LEG SLIDES IN TUBE

H.T. BOLT FOR AXLE

FIG. 13.4

suspension is effective, it also helps to give a scale appearance to the landing.

Making and fitting the oleo type of undercarriage legs may not present too many difficulties but one problem that does crop up on some designs (e.g. *Kaydet* and Stearman) is the treatment of the fairing between the oleo leg and the fuselage. Depending on the springing method employed there may be some fore and aft movement of the legs, making this joint particularly vulnerable. On the prototypes this fairing was often aluminium, although it did not have to cope with much fore and aft movement, but this is not a suitable material to use on the model. We require something with inherent flexibility and silicone bath sealant is absolutely right for this use. Leave a gap of $1/8$ to $3/16$ in. between the top of the oleo fairing and the fuselage. Mask around the oleo leg and the silicone fairing outline on the fuselage with thin plastic tape – it will follow the contours and sharp radii better than other tapes. Roughen up the materials to come into contact with the silicone to provide a good key. Painting white silicone bath sealant is not very satisfactory and it

This Sterling kit for a Stinson Reliant is a good example of both spats on the wheels and the big fairings at the top of the legs.

Opposite, typical "trousered" undercarriage favoured on Miles aircraft.

tends to chip off when the material flexes. Fortunately, the silicone can be coloured, including metallics, with glass fibre pigments and these should be mixed into the white or clear silicone rubber sealant. Do not over mix as the material 'goes off' fairly rapidly. Apply the silicone to the fairing area and build up the layers until the desired contours are reached, smoothing the surface with a dampened finger. When the silicone has finally cured remove the masking tape and you have a neat functional fairing.

Oleo legs were by no means always round, in fact these were more common on the retractable legs where drag was of no consequence. The streamline shape of oleo fairings can be made up from wood, but as the originals were normally from aluminium, we can also use thin aluminium plate or sheet for this purpose. A very useful and cheap source of aluminium sheet about 0.004 to 0.005 inches thick is litho plate as used by printing firms. As they discard much of this used material you will probably get it for nothing and it is very easy to form

into simple oval sections. Make a wooden former of the oval section and form the aluminium around it, trimming the rear edge so that there is no abutting joint at the trailing edge. It is possible to form an overlap joint but this is less sightly than a neat butt joint. The strut, or wire leg, must be roughened, epoxy or glass fibre putty pushed into the fairing and the fairing clamped and taped into position until the assembly has set. Where a fairing with a large chord is to be fitted, solder small piano wire 'U' reinforcements to the leg to prevent it twisting out of place. The tops of the oleo leg fairings can be formed with epoxy putty or silicone sealant as previously described.

Before retractable undercarriages were fitted, or in the interests of reducing costs and simplification, the designers were thinking up ways of reducing the drag from the undercarriage assembly. A simple expedient was the fitting of spats to the wheels or full, trousered fairings to the undercarriage legs and wheels. Spats, or wheel pants as they are called in America, have been used on many prototypes from the twenties to this day and they are reasonably effective in reducing wheel drag. Because they fit closely around the wheel, to reduce the frontal area, they are subject to fouling the wheel in rough landing areas, snow, long grass, etc., and for this reason were often removed from the aircraft. When produced in model form we suffer from the same limitations and we must, therefore, use a very tough thin material to withstand the knocks and bumps of landing without appearing too bulky. Glass fibre is most suitable for this application and it can be further reinforced by the use of carbon fibre at strategic points. The attachment point of the spats to the undercarrige leg must give a secure fixing and this can be achieved by silver soldering a plate to the axle, or leg, and screwing the spat to the plate. Nuts can be made captive on the inside of the spat by moulding them in during the glass fibre moulding process. See Fig. 13.5.

Undercarriage spats, or trousers, as opposed to fairings for the wheels only, were used on aircraft in the thirties to further reduce drag. Typical of the aircraft using these devices were the Miles *Hawk Speed Six* and Beechcraft *Staggerwing*. When designed for maximum drag reduction they left very little of the bottom of the wheel exposed, which was of little import when landing on smooth surfaces at the correct angle and without too much shock to the suspension system. Alas, the R/C flyer does not always achieve such results or have such ideal conditions. The close proximity of the spat and the ground spells trouble on some 'arrivals' and we must attempt to construct a robust fairing – and improve our flying. Glass fibre is again the obvious material to use, although ply reinforced with resin could be used, and

as an added precaution, the spats should be made 'knock-offable'. Glue a former, to the shape of the spat top interior, to the underside of the wing – spatted undercarriages were almost invariably fitted to aircraft using wing mounted undercarriage legs. The spat will house on to the former; it must be trimmed to fit the underside of the wing, and can be retained in position with fore and aft tension springs. Hooks can be moulded into the spat, near the base, and screw hooks fitted through the top spat former. Use a piece of piano wire, with a small hook formed at one end, to fix the springs in position and don't forget to reinforce the wing structure around the

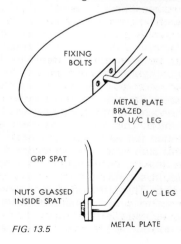

FIXING BOLTS

METAL PLATE BRAZED TO U/C LEG

GRP SPAT

NUTS GLASSED INSIDE SPAT

U/C LEG

METAL PLATE

FIG. 13.5

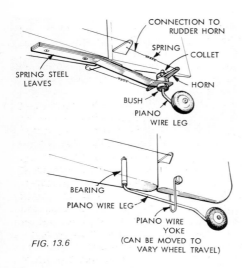

CONNECTION TO RUDDER HORN

SPRING

COLLET

SPRING STEEL LEAVES

HORN

BUSH

PIANO WIRE LEG

BEARING

PIANO WIRE LEG

PIANO WIRE YOKE

(CAN BE MOVED TO VARY WHEEL TRAVEL)

FIG. 13.6

spat area to prevent damage when it comes adrift.

Steerable tailwheels come in many sizes and types. Fabrication of the units, if none is commercially available, will require a little ingenuity, particularly if spring steel leaves are to be incorporated. Spring steel strip, i.e. clock springs, is another difficult material to use and although it can be detempered the retempering process is often less than satisfactory. With most applications it would be advisable to treat the leaf springing purely as cosmetic and to use piano wire as the main structural member. Steering of the tailwheel is often as a result of a direct coupling with the rudder. This is wrong as it will give too much tail wheel movement on the take-off run. Where a connection from the rudder to the tailwheel steering is needed it should be done as shown in Fig. 13.6. The amount of reduction of movement is proportional to the distance from the hinge line to the yoke position. Alternatively the steering can be catered

for, as with many originals, by using a small horn to the tailwheel bracket and separate control wire to the rudder servo output.

Some postwar light aircraft manufacturers, e.g. Cessna, have stopped using conventional construction welded undercarriages and have developed single leaf cantilevered undercarriage legs. This has been possible through the development of very high strength alloys with good flexibility values. The 'springiness' of the metal is in itself sufficiently shock absorbing to make any additional form of springing unnecessary. At present, the modelling field has no similar materials to offer and to attempt to use standard dural, in scale proportions, will result in failure – it does not have the necessary strength. Until a suitable material is found for our scale models we must resort to using two, or more, lengths of piano wire and fairing in between the wire.

RETRACTING UNDERCARRIAGES

The main disadvantage with retracting undercarriage systems is that they are necessary for scale flight where they were used on the prototype. In other words, if we could get away without using them we would for they can be a continual source of trouble. We have, as previously explained, to include more shock absorbing facilities in a model than on the full-size aircraft. Prototypes will allow for vertical loads to be taken care of but we often find it prudent to allow for rearwards springing as well. In making this allowance we build in the risk of misplacing the undercarriage leg and causing a malfunction of the retract system. It *is* possible to use only an oleo strut form of suspension but we must be both careful not to make the unit too heavy for the operating mechanism and to perform reasonably gentle landings. For reasons of scale we should not only make the undercarriage go up and down but also make it happen at a scale speed and in the correct sequence – undercarriage legs on aircraft do not necessarily operate in unison. To take the question of speed to the extreme, some aircraft such as the Avro *Anson* used a hand-cranked undercarriage retract system and this, depending on the fitness of the operator, would take a very long time to arrive at the up position. When we also consider the wide variety of operating and structural geometry employed to retract systems, it does become obvious that many of the subjects using them are not for the faint-hearted modeller. We are not only considering main wheel retraction, as prototypes also feature retractable nosewheels and tail-

wheels. Some arrangements of retract systems leave so little structural 'meat' of the wing or rear fuselage remaining that it is impractical to reproduce an exact scale copy in miniature. It is far from the purpose of this book to discourage modellers to aim for the highest achievements but there are times when prudence becomes a virtue. In respect of retracting undercarriage systems a little prudence in accepting your engineering limitations may save a lot of heartache. There are some excellent model retract units on the market, and for most modellers it would be discreet to use these, albeit with modifications, rather than attempting to start from scratch. Electric, pneumatic and servo operated units are available to cover the basic forms of retraction of main wheels and nose-legs. When you advance to the more complete folding and retracting

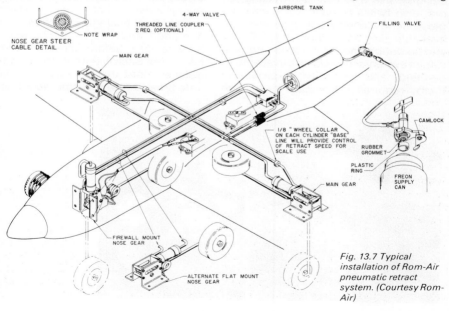

Fig. 13.7 Typical installation of Rom-Air pneumatic retract system. (Courtesy Rom-Air)

183

methods you are almost certainly on your own. Choose the system that is most applicable to your model's retract method of operation, modify it to suit the scale situation and build a test rig and operate it until you are *totally* satisfied that it operates *every* time. Of course, we are not finished with just the retraction of the wheels as there are often wheel well doors and hatches to incorporate as well. The actual design of operation of these doors and covers is not always too difficult, the difficulty is in ensuring that they stay firmly closed during flight, without adding a further load to the operating mechanism when the doors are required to be opened again.

Most of the commercial units have been designed for the main wheels to retract spanwise, inwards or outwards, through 90° or thereabouts. A number of prototype aircraft, principally American designs, use a rearward retracting leg that also twists through 90° during the movement. Commercial units are now available for this method of retraction, and no doubt many of the other forms of retract systems will become available as demand, and ingenuity in producing them, requires. They call for a high standard of precision work, gearing with a minimum of backlash, careful counterbalancing and the use of the correct materials for the various components. Installation must be equally precise and maintenance is important for the continued smooth operation of the retract system; the units should be checked for operation after each flight.

One of the hazards of a servo, or electric, operation of retract units, using a battery supply common to the receiver and other servos, is the risk of the system jamming. It only needs one undercarriage leg to be slightly out of alignment for it to fail to house into the well correctly and cause the servo motor, or electric motor, to remain in a stalled position. The increase in electric current being consumed from the battery will be sufficient to flatten it very quickly, and possibly without the operator being aware that it is happening. Suddenly, the pilot will realise that something is wrong, usually by the servos becoming slow in operation, and if he is lucky he will have time to land before catastrophe overtakes him. Such is the current draw from a stalled motor that there will be precious little time to take this emergency action

Inward and upward retraction (e.g. on some Grumman designs, amphibians, etc.) call for neat metalwork, also evident on steerable tailwheel shown.

and even the operation of the under-carriage to the down position may be sufficient to flatten the battery completely! An obvious solution, as normally used with electric motor operated retracts, is to use a separate battery supply for the servo/s actuating the retract system. A method of arranging this, using standard components, is illustrated in Fig. 13.9. It will be noted that the system includes a ground safety switch to prevent accidental operation of the retracts by the operator inadvertently knocking the switch on the transmitter. Many full-size aircraft incorporate a similar, automatic safety device which prevents the operation of the under-carriage lever to the 'up' position when there is a load on the undercarriage legs, i.e. when the aircraft is on the ground. This is all the more essential when the undercarriage and flap levers are adjacent and similar in feel and oper-ation. One of the first actions after land-ing is to retract the flaps and it is not unknown for the pilot to get hold of the wrong lever to do this. Unfortunately, in a fast taxi, the aircraft can occasionally 'leap' over a depression causing the solenoid preventing retraction to 'drop out'. If this moment coincides with the inadvertent operation of the 'wrong' lever the undercarriage will indeed retract – the author can vouch for this! Perhaps some keen scale R/C modeller would like to reproduce this system to see whether he can achieve the same results – it could be classed as a scale option.

One feature of standard retracting undercarriages, e.g. retracting outwards as with the *Spitfire* etc., is the geometry involved to obtain the correct slant forward of the leg in the down position and the rake back when it is retracted into the wing. Assuming the prototype

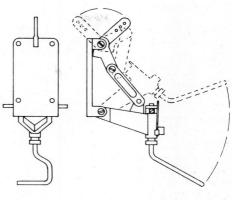

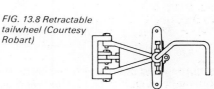

FIG. 13.8 Retractable tailwheel (Courtesy Robart)

does not use any sadistic methods of twisting the leg during retraction, the method of calculating the installation angles is not difficult. First we must measure the angle of the forward slant of the undercarriage strut relative to 90°

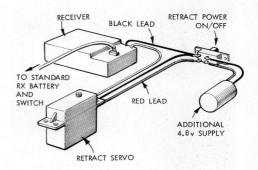

FIG. 13.9

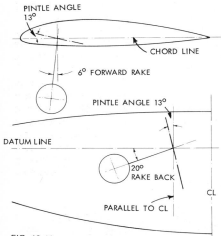

PINTLE ANGLE
13°

CHORD LINE

6° FORWARD RAKE

PINTLE ANGLE 13°

DATUM LINE

20°
RAKE BACK

CL

PARALLEL TO CL

FIG. 13.10

from the wing chord – let us assume the angle is 6° – See Fig. 13.10. Next we must measure the angle of the rake back of the strut position (the undercarriage leg) relative to the wingspan datum i.e. a line

from tip to tip of the wing. We will take that as being 20°. If we add these two figures together and divide by two it will give the pivot angles for mounting the retract system, i.e. $\frac{6° + 20°}{2} = 13°$. The unit must be mounted to give a compound pivot angle at 13° incidence to the wing and with 13° 'toe out' to the chord line. Providing the unit is accurately fitted to these angles it will result in the undercarriage having a true track and forward cant in the down position, and the undercarriage and fairings lying flat in the wing in the retracted state.

WHEELS

Wheels have developed through over three quarters of a century's flying from the fragile open spoked types to the magnesium hubbed, almost solid tyred wheels used by modern airliners that are capable of taking many tons load. Few individual items ruin scale effect more than having the wrong type, or size, wheels fitted to a model. Wheels a mere $1/8$ in. diameter too large or small will immediately look wrong to the trained observer – it is that noticeable. Using wheels of the wrong style will also destroy the scale illusion. A smooth tyre on the prototype requires a smooth tyre on the model – a ribbed tyre will 'stick out like a sore thumb'. The cross section of the tyre and hub must also be correct; some light aircraft used fat, low pressure tyres to minimise landing bounce and for operation from 'difficult' landing areas. To use a 'standard' commercial wheel to simulate these styles of wheels would create completely the wrong

Internal wheel well and door detail are essential on a good scale model.

effect. Tyres on full-size aircraft rarely have any sheen – let alone shine – unless they have gone through a 'bull' session by a devoted owner of a light aircraft. Most commercial wheels feature tyres made from plastic and not rubber that are quite shiny. This gloss must be removed by rubbing with an abrasive paper. There will be many occasions when there is no commercial wheel that is completely suitable for our scale model and we must adapt, or start from scratch. We will consider some of the wheels used through flying history with a particular emphasis on the older types where it is not possible to adapt existing commercial wheels.

Wheels for vintage scale models often present a problem to the modeller. There is a very limited availability of commercially produced open-spoked wheels and even the covered spoked wheels are often unobtainable in exactly the right size for *your* model. Micro-Mold, Veron and the American firm of Williams Bros. produce various sizes of W.W.1 type wheels, but as far as I am aware, open-spoked wheels are only made in limited sizes in this country at present. The reasons for the lack of variety result from purely commercial considerations. Tooling costs for the moulded wheels are extremely high and metal spoked wheels must be entirely hand-crafted and assembled.

A scale period model fitted with modern wheels looks totally ridiculous and, as a last resort, if you can't buy the correct article, the only alternative is to make it. When I started to build some 1/8th scale R/C models of Bleriots and Blackburn monoplanes I arrived at exactly this position. We had had some experience in producing spoked wheels for a 1/4 scale Bleriot, but these feature metal rims and spokes plus turned hubs.

This naturally involves considerable metal spinning, lathe and drilling work – I wanted to avoid these wherever possible. I knew that continuous 'laced' spokes had been made, both amateurishly and professionally, for lightweight free flight models and I decided to explore this method for R/C models. After a little experimenting I found that it was not only practical, but had the advantages of being not too difficult, of low cost and good appearance. The process is not over-lengthy and it should be possible to complete a pair of wheels in a couple of evenings.

MATERIALS AND TOOLS FOR OPEN-SPOKED WHEELS

Tool requirements should be generally covered by the average workshop, although a vertical drill (a portable drill in a drill stand is fine) will take the tedium out of the drilling operations. A long metal straight edge is also necessary for cutting the plywood strip.

Actual materials will depend on the size and style of wheel to be made, but the general principles follow throughout a size range from 2 in. diameter up to 6 in. The rims are constructed from strips of ply (0.4mm for wheels up to 4 in. diameter, 0.8mm for larger), and the ply should be obtained in as great a length as possible to avoid joints. Brass tube with an I.D. to suit the axle will be needed for the hubs, as will large diameter steel or brass washers to solder on to the tube for hub flanges. Spokes are formed from nylon monofilament fishing line (10 lbs. strain for the smallest wheels, up to 18/20 lbs. for the 4 in. diameter), but fishing traceline – metal cored – of 20/25 lbs. strength can be used for larger wheels. Should you be lucky enough to find some ready-made tyres of the correct size, e.g.

'O' rings for sealing steam pipes or rain-water downpipes, the problem is solved. If you have to make them, the simplest way is by end-glueing a length of rubber cord or tube to form a ring. I prefer the solid neoprene rubber cord to tubing as it is easier to glue together. Tubing, when used, must have a substantial wall thickness or it will flatten excessively on impact during landing. Apart from these items, you will only need a few short lengths of piano wire, scrap wood and a thick plywood/blockboard base for the jig.

DESIGN

A number of different methods were used in spoking early aircraft wheels, from the radial patterned, where the spokes travel direct from the hub to the rim, to the style where the spokes leave the hub flanges at an angle. The latter give the crossed spoke effect on the complete wheels. I have concentrated on radial spoking here; it may be possible to 'lace' up the spokes to give a different pattern, but the sequence of lacing becomes a little 'mind-boggling'.

Assuming that you have no drawing of the wheels, you only need to draw the outline of the tyre, rim and the hub flange (washer). The thickness of the rim — below the tyre — should be 4 × 0.4mm for up to 4in. diameter wheels, and equal to 3 × 0.8mm for larger wheels. Number of spokes per wheel varied considerably as many of the early wheels were only adaptations of existing types. In the absence of any more definite information, I would suggest using 36 spokes per wheel as this makes a 10° division per spoke. With the lacing method used, one hole in the hub flange serves two spokes and, therefore, we shall need nine holes in each flange, drilled at 40° separation.

RIMS

Cut strips of plywood to the required length (2 × 3.14 × radius of rim × number of thicknesses) and to a width slightly less than the diameter of the tyre, i.e. for a $^3/_8$ in. diameter tyre the rim width should be about $^5/_{16}$ in. Allow an extra ½ in. for chamfering the ends of the strip and trimming. If you have to join the strips to obtain the full length, use thin self-adhesive tape to join the ends. The rims can be formed around a ply-wood disc, cut to the internal diameter, or around pins positioned at close intervals around the circumference. Chamfer the edge of the strip — yes, it is possible to chamfer even 0.4 mm ply by sanding it with a fine sanding block. Dampening the ply strip will help it to bend easily and also help the adhesive to spread. Wax the former, or drawing, well and spread white PVA glue to the outside of the first three-quarters of the strip. Wind the ply strip around the former, or pins, making sure that each layer is tight on to the previous layer. Secure the end of the strip with a pin or cyanoacrylate adhesive and leave to dry thoroughly. Heat can be used to accelerate drying — over a con-vector heater — and the rim is then trimmed by sanding the external flanges on a sheet of glasspaper and sanding off the end of the strip to correspond with the internal chamfer. Before the top edges of the rim are added (see section) spoke holes should be drilled. To mark the holes, first take a strip of thin card, of the same width as the rim, and cut it to the exact length of the external circumference (wrap it around the rim and cut for the edges to meet). This card must now be divided for 36 hole positions, but remember that the two ends represent *one* hole and there must be, in effect, 37 marks. The simplest method of subdividing is to hold the card strip diagonally

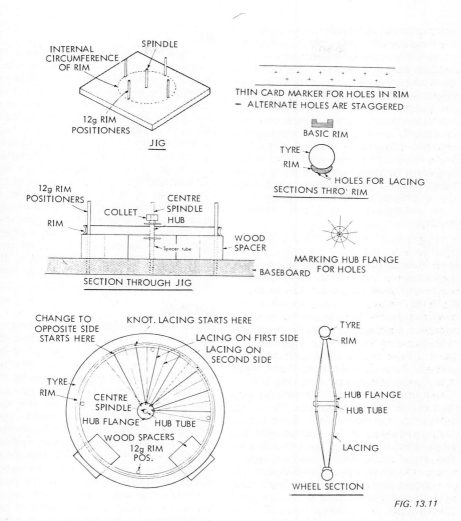

INTERNAL
CIRCUMFERENCE
OF RIM

SPINDLE

12g RIM
POSITIONERS

JIG

THIN CARD MARKER FOR HOLES IN RIM
— ALTERNATE HOLES ARE STAGGERED

BASIC RIM

TYRE
RIM

HOLES FOR LACING
SECTIONS THRO' RIM

12g RIM
POSITIONERS

COLLET

CENTRE
SPINDLE
HUB

RIM

Spacer tube

WOOD
SPACER

BASEBOARD

SECTION THROUGH JIG

MARKING HUB FLANGE
FOR HOLES

CHANGE TO
OPPOSITE SIDE
STARTS HERE

KNOT. LACING STARTS HERE

LACING ON FIRST SIDE
LACING ON
SECOND SIDE

TYRE
RIM

CENTRE
SPINDLE

HUB FLANGE   HUB TUBE

WOOD SPACERS
12g RIM
POS.

TYRE
RIM

HUB FLANGE
HUB TUBE

LACING

WHEEL SECTION

FIG. 13.11

across some suitably lined paper (lined
foolscap is O.K. for most wheels) until
the correct number of spaces correspond. Mark the hole positions on the
card, staggering the holes slightly as
shown on the sketch. Fit the card to the
rim, using a piece of Sellotape to join the
ends, and centre-punch the holes with a
bradawl or sharpened piece of piano
wire. Drill the rim with a fine drill ($^1/_{64}$ in.)
holding the rim vertically under the pillar
drill. The rim edges can now be added by
winding and glueing the thin strips of
0.4mm ply around the rims – three layers

are normally sufficient. Make sure that the strip comes right to the outside edges of the rim so that the edges can be sanded smooth easily. When the rim is dry it can be trimmed and sanded to section. A round section rasp is ideal for contouring the concave round for housing the tyre, but glasspaper glued to a piece of dowel is equally good. Rough trimming the internal edges with a sharp modelling knife will reduce the amount of glass-papering required. When the rims have been sanded smooth they should be thoroughly doped for additional strength – an alternative is to 'pickle' them in shellac.

HUBS

The hubs simply consist of a length of brass tube with a washer soldered on to each end. Cut the brass tube so that it extends about $1/16$ in. beyond the washers. Mark the hole positions on the washers and centre-punch the positions. It is possible to drill four washers at a time if they are bound together tightly with Sellotape. Hold them firmly with mole grips or heavy pliers during drilling. Clean up the washers after drilling, getting rid of any burrs around the holes. Soft soldering the washers to the tubing is quite satisfactory for most wheels, but silver soldering would be preferable for the larger sizes. I found the best way to solder the washer in position was to use a wooden clothes peg to hold the tubing and the peg then held in a vice. The tubing can be adjusted so that the washer sits on the top of the peg at the correct position. Stagger the hole positions in the washers by about 10° – the reason for this will become obvious when lacing the spokes. It is easier to paint the hubs and rims at this stage rather than when the wheels are complete.

JIG

A simple jig must be made to ensure that spoking is carried out to produce a true wheel. The sketch shows the method of jigging; the base board should be thick enough to hold firmly the piano wire verticals. A brass tube spacer is fitted to the centre spindle to lift the rim high enough off the base to allow lacing to be carried out to the lower half of the wheel – $1/2$ in. to $3/8$ in. is adequate. The four vertical positioners to the inside of the rim should be at 90° to one another, so that the rim can be adjusted for the holes to be clear of the positioners. If the rim is a slightly loose fit on the positioners, wind some Sellotape around the positioner to pack it out. Conversely, the positioners can be eased inwards if the fit of the rim is too tight.

LACING

Check that the holes are clear in the rims and hub and fit the hub and rim on to the jig; the hub must be retained on to the spacer tube with a collet. Note that the packing pieces for the rim must be the correct thickness to centre the rim and hub. The nylon monofilament line may be dyed black (ordinary nylon dye) before use, or the spokes can be painted silver on completion – a rather tedious job. Cut a length of line sufficient for *all* of the spokes *plus* the travel between holes, i.e. spoke length × 36 plus twice the circumference and a short length extra for tensioning. Tie a knot in one end of the line and feed through a hole from the outside of the rim. Take the line to a hole on the *bottom* hub flange, push through towards the base board, pull the line back and insert throught he next but one hole in the rim and pull tight. Take the line around the rim again to the next but one hole, push through and on to the next hole in the bottom hub flange. A pair of tweezers or fine nose pliers will assist in this operation. Continue lacing up in this way, tensioning at each stage. There is no need to glue the line as you go and it does not matter if the line goes loose as you are feeding it through the next hole. As you pull to tension at each stage it will tauten the previous slack spoke. When you have completed the lacing of the bottom side of the spokes, carry on to the next hole and commence the lacing of the top spokes. note that the wood spacers to the rim are not glued to the jig base board and can be moved slightly to allow for easier lacing. With the top lacing complete, take the loose end of the line and feed it back through the adjacent hole to secure it. Remove the wheel from the jig. At this point, the line around the outside of their im should be clued with cyanoacrylate adhesive and the loose end of the inside of the rim trimmed off.

TYRES

It is better to have a 'stretch' fit of the tyre on to the rim, so cut the rubber cord or tube about 1 in. less than the *external* circumference of the tyre (2 × 3.14 × radius). Cut the rubber with a sharp knife or blade, making sure the edges are 'square'. Join the edges with cyano-acrylate adhesive, holding them together until the glue has dried. Lightly glass-paper the joint – well done it will virtually be invisible. Check the tyre for fit on the rim; if it is not housing closely on to the rim it may be necessary to trim away a little from the inside of the tyre, particularly where the knot is. When you are satisfied with the fit, the wheel can be fuel-proofed and the tyre permanently fixed with cyanoacrylate.

There is no reason why it should not be possible to produce unequally coned wheels (with the spokes at a greater angle on one side than the other), although it is advisable to lace the steepest cone side first. There is plenty of room for experiment in the types and sizes of wheels, for example it might be possible to reinforce the rims by epoxy-ing piano wire rings around the top edges and using trace line or stranded wire for lacing.

Perhaps on reading this you have come to the conclusion that the whole process is far too complicated and time-consuming. Believe me, it is not. I completed my first pair of wheels in two or three evenings – from scratch. It is pleasant and exciting work and the finished article will surprise you, from both the appearance and strength points of view.

As an alternative to using the lami-nated plywood rims it is possible to form metal rims and, with piano wire spokes, this construction is more suitable for larger and heavier duty wheels. The rims can be fabricated in a number of ways:-
1. Turned on a lathe from a suitable size brass tube:
2. Spun from a metal disc (steel is O.K.) although this involves specialist equipment:
3. Building up the rim from thin sheet metal with reinforcing metal rod rings on either side of the rim.

The first two methods will obviously only be suitable for the modeller with metal working facilities available. Method number three should be within the capabilities of a modeller with a knowledge of silver soldering. It is imperative that silver soldering is used for spoked metal wheels, soft soldering is not strong enough to take the landing loads. The different melting temperatures

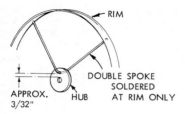

RIM

DOUBLE SPOKE
SOLDERED
AT RIM ONLY

APPROX.
3/32"

HUB

FIG. 13.12

of the various silver solders can be used to advantage when fabricating the wheels. Where 'tacking' is required it can be carried out with the high temperature range silver solder in the knowledge that, when it comes to 'fitting in' with the lower temperature solder, the 'tacking' will not melt and allow the component to move. If you are not familiar with silver soldering read, first, Chapter Five dealing with the methods and then practise on scrap metal to learn the technique. Cleanliness and the sparing use of silver solder is important, as in all forms of soldering. Commence the fabrication of the wheel rims by cutting a strip of 0.006 inch thick brass shim the full width of the finished rim and long enough to give a ¼ to ³/₈ inch overlap on the internal circumference (2 × 3.14 × radius, plus ³/₈ inch). Cut a thick ply circular former (6 or 9mm plywood) the exact diameter of the inside of the rim. Wind the brass shim around the former and silver solder the overlap. Take a bent wire metal coat hanger (or galvanised wire of about the

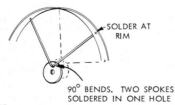

SOLDER AT
RIM

90° BENDS. TWO SPOKES
SOLDERED IN ONE HOLE

FIG. 13.13

same gauge) and straighten it by putting one end in the vice, the other end through a hole in a short piece of broom handle, and pulling *very* hard. Cut the wire to the correct circumferential lengths, no overlap, and form into circles round the plywood former. When you are satisfied that you have a true circle, tightly fitting onto the shim brass, tack solder the ends of the ring together. Position the first ring on to the brass shim, fitted on to the plywood former, and tack into position (with the outside of the ring lining up with the outside of the brass shim). The ply former can be held in the vice by mounting a nut and bolt through the centre of the plywood and gripping on the end of the bolt. Fill in the joint between the ring and the brass shim from the inside — capillary attraction will take the solder between the ring and the brass. Do the same for the ring on the opposite side of the rim, you will probably find that the plywood former will become charred and it is a wise precaution to have a spare prepared; dousing the finished solder joint with water from a spray gun will help to limit the effects of the high temperature. Remove the wheel rim from the former and file away the excess brass shim to form a smooth contour and finish with emery cloth and steel wool. The holes for the spokes are marked and drilled as previously described for the wooden rimmed wheels.

Piano wire spoking can be undertaken by two methods. Unless very large wheels are being produced it is impractical to drill a separate hole for every spoke in the wheel hub flange. One hole will suffice for two spokes but the size of the hole will depend on the method of spoke lacing employed. The first method involves the bending of spokes to be slipped through the hole in the hub flange and *only* soldered at the rim. See Fig 13.12. The second method uses single spokes soldered at the hub and rim but with the ends of *two* spokes being pushed into the same hub hole. See Fig 13.13. Naturally the holes in the hub flange for this method must be of large enough diameter to receive the two spokes. 20swg piano wire is adequate for sizes of wheels up to 7 inch overall diameter–the strength of a spoked wheel is quite surprising as some of the spokes are always operating under tension. Spoking arrangement will vary, the earlier types often used radial spoking but later versions utilised the more familiar crossed pattern. It can be quite a complex exercise working out the spoking pattern, and the fitting in the correct sequence; if you have any doubt of the positioning and directions of the spokes you should examine some full size examples – old motor cycle wheels etc. An arrangement similar to the one previously described, for lacing, can be used as a jig for spoking but it is suggested that the base be protected with asbestos and metal spacing blocks be substituted for wood. As before, the spoking is carried out one side of the wheel at a time, remembering to allow for any unequal coning angles of the spokes. Tack solder (soft solder can be used but they must be silver soldered later) three or four spokes in position around the area of the wheel. When you are certain that the wheel and hub are concentric, and you know the spoking procedure, the remainder of the spokes can be silver soldered in position. (It is again advisable to use a silver solder with a slightly lower melting point than that used on the rim.) Some of the tack-soldered spokes may have to be removed and replaced to maintain the correct sequence of spoking. On completion of one side, turn the wheel over, and complete the spoking of the second side. Trim the ends of the spokes in the rim well (they should be about ¼ inch longer than the finished length) and file the interior reasonably smooth. The ends of the spokes do not have to be absolutely flush with the brass shim, a little roughness will help to 'key' the tyre. Although the method of making the hub flanges with large diameter washers was previously described, they can be cut from sheet brass of 20–22g thickness if no suitable diameter washers can be obtained.

Clean off all of the flux from the soldered joints, and the wheel generally, with dope thinners or 'gun-wash'. Brushing with an old tooth brush will help to get into the difficult corners. There are plenty of firms that deal with plating, should you wish to have the wheels plated, nickel plating being the most reasonably priced. Painting is best undertaken with a spray gun but brushing is adequate as the surface areas concerned are small.

Prior to W.W.1, and after that period, spoked wheels were frequently covered with canvas covers. In normal operating conditions these were fine, but in the muddy airfield situations often to be found in France during W.W.1, they were sometimes removed. The mud would find its way inside the covers adding to the weight of wheels. It is, therefore, possible to have a scale subject with the spokes exposed, or covered, and retain scale authenticity. Canvas covers were usually hooked to loops formed in the wall of the tyre rather than the rim. This arrangement accounts for the typical appearance of W.W.1 wheels where the spokes show through the canvas near the hub of the wheel but because the covering is proud of the spokes, do not do so near the rim. See Fig 13.14. Some aircraft used conical metal covers, usually aluminium, and this method was continued into the twenties. There are some good facsimiles of W.W.1 wheels to be found commercially in the most popular scales, i.e. $3/8$th, $1/6$th and $1/4$scale. The tyres need 'matting' and detailing with the manufacturer's name and the wheel or tyre size. It is not possible to simulate the canvas attachment to the tyre but that is equally difficult to achieve when the wheels are made from scratch. When we get on to the larger sizes of wheels we must either construct them as spoked wheels – and it always seems a shame to hide all of that workmanship with covers – or we must improvise. Plastic pram wheels may seem to be an unlikely starting point but they do have one big advantage, the rims are already formed. If you can find a pair that have the correct rim dimensions they can be used as a basis for stand off scale W.W.1 wheels. Make 1.5mm ply 'spokes' to fit between the hub and rim, as shown in Fig. 13.14. These can be scalloped slightly towards the outside to prevent the covering from adhering to them. The hub may also have to be shortened to

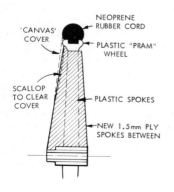

'CANVAS' COVER

NEOPRENE RUBBER CORD

PLASTIC "PRAM" WHEEL

SCALLOP TO CLEAR COVER

PLASTIC SPOKES

NEW 1.5mm PLY SPOKES BETWEEN

FIG. 13.14

end flush with the spokes. Glue the 'spokes' into position, both sides, using epoxy or some other suitable adhesive. Remove the tyre, it is doubtful whether it will be a close enough resemblance to the original to be usable. Cover both sides with nylon, checking first that the dope and plastic are compatible, taking the nylon over the top edge of the rim. Add details such as the reinforced valve access hole. Make up tyres to fit, from neoprene cord or thick wall tubing, but do not fit until painting of the remainder of the wheel is complete. If the tyre material is rather oversize in section the tyre should be made smaller in comparison to the rim circumference so that, as the tyre is stretched on to the rim, the cross sectional area will be reduced. The holes in the hubs will probably be over-large for modelling purposes and they must be sleeved. Look into your 'odds and scraps' box and see if you have a piece of thick wall aluminium tube, nylon or S.R.B.P. (synthetic resin bonded paper) tube to fit for sleeving purposes. As a last resort you can use wood dowel drilled to take brass or aluminium tube for the axle size.

During the inter-war period wheels continued to be made by the same processes but the tyre sections changed and the coverings were more frequently from metal. Larger wheels started to use metal hub construction with heavier section tyres and these gradually became the standard form of construction. With the wide selection of commercial wheels available it should be possible to find at least a size of tyre that is suitable for your project. Sometimes, however, the tyre will have a ribbed surface when a smooth finish is required. The ribbing can be removed by mounting a suitable nut and bolt through the axle hole, installing the bolt into an electric drill and applying coarse abrasive paper to the tyre surface. It may take a time to remove the ribbing, depending on the depth of tread — but nothing like the length of time my colleagues took to remove the 'knobbly' pieces of a grass track motor cycle tyre to transform it into a suitable tyre for a full size Sopwith *Pup* replica! Forming tread on smooth tyres is less easy. If there is ample wall thickness it *is* possible to cut in the tread pattern using a *very* sharp knife; the pattern should previously be marked with fine chinagraph pencil markings. Where only straight ribbing is needed the wheel can first be frozen, fitted in a drill or lathe, and the tread will cut much easier. The same freezing method may be adopted for making solid tyres from dense sponge rubber materials. First cut the approximate external diameter, freeze and drill the centre or fix in a lathe. Care is needed in shaping the tyre contours and refreezing may be needed, but it is one of the few ways that this type of material can be cut. Moulding on the tread to the tyre offers an alternative method of producing a tread pattern but it is also difficult to perform and obtain reliable results. A female glass fibre mould of the tread pattern, plus the tyre to be built up, is constructed so that the halves can be clamped together with the tyre inside. See Fig. 13.15. Roughen the surface of the tyre that is to receive the treaded area and place the tyre in one half of the mould, treated with a release agent. Pour silicone rubber, with black pigment added, into the gap between the tyre and mould and on to the tyre where the second half of the mould is to be fitted. Clamp the mould halves together, squeezing out the surplus silicone

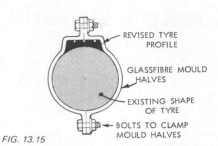

REVISED TYRE PROFILE

GLASSFIBRE MOULD HALVES

EXISTING SHAPE OF TYRE

BOLTS TO CLAMP MOULD HALVES

FIG. 13.15

rubber. It is, at the best, a hit and miss method with more than a fair chance that some of the tread will not be formed. There may well be better methods of producing some of the more exotic tyre patterns used, but apart from rotary moulding a complete tyre from an aluminium mould, it is difficult to find any alternatives.

Removing tyres from the hubs of commercial wheels can, at times, cause anguish. The use of a little warm water and washing-up liquid will make this task simpler. Making replacement scale hubs is easy if you have the use of a lathe, but without this facility or the aid of a colleague with one, you will have to adapt the existing commercial hubs. Inspect the prototype hubs and fabricate the hub caps, bolt heads etc., from plastic card, remembering to allow for the removal of the wheel at a later date, should it become necessary.

Fine detail on wheels should not be forgotten, e.g. the painted nut heads for checking whether any loosening has taken place — or castellated nuts and locking wires — white creep marks on the tyre and rims, the size and type markings on the tyre and the manufacturer's emblem on the hub cap, if fitted.

Chapter 14

Cockpit Details

To many modellers the detailing of the cockpit is one of the highlights of scale R/C model construction. For the scale competition addict it is not simply a matter of gathering extra points, although this cannot be ignored. The number of points awarded for cockpit detailing is barely commensurate with the hours of love and labour that are spent on some of the super-detailed examples to be seen. No, it isn't merely a case of winning points, it is the total fascination of finely reproducing the 'business office' of the machine being created. Everything in the cockpit is to the human scale, levers, switches, dials, all can easily be identified with. There is a completeness about a cockpit that is lacking in most other areas of the model and the builder is able, if he wishes, to scale down and reproduce *every* item involved. It is from the fact that we can imagine *ourselves* sitting in the cockpit, and flying the aircraft, that the fascination of detailing the cockpit must emanate.

There is so much more to a cockpit than a series of instrument dials on a dashboard, with a few additional levers and switches. Apart from the physical shape of all the equipment, seats, panels, there is *colour*. There may not be the strong primary colours used on some aircraft exteriors but most cockpits, apart from early aircraft, include a wide variation of colour and texture. Metal, wood,

cloth, glass, rubber, ceramics, plastics, paint, are all part and parcel of the make-up of the 'office'. It is the workroom of the aircraft and, as such, it will suffer from the knocks and scratches of usage as much, if not more, than the exterior of the aircraft. The finished cockpit interior must look inviting, it must give the feeling that if you were small enough, you could climb in, put your straps on, go through the prestart checks and fire the engine into life. No wonder so many modellers get carried away when it comes to detailing the cockpit interiors!

To be able to soak in the atmosphere of a cockpit (we have not yet found a method of reproducing the unique smell associated with cockpits) it is necessary to inspect the actual article. This may not always be possible and we will then have to rely on the evidence of photographs and drawings. Of considerable assistance, with military aircraft, are the series of reprints of Pilots' Notes covering military aircraft from about 1940 through to the 1950's. These publications have photographs and diagrams of the cockpit and, while not in colour, they form an excellent basis for the general layout. Cockpit layouts and finishes have gone from one extreme to the other during the development of aircraft. The very early aircraft featured nothing more than a wickerwork seat (or just a canvas strap or plank of wood) with one or two rudi-

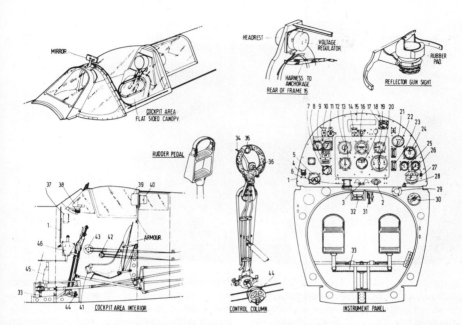

mentary engine instruments affixed to a convenient piece of fuselage framework. It was not until the first world war was well under way that instrumentation started to become regularised to any degree. At the end of the war the Gosport System of training, developed by Lt. Smith-Barry, was introduced in the R.A.F. and became the model for training pilots, military and civil, in many countries

Above, detail from the M.A.P. scale plans for a Spitfire MK.1

Right, the basic flight panel clearly identifiable on a Stampe aircraft.

A bit of history – cockpit of the four-engine 1949 Armstrong-Whitworth 'Apollo' one of the earliest turbo-prop airline projects.

throughout the world. The result of this training system was the development of a standard instrument panel leading up to the present Basic 'T' Flight Panel. On virtually any aircraft built over the past forty years you will find this standard basic flight panel, although some light aircraft may not include the artificial horizon instrument. Many smaller aircraft will have the panel fixed, and proud of, the fascia board, because it is fitted as a completed standard unit. Modern civilian aircraft can be positively 'lush' in their appointment, with deep pile carpet, expensive upholstery and plastic/cloth head linings. The effect is more comparable to a luxury limousine than an aircraft cockpit. Conversely, the interior of the cockpit of a modern military jet appears to be nothing more than an ejector seat surrounded by myriads of instruments, screens, switches, knobs and dials. The sophistication of modern electronics, communications and guidance systems, computers, etc., have made the cockpit of today's jets a cross between a Grand Prix racing car and a computer programming control panel. The civilian airline flight deck is little different, very utilitarian with instruments and controls on the floor, the sides, the front and the ceiling. Even the 'Jumbo' aircraft have deceptively small flight deck areas to allow immediate access to all instruments. About the only common features between the very early aircraft and modern ones are the control column and the rudder pedals. The control column may have developed from the simple 'pole' (still used on some light aircraft) to the two-hand grip now used, but the basic operation remains the same.

At some point, preferably at the beginning, we must decide just how far we are going in the art of deception with the cockpit interior. Are we going to be satisfied with a 'stand-off' scale representation of instruments, seats, etc., or perhaps no internal detail at all, or are we aiming for as near perfection as possible? In modelling terms 'near perfection' means a vast amount of detailing with numerous 'working' instruments. To give an example, Mick Reeves with his World Championship winning Fournier RF4 included the following 'working' instrumentation:- air speed indicator, altimeter, vertical speed indicator, R.P.M. and oil pressure gauge, stall warning lights, choke (operating receiver on/off switch) temperature gauge, magnetic compass, elevator trimmer and a genuine working communications receiver and headphones. That does not leave an awful lot of instrumentation left on the Fournier which does not move, light up or make a sound. Heaven help us if they ever devise sub-subminiature gyros and switches as Mick will no doubt be using these to operate all of the functions. Micro-chip and micro-processor developments will also be of interest to such fastidious scale innovators!

The probability is that you will commence with intentions of making a reasonable job of the cockpit area, but without *too* much detail. As you get embroiled in the intricacies of making the miniature instruments and components the sheer fascination of the project will lead you to elaborate to ever-increasing complexities. It should be remembered that the cockpit detail will almost certainly affect the basic structure of the model and this must be allowed for at the initial planning stage. The wise man will err on the cautious side and assume that full detailing of the cockpit may be undertaken as his enthusiasm for the work increases. Weight is still our enemy and we must be aware of it, but even the most complete of cockpit interiors does not have to add excessive weight, providing the materials are sensibly selected.

Drawing the whole of the cockpit area accurately to scale is every bit as important as the remainder of the aircraft for the super scale model. Side views, plan views, sections and isometric sketches showing the position and shapes of all equipment must be drawn at the initial planning stages and incorporated with the model structure. Individual detail drawings of isolated instruments and equipment, e.g. compass and emergency packs, will be necessary, and don't forget the items that the pilot takes on board separately – maps, log books, holdall, etc. It will quickly become obvious during the planning stage that it will be impossible to complete the basic model airframe and add all of the cockpit detail later. Most of the work will have to be built in as the construction of the model proceeds and the interior will be virtually complete before the exterior finishes are applied. This need not present problems providing we thoroughly protect the cockpit area with card, polythene sheet and masking tape, to prevent any risk of the ingress of dust and spray. There is an added psychological advantage in working on the cockpit area midway through the whole project. It gives us a spur to carry on and complete the model, at a time when our spirits may be flagging, when we begin to see some actual results from all of our hard labour.

Apart from the upholstered surfaces, window curtains, padded fascias, head-linings and the like, the materials and surfaces of a cockpit interior all tend to be of a 'hard' finish. This applies not only to the instruments and equipment but also to the visible bulkheads, stringers, metal panels and skinning. About the only exception is where the rear face of the external linen covering of the aircraft is visible from the interior. If we are using basic modelling materials such as balsa and ply for simulating the interior surfaces of the structure we must be most careful to prime and finish these materials to a smooth, 'sharp' standard to give a true scale finish effect. It will probably be easier and more convenient if we can mask the balsa construction with thin plastic card and use such materials as plastic straws and tubing to represent the structural members. Plastic sections, tube, angles, channels and rectangular section tube are used by railway model enthusiasts and have many applications for cockpit interiors – they can be obtained from good hobby stores. Watching weight is important at this stage as this is the point that excessive weight can build up. Paint the interior structure of the cockpit as you go – it will be difficult to get to many areas when other detailed items are fixed in position. As previously mentioned, the cockpit receives its fair share of abuse from the pilot's shoes – or boots – and the attention of the engineers during aircraft maintenance. To show these scratch and 'scuff' marks will make the cockpit interior 'live'. Where aluminium or dural is the base material the wood, or plastic, should be painted first with a silver metallic cellulose paint. On top of that we can paint the required cockpit interior colour which was often a grey/green or grey. The 'wear' marks can be simulated by scratching through the surface paint to the base paint. Use contrasting types of paint, i.e. oil paint on cellulose (but not the other way round) for this purpose as the bond between the different colours will be less integrated than may be the case with paints of a similar composition. Plywood floors were used in earlier prototypes and these are reproduced by using varnished thin ply sheet. Sand away the varnish where the floor would receive the heaviest wear. Aluminium sheet flooring was often patterned to improve the strength and wearing

qualities. The patterns can be simulated with vacuum formed plastic sheet, painted, or by scoring thin aluminium sheet – rub a little black paint into the score lines for 'dirtying'. Chequer or ribbed patterns were the most frequently used on aluminium floor patterns.

Seats for the pilot and crew are an essential part of the comfort necessary for efficiency but they are also designed for lightness. From the early 'Lloydloom' wickerwork seats to the aluminium bucket seats of piston engined fighters and, though they may not give that appearance, through to ejector seats – all are designed to minimum weight specifications. Wickerwork and cane chairs and seats of the 'early birds' can only be copied by using similar materials, and patterns to the scale required. It may be possible to enlist the help of a cane-work enthusiast for this project. Bucket seats came into use from W.W.1 onwards and miniature duplicates of these are easily formed from cardboard or thin aluminium. The seat pattern will depend on whether a back pack parachute was used or one in the form of a seat cushion. See Fig. 14.2. Ejection seats are fabricated from card, ply and balsa – a nice complex detailing job, particularly if you include all of the transferred notices. No doubt some over-zealous modeller will include a fully operational ejection seat in a model and use it as one of his competition optional extras! Modern upholstered seats can be constructed from close density foam (blue foam) carved, sanded and painted, or from foam covered with cloth or leather material. For a 'velour' finish try spraying the plastic with a 'flock' spray – the same type of finish as seen on wallpapers in Chinese restaurants. For a leather finish pick one of the simulated leather fabric-backed plastics. Peel away

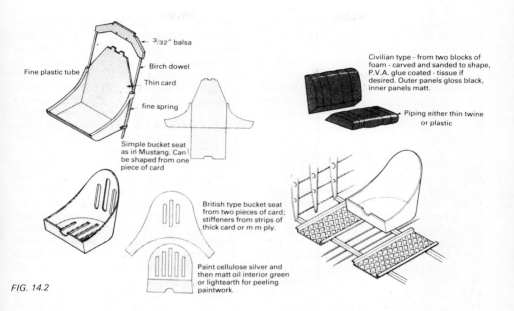

Fine plastic tube

3/32" balsa

Birch dowel

Thin card

fine spring

Simple bucket seat as in Mustang. Can be shaped from one piece of card

British type bucket seat from two pieces of card; stiffeners from strips of thick card or m m ply.

Civilian type - from two blocks of foam - carved and sanded to shape, P.V.A. glue coated - tissue if desired. Outer panels gloss black, inner panels matt.

Piping either thin twine or plastic

Paint cellulose silver and then matt oil interior green or lightearth for peeling paintwork.

FIG. 14.2

the cloth layer and you will have a thin and very pliable 'leather' material that retains the graining and mottled effect. P.V.A. or Copydex adhesive can be used for glueing the covering materials, including cloth, to foam, but check on scrap material before attempting to use any other glues. Corduroy covering can be scaled down by the use of a needle-cord material and the edged piping is imitated by the use of a thin plastic cord or tube to the appropriate colour. You will have to search through the drapery department for suitable material for safety harness belting material although flat shoe laces will suffice in some instances — and they are available in a wide range of colours. Buckles are fabricated from aluminium sheet anodised, as described in Chapter 5, or painted with lacquer coloured with blue Dylon dye. Where a full harness was employed

the strap fixing method must be duplicated. For Sutton harness eyeleted holes in the belt, a small rivet with a hole at the end and a split pin is all that is required. Later auto-lock fasteners will need spring loaded ball catches or a permanently fixed harness on to the model pilot. With a dual control aircraft with only one pilot aboard the spare harness straps were usually tied together in the empty seat to prevent them from swinging loose and the risk of them jamming some control system. Side panels of the cockpit area are often covered with fabric on civil aircraft and vinyl wallpaper can be used to simulate this material — the backing paper may be removed, by soaking in water, to give a 'softer' appearance. On the occasions when a quilted or 'buttoned' effect was used we must back the covering material with foam and card to achieve the right model appearance.

At the position of the buttons sew through the material, foam and card, and pull the thread tight. This will form the quilted effect and the thread should be covered with an appropriately coloured and sized 'button'. Headlinings, as with cars, are normally stuck to projecting structural members and not to an overall flat surface. To achieve compound curves it is necessary to sew, or in our case, glue or welt the panels together before fixing in position. Use thin card to make templates for the sizes of fabric – actual car roof lining material can also be used. Light public transport aircraft of the inter-war period sometimes fitted anti-sunglare thin curtains to the windows for the benefit of their customers. The curtains were fixed to an expanding rail top and bottom and could be opened or closed horizontally to reduce the glare of the sun. Modelling lightweight nylon, dyed light cream, can be used for the material, fitted to piano wire rods – they always look more effective in the open, concertina,

position. On more modern aircraft the pilot may have the benefit of a coloured Perspex anti-glare visor fitted just above the windscreen. If you can't find any thin Perspex (about 1/32 in.) use thick butyrate sheet and paint it with tinted lacquer – it must be applied very evenly or a streaky appearance will result. Operating door hinges can present a few problems; the extended hinges are best represented by using ply or paxolin hinge leaves with a pin pivot. Piano type hinges can be purpose made – see Chapter 15 – or small commercial leaf and pin hinges can be strung together on a long piano wire hinge, to form a continuous hinge. Safety and first aid packs, dinghy packs, etc., can be made from thin close woven fabric of the appropriate colour. Make the seams external, with the correct fabric side internal, turn inside out and stuff with kapok filling. Secure in position with thin strips of Velcro nylon fastening and inscribe with the instructions and notification emblems.

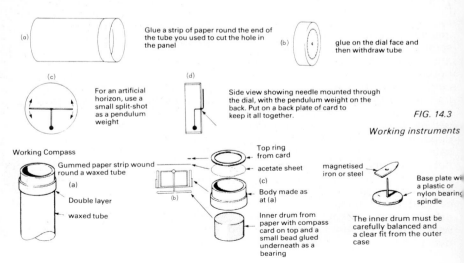

(a)

Glue a strip of paper round the end of the tube you used to cut the hole in the panel

(b) glue on the dial face and then withdraw tube

(c) For an artificial horizon, use a small split-shot as a pendulum weight

(d) Side view showing needle mounted through the dial, with the pendulum weight on the back. Put on a back plate of card to keep it all together.

FIG. 14.3

Working instruments

Working Compass

Gummed paper strip wound round a waxed tube

(a)

Double layer

waxed tube

(b)

Top ring from card

acetate sheet

(c)

Body made as at (a)

Inner drum from paper with compass card on top and a small bead glued underneath as a bearing

magnetised iron or steel

Base plate with a plastic or nylon bearing spindle

The inner drum must be carefully balanced and a clear fit from the outer case

Now for the most impressive part of the cockpit – the instrument panel. Many an excellent scale model has been spoiled by two basic errors on instrument panels.

1. The instruments have been given white faces with black lettering and numerals. Except for instruments on early aircraft the faces are almost invariably black:

2. The lack of 'depth' of instruments caused by the face being glued direct to the fascia.

If you add to these mistakes the lack of colour on instruments, such as red warning quadrants, for speed and temperature limitations, and yellow oil pressure gauges, plus incorrectly shaped or coloured bezels, you cover the majority of errors. Whether the instruments are made to operate or not (see Fig 14.4 for examples) the instruments should have 'depth' and this perception will be enhanced by the use of separate indicator needles.

Drawing the instruments to scale size, on black card, or with a needle and sharp pointed knife on black scraper board, is feasible on the larger scale models (¹/₅th and above). It does call for a lot of patience and care and the process will be made a little easier if a magnifying glass is used. A fluorescent paint is often used for the numbering on the black instrument face and this can be simulated by using a light grey/green paint applied by a *very* fine brush. If you have ever attempted to write the Lord's prayer on the back of a postage stamp you should be good at this small writing work. A much easier, if more costly, method of producing instrument faces involves a photographic process. The sequence to follow is:-

a. Draw the instrument face on white card in indian ink. Use a Rapidograph pen, compasses, Letraset and any aids that will make your work easier. Mistakes can be rectified by 'whiting' out with a liquid typing eraser. The size of the drawing can vary from full size (for ¼ scale and above) to three times the required size for smaller scales. Mark a dimensioned scale (the actual scale you require) on the side of the drawing to give the photographer a check measurement to work from:

b. Draw all of the instruments you will require to the same scale and mount them on a single piece of card – it is usually cheaper if the photographer is working from one piece of material:

c. Take your art work to the photographer and tell him that you require reversed black and white negatives, reduced to the appropriate scale, and prints from them on matt paper.

The results are extremely effective and any minor irregularities on the original art work are barely noticeable on the

(a) Instrument face drawn 3X scale size in black ink on white card. Draw a 3-inch line down the side of the card.

(b) Reverse negative. The black and white areas are the same as the drawing – unlike an ordinary negative where the tones would be reversed.

(c) On the final print the tones are reversed as we wish them to be. Note the line on the right – this will be 1 inch on the print.

(d) Draw all instruments on one card. The single one here is for illustration only.

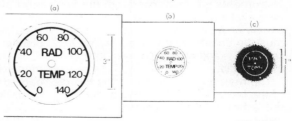

FIG. 14.4

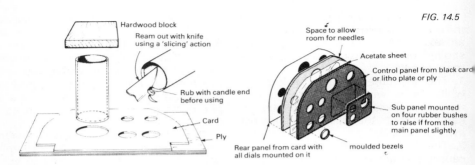

FIG. 14.5

Hardwood block
Ream out with knife using a 'slicing' action
Rub with candle end before using
Card
Ply

Space to allow room for needles
Acetate sheet
Control panel from black card or litho plate or ply
Sub panel mounted on four rubber bushes to raise if from the main panel slightly
moulded bezels
Rear panel from card with all dials mounted on it

reduced sizes. Of course, if you have a camera and enlarger you can have a go at doing the photographic work yourself, using a suitable reverse negative film and using the enlarger to adjust for the correct scale at the printing stage.

Printed commercial instrument faces are available in some of the 'standard' scales, e.g. $\frac{1}{6}$th and $\frac{1}{4}$ scale, and are usually sufficiently comprehensive to make a full instrument panel for most modern light aircraft models. With both the printed instrument faces and those produced photographically, the lettering, numbers and warning quadrants will be white. To obtain the fluorescent green colour a pale green spirit based felt pen can be 'brushed' over the digits. Don't overdo this colouring as the full size instruments are not glaringly green – wipe off the surplus green colour with a soft damp cloth. So, now we have the instruments we must construct the full fascia taking careful note of any sub-panels or panel joints. Separate panels must be constructed in just that way – separate – and attached, or let into, the main fascia.

The method of building up the layers of the fascia board is shown in Fig 14.5 but a few additional comments are in order.

1. The fascia panel and spacer must be identically cut. The holes may be cut by using spring-bow dividers (using one sharpened point for cutting the plastic card) or by punching the holes with a piece of sharpened brass tube. Cutting with the dividers offers a larger variety of hole diameters but limits you to working with a plastic material that is not too thick – you do not have to penetrate the plastic completely, heavy scribing is sufficient to allow the circle to be pushed out:

2. The internal edges of the holes should be painted matt black:

3. Instrument needles and pointers can be made from wire, plastic or thin aluminium and should be painted with the light grey/green 'fluorescent' paint:

4. The fascia should be finished to match the original. It may be matt black 'crackle' finish – use black Hammerite paint. Vinyl – use vinyl wallpaper. Aluminium – use litho plate or thin aluminium. Polished wood – use a suitable veneer or Contact simulated wood grain self adhesive plastic:

5. If you want to use working instruments you will have to allow for space behind the rear panel for the mechanical operation:

6. Bezels (instrument surrounds) must be the correct shape and size and the best method to date was developed by

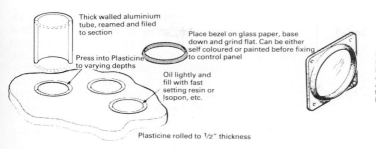

Thick walled aluminium tube, reamed and filed to section

Press into Plasticine to varying depths

Place bezel on glass paper, base down and grind flat. Can be either self coloured or painted before fixing to control panel

Oil lightly and fill with fast setting resin or Isopon, etc.

Some instruments are mounted so. The bezel is glued to a square of acetate and the bezel and the surround is then painted black, leaving the centre clear.

Plasticine rolled to ½" thickness

FIG. 14.6

Pete Ashmore and has been used successfully by David Vaughan on some of his superb models.

Start by rolling out a piece of Plasticine to about half an inch thickness. Sort out some thick wall metal tubing to the correct diameter of the bezel, aluminium or alloy is best, and ream and file it to the section of the bezel. Smear the edge of the tube with P.V.A. liquid *release* agent and make impressions in the Plasticine – of various experimental depths. Glass fibre resin can be coloured before filling the grooves or an aluminium filled epoxy can be used for producing the bezels. When the mouldings have fully cured, leave to set really hard, remove them from the Plasticine and sand the rear face flat on abrasive paper. This method can be used to make any kind of bezel including, in combination with plastic card, some of the military versions.

Reproducing the small aluminium instructional panel can only be done professionally by one method. Their size, to anything less than ¼ scale, is so small on the model that it is impossible to draw on the lettering to produce anything more than a 'squiggle'. The best way is to again use the photographic method described earlier but to substitute photo-sensitive thin aluminium

Championship Cup winner at a recent Model Engineer Exhibition was this D.H. 82a Tiger Moth by R.A. Chivrall.

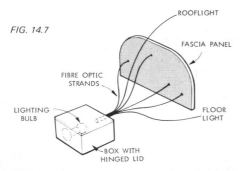

FIG. 14.7

ROOFLIGHT

FASCIA PANEL

FIBRE OPTIC
STRANDS

LIGHTING
BULB

FLOOR
LIGHT

BOX WITH
HINGED LID

sheet for the normal printing paper. When the correct exposure time for the plate is found, by trial and error, the aluminium is treated with the activator solution and the wording and edges will turn black. Original art work, because it is small, should be drawn to full size making use of Letraset or similar dry transfer lettering. Whether you have a standard reduced negative or a reversed negative will depend on whether the label lettering is silver on a black background or vice versa.

A slight bit of 'one-upmanship' can be indulged in with the use of fibre optics – the stranded glass used, amongst other things, for decorative table lamps. The ability of the light rays to follow the path of the fibre optics allows them to be used for fascia panel lights, roof lights, etc., with a single light source. See Fig. 14.7.

The coaming used around the cockpit edges of open cockpit aircraft was fitted

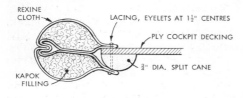

REXINE
CLOTH

LACING, EYELETS AT 1½" CENTRES

PLY COCKPIT DECKING

¾" DIA. SPLIT CANE

KAPOK
FILLING

FIG. 14.8

as crash protection for the pilot. Not all occupants were so fortunate and some prototype examples feature cockpit edges that were only reinforced with plywood and the edges wired together. To construct a typical bound leather coaming it is necessary to understand the constructional method employed on the prototype. A scale section of a Sopwith *Pup* coaming is shown in Fig. 14.8. A simplified leather coaming, suitable for average sized scale models, can be made by using a 2 inch wide vinyl 'leather' strip, cut about 3 inches longer than the total length required. Take a piece of thick cord and apply contact adhesive to the cord (use a piece of cloth impregnated with adhesive and pull the cord through it) and to the reverse side of the vinyl. Fold the vinyl over the cord and form the welt and trim the long edge to the scale width. Pin the coaming temporarily into position on the fuselage, trim the edges to length and mark the lacing hole positions. When you are satisfied with the fit of the coaming, glue in position using contact or cyanoacrylate adhesive. Drill the lacing hole positions to size to fit the smallest eyelets that you can obtain, or to scale size for the larger scale models. Clinching the ends of the eyelets can be difficult and you may find it easier to cut the eyelets to length first, or use a short eyelet. The coaming is finished by lacing with a suitable cord to the correct pattern.

Fixing curved windscreens to open cockpit aircraft often seems to create problems of fixing the windscreen *permanently* to the fuselage decking. Try the following method and you are unlikely to have a failure – see Fig. 14.9. Commence by taping a piece of thin card, ply or plastic card to the decking in the position of the windscreen, but overlapping all the way round. Cut a card

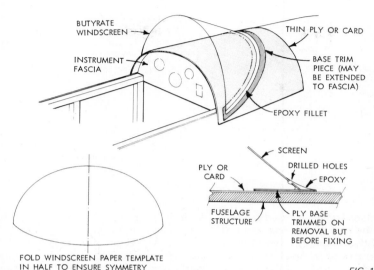

BUTYRATE WINDSCREEN

INSTRUMENT FASCIA

THIN PLY OR CARD

BASE TRIM PIECE (MAY BE EXTENDED TO FASCIA)

EPOXY FILLET

SCREEN

PLY OR CARD

DRILLED HOLES

EPOXY

FUSELAGE STRUCTURE

PLY BASE TRIMMED ON REMOVAL BUT BEFORE FIXING

FOLD WINDSCREEN PAPER TEMPLATE IN HALF TO ENSURE SYMMETRY

FIG. 14.9

template of the windscreen until you have the correct shape and fit. The template can be folded down the vertical centre line to check for symmetry. Cut the actual windscreen from a thick butyrate – a thin flexible windscreen never looks right as the thickness of the full-size screens is often in excess of $\frac{1}{8}$ in. Drill small holes around the periphery of the base of the screen and tack glue the screen to the card or ply-wood fitted to the fuselage. Cut a wind-screen base trimming piece, try for fit and mask the screen immediately above with tape. Apply the fillet, using slow drying epoxy so that the epoxy squeezes out slightly through the holes drilled in the windscreen – these will appear as rivet heads. Smooth the outside of the epoxy between the rim and the base with a dampened cloth to form a fillet. When the assembly is thoroughly set – leave for at least a day – remove from the fuselage and trim the front to the fillet line and the rear to coincide with the

cockpit opening. The top inside of the windscreen decking can now be painted – usually matt black – and any other detail applied (external rivets, wind-screen edging) before the assembly is finally glued to the fuselage.

Canopies come in so many different styles that one single method cannot be adopted for all types. 'Bubble' canopies must obviously be moulded, there is no alternative, but many earlier examples were constructed from straight or simple curvature screens fitted in metal frames. As soon as we meet a screen with a compound curvature then moulding is the only answer. One of the first decisions that must be made is whether or not to make the cockpit an opening type or permanently closed. Assuredly, if you have spent many hours detailing the cockpit interior, you will want the benefit of taking a closer, clearer look at the craftsmanship inside and an opening canopy will be featured. There are two basic types of cockpit access, the hinged

207

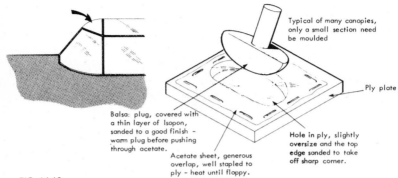

Typical of many canopies, only a small section need be moulded

Ply plate

Balsa: plug, covered with a thin layer of Isopon, sanded to a good finish – warm plug before pushing through acetate.

Hole in ply, slightly oversize and the top edge sanded to take off sharp corner.

Acetate sheet, generous overlap, well stapled to ply – heat until floppy.

FIG. 14.10

and the sliding canopies. Hinged canopy sections are the easiest to construct but have the disadvantages of being rather too flexible in the open position unless the framework is reinforced with ply, metal or glass fibre and carbon fibre. The aim must always be to keep this reinforcing as light – in visual terms – as possible or the illusion of a light structural framework will be lost. Hinges will be of the continuous piano type or individual flap hinges. More difficult to simulate are the canopy catches which are operated on the full size aircraft from the interior. Ball catches can be fabricated from brass tube, ball bearings and miniature springs, but these tend not to be too positive in fixing. It is also possible to include 'over square' type of springing to the cockpit although it is difficult to hide this from view, and the airflow effect over the canopy may tend to lift the hinged parts against the springs. If it is feasible to incorporate a piano wire rod, to locate with brass or aluminium tubes on the hinged part, this will provide a good positive security of the canopy hatch, but the end of the wire must be accessible and not too obvious. Canopy hatches are frequently restrained in the open position by a length of lightweight brass or chrome finished chain. The fine chain used on cheap jewellery is excellent for reproduction of this item.

When it comes to the construction of operating sliding canopies the first essential is accurately to draw and position the scale sliding rail positions. Unless these are to the correct dimensions it is unlikely that you will be successful in achieving a smooth operation of the sliding canopy or hood. The acknowledged master of this intricate and fascinating work is undoubtedly David Vaughan and it would seem pointless to do other than quote from one of his articles on the subject.

"Because of the limitations of home moulding I rarely make a canopy in one

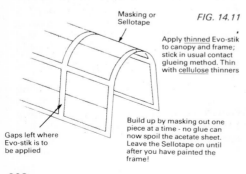

Masking or Sellotape

FIG. 14.11

Apply thinned Evo-stik to canopy and frame; stick in usual contact glueing method. Thin with cellulose thinners

Build up by masking out one piece at a time - no glue can now spoil the acetate sheet. Leave the Sellotape on until after you have painted the frame!

Gaps left where Evo-stik is to be applied

piece. Fortunately, it is often possible to restrict the moulding to just one section between frames, using the old plug and hole method. The rest of the canopy can then be made in sheet acetate. (Fig. 14.10).

Frames look better added as strips rather than moulded in. I have tried card, but it does not stand up to wear and washing very well. Strips of acetate sheet, scored against a straight edge and cracked off and then pulled through a fold of glasspaper, works very well.

To glue the strips in position I use thinned-down contact adhesive. It can be a messy business, but this can be overcome in the following way.

Mask out all the canopy except for the strips where the frame will go. Now all you need to do is apply the glue, nothing can now mar the rest of the acetate sheet. I would leave the tape on until the model is finished in fact. (Fig. 14.11).

The only snag with acetate sheet is that constant cleaning does wear the paint off. Best of all is to use thin aluminium. Its malleability makes it easy to form yet it is stiff enough to hold acetate sheet in shape, very useful where sliding canopies are concerned. Of

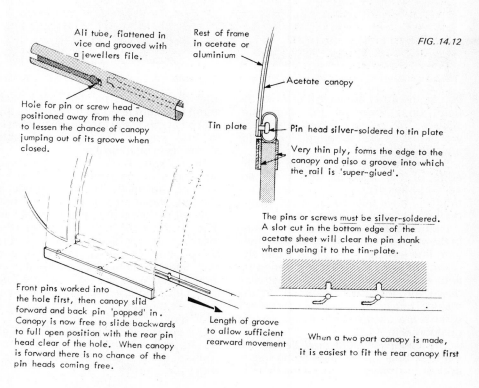

Ali tube, flattened in vice and grooved with a jewellers file.

Hole for pin or screw head - positioned away from the end to lessen the chance of canopy jumping out of its groove when closed.

Front pins worked into the hole first, then canopy slid forward and back pin 'popped' in. Canopy is now free to slide backwards to full open position with the rear pin head clear of the hole. When canopy is forward there is no chance of the pin heads coming free.

Length of groove to allow sufficient rearward movement

Rest of frame in acetate or aluminium

Acetate canopy

Tin plate

Pin head silver-soldered to tin plate

Very thin ply, forms the edge to the canopy and also a groove into which the rail is 'super-glued'.

The pins or screws must be silver-soldered. A slot cut in the bottom edge of the acetate sheet will clear the pin shank when glueing it to the tin-plate.

FIG. 14.12

When a two part canopy is made, it is easiest to fit the rear canopy first

The front of David Vaughan's 'Wirraway' is remarkably convincing.

course the other bonus is that when the paint does wear off the aluminium shows. The contact adhesive method works just as well for aluminium as for anything else.

Sliding rails have to be built into the edge of the fuselage and there are several ways of going about this. For the models I have built so far the following method has proved to work well.

I squeeze a length of aluminium tube in the vice to make it flat-sided and then, with fine jeweller's files, I cut a thin slot down the side. The slot is cleaned up with a scalpel until a pin will just slide down the tube with its head on the inside. Then either pins or watchmaker's screws are used to hold the canopy in position. (Fig. 14.12).

The canopy should now be on and painted, only a few units being left to add. Some may prefer to put the detail in after the model is painted, but I must admit that I am tempted to complete the cockpit at this stage for it leads to what is for me one of the most enjoyable moments in building a model.

The cockpit area is completely masked out and also the wing seating, so no paint can get inside. The whole model is painted, weathered and fuel-proofed. Now for the great moment. Using a hair dryer to soften the hold of the tape all the masking is removed. Suddenly the cockpit interior comes into view, and seen against the finished model, it is as though you were seeing it for the first time. Once more, with shaky fingers, you put it all together and settle down to a good gloat."

Our cockpit is, as yet, incomplete as we are still missing one vital piece of equipment – the pilot! This will be dealt with in Chapter 19.

Chapter 15

Covering

There are many methods of preparing, covering and decorating a scale R/C model and no one method is ideal for all subjects. The method you select for covering will have to relate to the size of the model, the amount of use it will get, the amount of time you have to spend and the degree of experimenting you are prepared to do. Regardless of the covering and finishing methods you adopt one thing is certain – the final result will only be as good as the initial construction and preparation. If you have an airframe with dents, gaps, low spots, high spots or any other blemishes, these, sooner or later, will show through on the finished surface. Any covering method will require a certain amount of learning of the techniques and skills involved. Don't get too upset if your first effort with a new material or method is less than perfect, remove the sub-standard area of covering and try again. Often the method is blamed by the modeller where the fault really lies with the lack of technique in applying the covering.

The basic covering materials and methods can be summarised as follows:-
A. Tissue and paint:
B. Nylon, or silk, and paint:
C. Tissue plus silk, or nylon chiffon:
D. Heat-sensitive plastic, polymer coverings:
E. Solartex or similar heat-sensitive fabric materials, with or without paint finish:
F. Resin, on sheeted surfaces, and paint.

There are other forms, or combinations of covering but these cover the principal types. They all have some advantages and some limitations and it is important to realise the merits and disadvantages of each type before selecting the method of covering.

A. TISSUE

Tissue, in the form of light or heavyweight tissue should only be used on *open* structures for very small scale models and where weight limitations are critical, e.g. tail surfaces of short nosed scale designs. The more common use of tissue covering, in lightweight, is for covering fully sheeted surfaces. One of the main advantages, albeit a somewhat negative virtue, is the repairability of a tissue covered structure after a crash. The limited strength of the covering allows the superstructure to break away and rapidly dissipate the energy generated in the crash. It has often been possible for a modeller to crash a model severely on the first flight of a competition, collect the pieces – *every* little piece – glue the bits together again as one would with a puzzle, and fly the model in the same competition. This is not recommended as a standard practice, but in an emergency situation and with the use of cyanoacrylate adhesives, it is possible. With stronger covering such as nylon, one tends to finish up with a complete nylon bag filled with a selection of broken pieces of the structure.

When the structure is complete, inspect it for any glue 'blobs' that may be proud of the surface and remove them with a sharp knife. Failure to do this may result, during the sanding phase, in the 'blobs' coming adrift, rolling under the sanding block and scoring the surface. Sand the surface to a smooth finish, working from a medium grit paper to a fine abrasive paper. The use of sanding blocks for all general sanding is of the utmost importance for a level, consistent surface. Curved areas may, where it is *impossible* to use a sanding block, be sanded with the paper in the *palm* of your hand. Do not use your fingers for supporting the abrasive paper as they are too flexible and will merely 'ride' over the high spots or harder surfaces of the wood. Clean down the sanded structure and inspect again for imperfections. Bruised or dented areas of balsa can first be treated by dampening them with

water. This action will cause the bruised fibres of the wood to swell to their original size and the area may be resanded when it has dried. For other holes and cracks, e.g. sheeting or planking joints, rib to trailing edge joints etc., the depressions must be filled and the area resanded. For filling we can use:-

1. Polyfilla (internal type) or Tetrion. These D.I.Y. materials are very suitable for model filling purposes as they sand easily and are not too heavy – although there should *not* be any large areas to fill. The bond strength to balsa is quite reasonable but not good enough for thin shallow depressions where the material may break away:

2. Resin and 'micro-balloons'. Not quite so easy to sand, and slightly heavier than some fillers, but gives a better bond and can be used for small, thin, areas:

3. Bonda Filler S.L.

4. Vinyl fillers. Good general fillers but not readily available and may not be compatible with some resin finishes.

An unusual subject, the Pomilio P1 WWI reconnaissance machine, built by Graham Smith. Note scalloped trailing edges and light rigging.

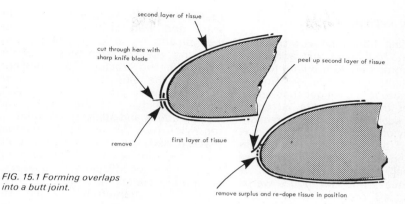

second layer of tissue

cut through here with
sharp knife blade

peel up second layer of tissue

remove

first layer of tissue

*FIG. 15.1 Forming overlaps
into a butt joint.*

remove surplus and re-dope tissue in position

Always leave the fillers to dry thoroughly before the final sanding and build up layers if shrinking takes place — it is wise to slightly overfill a hole or gap with filler to allow for some shrinkage. The preparation of the model to this stage is the same regardless of the type of covering to be employed. Cleaning down the structure after final sanding is best carried out with a compressed air jet, as this will dislodge any loose particles, but be careful to protect the eyes. A 'tackyrag' (3M manufacture or similar) is also a good method for removing loose debris from the structure. To return to the tissue covering —

The raw balsa surface must first be sealed by applying two or three coats of sanding sealer and sanding smooth with fine abrasive paper between each coat until a perfect satin smooth finish is obtained. The sealer may be the traditional dope and talcum powder, a car paint sealer or an epoxy filler. Epoxy fillers have the advantage of being non-shrink, flexible and durable but they are a little harder to sand. Apply to the smoothed sealer one coat of thinned (75% dope, 25% thinners) dope over the complete structure. The tissue is applied damp, in manageable panel sizes, e.g. one wing half top, and brushed on to the surface with clear dope. Wrinkles can be smoothed out by rubbing the area with a pad of tissue with a long stroking action. Compound curves must be covered in smaller sections with overlaps; cut down the centre of the overlap with a sharp razor blade and peel away the two loose strips of tissue — an accurate smooth butt joint will result. Take care not to get any air traps under the tissue. If it is impossible to remove them by brushing, remove the tissue and start again — there is nothing worse than the small 'blebs' caused by trapped air pockets on the finished surfaces. Sand lightly when the tissued structure has dried and apply a further coat of dope to any joint areas. Re-sand these parts only to remove any tissue 'fuzz'. Follow with two or three thinned coats of filler sanding with decreasingly abrasive paper and you should finish up with a superb surface that is ready for decorating. Apart from the advantages in repair, the tissue method is relatively cheap and light, providing your sanding has been efficient.

B. NYLON AND SILK

Silk is, in fact, little used as a covering material due to its high cost, and lower strength, compared with nylon. It does have a slight advantage on smaller models where it is stronger than tissue and lighter than nylon. For all open-structured scale R/C models of reasonable size nylon should be considered as the first of the alternatives. Its great strength and scale surface finish makes it an ideal material although it is relatively heavy and can induce warps unless applied correctly. Commercial modelling nylons, particularly the super-fine variety, are suitable for our purposes, but if you wish to buy the material from a market stall or a store, select material of about 1oz/square foot weight with a close texture weave. Open weave materials require too much dope to fill the pores and this adds considerably to the overall weight. Nylon can be dyed (Dylon dyes or similar) which is an advantage for early aircraft that used natural linen finishes – a light creamy buff colour will simulate the doped linen.

Two coats of full strength dope are applied to the structure to be covered and after complete drying (say, 24 hours) the surface is sanded smooth. Pay particular attention to the areas where dope may have built up, e.g. wing rib/leading edge, and take care not to catch vulnerable parts during the sanding, e.g. ribs and projecting formers. Nylon should be applied damp, soaking the nylon, squeezing it out and leaving to semi-dry to an even dampness. If the nylon tends to dry out too much during the covering of a large panel, it can be kept damp by lightly spraying with water. Dope is used as the adhesive for attaching the nylon to the structure and it is brushed through the nylon to fuse with the dope applied to the structure. Keep a check on the warp and weft of the material (the weave) and try to keep it straight by covering with an even tension of the nylon over the structure. Apply one end first, e.g. the wing root, pull the nylon taut lengthwise and stick the tip end. Stretch the nylon to the leading and trailing edges and adjust the position of the nylon (use thinners to lift material that is already secured) until it is smooth and free from wrinkles. The covering technique is not difficult, nylon adapts to compound curves very well, but may need a few attempts before first rate results are achieved – practise on the sports model first.

Nylon will only tauten once and this, in the case of covering with damp nylon, is at the initial covering stage. If, when the nylon has dried, the covering is not taut the chances of dope further tightening the material are minimal. Where wrinkles are evident the nylon should be removed and the area recovered, otherwise disappointment will result. The doping stage is the dangerous one for warps, and every care must be taken to avoid them 'creeping in' as the layers of dope dry. This is most important on wings with a thin aerofoil section where the torsional strength is low. To reduce the danger of warping we must dope the top and bottom surfaces concurrently and pin, or weight, the surfaces down during the drying period. After the final coat of dope has been applied the wing and tail surfaces should be held down for a minimum period of four days. The longer we can leave the surfaces held in their correct position the higher the chances of maintaining them warp free for the rest of their life.

Three or four coats of slightly thinned dope will probably be required to fill the surface pores of the nylon. Applying the

Simulation of the all-metal surface of this Tempest V is first class. It really could be a photo of a full-size aeroplane.

first coat is the most tricky as the dope tends to be brushed through the top surface to collect in a 'pool' on the underside. If this does happen hold the offending area above your head, facing down, and brush thinners over the area — this will draw the dope out to the top surface again where it can be brushed away. To overcome the risk of this happening entirely the first coat of dope can be sprayed on; the dope will only adhere to the warp and weft of the material but a light brushing with thinners will spread the dope over the pores and result in an even coating of dope. To check the porosity of the covering after doping try blowing cigarette smoke through the surfaces. If the smoke penetrates the surface a further coat of dope is required. It will sometimes be obvious after one or two coats of clear dope (full strength 'glider' dope should be used for nylon) that the covering is already very taut. Further applications of tautening dope may distort the structure and a non-tautening dope should be used instead. This type of dope is not readily available at model shops but it can be purchased at aerodromes that specialise in maintenance and repair of light aircraft. Failing that, a few drops of castor oil in a pint of clear dope will act as a

plasticiser and prevent overtautening.

For sports scale designs, where the model is likely to get a fair amount of rough usage, nylon covering is particularly recommended for both open and sheeted structures.

C. TISSUE PLUS SILK, OR NYLON CHIFFON

The purpose of applying silk, or nylon chiffon, to a tissue covered aircraft is to achieve a better strength/weight ratio than either of the materials have on their own. It will still not be as strong as standard nylon covering but it will be lighter and retain the authentic scale weave of the fabric covered prototypes. Covering with tissue is carried out exactly as previously described for *open* structures and the silk or nylon chiffon is applied *dry* to the tissue. Silk is, again, used very little because of the cost factor, but nylon chiffon (used for lightweight ladies' scarves) is a reasonable alternative although not so easy to apply. Iron the chiffon before using it to remove any creases. Cut an inch or so oversize and smooth over the area to be covered until it is as tight to the tissue as possible. Starting in the centre of the panel, brush with a soft sable mop brush thinned dope on to the chiffon and continue to brush outwards towards the edges. The important factor is to keep the material smooth and to avoid air traps – work slowly and methodically and try not to get the chiffon in a 'bunched-up' state. Keep overlaps to a minimum and trim them neatly. Only use *very* sharp scissors for cutting nylon chiffon or silk otherwise you will get into a terrible mess. When the model is covered in the chiffon only one further coat of dope is likely to be needed – we are not trying to fill the pores, simply reinforcing the tissue to prevent it splitting.

D. HEAT-SENSITIVE PLASTIC COVERING

Plastic film coverings of the 'Solarfilm', 'Monokote', types have become very popular with modellers over the past decade. Their virtues of speed, cleanliness, lack of smell, economy and self-finished surface are well known and appreciated by the sports modeller. For the serious scale modeller the film coverings are of less value. The shiny plastic finish is never quite true scale and it is not easy to apply the scale detail of rivets, panel lines, etc., that give the completed model that final touch of authenticity. However, for the sports scale enthusiast who requires a rapidly executed finish, on a model with a good basic framework strength, plastic film coverings can have many attractions. Many colours are available in the plastic film coverings, providing you look at the range of all of the manufacturers, including metallics. One can usually find a colour closely approximating to the scale subject's original shades and tones, but you must be prepared to sacrifice a little scale integrity on some occasions. It is possible to paint over some of the film coverings with oil based paints but this does defeat the object of the exercise somewhat. The adhesion between the paint and the film is slightly suspect and with the paint applied, one must be careful when retightening the film with a heat gun, or the paint will discolour. Normally, heat-shrink film is applied directly to untreated balsa framework whether it is fully sheeted or open. With open framework there is an immediate problem if a two tone colour scheme is used, as it is difficult to apply large areas of film on top of a lower layer of film. Attempting this will result in the formation of many small air bubbles between the two film skins. One way of making joints with different coloured film panels is to pre-cover the open framework components with tissue, as previously described. It is now possible to attach the first colour panels, use the lighter colour first, with an overlap allowance of $1/8-1/4$ inch. Iron in place and then apply the second colour panels, cut to exact size, with a small overlap on to the first panels. Use a solvent adhesive for attaching the overlaps to prevent the edges from peeling up. Using this method it is possible to produce sunburst patterns, large chequers and dual colour schemes of any style you require. It also has the advantage of preventing the grain marks of the balsa substructure from showing through the film skin – as will happen if you are too enthusiastic in your ironing onto the balsa direct. The tissue does not need to be doped when it has been applied, damp, to the airframe; it is acting only as a support for the film and the porous nature of the tissue will allow the air to be expelled during the covering.

Few prototypes have a surface finish as glossy and polished as that inherent with plastic film. The surface of the film can be made matt, after covering and tightening, by brushing on polyurethane clear varnish (matt or eggshell finish) to the surface. Silver 'Solarfilm', for instance, will give quite a reasonable impression of silver doped fabric when treated by this method. Applying the varnish will be made much easier if about 50% normal oil paint thinners is added.

E. SOLARTEX AND HEAT-SHRINK FABRIC MATERIALS.

In terms of method and strength, Solartex and its equivalents come between the plastic film materials and the conventional nylon and doping. Solartex is a biaxially orientated self adhesive covering material that is also heat sensitive. Thus it combines some of the advantages of nylon covering with the assets of the plastic film, with regards to ease of application, cleanliness, etc. It is not cheap, but if all the factors of time, fillers, primers, dope, brushes, etc., are taken into consideration the price differential is not as great as may at first appear. The material is available in plain form or a selection of colours, including a semi-transparent finish called 'Antique'. This closely resembles a natural linen finish and so is ideal as a basis for many of the early aircraft replicas. Another 'special' that is manufactured by Coverite is a ¹/₆th scale W.W.1 German lozenge pattern finish. Anyone that has had the unenviable task of individually painting on the different colour lozenges will fully appreciate the implications of this material. There is only one pattern/colour combination available and this is more suitable for the upper surfaces of the wings. The colours are rather on the bright side but they can easily be toned down by painting over with a 'dirty' clear dope or varnish. Similarly, the covering can be recoloured

with an 'orangey' tint when it is applied to the underside of the wings, to give a more authentic appearance.

In common with all 'new' materials experience and experiment will tell you what they are capable of and their limitations. Because the materials can be used in many ways, i.e. self finished, doped or painted, you should always test for compatibility of the various finishes before rushing on to the scale model. It is claimed that no pre-doping or priming of the structure is requird before covering and that the covering will not warp surfaces — it stops shrinking (when heat is applied) as soon as it reaches a half gramme resistance. The techniques used for covering are very similar to those employed with plastic film but it tends to be better for applying to outside and inside compound curves. Gentle persuasion with the heat gun, fingers and a soft cloth will help to negotiate these compound curvatures successfully. Overlaps are recommended, if less than scale, otherwise there is the risk of the joint opening up as post application tautening takes place. Air bubbles can be removed, as with other plastic films, by jabbing with a pin, reheating and smoothing down with a soft cloth. The added versatility of high strength, 'paintability' and variety of colours and finishes makes heat-shrink fabrics a strong contender in the scale R/C model covering league.

F. RESIN

Speed of carrying out the preparation stage of a model is an attractive proposition to any modeller. It represents an 'in between' stage where you have marvelled at the magnificence of the completed basic structure and you can't wait to see the finished results of the model. Preparation comes between these two realisations but we know that it is an

Colourful Curtiss Hawk P6E (41¹/₂in) is a Goldberg kit. Fuselage covering looks good.

important stage and if we skimp or rush now, the final result will be a disappointment. One method, for fully sheeted constructions, that is undoubtedly quicker than the preparations generally used for tissue and nylon coverings, involves the use of resins. Whereas the standard methods of preparation and tissue covering may take a number of weeks, a resin preparation can be completed in a matter of a few days. How is it possible to reduce this agreed boring period so dramatically? Principally by eliminating the tissue or nylon covering to the sheeted areas. The resin provides the priming effect and the strengthening of the balsa surface. Are there any drawbacks? Yes, although the resin does toughen the balsa to some degree it does not provide the same degree of antisplitting qualities that tissue, and certainly nylon, offer. There is a greater risk of joints opening, and splits occurring, through the general usage of the model and the effects of vibration. This may not be an important factor with small (0.20–0.40 cu.ins. engine) powered models but should be carefully con-

sidered for large aircraft. Of course, resins can be used in conjunction with tissue covering but then their main advantage disappears. The resins are specially formulated for quick drying, easy sanding and easy application. They are available as commercial modelling items and may be stocked as a standard product for use in the automobile industry. Normal glass fibre resins are not suitable for this purpose as they cure too hard and are extremely difficult to sand.

The first coat is applied with a stiff brush and is brushed hard in to the surface of the wood. Good adhesion and penetration are more important for the first coat than obtaining a smooth consistent coat. When the resin has hardened – don't leave it too long for this layer – sand to a reasonable smoothness. It doesn't have to be a super-smooth surface at this stage. Apply the second coat with a soft brush in long flowing brush strokes to achieve a smooth even coating to the surfaces. Allow to dry and sand with reducing grades of wet and dry abrasive paper. A third coat may prove to be necessary or it may only be a case of filling up some low spots and resanding. Test the resin for compatibility with the finishes to be used although it has proved satisfactory with the majority of paints.

To give an indication, and it can only be that, of the comparative weights of some of the preparation and finishing methods that can be employed, a table is illustrated in Fig. 15.2 below. The actual weights involved will depend on how liberal you are with fillers and primers and how much 'elbow grease' is employed in removing the surplus before final painting.

NYLON WING BAGS

The method used to cover open structure wings of full-size aircraft such as the D.H. *Tiger Moth* is first to make up a linen wing bag. This is, in essence, very much like a pillow case with one end sewn up, shaped to the tip outline and the root end left open. When the bag has been sewn up it is turned inside out and pulled over the wing, removing as many creases as possible. At every rib station the material is sewn round the rib to prevent the upper surface from lifting in flight, due to the low pressure, and to retain the material to the undercamber of the lower surface. When the wing has been doped rib tapes are doped over the stitching to give a neat, practical finish.

The same system has been used on scale R/C models featuring thin undercambered wings with complete success. Providing the nylon bag is accurately sewn to the weave of the material it has a number of distinct advantages. When the bag is positioned, dry, on the wing it can be adjusted so that the warp and weft are in line with ribs and the spars respectively, thus reducing, as far as

humanly possible, the risk of warping through uneven tensions of the material. No overlaps or trimming are required and there are no difficult adhesion problems on small wing tip or trailing edge sections. It is ideal where a wire trailing edge is used as it is unnecessary to glue this area at all, the tautening action will provide natural concavity at the inter-rib stations. We do not have to sew the nylon to the ribs, as dope adhesion is quite adequate, but the undercambered area of the ribs should be smeared with balsa cement, rubbed in with the fingers, before the covering is applied. This will give a stronger bond between the dope and the ribs over this area. It will be helpful lightly to water-spray the nylon over this area when doping through to attach the nylon to the ribs. Apart from fixing the nylon to the root rib, and the undercamber, there is no need to stick the nylon to any other parts of the structure. Indeed, it is better not to as the nylon can tauten over larger areas, again reducing the chances of warping. The sewn seam should be kept to the leading edge where it will be less obvious. Doping is carried out by any of the normal methods. With the very early aircraft modellers are apt to make the covering on their replicas too good; most of the prototypes had numerous wrinkles in their covering but it is a brave man that incorporates these in his model. His colleagues will inevitably comment that they are there by accident!

METAL COVERING

Covering large panels, even complete aircraft, with aluminium has been successfully undertaken by a number of modellers but it is generally agreed that it is not the easiest of processes. The problem areas are the joints, e.g. fuselage panels, wing trailing edges, curved leading edges and compound curves. Simulating polished aluminium has limitations when using any other method than thin aluminium sheet glued to the structure. Silver paints never look absolutely right and the aluminiumised papers, e.g. paper backed aluminium foil, are only suitable for straight or single curvature panels. Aluminium foil of the kitchen roll variety is far too thin and will show every speck of dust on the structure, through to the surface. Even on a perfect surface it is nearly impossible to apply the adhesive without scoring and marking the surface of the aluminium. By elimination, therefore, we find ourselves having to consider the use of thin aluminium sheet as the only practical alternative. As nearly all prototypes incorporate a number of panels with compound curves, and fairings and housings that are panel beaten, we must be prepared to do some 'tin bashing'. Unless you are very keen to work in metal it would be advisable to ignore the all-metal, unpainted, prototype, but

smaller areas of aluminium present quite a pleasant challenge. The difference between an aluminium-clad aircraft that is subsequently painted silver, and the prototype that is left with the aluminium panels untreated, should clearly be understood. There are many examples of the former and these can be well reproduced by using sprayed silver finishes; even the dull aluminium panels can be represented in this way. It is the polished aluminium panels that have to be copied in the same materials for scale model work.

For aluminium panels we can use a material known as Alu-foil. This comes in a variety of thicknesses, but for our purposes the 0.06mm and 0.1mm sizes are the most suitable, the former for small models and the latter for larger scale R/C designs. It is available in rolls of approximatley two feet wide and to any length required. Being a 'half hard' material it has a certain degree of natural temper and is only suitable for straight panels and simple curvatures unless it is detempered by heat treatment. During the rolling process of manufacture oil is

Good representation of nose panelling on a Hawker Fury, though sprayed shadow lines are a little too marked.

used as a lubricant and this *must* be removed if a satisfactory glueing bond is to be achieved. Use cellulose thinners for the degreasing operation, pouring some on to a soft cloth pad and rubbing the surface of the alu-foil thoroughly until all traces of the oil are removed. Surface marks are easily made on the surface of the foil and it is also easy to crease or 'cockle' the material. Work on a smooth, flat, clean surface clear of every scrap of loose material, glue 'blobs' and other blemishes.

The alu-foil can be cut with conventional tools, i.e. knives, razor saw, scissors, shears, but the last-mentioned tools will cause the metal to curl as you cut it. Always fit the concave side, even after further flattening, to the structure to be covered. Cutting with a knife will give a clean *sharp* edge – sharp enough to give a nasty flesh wound. Special adhesives can be purchased for glueing the foil to a variety of materials, it is also necessary to purchase some compatible thinners. The adhesive is of the 'contact' type and should be used with the same caution as similar adhesives, i.e. warm dry conditions but with *plenty* of ventilation.

Alu-foil can be used in a similar manner to wood veneers and micro-ply. A polystyrene foam wing core can be covered direct with the foil using the same techniques as with obeche veneer, although a little more care is needed in rolling the core on to the metal to prevent trapping air bubbles. The foil is distinctly non-porous and the cellular composition of the foam equally so, and air trapped between the surfaces will remain there. Check that the leading edges of wings and tailplanes are truly straight, and that the section is constant or *progressively* changing, otherwise you will have some unsupported areas of foil. Balsa can be equally well covered with the foil and normal, untreated preparation is all that is required. To both foam and raw wood a thinned coat of adhesive should first be applied to seal the surface – this improves the bond considerably and should not be omitted. The same technique will improve bond strength when a foil to foil adhesion is required. For all sealing *and* adhesion glueing the adhesive should be thinned to the proportions of three parts of adhesive to one of thinners. Mix only sufficient thinned adhesive for the

Variety of surfaces on an HP42. Metal engine nacelle panels with fabric fairings, corrugated fuselage, fabric wings etc.

immediate purpose as the thinner will evaporate rapidly; brushes are cleaned in the same thinners. Foam cores and balsa structures must be totally free from dust and particles and smooth. As with other veneering methods the adhesive must be spread thinly and evenly and allowed ample time to become dry before joining the covering and substrate. To give an indication of comparable weights, an obeche veneer weighs about three quarters of an ounce per square foot, 0.06mm thick foil weighs about 0.7 of an ounce and 0.1mm thick (4 thou.) is around 1.25 ounces per square foot. Bearing in mind that the alu-foil requires no further covering the weights are quite competitive. Open structures can be covered and there is no immediate visible definition of the structure below but take care not to handle these areas too aggressively or the 'ridges' will become apparent.

Detailing panel lines and rivets may be applied to either side of the foil, depending whether raised or relief detail is required. The material must be handled with care and marking should be made over a semi-hard surface, such as 'K' quality hardboard, using a hard pencil as the incising instrument. Overlaps will obviously show on the finished surfaces and are to be avoided where possible. A wise precaution would be to paint the surface under the butt panel joint with a fuel proof silver paint to make the joints less conspicuous. The alu-foil surface is compatible with all standard paint finishes, film coverings and fuel proofers. The cost is directly comparable with obeche veneers and cheaper than micro-ply. The limitations arise, as previously stated, with compound curves but some of the methods of overcoming these problems are covered in Chapters 5 and 16.

COMPARATIVE WEIGHTS OF COVERING MATERIALS
Weights quoted in ozs. per sq. ft.

	Covering base	3 coats dope	4 coats dope
Lightweight tissue	.037	.096	.118
Heavyweight tissue	.079	.150	.180
Nylon *†	.216	.288	.317
Plastic films‡	.26–.36	–	–

1. * Average figure-weight will depend on weave of nylon and quantity of dope to fill pores.

2. † Heat-shrink fabric similar.

3. ‡ Weight variation will depend on thickness of film and colour of pigment.

Chapter 16

Engine Details

Unlike large scale plastic *static* model aircraft ($\frac{1}{32}$nd scale) it is rare for the scale R/C model to have a dummy engine fitted *except* for the exposed areas of the engine. So, for a fully cowled, water or glycol cooled engine (e.g. Rolls Royce 'Merlin' engine in a *Spitfire*) the modeller will limit his detail to external details of exhaust stacks, cowl panels, etc. Having stated that fact, no doubt some modeller will now produce a model with hinged cowl panels opening to reveal a dummy in-line engine in full detail. For the purpose of this chapter, however, we will concern ourselves only with the externally visible engine items and ancillary equipment.

Engine cylinders, spark plugs, valve gear, rocker boxes, etc., offer tremendous scope for the ingenuity of the scale modeller to imitate the shape and finishes of the originals. It also gives scope to the 'jackdaw' instincts whereby any small metallic and plastic items that look as if they could be pressed into service in representing a part of an engine are avidly collected and stored. For those modellers with access to a lathe, and other metal working tools, life will not be too difficult, but for most of us it really is a matter of searching around to find the most suitable basis for a particular component. Virtually every part of the engine system, apart from hoses and bellows, has a 'hard' finish and we can best represent this with a

Neat engine cowl with engine-turned finish and simulated engine add considerably to this Sopwith Triplane.

Modern engines, except those used in light aircraft, can mostly be ignored by the scale modeller as they are well hidden from view. Fortunately, the older engines are well documented and it is possible to see actual examples of many of them in museums and collections. Photographs and detailed drawings are also available in books and magazines contemporary to the subject, so that we should not be short of information to design our dummy engine. Serious thought has to be given to the fixing of the dummy engine as it will be situated in an area of high vibration levels; for the same reason the assembly must be reasonably robust. Apart from the wings it will probably be the most removed part of the aircraft – to allow for cleaning and servicing of the real engine. Dummy engines and cowls may not be 'working', in the real sense, but they certainly must be functional.

metal or plastic. It *is* feasible to use balsa and ply, and often we *have* to resort to the use of these, but they must be very well prepared and painted to give the desired effect. There are very few full size 'fuzzy' cylinder heads in existence! For some engine types, at some scales, commercial cylinder head assemblies and crank-cases are available, moulded from plastic. These are mostly for the rotary and radial engines where much of the engine was exposed. A lot of time will be saved by using these items and most of them have great scale accuracy and realism, but in the majority of instances we shall be working from scratch. Before we can start to build the dummy engine we must first give consideration to the working model engine. All of the practical requirements of cooling, accessibility etc., mentioned in Chapter 9, must be given prime consideration. There is no point in having a most beautifully detailed dummy engine on view if it prevents the real engine from performing correctly.

ROTARY ENGINES

The rotary engine, where the cylinders rotate around a static crankshaft, was an amazing design concept that remained in service until the end of W.W.1. The design of the rotary engine required very high standards of engineering, and frequent overhauls, but did have some advantages. Smooth running was a feature of some of the makes and the spinning cylinders got rid of any cooling problems. As radial and in-line engines improved the rotary could not match them in economic or performance terms and disappeared from the scene.

From the scale modeller's aspect the rotary engine presents more than a few perplexing questions. Shall we make the engine to revolve? Shall we fit a non-rotating dummy engine? Our difficulties are not made any easier by the fact that the prototype engines operated at low R.P.M., swinging a large propeller. There is little doubt that the use of a slower-revving petrol engine, or geared unit, will enhance the simulation of these early power units, although even these will be turning at excessively high scale speed. The appearance of a slow flying Bleriot and the sound of a glow motor turning at 10,000 R.P.M., is incongruous but difficult to correct with a two-stroke engine. One aspect of engine noise simulation that has not been sufficiently explored is the modification of frequency of sound of the exhaust note. We want to give the *impression* of an engine turning at slower speeds, and as the exhaust accounts for the major part of noise emission on most aircraft engines, it is in this region that we should be exploring. Fig 16.1 illustrates a method for adapting a silencer to 'pulse' the exhaust emission to a lower frequency and it should also have the benefit of quietening the exhaust note. The speed of the pulses can be adjusted by bending the ends of the tabs on the disc to a lesser or greater degree. This proposal is one of theory only and has not, at the time of writing this book, been put into practice.

Because of the bulk of the rotary engines, and because – on many aircraft at least – some of the engine is exposed, it is impossible to build a complete dummy engine around the working engine. Not, that is, if we also want the dummy engine to rotate. To achieve this state of affairs we almost certainly have to use an extension shaft, from the engine to the propeller, and mount the dummy engine around that shaft. The shaft must not be too long as it will be impossible to support the front end,

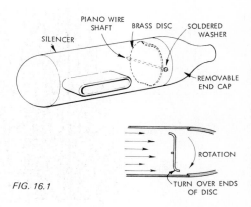

FIG. 16.1

unless the prototype used a similar support, e.g. Bleriot, Sopwith *Tabloid*. Positioning the working engine further back will almost certainly introduce another problem for the scale modeller. Rotary engines were pretty hefty pieces of machinery and, therefore, the nose moments of the aircraft that had rotaries fitted were quite short. At a time when we are trying to get as much weight as possible at the nose end of the model we negate the situation by moving the engine *rearwards.* Assuming that we do opt for this situation we now have to devise a method of reducing the rotational speed of the dummy engine. All things are possible – or nearly all – and no doubt a gearing system could be devised for achieving the required reduction (average 800–1,200 R.P.M.). It would, however, be a complex engineering undertaking and anyone prepared to set forth on such a project would have the expertise to design such a system. For the average modeller there are no short cuts as the mass of a light dummy engine rotating at 1,000 R.P.M., is considerable and must be accurately engineered. Much better to select a prototype where the engine is fully cowled in, i.e.

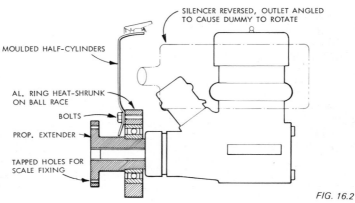

SILENCER REVERSED, OUTLET ANGLED
TO CAUSE DUMMY TO ROTATE

MOULDED HALF-CYLINDERS

AL. RING HEAT-SHRUNK
ON BALL RACE

BOLTS

PROP. EXTENDER

TAPPED HOLES FOR
SCALE FIXING

FIG. 16.2

Sopwith *Pup* or *Camel* or one that uses a non-rotary engine. It is interesting to note that on a full size aircraft fitted with a semi-exposed engine, (i.e. Blackburn Monoplane) it is virtually impossible to see the engine cylinders in flight – at the most they appear as a blur! This should add some credence to the suggestion of fitting a dummy rotary for static viewing and to remove it for flying. Cowled rotary engines do present less scale difficulties because it is even more difficult to detect whether the engine is rotating in flight; in these circumstances it is reasonable to fit a dummy rotary engine 'front' and hide the working engine behind – the dummy engine could remain fitted for flight providing no cooling problems would result. In Chapter 14 it was stated that we could not, as yet, reproduce the characteristic 'smells' of a full size aircraft. Rotary engines are one of the areas where we *can* produce authentic smells as the full size engines also used castor oil as the non-recirculating lubricant. The smell of burnt castor oil must be highly evocative to any pilot that has flown prototypes powered with rotary engines.

Static plastic kits of rotary engines – and radials – can provide excellent references for producing our dummy engines. Although they are rarely to a

Plastic model Le Rhone rotary engine available as a Williams Bros. kit.

large enough scale to use directly on our models, they provide a permanent guide for enlargement purposes. As previously stated, the method of producing the cylinder heads, valve gear and inlet tubes, will be the consequence of your engineering facilities. Even without the use of a lathe it is possible to 'turn' a cylinder head from birch dowel by fitting it into the chuck of an electric drill. The slots are cut by holding a hacksaw blade against the revolving wood, the positions being previously marked with soft pencil. Alternatively, the cylinder head and finning can be constructed by building up from a series of circular blanks of varying diameters, glued together. Valve gear can be reproduced with the use of small typewriter springs and plywood 'rockers'. Fuel and air inlet pipes, normally from copper, have bends incorporated and it is necessary to experiment with the bending of aluminium tube to simulate these. If you really are trying to build up the weight of the model at this end you could use genuine soft copper pipe for scale induction tubes. We would not normally consider this type of tube because of its high weight/low strength but it has good ductability and is highly suitable for this purpose. Various sizes can be obtained from model shops dealing with marine modelling.

RADIAL ENGINES

Radial engines have many of the same problems, and attractions, as the rotary but at least we don't have to concern ourselves with the revolving dummy engines. The 'plumbing' and valve gear operation tends to be more complicated with radial engines, particularly the later versions, and this will involve more work on the dummy engine. Rocker box covers and parts of the crankcase are best vacuum formed from A.B.S. plastic sheet and painted to a silver colour, or the matt black finish that was often used. Pushrod covers to the cylinder head valves were usually from aluminium and round or oval in section. Aluminium tube is fine for this work and it may need to be flattened in a vice to form the oval section. Induction and exhaust pipes are sometimes of the 'Y' branched variety and it is very difficult to fabricate these from metal tube. The use of mouldings may also be the best answer here, but they can be carved from balsa. Certainly, where there is considerable duplication of an item the moulding method will give quicker overall results – and greater consistency. There are normally advantages, for both rotary and radial engined proto-

Many famous radial engines were built by Wright. Another Williams Bros Kit.

types, in using a rear induction glow motor. The carburettor and throttle control are then well away from the dummy engine crankcase area and there is less likelihood of any 'fouling' of the dummy engine casing. In the same way, it may be easier to use a rear exhaust outlet engine; you must sketch the alternative arrangements at the planning stage before making this decision.

COWLS

Radial cowls on full size aircraft are nearly always fabricated from aluminium and often they were left unpainted. To copy the natural aluminium finished cowl we have little option but to use one made from the same material. There are two easy ways of doing this. One is to buy a commercially produced spun aluminium cowl of right diameter and shape – it may be worthwhile slightly adjusting the scale of the model, at the design stage, to accommodate a commercially available 'ali.' cowl. Secondly, a visit, or more likely, many visits, to hardware stores may secure for you an aluminium tea pot or saucepan of the ideal diameter and shape. Take a large pair of callipers with you and a template of the curved section and check all of the available pots and pans. Of course, the assistants will think you are completely

mad, but as a scale R/C modeller you should be used to this by now! Failing success with either of the above methods you will have to resort to making an aluminium cowl from basic materials. You could make one from G.R.P. and this is more than acceptable for painted prototype cowls, but you will never be able to get that 'true' aluminium finish – even by using aluminium pigment in the gel coat resin.

To make an aluminium cowl you must first produce a hardwood male mould that measures the thickness (say 20 s.w.g.) of the aluminium less that of the finished size. Use a close grained hardwood and it is strongly recommended that you obtain the services of a wood turner to produce the male mould. He, or she, will be able to turn the mould in a fraction of the time that you would take in hand carving it. Use aluminium sheet and not an alloy for the fabrication and this must be annealed (or normalised) before work is commenced and probably during the beating operation, as work hardening takes place. Cut a strip of aluminium long enough to give a small overlap around the circumference of the cowl and wide enough to allow the front edge to be beaten around the radius to the inside trim edge. With this method of forming the cowl there will inevitably be a visible joint – unless you are a superb welder of aluminium and they are about as common as icebergs in the desert! Many of the radial cowls on prototypes had hinged panels and these offer an obvious position for a joint, but if the original had no separation lines, make the joint on the underside and make as neat a job of it as possible. Clamp the aluminium around the wooden plug with the rear edge lined up with the base of the plug. Trim off the overlap to make a snug butt joint. Using a hide or plastic

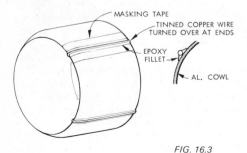

MASKING TAPE
TINNED COPPER WIRE TURNED OVER AT ENDS
EPOXY FILLET
AL. COWL

FIG. 16.3

The underside of the Wirraway cowling with carb intake etc. Wheel well fairings also visible.

mallet, start forming the aluminium around the wooden former working *very* gradually around the curvature. Tap the aluminium sparingly and work consistently around the circumference gradually working the material to the front face. The metal will naturally try to 'bunch' as it gets towards the smaller diameter and the skill in beating is to prevent the formation of creases. If the formation of a crease becomes unavoidable it is better to make a neat 'V' cut in the metal and beat the aluminium to produce a close butt joint – it can be reinforced with scrap aluminium and epoxy (or glass fibre resin and cloth) on the rear side. Aluminium cowls on full size aircraft often have to be patched and riveted – take a look at some vintage aircraft nose cowls – and this feature can be used as a method of covering up a 'mistake' on cowl beating. When you are satisfied with the shape of the cowl, remove it from the wood mould and reinforce the joint with aluminium and epoxy or glass fibre. Trim and file the internal edges and smooth out any irregularities on the cowl surface with

wet and dry abrasive paper and metal polish. Work down to a No. 600 grit and finish with a good polish. The cowl may be finished in this state or it may require further surface detail. Perhaps the original cowl had the 'engine turning' effect on the aluminium surface and this can easily be reproduced by the use of a piece of dowel, or round ink rubber, fitted into the end of a piece of brass tube and held in the chuck of a power drill flexible drive. With the drill revolving, just dab the end of the dowel, or rubber, on to the aluminium and an effective engine turning simulation will result. Use a diameter of dowel to suit the scale you are using and work methodically to the same pattern as the original. False hinge lines can be simulated by using tinned copper wire, pulled straight in a vice, laid on to the cowl and the edges bent around the front and rear edges of the cowl. See Fig. 16.3. Mask off close to each side of the wire and smear an epoxy fillet around the wire. Leave the epoxy to set and then remove the masking tape. This method is, naturally, more suited to a painted cowl but is acceptable on a

Not only radial engines have details. Nose of Westland Widgeon by Ross Woodcock with hand-formed cowling.

polished aluminium one providing a clear epoxy is used. One surface finish that is not easy to emulate is the patterning left on the metal surface from the full size moulding operation. The appearance slightly resembles a 'paisley' pattern cloth consisting of scrolls and curves; it featured mainly on German radial cowls of aircraft in W.W.1. There would appear to be no alternative to painting these marks on with a tinted lacquer, followed for protection by a clear fuel proof lacquer over the whole cowl.

Double curvature aluminium panels and rounded covers in aluminium can be formed by panel beating in a similar manner, using a male or female wood mould – whichever is the more suitable. Panel beating is an art, so don't be surprised if it takes some time before you master the techniques. For thinner gauges of aluminium a slightly different method can be employed for forming rounded panels. Instead of beating, the aluminium, annealed, is 'boned' to shape

using the rounded surface of a spoon or similar implement. On a semi-hard surface keep rubbing and stretching the material until you have formed the correct curvature of the panel. Trim the edges and glue the panel to the prepared structural surface as previously stated.

VERTICAL RADIATORS

Upright, car type radiators were often fitted in front, or remote from, in-line water-cooled engines in aircraft of the W.W.1 period and slightly later, e.g. D.H.4. The front large upright radiator is ideal for the scale modeller as it makes the mounting of an upright, standard engine arrangement ideal. All of the engine and the ancillary equipment can be easily accommodated in the generous cowl areas which often consist of simple curves. The slatted radiators, or honey-combed grill, can be constructed to allow sufficient cooling air and there are normally enough vents and louvres to take care of the extraction of warmed air.

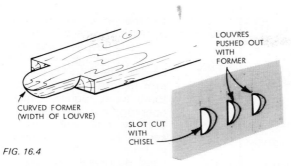

LOUVRES
PUSHED OUT
WITH
FORMER

CURVED FORMER
(WIDTH OF LOUVRE)

SLOT CUT
WITH
CHISEL

FIG. 16.4

Where a metal radiator surround was featured on the original this can be reproduced by a panel beating method similar to that described for radial cowls. Brass was used on some radiators and this metal has the advantage that it can be beaten *and* silver soldered. For sharp radii it will be found to be easier to form using a small hammer rather than a mallet but do not allow the metal to become too work-hardened. Fabrication of the shutters is from strip metal; set them at about 30° to the horizontal for a good visual and cooling effect – unless you are prepared to go for a fully operating shutter system. Brass shutters may be silver soldered to a brass surround but aluminium joints must be epoxied in position. To simulate the honeycombed radiator construction use a fine mesh brass gauze which will also allow the passage of cooling air – although not as much as you might think, as the free air area of the gauze material is not great. Where metal components are to be epoxied together cleanliness is imperative; thoroughly degrease the surface and roughen it with emery paper and use heatproof epoxy where there is any actual contact with the engine.

The top and bottom cowlings should also be formed from aluminium as these frequently have louvres and scoops formed in them. We will probably need the louvres (facing rearwards), and possibly air scoops (facing forward) to be operative for cooling the engine and a ductile sheet material is ideal for forming them in situ. Cut the panels exactly to size using a card template for trial fittings, and bend them to the curvature required to fit over the fuselage formers. Mark on the position of the ventilation scoops and louvres with a soft pencil and cut the vertical front or rear edges with an appropriate sized chisel. The curved parts of the vents are formed by using a hardwood former, as shown in Fig. 16.4 and pressing down on a hard rubber pad. Little cleaning up is required and it should be possible to form the vent in one operation, but take care not to tear the edges. Work from one end, in sequence, to the opposite end so that the finished vents are not squashed.

FASTENINGS

The method of fixing removable metal cowls and panels must approximate, as near as practical, to the full size fastenings. For instance, the radial cowls on many Sopwith aircraft are held in position by a stranded metal cable around the circumference of the cowl, at the rear, tightened by a screw clamp device. Other forms of fastenings include the 'turn through 90° type' which are not easy to copy as they would probably

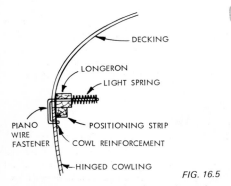

FIG. 16.5

require the reinforcing of the slot, where the turn button pushes through. The simple 'U' sprung fasteners as used on the *Tiger Moth* are easier to construct but suffer from the same problem — it really depends on the gauge of aluminium you are using for the cowl. See Fig. 16.5. On later aircraft the most used forms of cowl retention, and inspection panels, are the Dzus and Oddie types of fasteners. The latter type was a great advance on previous methods because of the speed with which the panels could be replaced. It simply involved position-ing the panel and banging the Oddie fasteners home with the side of your hand and the panel was securely home — a big advantage in active service con-ditions. The Dzus fastener requires a 90° turn to locate it in the closed position (both types require a quarter turn for opening) but it probably offers better security than the Oddie type under certain conditions. Either counter-sunk or mushroom head configurations are used dependent on the surface finish style of the aircraft. It is possible to purchase small sizes of these excellent fasteners but they are not normally small enough for scale representation. With a little ingenuity we can, however, make our own 'Oddie' style fasteners without having to resort to expensive tools. For the male portion we use a countersunk bolt and for the female side of the fastener a female half of a press stud (e.g. Newey type). A 4-40 bolt and No.1. Newey fastener are compatible and approximate to one sixth scale. The bolt should preferably have a shank without thread to the full length of the fastener

Simple mono-curve cowling panels with separate hinged louvre panel. Absence of flying wire "ends" is noticeable.

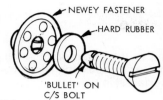

NEWEY FASTENER

HARD RUBBER

'BULLET' ON
C/S BOLT

FIG. 16.6

fixing. Calculate the distance from the bottom of the head through the panel and the fastener and allow about $^3/_{16}$ in. beyond this for the length of the bolt. Make allowance for the use of any rubber padding that may be incorporated to assist with the seating of the cowl. Cut slots on opposite sides of the shank at the Newey fastener position and shape the portion of bolt from the slots to the end to a 'bullet' form. The Newey fastener is bound and epoxied (avoiding the spring action) to a ply plate and this is suitably affixed to the fuselage structure. Form an indentation in the aluminium cowl at the precise position of the fastener and insert the shaped bolt. A small hard rubber washer pushed on to the inside of the bolt will retain it in position and add a little 'cushioning'

effect for the cowl. Make sure to line up the Newey fasteners so that all the bolt slots are correctly aligned — inspect photographs of the prototype for directions of slots. See Fig 16.6 for details.

HINGES

The piano type hinge used on many metal cowls can be fabricated from metal, although it is obviously easier to do this as a separate item rather than trying to form it as part of the edges of the actual cowls. A metal hinge for cowl parts is to be preferred to the nylon hinges previously described, as the fixing is easier and the scale of the pitch of the hinge parts is more accurate. Cut two strips of tin about one inch wide and slightly longer than the full length of the hinge. Ordinary baked bean or similar material is quite satisfactory. Two three millimetre ply strips are also cut to the same length and width. The tin strips are sandwiched between the plywood, with the edges all level, and this must be clamped between two metal bars. Mild steel bars about $^3/_8 \times \frac{1}{4}$ in. section will be quite adequate; make them an inch or so

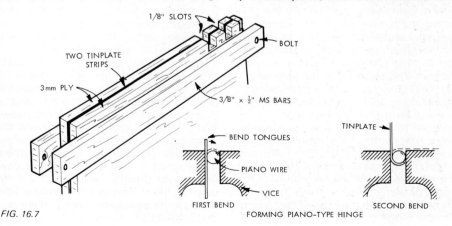

1/8" SLOTS

TWO TINPLATE
STRIPS

3 mm PLY

BOLT

3/8" × ½" MS BARS

BEND TONGUES

PIANO WIRE

VICE

FIRST BEND

TINPLATE

SECOND BEND

FIG. 16.7

FORMING PIANO-TYPE HINGE

233

Large glass-fibre cowling for small in-line engines such as the Gipsy series.

be fitted to the panels with small nuts and bolts or by epoxying (slow drying – clean surfaces) in position.

GLASS FIBRE COWLS

Few of the aircraft after the 1930s used polished aluminium cowls, unless you include airliners, so, for the small modeller, these areas do not have to be reproduced in metal. We can use wood construction or G.R.P. for the fixed or removable cowl areas. Balsa, reinforced with ply, can be satisfactory but the nose areas are some of the most vulnerable and the surface will soon become dented and scratched with use. Glass fibre is an ideal material for engine cowls as it can be moulded to any shape and the thickness of the material adjusted for weight and strength considerations. Surface detail, such as rivets, panel lines, bulges, can be moulded in, the techniques for moulding the glass fibre cowls being principally the same as previously described for fuselages. Cowls must have a close, smooth fit with the basic fuselage structure and this can be achieved, prior to the finish being applied, in the following fashion.-

longer than the hinge length and drill at each end to accept $^3/_{16}$ in. clamping nuts and bolts. Select a flat file that has a cutting edge at least $^1/_8$ in. wide and mark down the length of the ply equal spacings slightly wider than the file. Commencing at the right hand end, with the bars held in the vice, file slots about $^1/_8$ in. deep at every other marked position until the complete sandwich is filed in castellated fashion. As the projecting metal tongues have to interleave the gaps can be made slightly larger than the tongues to ensure them fitting. Remove the pieces of tinplate, take one of them and clamp it in the vice with a piece of 18 swg piano wire positioned as shown in Fig. 16.7. Tap the metal tongues over the wire and continue to move the material round in the vice, tapping the hinge parts until the tongues are fully rounded. Remove the piano wire and repeat the operation with the second half of the hinge. Check the two halves of the hinge for correct mating, insert the hinge pin, cut and crimp the ends of the pin and trim the hinge to length. The hinge may

Trim the rear edge of the cowl accurately to size, filing the inside edge of the cowl to remove any surplus material. Check fit the cowl on to the fuselage lip that is to act as the seating for the cowl. Put a bead of epoxy filler around the seating area, treat the inside edge of the cowl with release agent or a good smear of petroleum jelly and push the cowl firmly into position, squeezing out the surplus filler. Remove the excess filler with a knife and damp cloth and leave to dry, making a final check that the cowl is

Very closely fitted spinner on a late mark of Spitfire. Perhaps a shade more emphasis on panel lines would look better.

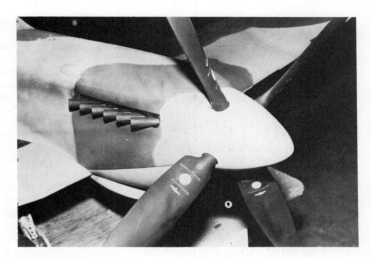

well and truly home. When the filler has hardened, but before it has fully cured, remove the cowl; trim off any internal loose edges and sand the external surface carefully to blend in with the general fuselage contours. The final fixing of the cowl to the fuselage will depend on the fixing points available on the fuselage and the use that can be made of scale features for fitting access.

SPINNER FITTING

Fitting a spinner to a glass fibre cowl does not leave much room for error and the engine positioning, angling and the length of the cowl must all be accurately determined before final fitting is reached. Some engine side and down thrust adjustment may be available, but as a *final* resort it may be necessary to make the holes in the engine lugs into slots. It should be repeated that this should only be considered as an absolutely *last* resort as this type of treatment is to be discouraged on any engine and particularly on large engines where accidental movement could take place. Balsa nose

areas are easier to cope with for final spinner fitting as we can utilise the adaptability of the material to our benefit. Assume the engine is fitted temporarily, but firmly and accurately, in the fuselage and that the ply nose ring has not been glued in position; final shaping of the nose area is also to be undertaken. Take the backplate of the spinner and tack glue to it a piece of $1/_{32}$ in. balsa – or whatever gap you finally require between the fuselage and spinner. To this packing piece tack the ply nose ring of the fuselage. Screw the propeller/spinner assembly on to the engine and tighten it up. You may have to trim some wood away from the front of the fuselage, or, alternatively, it may be necessary to build it up with scrap balsa or filler. When you are satisfied with the fit of the nose ring it can be permanently glued in position – it should be just possible to rotate the propeller. Remove the front of the spinner and the propeller when the adhesive has dried, protect the edge of the spinner back plate with Scotch tape and carve and sand the front of the fuselage to shape. Break away the spinner backplate, clean off the packing piece and the fitting is complete. The balsa nose area can be 'toughened' by treating it with epoxy filler or glass fibre resin, the latter being the most difficult to sand smooth. Internal surfaces can be strengthened with glass fibre cloth and resin.

PROPELLERS

It is not always practical to fly a scale R/C model with a scale propeller due to the comparative speed differences of the model and prototype engines. For static scale appearance, however, we do want to have a scale propeller fitted to resemble the prototype aircraft closely. Propeller types vary from the early laminated wood variety to modern variable pitch or constant speed versions. Dummy three, four and five bladed can be made up from old broken blades – we knew there would eventually be a use for all of those broken propellers – with the hub and pitch mechanism constructed from scraps of dowel, epoxy putty, small nuts and bolts etc. As these later propeller units were all metal it is important to seal and sand all wood surfaces thoroughly, since wood grain showing through on the finish totally ruins the illusion we are attempting to create.

Early laminated propellers were both functional and beautiful and they are now prized collectors' items, to use as decoration in clubs and homes. The timber was carefully selected for its density, straightness of grain and moisture content, and the propellers were manufactured under controlled environmental conditions. Mahogany, walnut, silver spruce and ash were the woods most commonly used and it was the combinations of these timbers that gave the very attractive appearance. The leading edge was usually reinforced with a brass strip screwed in position and the whole of the propeller was sometimes sheathed in a linen or canvas material. More often this fabric reinforcement, hot glued in position, was restricted to the tip area where the blade thickness was at its minimum. Varnish was applied to all but the hub area of the propeller resulting in finishes varying from 'satin' to a full gloss.

For our two-bladed model propeller, flying or static, we must first draw the outline of the propeller and cut out the rough blanks or laminations. The width of the blade and the thickness of the laminations will determine the pitch of the propeller and it would be useful to have a propeller pitch gauge to assist in

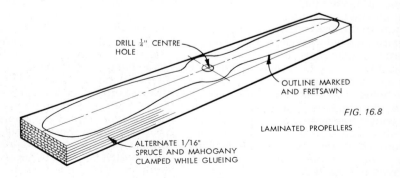

DRILL ¼" CENTRE HOLE

OUTLINE MARKED AND FRETSAWN

ALTERNATE 1/16" SPRUCE AND MAHOGANY CLAMPED WHILE GLUEING

FIG. 16.8

LAMINATED PROPELLERS

the carving and shaping of the propeller. This, of course, is only necessary if a flying propeller is to be carved and even then, a little practice and experience will allow you to make reasonably efficient working propellers. Cut four mahogany and three spruce blanks from $\frac{1}{16}$ inch thick material to the size required, i.e. for a 12 × 6 inch propeller the size of the blanks should be approximately 12¼″ long by 1³/₈″ wide, allowing for some trimming of the propeller. Sand the laminations flat, glue them together with Cascamite or Aerolite glue and clamp firmly together. Use individual 'G' clamps, with protective plywood each side, to hold the laminations *firmly* in position until the glue has set. Drill a ¼ in. hole in the centre, it must be square, and cut the outline of the propeller accurately to shape on a band saw or a fretsaw. An efficient propeller will have a *flat* rear surface and convex front surface — similar to a Clark 'Y' wing section. Don't be confused by pictures of some of these early propellers, the direction of rotation and shape of the leading edge can be deceiving. There is nothing to say that a propeller should not be the original 'scimitar' shape, in fact there is a school of thought that suggests that it may be more efficient than our 'standard' shapes. Eric Clutton, well-known modeller and aviator, produces an excellent booklet on designing and carving propellers for light aircraft which is most useful for the scale modeller.

Commence carving by tapering the rear of the blades from the leading edge to the top edge of the trailing edge. Use a small plane, knife and sanding blocks

and keep the surface flat — check the pitch of the blade down its full length with a pitch gauge. Round off the front surface of the blades, cutting, filing and sanding as before. Naturally, the left and right hand blades must be symmetrical but the laminations will give you a good visual check for regularity. Sand smooth by using gradually finer grades of sanding blocks, with a hard rubber backing, and balance the propeller. Give numerous coats of clear dope, rubbing down between coats, and dope on nylon to simulate the fabric reinforcement and glue brass shim into position on the leading edge. If the propeller is to be used for flying it will be more practical to paint the simulated brass leading edge. Complete the propeller by giving one or two coats of fuel proofer, checking the balance again between coats.

Cowl and undercarriage details of a full-size Stampe. Laminated prop, too.

Pity the cylinder heads are so obtrusive on this smaller HP42, but the four-blade props improve looks.

Four-bladed propellers can be fabricated using the same method by alternating the 'full' and 'half' blades between each lamination. The resulting propeller, properly glued and clamped during construction, will be sufficiently strong to use for flying at moderate engine speeds.

Modern wooden propellers, although laminated, need not be made in this way. We can use standard wooden model propellers as our basis which considerably reduces the time element — so much so that it is reasonable to use them for all flying. Because of the risk of damaging and breaking the propellers occasionally, it is sensible to prepare a few propellers at one time. Using dope thinners, or Nitromors paint stripper, remove the varnished finish, if any has been applied to the commercial propeller. Modify the tip shape if this is necessary but try not to change the width and shape of the blade generally any more than is vital — choose the commercial propeller shape that most suits your needs. Smooth out the machined edges of the hub. Sand the propeller really smooth, keeping the rear of the propeller flat, and check the balance. Give sufficient coats of clear dope to obtain a satin smooth finish, sanding lightly between coats. Mark with a soft pencil

the separation lines of the laminations, four or five separations, i.e. three or four lines are enough. Use your middle finger on the propeller leading edge to guide the pencil for the separation lines; they do not have to be perfect because the wood laminations of the full size propellers never finish to a positive line. Also mark on the metal leading edge and the fabric covering, where that is used. Now the laminations must be painted in using a very thinned yellow ochre coloured dope for the first layer, brushed over the whole of the propeller. The dope must not be too dark and it must remain translucent — we are only trying to obtain a slightly darker effect than the maple or beech propeller. Add a small amount of red dope to the basic yellow colour to change the tone *slightly* and paint this on to one lamination. A further slightly changed colour can be painted on to successive laminations. Paint on the metal leading edge, which may have a painted finish or metallic one, and the fabric covering using oil based paint, i.e. enamels. Any manufacturers' emblems should also be painted on at this stage with enamel paints. The propellers are finished by coating them with two part clear gloss fuel proofer and final balancing.

Chapter 17

External Details

The range of possible external detail items is so vast that it is impossible to cover them all and it will be up to the inventiveness of the scale R/C modeller to think of ways of reproducing most of them. Where there is a specific, and unusual, item to be moulded, draw it to scale, study the drawing and photographs of the prototype and think hard whether there is any item that you can use as a basis for the miniature representation. It may be a tooth brush holder, the top of a 'bubble' pack, a hair roller, a part of an old watch or clock, something from a child's toy, a piece of jewellery – anything that will save you making the item totally from scratch will be less work and will probably result in a more convincing finished article. The external details, plus the quality of the finish, are responsible for giving the model 'believability'. A well finished model that is devoid of these final details – the aerials, venturis, fuel cocks, gunsights, bombracks and many other small but important details – may look *nice* but it will not be *convincing*.

One of the biggest aids to producing many of these items is a vacuum forming device. Commercial machines are too large and equipment devised for the modeller may not be readily available, but it is not a difficult job to make your own vacuum former as on page 69.

The A.B.S. and styrene sheet used for vacuum forming is also a very useful material in its own right and has many uses on a model for panels, brackets, plates, etc. Equally useful are the plastic sections, tube, rod, channel and angles that are sold in model shops; polystyrene adhesives, or a solvent, can be used for glueing the plastic. The model world of the scale boat builder and the model engineer can produce useful metal fittings that are readily adaptable for our purposes. Miniature eyelets, stanchions, gear sets, cleats, plus the range of tiny B.A. nuts and bolts, will all have their uses on some scale R/C aircraft models. We must also remember that there are plenty of specialised scale items produced specifically for radio control models. Both plastic and metal fittings are available and the latter include brass turnbuckles, brackets, plates and pulleys. Look at these items with a discerning eye before incorporating them in your model, they may *appear* to be just what you are looking for but are they truly authentic in shape and scale? It is also possible to incorporate commercial R/C accessories into the model, not as a representation of a scale item but as an aid to fixing the scale components, e.g. wing struts. Some examples of the use of 'Du-bro' fittings are shown in Fig 17.1.

Modern aircraft are relatively free from external protuberances as they tend to add unwanted drag. The inclusion of these sparse external details become,

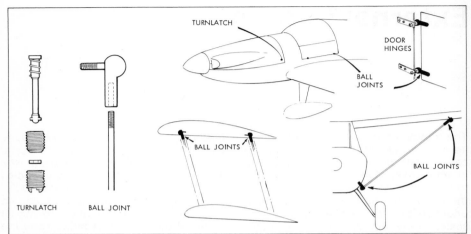

therefore, all the more important if we wish to get away from a very 'stark' effect. Careful modelling of the pitot tube, venturis, radio aerials, etc., is essential, together with a 'used' aircraft finish if we are not to end up with a model looking more like a toy than a scale replica of a *flying* aircraft.

Models of earlier prototypes do not have the same problems as there is often a wealth of external detail, including bracing wires, to assist in creating the atmosphere of the original. If we take, for instance, the W.W.1 period we can include the following items to improve the scale authenticity of the model.

1. Rigging turnbuckles. We have already discussed the possibility of using working turnbuckles and concluded that for

the majority of models, dummy turnbuckles are a better proposition. These can be reproduced, in slightly simplified form, by slipping a tiny nut (to scale size) on to the rigging wire followed by a length of brass tube, rounded at the ends, and a further nut. Epoxy the three items together at the required position on the rigging. See Fig 17.2. Don't forget to drill a small hole through the centre of the brass tube.

2. Cable operated controls. The same method of fitting dummy turnbuckles can be used if the controls are of the working type. Where alternative, internal control linkages are used the dummy cables can be made even more lifelike as we are not concerned with the function of the cable. Instead of using stranded flexible cable we can use, for short cables, piano wire that merely penetrates the exit hole on the fabric (usually reinforced with plywood or fabric). Allow sufficient wire to enter the fuselage or wing so that it can be 'sprung' into position but will not come out when full

FIG. 17.2

BRASS TUBE (ROUNDED ENDS)

EPOXY PARTS
ON RIGGING
LINE

SMALL NUTS

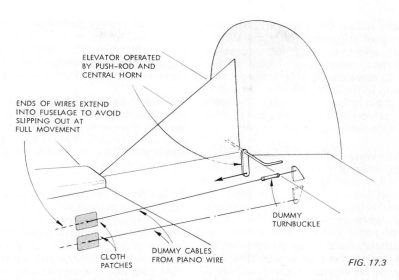

ELEVATOR OPERATED
BY PUSH-ROD AND
CENTRAL HORN

ENDS OF WIRES EXTEND
INTO FUSELAGE TO AVOID
SLIPPING OUT AT
FULL MOVEMENT

DUMMY
TURNBUCKLE

CLOTH
PATCHES

DUMMY CABLES
FROM PIANO WIRE

FIG. 17.3

movement of the control surface is given. See Fig 17.3. Build up, on to the piano wire, the scale detail of the turnbuckle.

3. Lacing. Inspection panels on fabric covered aircraft originally took the form of laced panels, i.e. the removable fabric was stretched tight by lacing pulled tight, through eyelets, to join the fabric edges. The neatness of the laced joint depended on the skill of the manufacturer and, subsequently, the airframe fitter responsible for maintenance of the aircraft. Results varied from the extremely tidy to the very wrinkled fabric effect so noticeable in some photographs of aircraft of that period. We can simulate the neater versions quite simply with the use of pins and thread. It is a system that has been widely used on scale models and the method is illustrated in Fig 17.4. The eyelet effect is produced by wrapping the thread once or twice around the pin. Dope the thread thoroughly in place, allowing it to soak well into the thread, and allow to dry before removing the pins.

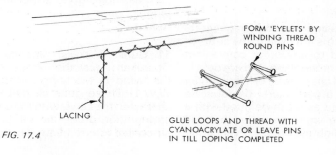

FORM 'EYELETS' BY
WINDING THREAD
ROUND PINS

LACING

GLUE LOOPS AND THREAD WITH
CYANOACRYLATE OR LEAVE PINS
IN TILL DOPING COMPLETED

FIG. 17.4

241

4. Drain holes. On the rear underside surfaces of the wings of some W.W.1 aircraft, and many later fabric covered prototypes, were small holes in the fabric to equalise the air pressure inside the wing to the external pressure and to act as drain holes for moisture. The holes were reinforced by a linen patch and, later, with clear plastic surrounds.

5. Clear view inspection panels. Look at photographs of many fabric covered aircraft and you will see, on the tops of the wings in front of the ailerons, small triangular, round or oval clear view panels. These were situated over the aileron control cable pulleys and allowed an immediate visual check on whether the cable and pulley were operating correctly. On our scale model we can feature the panel and the pulley and cable below.

6. Elevator control cable cranks. Projecting from the side of the fuselage, in the cockpit area, there was often a tube to which was fitted a 180° crank. The tube was fitted directly to the control column and the crank, connected to the elevator cables, would rotate to move the elevator up or down. Ideally, this arrangement should be incorporated on the model as a working feature, and it is usually possible to do so, as the realistic effect of the cable controls working is extremely convincing.

7. Pitot tubes and wind driven generators. These items are fixed to the struts of biplanes, and to any other convenient position on a monoplane, and are details that are full of character. The wind driven generator is a particularly useful scale embellishment as it can be fitted with a free wheeling small propeller that will turn in the slightest breeze. Even when the model is static parked on the runway, or judges' table, there will be that all important bit of movement that attracts the eye. Full size examples of the above items are illustrated in the photographs.

8. Flight Leaders' Pennants. Having the same benefits as the moving propeller on the generator, the small cloth triangular pennants, fitted to the interplane struts, will flutter in a breeze. Make from coloured nylon.

9. Ignition Switches. Sometimes fitted outside the cockpit on the decking, the early versions were of the brass domed, white porcelain, toggle action type. Use half a plastic ball from a 'pop bead' necklace for the dome and a pin from a shirt pack for the toggle. White plastic can be used for the base.

10. Bomb Racks. Bombers, and some fighters, (e.g. Sopwith *Camel*) carried their bomb loads externally. Release mechanisms were very simple and usually cable operated. They are not difficult to duplicate on a model and add another interesting function. Bomb types ranged from the small 20lb bombs to considerably larger devices but the shapes should be faithfully reproduced to get the full flavour of the period. An out of scale, or inaccurate bomb will be just as noticeable, especially to the judges, as a wrong shaped fin and rudder.

11. Guns. Vickers, Spandau, Lewis, Oberliken – just the names conjure up the 'wind in the wires' atmosphere of W.W.1! These guns all had their own character, the Lewis with its top mounted ammunition drum, the Vickers with its air cooled louvred barrel surround, and

they deserve to be accurately modelled. Williams Bros. manufacture excellent plastic kits of the above guns to one sixth scale and the Vickers gun to one quarter scale. Even if the scale does not corresponds to your model they are useful as a three dimensional reference. Many drawings have been produced of the different types of guns and examples can be viewed at War Museums and other collections. Where an external belt feed is used for the bullets this may be modelled by using a strong fabric webbing with slots cut in to receive the individual bullets. Metal cartridge links were not used until quite a bit later. To simulate the gunmetal finish on guns a mixture of silver with black and blue added will give a reasonable representation.

The observers on British aircraft had Lewis, or twin Lewis guns to operate and these were most frequently mounted on a 'Scarfe' ring. The latter device allowed the gun/s to be rotated on the ring and elevated on ratcheted quadrants. Try to use light materials for the construction of the guns and their mountings, i.e. the Scarfe ring and the Forster top wing

Above, bomb racks, tip skids, attachment plates and many other details add to Eric Coates' Martinside Elephant.

Right, more Williams Bros. accessories of high standard.

mounting, which allowed the pilot to reach the Lewis gun and pull it down on a rail to change the ammunition drum. Aluminium tube and sheet is to be preferred for the fabrication although tinplate and brass are easier to solder together.

And so it becomes obvious that the aircraft up to the 1930s have a lot to offer in the way of interesting exterior detail and this probably accounts for the considerable interest in modelling aircraft of this period. For the scale enthusiast with a flair for constructing small, detailed ancillary items, these aircraft present many challenges. The later 'cleaner' aircraft present more challenges on the decoration and finish side rather than detailing physical items. Colour schemes, lettering, symbols, squadron markings, roundels and flashes contribute far more to the external atmosphere of the scale model and greater attention must be paid to the weathering effects. One area where we can add a little extra working detail on the more up-to-date aircraft models is with the use of working navigational lights.

Very small light bulbs are obtainable and these are suitable for wiring into our model during the constructional stages. For instance, model railway enthusiasts use small pea bulbs, nominally rated at 12 volt but satisfactory on 6 volt, that are produced in red, green and white. It is also possible to colour clear bulbs by coating the glass with fuel proofer to which has been added some colour dye. Radio spares catalogues are an 'Aladdin's Cave' for scale model aircraft constructors. In addition to the hundreds of functional items ranging from nicads, miniature and sub miniature toggle, slide and micro-switches, plugs and sockets, wires, tags, circuit board, etc. etc., there are also items that could be used for scale detail because of their appearance. Included in catalogues are a number of sub-miniature bulbs such as sub-miniature flange bulbs with a diameter of 4mm and length of 9mm. They have a 5 volt rating (ideal for a 4.8 volt 225 mAH nicad) and a current draw of 60 milliamps. Holders are available requiring an 8mm. mounting hole. Operation of the navigational lighting system (red for port, green for starboard) can be from a fixed switch on the model or through a micro-switch operated by a servo. At dusk, or in dull conditions, these lights will show up very well but remember that this is also the most dangerous time to be flying — it can suddenly get very dark at ground level, without you fully realising it, and that makes for difficulties on the approach and landing.

Landing lights, housed behind a clear glazed panel in the leading edge of the wing, are also a feature of many civilian and military aircraft. To simulate the full size in operation the bulb on the model would have to be very powerful. Some reversing lamps are the right style to represent, statically, the typical landing light but these silver reflectored bulbs are rated at 12 volts with a 5 watt current drain! Obviously these lamps are more suited to non-operational use, although it may be possible to wire them up for short period operation on a large model with a suitable battery source.

OVAL TUBING

A common feature on aircraft from the early days to present times is the use of oval sectioned tubing. As previously stated, it is not always possible to procure tubing of the correct size for our models, but we can fabricate our own sections using standard round tube as the basis, following the method described in Chapter 6.

CONTROL SURFACE 'RIBBING'

Aluminium clad control surfaces frequently have the rigidity of the surface enhanced by the pressing-in of raised corrugations. To simulate this effect on our model (when applied to a sheeted structure) we can use an adhesive backed aluminium foil, of thickness to suit the control surface size. With the covering marked out to size place the aluminium face down on a piece of hard rubber. Use a piece of hardwood, slightly narrower than the corrugations, and press down on to the adhesive side of the aluminium. Draw the wood along the length of the corrugation, easing off the pressure at the ends. The aluminium is now ready for fixing to the airframe.

Drawing external details to scale by studying photographs can be rather frustrating; it seems that there is always one 'shot' that is missing and we are left to our own devices to interpret the information that is lacking. It may help us considerably if we try to understand the function of the item being modelled. Are any of the parts 'moving'? What material was the item constructed from? What function does it perform? Is it controllable by the pilot or is it a fixture? Is it connected to, and working in conjunction with, any other component or piece of equipment? Often, by studying the function we can make a reasonable guess at parts of the item that are not totally clear from photographs and drawings. Of course, there is no substitute to inspecting the real thing and this may be possible in collections such as can be viewed at the Smithsonian Institute, Confederate Air Force collection or Cole Patten's Rhinebeck Airfield in the U.S.A., or the Science Museum, Imperial War Museum (both in London), the R.A.F. museums at Hendon and Duxford, the F.A.A. at Yeovilton and the Shuttleworth Collection in England, and similar institutions in other countries. An hour's perusal of the full-size aircraft will resolve all of the queries relating to 'unknown' detail areas.

Fred Coulson's Grumman Skyrocket has very little exterior detail to copy but what there is is all nicely modelled and the panel lines are just right.

Chapter 18

Finishes

To achieve a high standard of finish on a scale R/C model aircraft is of vital importance, none more so than for competition work. Finish does not simply mean obtaining smooth surfaces and the use of correct colour schemes and insignia: that is but a part of the deception we are attempting to perpetrate. We must try to represent the full-size finish in colour, texture and atmosphere. We must *think* about the materials we are portraying. Is the surface hard or soft, smooth or rough, solid or fragile, natural or artificial? All of these characteristics we must aim to reproduce in miniature on our scale model. Imitation, it is said, is the sincerest form of flattery, and with our chosen prototype we want to flatter it to the extent of including every small scratch mark, paint fading and any other device that will improve the illusion of a full-size aircraft that has been miraculously reduced in size. It is an art — and that is not an exaggeration — that must be worked at to achieve the highest standard, but is endlessly rewarding.

Before entering into more detailed descriptions of the methods of producing various forms of finishes, a word of warning. Modellers often use colour print photographs as the basis for painting their scale models. This may seem to be an obvious source of colour information but there are dangers. Colour prints are not necessarily an accurate representation of the actual colours and they can be quite misleading. Different makes of colour film, film age and storage temperature, and the light conditions at the time of taking the photograph, will result in different biases of colour. For the want of a better description, you may have prints with 'Kodak' colour or 'Agfa' colour, and if you took identical photographs of the same subject, with different films, the colour results would not be the same. For competition work there is no substitute to viewing the original example — with contemporary aircraft you may be able to obtain some of the original paint as a sample, or to use for painting the model. The sports scale modeller will not be so worried about an exact match to the original colours, and for prototypes no longer in existence some intelligent guesswork, based on research, will have to suffice.

Because there are so many different methods of finishing a model and paint types it will not be tenable to include every variation. The basic methods will, however, be covered with notes regarding the fabric covered aircraft and the later wood and metal-clad prototypes.

DOPES

Applying a finish to a model normally has two basic functions, to seal the surface and make it airtight, and to provide the decorative finish to resemble the finish of the prototype. With modern heat-shrink materials – films and fabrics – it may not be necessary to seal the surface, although most of the iron-on fabrics will benefit from a couple of thinned coats of clear dope before the colour is applied. Methods of clear doping, using shrinking and non-shrinking types, have been covered in Chapter 15 and the painting of plastic films with coloured cellulose is not recommended – enamels are preferable for this purpose.

Before colour dopes are applied to any surface intended to represent a 'hard' material on the prototype the doped tissue or nylon must be filled and sanded, to a perfectly smooth finish. Modelling cellulose fillers, primers and sealers, or commercial (car) types may be used and the number of coats required will depend on the standard of substructure finish and the porosity of the covering. Tissue covering on a smooth structure should not need much in the way of filling but nylon, with an open weave, will inevitably need more attention. It is important to realise that a good base to any colour finish is obtained as a result of working down to a fine surface rather than building up to a satiny finish. After the filler has been applied it must be rubbed down until only the low points remain filled. This process is repeated, using finer grades of 'wet and dry' abrasive papers on successive applications, until the complete surface is smooth and without blemish. Unless great care – and plenty of 'elbow grease' – is employed at this stage of the preparation there will be a considerable build-up of weight.

Fabric covered prototypes do not usually possess such a high standard of smoothness as the metal clad aircraft (although some of the high performance aerobatic types, e.g. 'Pitts Special', feature a many-coated smooth finish). Where the full size version has an obvious fabric finish it is not necessary to fill the pores of the nylon covering to the same extent and only light sanding of the filler will be necessary to avoid 'fluffing-up' the strands of nylon.

Prior to the brushing or spraying of any colour dope or cellulose to materials other than a standard doped and filled

Finish on the author's $^1/_6$ Avro 504K represents an aircraft in 'normal' condition.

structure it is prudent to carry out some experimental tests on scrap material. Even though the cellulose dope may not adversely react with the material (as it *does* with expanded foam or rigid styrene) the adhering qualities of the dope to the material may be poor. Metals can be etched or primed with metal primers, but plastics are not so easy to deal with. G.R.P. mouldings will accept cellulose finishes if they are well cleaned and rubbed with a fine steel wool to give an improved key for the finish. This is not the case with all plastics; A.B.S., polypropylene and 'Fablon' type materials do not form a good base for cellulose finishes − even when 'keyed' − and alternative paints should be considered. With so many different types of plastic material now being used in modelling it is important to investigate the compatibility of the finishes and the probable cohesive qualities. It is very frustrating to complete the painting of part of the model only to find that the paint is unsuitable for some of the other areas.

Where cellulose finishes are to be used in conjunction with other paints it is equally important to check their compatibility, if there is any over-painting of the finishes. For instance, enamels can be painted over cellulose finishes but not vice-versa. Cellulose finishes (nitrate based) are only fuel-proof to petrol based fuels and for glow or diesel fuels the finish must be protected with a fuel proofer. Virtually all of the regular fuel proofers can be used on cellulose finishes but problems arise when repairs have to be made; the proofer must be totally removed over any area that is to be repainted with cellulose, or 'pickling' will take place.

Cellulose paints, particularly those from automobile sources, are normally supplied in gloss colours; colour dopes specifically produced for modelling purposes can be obtained in matt finishes. It is a common characteristic of dopes and enamels for the gloss varieties to have better adhering qualities than the matt and semi-matt types. Matt paints have a higher proportion of colour pigment (good for colour covering abilities) and less effective base material to give the necessary 'stick' to the object being painted.

Because cellulose paints are rapid drying, and also because they are easily softened by the application of subsequent coats, they are not very suitable for brush application. It is not impossible to apply modelling colour dopes with a brush but it does take a lot of practice to obtain reasonable results. Spraying techniques are highly recommended if a decent finish is to be expected. Commercial cellulose paints are virtually impossible to apply with a brush and, as these are readily available to the modeller (the colour range is infinite as a car paint factor will mix any colour desired) spraying does give many advantages. Non-blushing cellulose thinners will be needed for reducing the consistency of the paint for spraying and also some cellulose-based cleaner for cleaning out the spray gun etc. − this is cheaper than the thinners.

OIL BASED PAINTS AND ENAMELS

Enamels are similar to domestic oil-based paints except that the colour pigments are more finely ground and they are, therefore, more suitable for model work. Plastic kit modellers use enamels (cellulose finishes attack the moulded plastics) but the common size of ½oz or 14–15ml tinlets are not generally suitable for large scale R/C models. Larger tins are usually available in limited colour ranges − try hardware and cycle stores −

or they may be stocked as household enamels. Brush application is more feasible with enamels as they have a slower drying time (typically one hour) and two or three thinned coats will give a superior finish to one heavy coat. The paint may be *lightly* rubbed down between coats. Spraying of enamels is quite satisfactory, although care has to be taken with obtaining the right consistency and the correct application; separate thin coats are again to be preferred to attempting to cover in one go. White Spirit can be used for the thinning agent.

Although enamels are resistant to methanol/castor based glow fuels and diesel fuels they are not proof against nitro-methane and some of the other additives included in fuel mixes. Enamels give a tough finish but also tend to be heavier than cellulose paints; the slower drying time may be a disadvantage for the modeller with limited workshop facilities.

ACRYLICS AND POLYURETHANES

Acrylic and Polyurethane paints are produced in two basic types, one pack and twin pack (resin and hardener). The latter version are more fuel-proof than the single types and they rely on a chemical reaction for setting – for this reason they also produce a heavier finish than the solvent based paints, when applied to the same thickness. Single part paints have a drying time comparable to enamels (the acrylics slightly the more rapid) and the two part types can be adjusted by the resin/hardener ratio and the ambient temperature during application – the hotter it is, the quicker will be the drying time.

Both types of paint can be applied over cellulose based finishes but adequate drying time must be allowed to ensure that the cellulose solvents have dispersed. Leaving plenty of time between the application of subsequent coats of paints, irrespective of the type to be used, is good practice in every respect as it minimises the risk of any reaction between the different layers. Special thinners are required for the two-pack acrylic and polyurethane paints.

EPOXY PAINTS

Until recently epoxy paints have been considered as a two part paint only but now, thanks to the miracles of science, it is possible to purchase aerosol spray cans of epoxy paint. The use of epoxy resins for preparation of the airframe has been covered in Chapter 15 and this method makes an ideal base for an epoxy paint colour finish. Applying epoxy paints to cellulose finishes is also satisfactory; they may not be compatible with other types of paint.

Epoxy paints have the virtues of being almost 100 per cent fuel-proof and of giving a tough, abrasion resistant finish. Modelling ranges such as America's Hobbypoxy include a number of standard aircraft manufacturers' colours and they may also advise on the precise mixes of their paints to obtain specific camouflage colours. Matting agents are produced for adding to the normal gloss paint although this may reduce the fuel-proofing effectiveness of the finish. Undoubtedly epoxy paints are very suitable for R/C scale aircraft though the major problem may be in finding a well-stocked source of these products – they are not generally available outside of model shops. Inhalation of spray dust must be avoided at all costs.

FUEL PROOFING

Fuel-proofers are based on the types of paints that offer resistance to the effects of destructive fuels i.e. polyurethanes and epoxies. Gloss finishes always provide better protection than matt varieties and where appearance is of no consequence i.e. in engine and fuel tank bays, this type should be used. High gloss finishes seldom look authentic on scale models (even when the prototype had a gloss finish) and some means of reducing the gloss of the fuel-proofer must be sought. There are single pack matt fuel-proofers on the market but these are only suitable for use with 'mild' fuels. A compromise is to apply a coat of gloss fuel-proofer followed by a matt proofer; this will at least prevent the fuel from attacking the colour finish if the top layer of proofer is breached.

Single pack proofers also tend to 'yellow' with age and this becomes particularly noticeable over white and light colours. Two part fuel-proofers, such as 'Tufkote', are less prone to this ageing process and they produce a hard, high gloss finish that has excellent fuel resisting qualities. To matt this type of finish it is possible to scour the surface with steel wool – a laborious process – or to spray the proofer on to the model from a distance. The minute droplets of proofer will have partially dried before they contact the surface, resulting in a matt, or semi-matt finish (depending on the distance and temperature). Using this method will leave the model having a rough feel to it, which can be removed by rubbing down with fine wet and dry paper, although it does not spoil the appearance.

SPRAYING TECHNIQUES

Five essential prerequisites for satisfactory and safe paint spraying are:-
1. Warm atmosphere – spraying temperatures will be recommended by the paint manufacturers.
2. Dry atmosphere – high humidities may cause 'blooming'.
3. Clean atmosphere – small dust particles in the air will invariably find their way onto the sprayed surface and ruin the finish – more important with the slower drying paints.

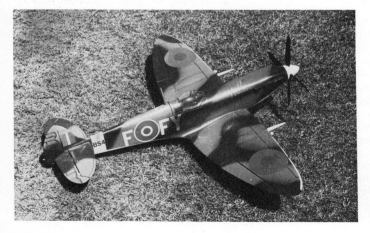

A simplified, semi-scale Spitfire made to look much closer to scale by a clever spray finish by Ian Peacock.

4. Adequate ventilation – some of the paints are toxic and those with volatile solvents can cause headaches, fainting and nausea. Wearing an efficient mask is imperative.

5. The correct equipment.

The whole subject of spray equipment and spraying technique is too complex to deal with in this book. There are some excellent specialist books on the subject; one written with the scale modeller in mind is 'Airbrushing and Spray Painting Manual' by Ian Peacock, published by Argus Books. Whether you opt for spraying (other than by small aerosol cans – not very economic) will depend on the facilities, with respect to suitable accommodation, and the financial implications. Do not embark on the purchase of spraying equipment without fully researching the subject, as it is all too easy to make a considerable outlay on equipment that you will quickly realise is not ideal and has too many limitations. Spending a few pounds on a book on the subject is a wise investment.

World class models have been brush painted but, having said that, there is no doubt that a spray finished model represents the pinnacle to aim for in top quality scale models. After all, few full size aircraft are brush painted and when 'soft' spray overlap techniques are used on prototypes (as in many camouflaged aircraft) the only way of reproducing this effect is by spraying the model.

FABRIC COVERED AIRCRAFT

In Chapter 15 the method of covering undercambered wings, and the full size stitching of the fabric to the ribs, was mentioned. The methods of stitching the fabric were, and are, fairly consistent and the style of stitching and knotting are shown in Fig. 18.1. Rib tape was often placed over the rib before the main covering so that the final fabric 'sandwich' over the area of stitching consisted of a rib tape/wing covering/external rib tape. Look at a fabric covered aircraft, even recovered original examples of early types, and the chances are that the external rib tape is of the serrated edge type. This may or may not be correct because before the 1920's a plain edge tape was used and the serrated edge linen tape had not been developed. It is

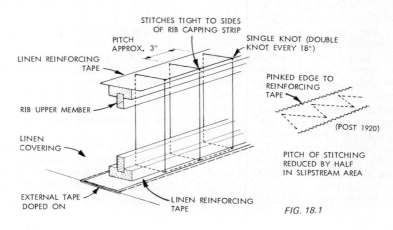

STITCHES TIGHT TO SIDES
OF RIB CAPPING STRIP

PITCH
APPROX. 3"

SINGLE KNOT (DOUBLE
KNOT EVERY 18")

LINEN REINFORCING
TAPE

RIB UPPER MEMBER

LINEN
COVERING

EXTERNAL TAPE
DOPED ON

LINEN REINFORCING
TAPE

PINKED EDGE TO
REINFORCING
TAPE

(POST 1920)

PITCH OF STITCHING
REDUCED BY HALF
IN SLIPSTREAM AREA

FIG. 18.1

251

Neat fabric lacing and cockpit coaming plus barely visible rib tapes on the Martinside Elephant.

unlikely that the modeller will want to go to the extremes of sewing all the rib positions with a thin cord, but for those that are building a large scale model and wish to incorporate fine detail, the pitch of the stitching was generally about three inches. This was reduced in later aircraft to about half that pitch in the areas of the propeller slip-stream only. For the smaller scale model the knot positions may be simulated by applying spots of white P.V.A. glue, from a hypodermic syringe, before applying the external rib tape. Early plain edged rib tapes are copied by using strips of heavyweight tissue, cotton tape or nylon 'baby' ribbon. The latter looks effective but is rather thick for anything bar the large scale aircraft — our covering materials are mostly overscale anyway. Serrated edged tape cannot be purchased in model sizes and the pitch produced by pinking shears is far too large. You may be fortunate in finding a serrated edged cutter, from a roll of kitchen foil or plastic, that is about the right scale (the pitch of the tape serrations for full size aircraft is about

$3/16$ in.). By marking the straight edge of a piece of thin steel to the required pitch and filing the notches with a square section file, you can make a template suitable for tearing paper rib tapes. Use a white, fairly soft paper for the tapes and it may be helpful to dampen the paper slightly. Mark the width of the tape at both ends of the paper, leaving a wide margin, and place the template over the first marks. Hold down the template firmly and tear upwards and slightly inwards, the free end. Reverse the template on to the second set of marks (i.e. the width of the tape) and, holding down the template very firmly, tear upwards the free area of paper. You may have to experiment with a few different papers, and dampening, before you obtain acceptable results. The tapes, paper or fabric, are doped in position after the wing has been given its first full coat of dope.

Seams in the wing covering material where the chord was wider than the full width of the material, were made chordwise, as in the case of some preprinted lozenge pattern fabric. On some early aircraft, however, the seams in the covering were made diagonally (e.g. Bleriot XI). Close inspection of prototype photographs should reveal the method used.

GERMAN CAMOUFLAGE FABRIC

The Allied aircraft in W.W.1 were mostly of natural linen finish, silver doped or the chocolate to dark green colour dope of the R.F.C. aircraft. There were examples of Allied machines with more garish colour schemes but these were few and far between and were generally frowned upon by the military authorities. German aircraft were originally natural fabric finish, or dyed a grey/blue colour giving a translucent effect, as used on the early Albatros reconnaissance aircraft. As the importance of camouflage was realised the German aircraft were painted with large hexagonal patterns of beige, dark green, mauve and browns, to a random pattern. The manpower involved in this work, and the variable results, led the authorities to adopt the use of printed fabrics which also resulted in weight saving compared with the painted surfaces. Not all aircraft were left in the camouflaged finish, thankfully for the less fastidious modellers, and parts or all of the fabric were overpainted in colours of the pilot's or squadron's choice.

Two main basic geometric patterns were adopted by the German armed services, although further examples were introduced for larger bomber aircraft at a later stage of the war. One of the fabrics used a four colour scheme and the other employed five colours. Differing colours, but not patterns, were used on the upper and underside surfaces, viz. Four Colour: Light underside pink, blue, light ochre, green. Dark upper surface sage green, blue-grey, ochre, blue-green. Five Colour: Light underside pale violet, ochre, blue, green, pink. Dark upper surface violet, dull ochre, blue-grey, blue-green, sage green. Colour references have been established by the Heathrow (London) Group and Historic Maintenance Group.

INTER-WAR FABRIC COVERED AIRCRAFT

The covering techniques used up to 1918 continued to be used until the introduction of metal-clad airframes. Even today the same basic methods are employed in fabric covered light aircraft, although the Irish linen has to a large degree been superseded by closer weave, lightweight fabrics such as 'Medapalin'. The aircraft after W.W.1 tended to have a higher standard of fabric finish and this can be recreated by mixing some filler with the later coats of clear shrinking dope. Access to the fuselage cockpit/s often entailed traversing the lower wing root and special walk areas were created, using a non slip black rubber or compound material. To simulate this non-slip surface the modeller can use emery, or a carborundum coated abrasive paper. The area was usually trimmed with thin sections of hardwood and adjacent to the wing walk would often be the words 'No step'. Remember to fuel-proof the wing walk area with matt clear fuel-proofer.

CHEMICAL COLOURING OF METAL COMPONENTS

It takes a long time for metals to reach a naturally oxidised state where the patina or discolouring of the metal gives that characteristic aged appearance. We can accelerate the effect by treating the metals with certain bleaches and acids or we can artificially colour the metals to some degree. Anodising aluminium is a

FIG 18.2 CHEMICAL COLOURING OF METALS

Effect	Metal	Chemical	Comments
	Steel	Steam	Heat to red heat and hold in jet of steam from boiling kettle.
	Brass	Copper Nitrate	Immerse for a few minutes.
Dull	Copper	1 oz. Water 3 oz.	Does not flake or chip.
Black	Iron & Steel	Hypo-Photo-graphic fixer.	Immerse – boil for short while
	Zinc	Antimonious Chloride.	Immerse.
Shiny	Copper	1 part ammonium	Immerse for a few minutes.
Black		sulphite 4 parts water	Brass goes steely grey colour
	Copper	Sodium sulphite solution.	Depth of colour depends on concentration of solution.
Antique			
Brown	Brass	Lime and Sulphur	Mix into a paste with water. Cover and heat gently.
	Brass	Vinegar, salt and sugar.	Brush over daily until satisfactory.
Green			
Patina	Copper	Washing soda water and vinegar	Suspend articles in closed container. Pour vinegar on to soda.
Dull	Aluminium	Caustic soda	Use hot, moderately strong solution.
coloured		(sodium hydroxide) oxide).	Immerse for a few seconds.

DANGER:-Treat all chemicals as being potentially poisonous; avoid unnecessary contact with the skin and clothes.

reasonably permanent method and, of course, it is possible to have metal parts plated by commercial concerns. For home anodising we require a 'bath' (a plastic bowl will suffice), a wire-wound variable resistance of ten watts, a car battery, some sulphuric acid and some aluminium wire to connect up with. Attach the article to be anodised to some aluminium wire to conduct electricity to it, and to suspend the item in the bath. The article must first be thoroughly cleaned with detergent and etched in a caustic soda solution. Pour into the 'bath' a 10% sulphuric acid solution, connect the aluminium wire via the variable resistance to the car battery positive and to the negative pieces of scrap aluminium – the scrap and the article being on either side of the 'bath'. Increase the current until fine bubbles are emanating from the article to be anodised. Leave for about twenty minutes to allow for a fair depth of film and then dye to the chosen colour. Should the material being anodised start to blacken the current must be reduced. Great care must be taken when using any potentially dangerous chemicals where skin damage and the

breathing in of noxious fumes can be injurious.

In Fig 18.2 is a list of methods, and the chemicals used, for the chemical treatment of metals. Some of the finishes are relatively permanent and others less so but they should all be superior to attempts at painting on the equivalent finish. For colouring anodised aluminium or treating aluminium previously etched in a hot caustic solution, the articles should be boiled for a few minutes in a strong solution of nylon dye. Nylon dyes are suitable for this application and are available in a wide range of colours.

WEATHERING EFFECTS ON FABRIC AND WOOD AIRCRAFT

No aircraft stays in a pristine condition for long: within a few weeks of operation it will start to gather dust, dirt and oil. In war conditions the situation will often dictate that the aircraft maintenance is restricted to the more essential mechanical servicing, refuelling and rearming, and cleaning of the airframe becomes the lowest priority. Aircraft take on a well-worn and used appearance and it is this atmosphere that we may wish to emulate for maximum realism. The mere thought of having to 'dirty up' a model is anathema to many modellers after they have spent so many hours in completing the model to the painted stage. They will have severe doubts about their ability to make a convincing job of applying the weathered and dirty appearance and will be tempted to bypass this operation and leave the model as an 'ex-factory' example. Fortunately, for the fabric covered models – and to some extent for the metal-clad examples too – we do not have to take any risk and errors can be quickly rectified. Assuming that the covering has been already treated to give the correct background colour, natural or painted, we are only concerned with the 'dirtying' effect. The theatrical profession use hair lacquer spray cans that are used to tint the hair and these have the great advantage of being water soluble. In practical terms this enables us to wipe off the spray from the model with a damp cloth should we be dissatisfied with the results – a much safer proposition than spraying on a

'permanent' paint. The model can be completed before the dirtying operation is carried out but you will probably find it easier to dismantle it for spraying. A can of dark brown and one of dark grey or black will suffice for the effects we require. Think logically before commencing the spraying of where the dirtiest areas are likely to be. There are the obvious places around the engine cowlings and exhaust areas but there are also some less obvious positions. When the aircraft is being cleaned down, often in a hurry or by a none too enthusiastic mechanic, there will be some parts that will be missed, or avoided, because they are 'difficult' areas. Near to a rigging fitting where the rigging wire obstructs the fitting is one area, and no one is ever keen to get on his back to clean the underside of the fuselage. The lower surface of the wings, adjacent to the undercarriage, is likely to become spattered with mud during take-offs and landings and oil or grease will leak from the wheel axle on to the wheel covers. Aircraft have to be ground handled and

The Hawker Fury shown earlier. Nicely built but a little strong on the dark spray which contrasts too much with the excellent general finish.

255

Torpedo is just visible on this Blackburn design. Nice scale look; turn near ground is telephoto effect.

the mechanics responsible for this work are hardly likely to have 'lily white' hands. Grease and dirt marks will show on the wing tips, the struts, the leading edges of the wing and tailplane and the undercarriage at the positions where the aircraft has been pushed for manoeuvring. Spray these areas gently, building up the darkening effect, until you are satisfied with the result – it is very simple really! Leave the spray to harden off for a day or two before fuel-proofing with a matt polyurethane varnish to the fabric areas. Spraying the fuel-proofer is recommended but if it is brushed on do not be too vigorous with the brush action or it may 'spread' the hair lacquer *and* make the varnish dry with a gloss. A word of warning, the hair sprays are quite scented, so do warn the wife of what you are doing or she may jump to the wrong conclusions! Further embellishments such as 'scuff' marks, tears, patches, etc., may be added – for military aircraft the addition of a few bullet holes may improve the authenticity, but do back up the holes with some black material to prevent the ingress of oil. Modellers are naturally loth to allow their models to get oil-stained, but within reason the

effect can be quite realistic on the old, plain fabric aircraft models.

PLYWOOD COVERED AIRCRAFT

One might consider ply covering as an intermediate stage of finish between fabric on an open structure and the sheet metal cladding. Ply is nearly always covered with fabric to strengthen and protect the wood finish, and this will occasionally cause a slight 'cockling' of curved areas e.g. the rear turtle decking of the *Tiger Moth*. The paint finish on fabric covered ply is frequently, but not invariably, less glossy than one would expect with a metal aircraft. Much will depend on the amount of fabric filling that is applied but the weave of the fabric is often visible under the paint. Certainly, the best method of denoting a change between metal and ply construction is in the texture of the finish.

METAL SKINNED AND GLASS-FIBRE SURFACES

Whatever method we use to obtain the finish, including the panel lines and other surface detail, the model must give the impression of having a hard, 'solid'

Plainness of simple S6B nose is offset by spraying of panel/shadow lines which aid 3D effect.

surface. We shall only achieve this by having a well-filled smooth surface with no signs of the substrate showing through.

There are four basic methods of applying the panel details.

1. By painting the model and drawing on the panel lines with soft pencil or incising with a knife – helped by a little spray shading where necessary:

2. By recessing the panel lines, using thin masking tape, painting over and then removing the tape:

3. By using subtle colour gradings of adjacent panels to simulate the separate panels:

4. By applying actual dummy panels cut from paper.

Obviously, there are other refinements, or combinations of these four methods, but these cover the general principles.

Before considering these methods in more detail we will take a look at the ways and means of producing scale looking rivets and hatches and the general planning of the finishing schemes. Rivets come in two types, countersunk and raised (or dome headed) and any aircraft will use a

predominance of one or other types. Modern jet aircraft always use flush rivets to reduce drag, but W.W.2 aircraft were varied in their use. It is not enough to know the type of rivets but also the head diameter (one aircraft will use numerous sizes of rivets) and the pitch of them. Look at most modern aircraft and you will see that the rivets are neatly made, regular and precise in their location. In most cases the panels will not have been distorted by the application of the rivets and the surfaces will follow a smooth contour. Look at some examples of W.W.2 aircraft and you may find a very different situation. Rivets, even so called flush rivets, will vary between being quite proud of the surface to being countersunk to the extent of the aluminium panel being recessed and pulled in. The two finishes will obviously require different techniques to reproduce scale finishes. Dome headed rivets must be applied before the paint finish and the method almost universally used is to apply them as white P.V.A. glue from a hypodermic syringe. The secret of quick and regular application is in having the P.V.A. glue at the right consistency so that it will feed

Good representation of pop rivets in Volksplane tailplane. Horn also provides scale "feel".

smoothly from the needle but not run on the surface of the model. It does not take long to get the feel of producing P.V.A. rivets and the method is not as time-consuming as might be imagined. Soft pencil lines must be drawn on the model for guidance to position the rivets and you will probably find it an advantage to also mark the pitch of the rivets. As the rivets are produced from an aluminium alloy, and as they are likely to show some wear on the aircraft, it must be advantageous to start off with metal coloured glue rivets for our model. If we do this any accidental or artificial rubbing away of the paint surface will reveal an aluminium coloured rivet rather than a clear blob of P.V.A. glue. Silvered rivets

can be produced simply by adding silver paint to the P.V.A. glue and leaving it to reach the right consistency, or accelerating the thickening process by heating with a hair dryer. Don't mix too much glue at a time as keeping it at the correct consistency is important, and in any case a little glue makes a lot of rivets.

Countersunk, or flush, rivets are applied *after* painting the structure of the model. The impression of the rivet head is made by pressing and revolving a suitable sized piece of tubing into the surface. Surprisingly, the wear rate on the tubing is quite high and for this reason, and the fact that it leaves a black mark, brass is not suitable. Obviously, aluminium and copper tubing are

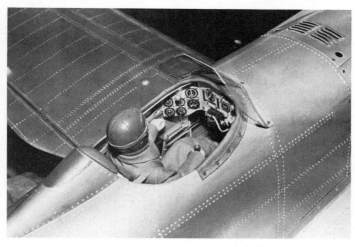

PVA rivets applied straight and even but needed tinting or subsequent colour washing to reduce prominence.

unacceptable for the same reason. Steel is far more satisfactory, particularly if it is hardened, and stainless steel (available in many sizes of small diameters) is also excellent. Dzus fasteners can be similarly denoted, with the screw head being inscribed with a jeweller's screwdriver. Remember to line up the slots of the Dzus and Oddie fasteners to the same directions as the prototype. Moulded rivets can be purchased but these are only really suitable for the larger scale models. They will give a very consistent rivet pattern and, therefore, will give better results for the prototypes with a high standard of dome headed riveting.

Hatches, by design or because of their less accurate fitting, are often proud of the surrounding panels. Some hatches are totally removable and others are hinged, so the latter should have the hinges indicated on the models. The hatches can be represented by a variety of materials including paper (writing paper quality), thin plastic card, 'Contact' or 'Fablon' self adhesive vinyl sheet or aluminium litho plate. Litho plate has the advantage of being suitable for making indentations, from either side, to represent rivets and other securing devices. As an alternative to gluing a complete hatch plate to the surface it is possible to build up the additional thickness by masking and applying a coat of sanding quality resin. This method has the advantage of allowing the panel to be 'faded out', leaving one edge proud and the other flush with the adjacent panels. Mask the 'proud' edge and part of the side edges with a thick self adhesive plastic (Fablon or similar), apply the resin and when it has just dried sand the hatch smooth, grading it down to a feather edge.

A very necessary preamble to the finishing process is the detailed study of the prototype and the planning of the application. As stated many times previously there is no substitute for inspection of the actual prototype, providing it is in authentic condition. The highly 'bulled' and repainted examples to be found in some collections and museums are a tribute to the refurbishing attempts

Riveted headrest, aileron push-rod hatch etc. Very neat on this Widgeon. Wear patches on centre-section not where expected?

of the workers but are not the type of finish that, if emulated, will result in a model representing a full-size operational aircraft. However, if it is feasible to examine the genuine article do so and make copious notes and take photographs to provide yourself with a complete record of details, finishes, colours and surface imperfections. Without the prototype to hand you will have to satisfy yourself with thorough inspection of photographs. Half tone reproductions, as featured in magazines, are only useful as general references; when you try to investigate them closely for a particular detail you will only find a series of different tone dots! Real photographs, glossy if possible, are the only type that are completely satisfactory — colour and black and white. What are we looking for? Almost everything! We are searching for the position of panel lines, rivets, hatches, fillets, fasteners, fuel tank caps, fairings, lettering, insignia, scratching, fading, chipping, in other words the complexities of the finish and the character and 'feel' of the surface. All of these details should be marked on the drawing as a permanent reference – you may wish to build another model of the same prototype – although it can be marked directly on to the model.

With the model researched, the next decision must be the method to be adopted for painting it. How many colours are to be used? Are the paint chippings to be applied before or after the final coat? Will transfers be used for the insignia or will they be painted direct? In general terms the light colours should be painted first, working up the tones to the darkest for the final coat. Using this method slight areas of overspray, or going beyond a defined line with a colour, will not be too critical – the darker colour should cover the lighter

one without it showing through. The white areas on insignia sometimes give rise for concern, especially when they are within a dark background. Some modellers treat the insignia and lettering as part of the overall colour scheme, painting them in and masking them as the general painting proceeds. There is nothing against this method except that it does make the work a little more complicated and leaves no room for errors. As the full-size aircraft invariably have the insignia and lettering painted on *after* the general colour scheme is complete it seems logical to treat the model in the same way. It may need a few extra coats on the white and light coloured areas, but no doubt the painters of the prototypes had the same difficulties. A word of warning regarding silver paints. For some reason silver finishes never seem to have the same adhesive powers as other colours and tend to pull away from the primer coats rather easily. This is not bad enough to present problems in the ordinary way of flying but can be troublesome during the painting stage. Try to organise your painting schedule so that any substantial areas of silver are painted after the other colours. By working to this order any masking tape used for separation of colours will be attached to the standard colours and not the silver paint. To reverse the order may well cause the silver paint to be lifted with the tape. The 'scuff' and wear marks can be added after the general colour scheme has been completed with the assistance of a dry brush to stipple on the silver plus a fine (000) brush to work in the fine detail. Afternatively the general colour can be applied over a silver base and the marks made by scratching through with medium grade glasspaper and careful use of a sharp knife blade. If you adopt this method use

The technique of scraping away the top paint to expose a silver undercoat should not be overdone.

a silver paint that will 'take' well on the primer and is not likely to be dislodged readily, i.e. silver dope. Compatibility of paints for finishing is most important, to avoid 'pickling' and other disastrous happenings. The enamel-over-dope technique is ideal for the paint chipping and flaking process as the dissimilar paints leave a natural barrier when breaking through the top surface. Further enhancing of the silver paint can be made by rubbing the areas to be treated with steel wool to give the grain effect often found on aluminium. Study *very* carefully how the scratches take place and where they occur. Just chipping and scratching in an indiscriminate fashion over the whole aircraft will *not* give a convincing result. There is a reason why the paint has been worn away, i.e. walk areas, moving parts, constant abrasion on the leading edges etc. Write out the sequence of colours to be painted or sprayed and the types of paints to be used.

To return to the methods of marking the general panelled areas.

1. PENCIL LINES

This technique must be used over matt finishes as soft pencil will not take on a gloss surface. In point of fact matt paints can always be used for painting the model as the gloss finish, if required, can be achieved by using a clear gloss fuel-proofer at the final stage. Matt paints generally have a much better covering facility as more pigment is used and less varnish, compared with gloss paints — they also dry quicker but have less adhesion over gloss surfaces. Never use a black ink for marking the panels, etc., which looks totally artificial and will ruin the finished effect — we are only attempting to represent small gaps or height differences in the surface. Mark the pencil lines with the aid of a flexible clear plastic straightedge; you can augment this method by using a hard pencil or knife to incise some of the more prominent lines. The soft pencil can also be used for shading on the light 'shadows' to the rear and bottom edges where grime and dirt would be likely to collect on the full-size aircraft. Marking the surface by this technique is really more suited to small

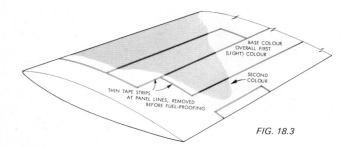

BASE COLOUR
OVERALL FIRST
(LIGHT) COLOUR

SECOND
COLOUR

THIN TAPE STRIPS
AT PANEL LINES, REMOVED
BEFORE FUEL-PROOFING

FIG. 18.3

scale.models where the amount of detail to be applied is limited. Better shading effects can be obtained with the use of an airbrush and masking the areas involved with well wetted paper. Cut the paper mask to shape from a heavy absorbent paper and soak in water, apply to the airframe and allow to dry. Spray on the shading (e.g. lines of fabric covering on the tail surfaces of W.W.2 aircraft) with great restraint with darker tones of the base colour, and possibly a little grey added. Fade out the edges very softly and don't spray too close to the paper or it may lift. As soon as the paint has dried remove the mask – the water will not damage the base colour paint.

2. RECESSED PANEL LINES

This system is particularly suitable for models of modern, smooth-surfaced jet aircraft although it can also be used on other types. It is suitable for glass fibre fuselages and for sheeted surfaces that have been covered with glass fibre cloth and resin. (The latter should be filled with sandable resin, sanded to a smooth finish and primed and sanded.) Mark out the colour separation lines lightly with a pencil – unless you are a natural artist with a spray gun – and spray on the first, lightest colour. Spray on the second and third coats (assuming a camouflaged pattern) masking the other areas as

necessary. If you look at the painting of the colours on full-size aircraft you will note that the separation is not in the form of a 'hard' line, but you should also notice that the fading out width is quite small. Many modellers make the mistake of making the separation *too* soft – remember the scale factor. When all of the base coats have been applied, and we are only looking for a light spray at this time, the whole of the surface can be rubbed down using a number 400 grade wet and dry paper used wet. The panel lines are now marked out with masking or chart tape about $1/_{64}$ in. wide. If you are going to use the chipped paint technique, where the top paint layer is removed, now is the time to apply silver paint to the areas to be treated. As an alternative to scraping and scratching through at the later stage the silver can be 'painted' with liquid masking and cut to the desired shapes of chips etc. The liquid masking is removed after the final painting has been finished. Spray on the final coats of paint, add the insignia and lettering (painted – not transfers) and when dry, remove the tapes. A final coat of fuel-proofer, unless fuel-proof epoxies have been used, will complete the basic colouring and panel line stage. Dirtying, oil marks, gun firing powder stains, etc., may be applied before the fuel-proofing although if applied after proofing it gives the advantage of being able to remove them more easily if a mistake is made.

3. COLOUR GRADING

This is a system devised by champion scale modeller David Vaughan, and if carried out with flair and artistic ability, can give superbly realistic results. To achieve the 'aged' effect of well-used service aircraft, where the paints have faded and dirtied, there is no better method. It *must* be used with great restraint, and that is true of most methods, and there is always the temptation to overdo the first areas to be treated forgetting that it is the total effect of a build-up of subtle gradings that will give the result we require. The model is painted in the usual way, including insignia etc., with matt finish paints and the panel lines are lightly marked on with soft pencil, where these are not obvious. For the shading of the panelled areas,

etc., we shall be using Artists' Oil Pastels of the type marketed by such firms as Reeves and Cray-Pas, available from any good artists' materials retailer. These pastels are very soft and are not to be confused with the children's types — artist quality are the most suitable. If you can purchase the sticks separately just concentrate on the black, white, dark grey, olive, yellow and earth colours, although you will probably have to buy a full or half set. David suggests that the best instrument for applying the pastels is the tip of the finger — a technique not unknown to the artist. The pastel is applied to the area to be 'weathered' with the finger tip and smeared out to a gradual fading. Stencils and masks from cartridge paper can be used to define edges accurately and, fortunately, mistakes can be wiped off with the aid of a soft clean cloth dampened with turps. Use the pastels and colours sparingly; it is safer to start off with an understated effect — the staining and darkening can

The Mustang by David Vaughan, whose method of colour-grading with pastels is described above.

always be increased at a later stage. Although aircraft did get dirty and, therefore, darker as a result, the paint often faded also. Dirtying and shading the model by the use of pastels will, overall, darken the base colours and it may be advisable to consider this when painting them, possibly opting for slightly lighter shades initially. Dirt areas are treated with dark grey or black and a smear of pastel to the rear of a line of rivets will immediately 'bring them to life'. The precise application of the colours and positions will only be found out by experiment, and reference to the prototypes, but the techniques are within the scope of most modellers. Taking the first step is probably the most difficult but, bearing in mind that the poorer efforts can be wiped away, you should quickly get the hang of it and probably wonder why you haven't used the method before. When all of the fading and dirtying has been completed it only leaves the addition of the oil stains (glossy) before fuel-proofing. It is *imperative* to spray on the fuel-proofer (this applies to soft pencil technique

also) as brushing will certainly 'drag' on the pastel and smear it. Matt or egg-shell finish clear polyurethane varnish is suitable although it is not 100% fuel-proof with nitro glow fuel. Another technique is to spray one coat of two-part gloss fuel-proofer in the normal manner, followed by a second coat sprayed on at a greater distance. The minute drops of proofer virtually dry before they hit the surface of the model and the result is a nearly matt finish.

4. APPLYING DUMMY PANELS

Apart from the panel beaten, or moulded, metal parts an aircraft consists of riveted panels with, at the most, simple curves. There is, therefore, no reason why we should not duplicate these on the model by using thin panels glued directly to the surface. Use a medium weight paper (about the thickness of writing paper) for the majority of the panels, though you can incorporate some thicker panels where this is justified, glued to the surface using a thinned down P.V.A. glue. The paper may be

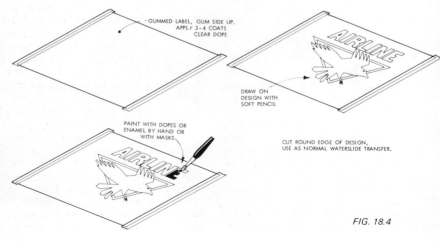

GUMMED LABEL, GUM SIDE UP.
APPLY 3 - 4 COATS
CLEAR DOPE

DRAW ON
DESIGN WITH
SOFT PENCIL

PAINT WITH DOPES OR
ENAMEL BY HAND OR
WITH MASKS.

CUT ROUND EDGE OF DESIGN,
USE AS NORMAL WATERSLIDE TRANSFER.

FIG. 18.4

dampened to improve its ability to follow the curves – don't worry if there is a slight shrinkage, the effect will be quite acceptable. Where the prototype shows indications of double layers of cladding, e.g. wing and tail fairings, a double layer of paper should be used. The curvature of the fairing can be built up with balsa, fillers, epoxy putty etc., and sealed. With all of the panels applied and checked for security, the complete surfaces must be sealed and sanded until all 'furry' edges have disappeared. From this position the remainder of the finishing, i.e. rivets, details, painting, can follow the standard methods.

AIRCRAFT MARKINGS

As aircraft markings are applied by painting on to the airframe, earlier examples by brushing, and later aircraft with spray techniques, it is entirely reasonable that we should emulate this system. Decals (transfers) are supplied with many kits and the best examples have excellent colour rendering. They are, however, a poor substitute for the hand-painted article as they are less permanent in their adherence to the airframe, have thickness and have to be weathered in to match the remainder of the decoration. Where cellulose finishes are being used for painting and weathering these may affect the transfers and cause pickling and you should experiment before risking this process. Water-slide decals normally have a border to the markings that is supposedly transparent – it will not be so when it is affixed to the model – and this surplus edge should be carefully trimmed away before the decal is used. The same applies to self-adhesive decals and trimming is best undertaken before the decorative elements are removed from the sheet.

Fitting any form of decals to double curvature surfaces is virtually impossible and these areas must be hand-painted. A good example of this problem is when fin stripes are expected to curve around the leading edge of the fin and part way down the curved fillet at the base. Trying to use a decal for this position will inevitably end in failure.

Fortunately it is not difficult to mask and paint markings; hand-painting without the assistance of masking or templates should be within the capabilities of most modellers for small items. Although decals can be produced by the modeller they are only suitable for small markings, though they do have the advantage of allowing an intricate design to be worked on a flat surface where it is easier to operate. The method is quite simple: tape down a gummed label to the drawing board, give it two or three coats of clear dope, draw on the pattern and paint in with cellulose or enamel paints. Application is then the same as with commercial decals, the outline is trimmed, the transfer immersed in warm water, removed and placed face down on newspaper to remove the surplus water and the decal transferred to the model. Adhesive on the original gummed label will stick the decal to the model. Similar results may be obtained by painting on to white or clear self-adhesive vinyl sheet – the type used for covering books is suitable – but this is a thicker material than is desirable.

There are commercial products on the market for softening transfers (e.g. 'Micro-Set' and 'Micro-Sol') and these certainly assist in positioning the water-slide decals to a curved surface without tearing them. Plastic kit modellers use these materials extensively as they allow the decals to 'form' over details such as panel lines and rivets, and similar advantages will be obtained when they are used on R/C scale models.

LETTERING

1. Dry print commercial systems

Pressure sensitive lettering forms such as 'Letraset' and 'Meccanorma' have come to the rescue of many scale modellers. The range of lettering styles and sizes is now very extensive and there is a reasonable chance that there is a type available to suit your purposes. Catalogues of the various makes are viewable at graphic artists' stores or if you can obtain the catalogues separately, the sheets of lettering are available by post. Sheets of these dry-print lettering schemes are expensive and the larger lettering sizes may only have one example of each letter and numeral, so where you have repeated letters or numerals it can cost you a small fortune to decorate the model. The results though are excellent and superior to virtually all other methods. Modification to dry-print lettering is not difficult *providing* that it only entails *removal* of material and not adding to it. Using a very sharp knife or razor blade the surplus material may be removed by cutting on the rear of the top sheet and scraping away the unwanted area. If sizeable areas of surplus material are to be removed only the cuts need to be made and care taken not to press on these when the letter, or numeral, is being fixed to the airframe. Typical W.W.2 stencil lettering may be simulated using this method, leaving the stencil 'gaps' on the sheet. Some dry-print lettering, particularly if it is fairly old stock, can require fairly high pressure on the top surface of the sheet before the character will adhere to the surface. This may not be acceptable when the print is

being applied to a soft surface, as the pressure marks from the stylus, pen or whatever is being used, will be transferred to the model surface and ruin the finish. To obviate this potential disaster it is possible to pre-release the characters from the top sheet by pressing on to the backing sheet. Full instructions are given for this method with each sheet but it is a technique that requires considerable experience before it can be perfected. Where dry-print characters are to be oversprayed a check should be made on a spare letter to ensure that the materials are compatible. What if the lettering on the model is in a colour that is unavailable in the dry-print process? At least we can use the characters, providing they are the correct outline and size, as patterns for producing masks and hand painting.

2. Direct painting

Confidence is one of the chief assets to painting direct, without masks or templates, on to the semi-completed airframe. The fear of failure is more likely to cause mistakes than the certainty that it will be satisfactory. This confidence can be increased if the paint is dissimilar to the base colours and will not affect them, i.e. enamels on to cellulose finishes, because there is always the knowledge that mistakes can be rectified. Equipment that is essential for direct painting includes draughting pen (the old-fashioned variety with two 'blades'), ink compasses of high quality and sable brushes. Paint applied from a pen must be thinned slightly or it will not flow smoothly; enamels are superior for this purpose, cellulose paint tends to dry too rapidly in the pen giving inconsistent viscosity of the paint. Roundels, using an ink compass, are very simple to create if the paintwork is to be brush applied. Start by

A smart 58in. kit model of the Czech aerobatic Zlin 50L Nice finish without over-fussy decor.

taping a small square of ply to the central area of the roundel, to prevent the point of the compasses from digging into the surface of the airframe. Thin lines are quite acceptable for the rings of the roundel – providing there is *something* to paint up to, the brush can be swept boldly up to the line without fear of over-painting. Paint the inner and outer rings of each colour, leaving sufficient time for the paint to dry before proceeding on to the adjacent colour. Remove the centre plywood piece and fill in the colours with normal consistency paint. Using this method the results will often be more authentic than a sprayed finish as roundels were frequently hand-painted on service aircraft. Straight-edged markings are accomplished with use of a draughting pen and straightedge to map in the outline. A flexible material straightedge is useful when drawing lines on a curved surface, but the edge must be very smooth and tolerably thick. Corners must be neatly formed, neither crossing the lines or stopping short, and even pressure and a constant speed are needed for a consistent thickness line.

A well-weathered Zero, also from a kit. Weathering seems to have gone a little too far?

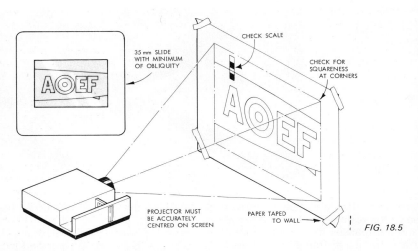

CHECK SCALE

35 mm SLIDE
WITH MINIMUM
OF OBLIQUITY

CHECK FOR
SQUARENESS
AT CORNERS

PROJECTOR MUST
BE ACCURATELY
CENTRED ON SCREEN

PAPER TAPED
TO WALL

FIG. 18.5

Paint that is too thick will leave an excessively high ridge and over-thinned paint will tend to spread over the surface. Freehand painting of irregularities is naturally the most difficult, but with care and practice the results can be far superior to those anticipated. First map out the design on the surface with a *soft* pencil, when mistakes may be rubbed out with a rubber or by rubbing with a little lighter fuel (petroleum spirit) on a rag. Separate the different colours and start to paint using a fine sable brush. It is not necessary to go to the smallest size of brush available (unless the work has very fine detail) as larger brushes will take a fine point. Try to use smooth strokes of the brush, using more or less pressure on the brush to carry the paint to the required line by spreading out, or contracting, the 'mop' of the brush. Avoid 'dabbing' the paint on to the surface; the brush should be held at an angle to the work and the paint 'stroked' on to the surface. It is true to say that some modellers will never become proficient at hand painting, perhaps because of an unsteady hand, but most of us can master the technique by perseverance – Leonardo da Vinci probably made a mess of his first painting!

3. Masking and airbrushing
For the less expert at freehand painting, or the more cautious, there is fortunately an excellent alternative; that of masking the area to be painted and airbrushing the colour in position – although brushing may also be used. Most modellers are aware of the use of cellulose adhesive tape for masking 'cheat lines' on models but this is not an ideal material for masking and there are far superior products on the market. We are looking for an adhesive film that is thin, has low tack properties, is transparent and can be easily cut. Such a material is available from artists' and graphic stockists under such brand names as 'Frisk film' etc., and may be purchased by the roll. As it is specifically manufactured for masking graphic illustrations and the like, it has the correct degree of adhesion without the risk of paint creeping under

the edges or for the base coat to be removed when the mask is removed. It is also intended to be applied over a design that is already drawn but this will not be the situation for our work. You have the choice of drawing the design on the film before removing it from the backing sheet or applying the film to the model and then drawing the design. The former method allows you to work with the benefits of the drawing board but complicates the precise positioning of the design. Either way the unmasked area is cut away with the film adhering to the model, leaving a reasonable margin around the outsides. Special knives (they look like a cross between a screwdriver and a ball point pen) are available for cutting the film and it is strongly recommended that one of these be purchased; it is possible to use a razor blade or sharp modelling knife, but it is more demanding. Assuming that more than one colour is to be applied, the mask is cut in the sections corresponding to the first colour to be used, the pieces of film removed returned to the backing sheet and retained for remasking purposes later. The colours are added, one at a time, cutting away the new sections and replacing the other pieces of film until the whole of the design is complete. Accuracy of marking, cutting and replacing the masking pieces is an essential part of the exercise so do not be in too much of a hurry to see the final result. Any shapes, sizes and patterns may be painted in this fashion and it is often used in conjunction with masking tape (available in a range from a few thou.

wide up to an inch) where 'cheat' lines terminate in a more complex shape. Where one colour line abuts a contrasting colour it is vital not to allow any of the base colour to appear in a gap between the colours as this can spoil an otherwise excellent piece of painting.

Drawing out the roundels, stars, crescents, crosses, swastikas, letters, numerals, chequers or whatever can be time-consuming when measuring up from a small scale drawing or interpolating from photographs. Prototypes that are available for inspection and photographing offer a quick way round this problem. By photographing the insignia square on and (with a ruler beside to give scale) the transparency can be projected on to a screen, adjusted for scale and the respective area traced (Fig 18.5). Tracing paper or film can be used as the screen itself and the insignia drawn direct to the rear of the screen. Draw in also some of the associated structure of the aircraft so that the location can be accurately made. Wrong positioning of insignia is a major fault with many scale models — take a look at the 'model and full-size' photographs and you will often be able to see discrepancies in this direction.

Viewers of your scale model will only be able to judge it by the external appearance and finish, therefore it is very important. Remember also that the finish will only be as good as the construction and preparation, and even if it is given a cosmetic 'face lift' you will know whether the construction is good or not. Self satisfaction is more important than the views of others.

Chapter 19

Pilots

Pay a visit to your local flying club, an air display or even a major airport and take a look at the aircraft flying; none, it could be reasonable to assume, will be airborne without the assistance of a human pilot. In some cases, in open cockpit and light aircraft, the occupants will be obviously visible, but in larger aircraft, less so. Aircraft and pilots are synonymous, neither can fly without the other and to have a scale model flying without a scale pilot must be a contradiction of terms. Why is it then, that we see so many scale models taking to the air without the benefit of a dummy pilot? It is not difficult to understand the reason, commercial model pilots are not always available in the scale desired and modellers tend to dread the thought of manufacturing their own human facsimiles. In common with many other aspects of scale modelling, it is the thought of the action that is terrifying and not the execution, as once embarked on the project it ceases to be the ogre that we imagined. Perhaps the only sight worse than not having a pilot in the cockpit is the fitting of a 'Mickey Mouse' or 'Donald Duck' effigy. These may be acceptable in a sports or fun model but they look totally ridiculous in a model purporting to be a scale representation of a real flying aircraft. There would seem to be a total lack of logic in spending hundreds of hours in

Attractive Free French Tempest V but would it be left running unattended with no pilot?

producing a miniature scale masterpiece only to desecrate it by installing a 'Disneyland' cartoon character in the cockpit – or no pilot at all. This fact becomes increasingly important as the scale of the model increases, where the standards of pilot representation must be high to give authenticity. With a ⅓ or ¼ scale open cockpit model design the pilot must be convincing and detailed – warts and all! They must appear to be flesh and blood and to be capable of climbing in and out of the cockpit, not just sat in the cockpit like a piece of immovable stone. We may be able to get away with a simplified and stylised figure in a $^1/_{10}$ scale *Mustang* or the dark recesses of a B-17 *Fortress,* but the larger scale models require the same degree of modelling skills as are applied to the remainder of the airframe and finishes.

Few of us are natural born sculptors but we may have to face the fact that we are going to have to try our hand at becoming, if not Epstein, at least an observer of the human form and portrayer of its characteristics. Repro-

ducing an intricate retracting under-carriage, or a complex cockpit interior, is tackled with enthusiasm; ask a modeller to reproduce a head or the limbs of a pilot and he rarely knows where to start. It is really not as frightening as might be supposed and it does have the intrigue of being a 'different' aspect of scale modelling – the ultimate in scale satis-faction must be to have a recognisable miniaturisation of the builder in the cock-pit of the model.

Before considering the different approaches to producing the scale pilots let us list the qualities needed to provide the convincing 'human touch'.

1. Realism One instinctively knows when the model pilot looks right in the cockpit of a scale model but it is less easy to define the reasons. That air of 'belong-ing' probably results from a combination of virtues that include the shapes of the figure, the authenticity of the colouring, the representation of the clothing and the belief that the pilot is actually con-cerned with the operation of the aircraft.

Pilot adds realism to this Sopwith Baby, which could be taken for full-size, surely an object of scale?

271

2. Appropriate to the Period Pilots of Cessnas and Pipers do not go around wearing 'Bone-domes' or leather helmets and goggles and, equally, W.W.2 fighter pilots *did* wear face masks fitted with an oxygen supply. Different countries and different air forces have their own style of flying equipment and the variations are immediately apparent. You must be prepared to research the era of the prototype for information on the pilot and his appendages, to the same degree that you would for the aircraft itself. Pilots out of context are just as much an anachronism as a jet aircraft fitted with wire spoked wheels.

3. Scale Scale pilots that are too small or too large are never believable, they produce a toy-like effect with the model. If you have to settle for a commercially produced pilot that is not completely in scale with the model, opting for a slightly oversize example will give a slightly more plausible effect.

4. Pose Regrettably, many of the manufacturers responsible for producing miniature airmen seem to assume that a pilot sits bolt upright in his seat with a fixed stare ahead. Such is rarely the case, the pilot is constantly turning his head to scan the horizon, looking at his instruments and peering down at the ground to see where he is going. Although there may be some technical manufacturing reasons for these "look straight ahead and trust in the Lord" examples, a pilot with a tilt of the head and looking to the side, is bound to be more convincing.

5. Weight Competition scale models have a habit of accumulating weight to an unexpected degree during the constructional and finishing stages, so much

so that there is little outstanding balance for the extras such as the pilot. This should not be the basis for a legitimate excuse to omit a model pilot, as this can be done with the addition of only a few grammes for a head and shoulder representation.

At the outset let us eliminate two possible varieties of pilots for the serious modeller. Dolls, of the children's baby doll type, are not a suitable basis for an adult pilot; their proportions and features are entirely wrong. Nearly as bad are the ready painted, oriental style pilots that look as if they have come out of the Christmas stocking. These brightly painted effigies are totally unconvincing (although there are some superior painted model pilots on the market) and their almond eyes are more suited to the eastern areas of the world. Perhaps, in a small scale *Zero,* and with some reworking, they would pass as acceptable, but for more serious work they must be discounted. Of the 'toy' type figures the only ones worthy of consideration are the 'Action-Man' series and types of similar, superior design. Having the added advantage of movable limbs and a wide range of clothing items and accessories, these model toys make an excellent basis for a pilot of models of corresponding scale. Realistic hair, and a beard if required, is fitted to the 'Action-Man' models and this can be considered as a definite bonus; the face only needs a small amount of 'touching-up' with paint to give it individual character. Resist the temptation to use some of the accessories, i.e. goggles, helmets, etc., that are not scale and will spoil the final effect; these must be individually made, as described later. Excessive weight is the one objection to many of these figures, since they are constructed from injection moulded plastic of robust proportions

Of course, if you build something like Martin Fardell's D.H.10, you have extra crew figures to make!

(they have to be to withstand the pounding given by some of our less considerate junior brethren). It is not necessary to use the complete figure as the parts can be dissembled and the mouldings below the waist discarded before the upper limbs are reconnected. Stronger rubber bands can be fitted at this stage to prevent the head and arms from being blown about in the slipstream, and the torso can be fitted to a plywood plate to allow the figure to be rotated.

Commercial scale model pilots are either injection moulded or formed from plastic sheet by a vacuum forming process. Injection moulded types are normally ready assembled (they may be moulded in a urethane foam or from two halves of a styrene moulding joined together) and only require cleaning up and painting. Vacuum formed scale pilots are more often supplied as two halves, integral with the sheet of styrene or ABS plastic. The forming process can be from a male or female mould but the latter is superior as it imparts the surface

detail where it is required, i.e. on the outside and not the internal surface. Where weight is an important consideration the vacuum-formed variety have much to commend them, as even the largest scale head and shoulders, fully painted, should not weigh more than an ounce or so. Model pilots are more capable of withstanding the stresses imposed on them than are their full-size counterparts — which is just as well, otherwise there would be more than a few 'black-outs' during the flights of some scale models! Strength is not a vital consideration, but appearance and possibly weight are. Cutting and trimming the two vacuum-formed halves from the surrounding plastic sheet must be carefully undertaken (nail scissors and a sharp knife) until the joint area is a good fit. Due to the forming process, the high points of the moulding, e.g. tip of the nose, where the draw of the plastic is at its greatest, the plastic may be excessively thin. Reinforce these areas with a spot of five minute epoxy. Join the

273

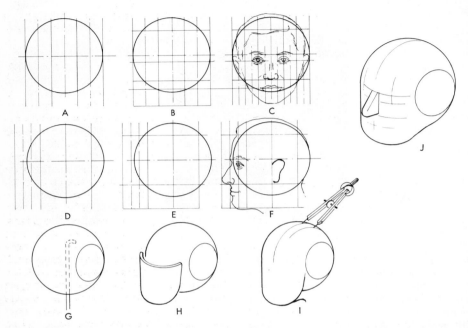

FIG. 19.1 Basic Head (after Wally Batter, 'World War 1 Aeroplanes') From front. A. Circle divided into sixths. B. Mark ⅓ diameter above C/L, ⅔ below. Add eye and mouth lines. C. Sketch features; bottom area divided into twelfths helps.
From side. D. Divide in thirds, ⅔ left of C/L, ⅓ right. E. Space ⅓ above C/L, ⅔ below, divide left third into three. F. Draw profile.
Moulding in clay. G. Form ball, flatten sides. H. Add spade shape and smooth in 1. Fill behind spade to form jaw. Use dividers to mark lines from sketches lightly on clay. Add wedge for nose (J), remove or add clay for eye sockets, mouth, etc.

halves with polystyrene cement starting at the centre top of the head and working down the seam. The plastic may be softened by the cement and this will allow minor discrepancies in the joint to be resolved as the two edges of the plastic are fused together. Any gaps, or low points, are filled with epoxy putty and this material (or similar epoxy fillers) can also be used for reinforcing the internal joint. Leave the assembly to dry thoroughly before smoothing the external joint area with fine abrasive

paper and trimming the base. Filling the inside of the ABS pilot with a two-part urethane foam mixture will strengthen the moulding – do not use too much mixture or it will foam everywhere! Trim the base where excess foam emerges.

Carving pilots from block balsa is one of the most difficult methods of producing an authentic looking pilot. It can be done and some modellers have carved balsa pilots with a lot of character and interest, but these modellers had a natural affinity with wood carving and an innate artistry. The problem is, apart from obtaining the correct shapes and attitudes, that balsa has a relatively coarse grain and is not easy to carve in all directions. Achieving a good finish, without resorting to fillers and sealers, is virtually impossible by carving alone. Other timbers, e.g. boxwood or jelutong, are more suitable for carving as they are close-grained timbers and not too hard; inevitably they will result in a heavy model pilot. Unless the carved pilot, using a suitable wood, is to be used as a basis of a mould it would probably be prudent to avoid this method.

Sculpting in clay, followed by moulding, offers the advantage of working on the figure, adding or cutting away, until you are satisfied with the results. Using a commercial modelling clay (the type we used as children, or as balance weight on our early free flight models) allows the modelling of the subject with the use of simple tools, no smell or mess and as many efforts may be made with the same piece of material as may be necessary. We would never consider starting to build a model of an aircraft without first researching the subject and producing some scale drawings. Exactly the same applies to the human figure, and close observation is essential — you may think you know exactly what a human face looks like, but when you prepare a drawing you will be surprised by the exact disposition of the component parts. Viewed in isolation the head is a most peculiar piece of engineering and a space visitor would probably find it even more amusing and strange than we do with the 'little green Martians' depicted in fantasy illustrations. Unless there are specific reasons for doing otherwise it is sensible to restrict first efforts to the head and bust only; to sculpt and mould a full length figure presents problems at

the moulding stage. We can literally measure the head and bust of a colleague, but measured drawings of the head are far from simple. There is an easier way — by taking a series of photographs of the head and shoulders at 30° divisions, through a full 360° — similar to police file photographs, but more of them. Ask your 'model' to sit on a revolving stool, dressed in the appropriate flying equipment if possible, and set up the camera at the same height as the subject's head. Take each photograph in turn, rotating the stool through 30° after each shot and ask him to hold a ruler by the side of his head for every position — this will act as a scale reference later. When the film is developed the prints, black and white or coloured, should be enlarged to the desired scale. You now have an immediate reference for modelling the subject, plus, if you require it, the opportunity to look in the mirror to gain more information. Observation is the keynote to success, don't sculpt what you think is the shape of the nose — take a good look at it and model it as it actually is, and where it is. See Figs. 19.1 and 19.2 for head detailing.

Cut a ply base large enough to take the lower section of the torso plus a half an inch clear all round. Fix a wood screw through the ply from the underside to act as an anchor for the modelling clay. Start to build up the rough form of the bust and head, using measurements taken from the photographs until you have the bulk of the proportions correct and the angle and inclination of the head as desired. (It is assumed that the photographs were taken with the head positioned in an 'interesting' attitude.) Engineer's callipers are handy for checking dimensions from the photographs of the model. Using any convenient tools, modelling knife, spoon handles, knitting pins, carved pieces of hardwood, proceed with forming the area from the neck downwards. Aim to create the folds in the clothing and the texture of the materials by incising and puncturing the surface with a sharp point. Loose items, e.g. scarves, are best added to the moulding at a later stage, with material to represent the cloth. Continue with the sculpting of the head; much will depend on the headgear and equipment worn by the pilot, and in some cases none of the face will be visible. Where oxygen supply tubes, microphone and earphone leads and other similar connections are part of the impedimenta, a decision must be made on when to exclude these items from the model. Generally speaking, it is easier to make up these flexible items separately and add them to the moulding at a later stage. Concentrating on the attitude as well as the shapes and sizes. When you reach the stage of final detailing you will probably find it difficult to achieve a good finish and fine detail due to the modelling clay being too soft and tending to 'pull'. Two ways of overcoming this difficulty can be employed: (a) add beeswax to the clay to stiffen it or

(b) put the work in the refrigerator for a few hours to harden off. Select the surface finish to suit the original material. Hard surfaces such as visor screens should be smooth and without blemish, softer materials, e.g. leather, should have a lightly textured surface and not be too even. Goggles may be treated as a separate item if they have a simple form, or can be carved integrally with the face. Fitting clear plastic to the goggles has a much greater obscuring effect than the glass in full size goggles and it may be impossible to view the eye detail behind the 'clear' plastic. Moulding the goggles integrally, with the eye detail internally, and omitting the 'glass' from the model is a reasonable compromise. The eyes probably present one of the most difficult parts for the modeller to cope with. In addition to inspecting the photographs, and your own eyes in the mirror, you can observe the methods used in 'proper' sculpture, ancient or modern. Hair is also difficult to represent and gluing real hair to the moulding may not give a very good simulation, unless you like straight 'spiky' hair. Treating it in a bold simple manner is the best answer,

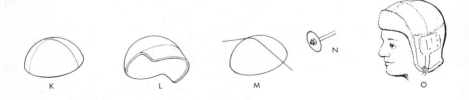

FIG. 19.2 Helmet. K. Mould and fit four thin panels of clay for crown. L. Add nape (in two pieces). M. Smooth joints, then mark seams with thin thread pulled back and forth to form grooves. N. Use a wheel from a scrap watch rolled along stitch lines. O. Add bulges at ear positions plus appropriate covers. Note: head should be fired before adding helmet, helmet/head then fired before adding fur, which can also be mdelled in clay.

276

and some degree of individual hairs can be suggested at the painting stage. No undercuts are permissible if a solid mould is to be taken from the model and there must be no holes, e.g. between the arms and body, if a flexible mould is used, as described below. The only reason for taking a solid mould (resin casting) would be to obtain vacuum formed or light glass fibre mouldings. Unless it is anticipated that relatively large numbers of vacuum formings are to be produced, the following methods should be used.

Liquid silicone rubber is the material to be used for forming the mould and this is available from children's toy stores as the substance used for forming moulds for plaster casts. It consists of solid pieces of silicone rubber that liquefy when heated in a pan — full instructions are included with the moulding kits. Make a small dam around the plywood base, heat the silicone rubber slowly and thoroughly and then pour or ladle the rubber over the clay model. The objects of this exercise are (a) not to burn yourself and (b) to finish with an even, but not overthick layer of rubber over the complete model. Pay particular attention to the underside areas, i.e. nose and chin, to ensure that the rubber is applied equally thickly to these areas. When the rubber has thoroughly set and cooled the plywood base is removed and the bulk of the modelling clay dug out. Turn the mould inside out (it is flexible and it won't tear) clean the remainder of the clay away and wash thoroughly. The mould is now ready for use; it does not require the addition of a release agent, it is suitable for most resins and adhesives and it can be used many times.

Numerous materials can be experimented with for forming the finished moulding. For very large pilots it is possible to lay up a glass fibre shell but this is not practical with smaller sizes. Expanded polyurethane foam, produced by mixing equal parts of base and activator liquids, is an excellent filler material but it will not produce the surface and detail from the mould for a suitable finish. We must, therefore, form an initial outer skin before using the foam (it is used for buoyancy compartments in R/C model boats) as a filler.

Hair is a problem, though short and curly like this is not too bad. Nice harness and panel details.

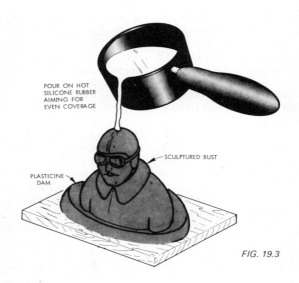

POUR ON HOT
SILICONE RUBBER
AIMING FOR
EVEN COVERAGE

SCULPTURED BUST

PLASTICINE
DAM

FIG. 19.3

Polyester or epoxy gel resin will form a tough, dense and thin coating to the mould; pour a small quantity into the mould, swirl it around and keep it moving over the complete internal surface until the set has commenced. Placing a piece of plastic laminate over the base of the mould will assist in this operation as it will allow the mould to be rotated through a full 360° until the resin has started to gel. Be warned that the polyurethane foam bulks to very many times its original mass when it fully expands. Providing the liquid is placed in the mould immediately it is mixed the surplus foam will be ejected from the top of the mould and can be trimmed away later. As soon as the liquid polyurethane is in the mould continue to tap the base and revolve the mould to eliminate any air pockets. Leave the moulding to set completely, preferably overnight, before you attempt to peel off the rubber mould — of course you want to see the results as

soon as possible but a little patience is necessary. When you do 'strike' the mould your initial reaction may be one of slight disappointment; if you have used a clear resin the general effect is likely to be somewhat motley. However, the important consideration is whether the surface is consistent and well detailed — painting will take care of the rest. Do not remove the surplus foam on the base at this stage, as it will be useful for holding during the painting stage.

Matt enamels are the most suitable paints for using on resin, styrene or ABS plastics, since they are dense, easily mixed and dry relatively quickly. Cellulose paints will affect some of the materials. It is useful to have a large range of colours but it is even more important to have a sound knowledge of the effect of mixing various basic colours. Armed with this information you can obtain any colour and shade that you want from little more than the three

Two-part moulded figure. Joint flash can be scraped away before painting

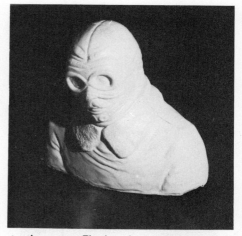

primary colours, (red, yellow and blue) plus black and white. Some of the results of simple mixes are shown below but experimenting will soon show you what other variations can be achieved – mix sufficient different colours together and you will nearly always finish with a muddy brown!

Blue/Yellow	– Green
Red/Yellow	– Orange
Red/Blue	– Purple
Red/Green	– Dark Green (Olive drab)
Red/Black	– Brown
Yellow/Green	– Pale Green

Mixing primary colours may result in strong, bright colours and these should be avoided for painting of the pilot. Colours can be toned down by the addition of black and/or white.

High quality brushes, sable hair, will make the job of painting the moulding much easier – there is nothing more frustrating than to have hairs constantly coming out of the brush, or being unable to get a decent point on the tip of the brush. Apply the light toned colours first, allowing for the next colour to overlap slightly – base material showing through between colours is abhorrent. Where the eyes are visible commence painting with them, colouring the whole area of the eyes an off-white. Inspection of your eyes in a mirror will show you that when looking straight ahead or slightly down, all of the bottom half of the pupil is visible but part of the upper edge of the pupil is obscured by the eyelid. Paint in the pupils to a blue/grey colour, or if you insist, to a brown or hazel hue, followed, when the paint has dried, by a small black circle representing the iris. A pin point of white on each iris, to represent the reflection of light, will add a 'sparkle' to the eyes. Flesh colour can be bought by the tinful but it is only a synthetic looking pink! Real flesh is far more subtle than that and contains a whole range of colours, depending to a large extent on the quality of light shining on it at the time. Take a close look at some of the Impressionists' paintings, you will see used on the 'flesh' all manner of colours, *including* blues and greens. Step back, and the overall effect is a very convincing representation of flesh! It is not suggested that you should try to produce an 'Impressionist' model but it does indicate that flesh is more than a single anaemic pink colour. Put on the base colour and with the paint still wet, brush in white to highlight the prominent top surfaces, i.e. cheek bones, bridge of the nose etc., and darker pink/brown in the shaded areas under the chin, eyebrows, lower lip, etc. Experiment by brushing in small quantities of yellow, red and green into the wet base colour to give the more mottled effect of flesh. Lips, unless they are artificially made-up, are not bright red but a medium tint of red/brown, with the inside of the lips being painted a

Figure from previous picture part and fully painted. Fur-edged goggles unusual.

still — the natural shadow effect is less with a small scale model. A thin wash of a light tint of the fur colour will help to take away any too obvious stippled effect.

Leather has always been a popular material for pilots' helmets and coats, and as it becomes worn it begins to show scuff marks, creases and dirt. We will not be able to represent this effect by using a single colour of brown — it is necessary to use a constant variation of tones of the base colour and to accentuate the creases by darkening them, and the high points by lightening them. Use a palette (any piece of wood will do) with browns, reds and black and merge the colours as you apply them to the 'leather' areas. Where you have leather on leather, goggle straps on the helmet for instance, use a slightly contrasting leather colour so that the difference is more obvious. Remember, at all times when painting the pilot, the effects of light and shade; we are aiming to accentuate the shading and highlights, otherwise it will appear too flat and dull. Metal parts can be painted with metallic paints, i.e. silver or brass, but tone them down slightly or they will look too artificial. Matt enamel paints are not fuel-proof and the pilot must be protected from the ravages of methanol and nitromethane. The last thing we want is a glossy pilot, so matt fuel-proofers must be used. Choose your favourite type, but if you are brushing on the proofer, avoid excessive brushing, it may start to remove the enamel and it may produce a semi-gloss finish.

Working from a basic figure, clothing it and adding goggles, masks, leads, straps and scarves can produce better

slightly darker tone. Painting around the pupils of the eyes must be accurate, but elsewhere you can rely on overpainting to form the required line. To emphasise the eyes a *very* thin line of dark brown, as the shadow of the eyelid, may be painted around the eye, and especially on the inner corners.

Flying helmets, fortunately, often obscure the hair but when it is visible you should apply the general base colour, darken the partings and lighten the high points. Applying very thin streaks of white can simulate hairs to some extent, but it is never an easy task — perhaps there should be more bald-headed pilots about. Fur can be 'faked' by applying the base colour and stippling darker tones to the surface, edges normally in shadow are stippled darker results than a fully painted figure, provided that the work is very neatly and expertly carried out. Clothing seems to cause most problems, in nearly all cases because actual cloth materials are used instead of scale materials. For cloth on a model to have any hope of taking up the folds and drapes of the original, it must have a scale thickness and weave or as close as possible. We must, therefore, select ultra thin materials such as nylon and chiffon, although they must also be opaque where this is applicable. For items that are intended to move as a result of the slipstream effect, e.g. a scarf, nylon chiffon will give an excellent impression; the light material trails freely in the wind and has the bonus of giving movement in the cockpit area during flight. Simulating leather creates similar problems and it is only by using very thin leather, or 'plastic' leather, that we shall have credible results. Imitation leather is usually manufactured from P.V.C. plastic with a cloth backing, and the backing can be removed in some cases, leaving a thin layer of plastic. Reducing real leather is also feasible by a technique known as skiving i.e. scraping the rear side of the leather with a sharp blade until it is of the required thickness. You may be fortunate enough to find some pieces of chamois leather that are sufficiently thin to use without further working, except for darkening the leather by applying aniline dye or special suede dyes. Unless the figure is reasonably large, sewing internal seams is too intricate and it is safer to glue the material in position, leaving a butt joint to represent a seam. Collars and coat fronts are reproduced by overlapping the leather and ear flaps are added as separate items. Fur collars and trimming can be made by using a fine grade of synthetic fabric fur material — avoid making it too plush — fur on the real sheepskin coats is not too thick. Sequins can represent buttons (covered with leather if necessary) and buckles can be made from scrap aluminium; the 'blued' effect is obtained by mixing a little blue cellulose paint with clear dope, or by anodising as previously explained.

Goggles and visors must be made from scrap materials, i.e. leather, card, clear plastic and aluminium sheet. Do take the trouble to investigate the real article thoroughly — most air museums have examples of the full range of pilots' accoutrements. Flexible hoses are easily made by using a light spring covered with heat shrink plastic tube and electrical leads can be made from *flexible* thin diameter plastic covered wire, plugs with sockets suggested by a thicker plastic tube slipped over the wire.

Animation of pilots is already here, as more than one modeller has taken functionability to the full extent by having the pilot's limbs radio controlled and operating the controls in full-size fashion! Just the movement of the head or arm will help to give realism in the air and this can be achieved by connecting the limbs to control surface servos or a separate servo. How long will it be before a fully radio-controlled model pilot actually walks out to the aircraft, climbs in, starts up and takes off?

Pre-flight Checks and Test Flying

It may seem strange that in a book with over twenty chapters only two chapters deal with flying to any great extent. Emphasis has been placed on the importance of flying, otherwise we may just as well construct a solid scale model, so why is so little written about the practical aspects of flying? There are two reasons for this apparent omission, (1) that it is assumed a modeller seriously intending to take up scale R/C modelling will already be a competent R/C flyer and (2) there are limits to the amount that can be taught in respect of flying; most of it has to be learned the hard way – on the flying field. Flying a scale model can be more difficult and challenging than experiences with a training or sports design and for this reason, some of the basics of flight are reconsidered and equally important, the preparation and pre-flight checks reiterated.

Checking a model thoroughly before going out to the flying field means just that – a thorough check of every item associated with the model, right down to ensuring that you have a clean piece of rag in the field box. Item number one on the check list is the airframe design/construction relation. The model has been designed to certain parameters and specifications and before flying we must check that the model meets these criteria. Not in order of importance, because all of the factors are important – we will put weight at the top of the list.

WEIGHT

It is far more likely that the target weight will be exceeded than the other way round; if the model does finish up lighter than scheduled just breathe a sigh of relief and consider yourself very fortunate. Experienced modellers are often plied with the question "my model has come out well over the specified weight, what shall I do?". The simple answer is – "Nothing". Short of stripping off all of the covering and trying to apply a lighter finish we are literally stuck with what we have got – you cannot add lightness. Knowing that the model has a heavier wing loading than the design limitation does give us a warning of what to expect; the stalling speed is going to be higher, the acceleration poorer, the overall performance worse, i.e. it will be more critical to fly within the safe limits. At worst, it may so change the flying characteristics that it becomes very unpleasant to fly, with the margins between the stalling speed and flying speed minimal. Increasing the engine power may help in some respects but it will not recover the more pleasant aspects of the flying. Moral! Avoid excess weight like the plague.

CENTRE OF GRAVITY

We are more concerned with the longitudinal and lateral balance points than the true Centre of Gravity (the point at which all the moments of the aircraft are in balance). There is little we can do to adjust the vertical position of the C of G, apart from positioning the radio equipment higher or lower in the fuselage and this will have only a minimal effect. Lateral balance, whether one wing is heavier than the other, can be adjusted by adding weight to the wing tip of the lighter side. Lateral balance is often overlooked in all forms of R/C models but making sure that it is correct will help to ensure that the model flies true. Longitudinal balance is of vital importance and if we try to fly the model with a rearward balance point we can almost guarantee disaster. A forward balance point is far less likely to end with dire results, though it may result in less elevator control, giving rise to embarrassment at the time of flaring out for a landing. Despite the many times warnings have been given about the risks of flying with an incorrect balance point there are many modellers that seem prepared to take the risk — on the false assumption that their flying skills will more than compensate for the poorer flying characteristics. Maybe pride comes into it and, perhaps, the impatience to get the model into the air; a third factor that certainly contributes to the failure of attaining a correct balance point is the ignorance of how to determine and adjust it. Assuming that the balance point is indicated on the plan (if there is a C of G 'range' shown, choose the forward point for initial flights) we must also know that this must be determined with the tailplane horizontal — even if the tailplane is set at some degrees positive to the datum line. Armed with this knowledge we can now scientifically calculate the distances from the actual balance point and weights of ballast that must be applied

for given corrections i.e. if we have to move the balance point 0.6 of an inch forward how much lead must we fix to the front of the bulkhead? We need to know three factors before we can make our calculations:

a. The distance and direction of the change of balance:

b. The existing balance point:

c. The total weight of the model.

We can use any units we may choose for calculating the moments (distance × weight) but cms. and grammes or inches and ounces are the most suitable for model work. The method can best be described by quoting an example, so let us assume that we have a scale model with a longitudinal balance point that is 0.6 inch too far aft and the distance from the desired balance point to the front of the bulkhead (the most convenient position for fitting the lead weight ballast in this instance) is 10 inches. All up weight of the model (less fuel, because the model should still be capable of flight with an empty tank) is 66 ozs. Referring to Fig. 20.1 we can see these factors in diagrammatic form. The formula for calculating the weight required to be fitted to the bulkhead is

$$W^b = \frac{W^t \times D^c}{D^b}$$

Where W^b = Weight of the ballast

W^t = Total weight of model

D^c = Distance the balance point is to be moved

and D^b = Distance of the ballast from the required balance point

From our example:-

$$W^b = \frac{66 \times 0.6}{10} = 3.96 \text{ ozs} - \text{say 4 ozs.}$$

It should be noted that if the *total*

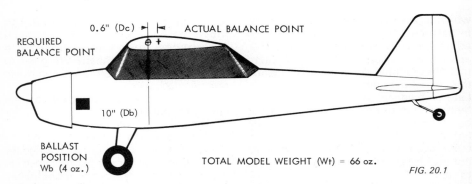

0.6" (Dc) ACTUAL BALANCE POINT

REQUIRED
BALANCE POINT

10" (Db)

BALLAST
POSITION
Wb (4 oz.)

TOTAL MODEL WEIGHT (Wt) = 66 oz.

FIG. 20.1

weight of the aircraft was reduced to 50 ozs the ballast weight would only be 3 ozs. so it obviously pays to build light for this reason also. This formula can be adapted to compute the distance a fixed weight object, say a battery pack, must be moved to correct the balance point position. Although it is regularly written in articles that the balance point should be corrected by moving around the radio equipment this is rarely practical. The only item that can be moved with any degree of ease is the battery pack and even this relatively heavy mass has little effect on the balance when moved within the wing chord area, or just forward of it. Adjusting for a nose heavy model is obviously less serious, both from the flying characteristics point of view and the amount of ballast we must add; the tail moment has a much larger distance component than the nose. Once again, the lessons to be learned are irrefutable, build as light as you can and keep the tail end especially light.

Incidences Design of a scale model should include a good force arrangement including specific wing and tail-plane incidences and engine thrust line deviations from the datum. If it is feasible, and does not show on the completed model, the front and rear

horizontal datum points should be marked on the fuselage as these can act as useful reference points for checking the rigging of the model. The front mark can normally be indicated somewhere under the cowl and the rear mark by a pin hole in the stern post, on either side of the fin if this extends to the bottom of the fuselage. One factor regarding incidence lines is often misunderstood. Irrespective of whether the aerofoil is symmetrical, semi-symmetrical or flat bottomed, the incidence line is taken from the centre of the leading edge radius to the centre of the trailing edge (pointed, square or round). In building the model we obviously do all that we can to keep to the designed incidences and engine thrust lines but it is prudent to check these before we attempt to fly the model. It may be that there is little we can do to alter the positions if they are wrong (unless they are grossly out and then we must resort to desperate action), we shall, however, be prewarned of what to expect and can make control surface adjustments to compensate for the probable effects.

Commercial incidence measuring meters are available and these are excellent for their purpose. The Robart incidence meter will, for instance, cope with wings up to 16 inch chord and will

FIG. 20.2

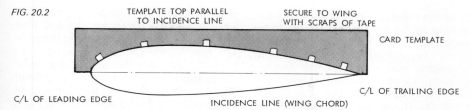

TEMPLATE TOP PARALLEL
TO INCIDENCE LINE

SECURE TO WING
WITH SCRAPS OF TAPE

CARD TEMPLATE

C/L OF TRAILING EDGE

C/L OF LEADING EDGE

INCIDENCE LINE (WING CHORD)

also measure the downthrust of the engine. It is easy to use and accurate, and measurements are given in half degree increments. For those modellers who do not possess such a piece of equipment it is not too difficult to check the incidences and thrust lines using basic equipment. First we must prepare the model by determining the centre points of the leading and trailing edges of the wing and tailplane, either by sticking pins in at these positions or by cutting a cardboard template of the top surface of the wing and tailplane, cut square at the incidence line and fixed in position – See Fig. 20.2. Block the assembled model clear of the table, or the floor if it has a flat hard surface, until

it is level; that is to say, the tailplane incidence line is parallel to the supporting surface. We can now measure the centre lines of the wing leading and trailing edges to the table or floor. Checking the actual incidence can now be implemented by trigonometry or by drawing the resultant incidence line on the plan, measuring the chord of the wing at the point of measurement. Downthrust can be measured by substituting a piece of flat wood for the propeller and using a set square to indicate the difference of distance at the tip and the engine centre line. See Fig. 20.3. Sidethrust measurements are not quite so easy and it is necessary to strap a length of straight wood with one edge down the centre

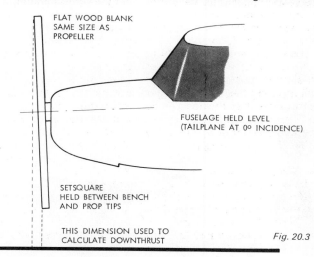

FLAT WOOD BLANK
SAME SIZE AS
PROPELLER

FUSELAGE HELD LEVEL
(TAILPLANE AT 0° INCIDENCE)

SETSQUARE
HELD BETWEEN BENCH
AND PROP TIPS

THIS DIMENSION USED TO
CALCULATE DOWNTHRUST

Fig. 20.3

285

line of the fuselage (plan view). This can then act as the guide for a square to be positioned, for measuring the tip distance compared with the distance at the engine centre line of the dummy propeller. Control surface throws are normally indicated on the plan of the model and these can be checked whilst the model is blocked up. Where no measurements are shown, or if it is your own design, be guided by models of similar design; rudder movements can normally be quite generous, elevators less so and ailerons moderate throws with more up movement than down. This, however, is only a generalisation and it is much safer to obtain more positive information.

Having satisfied ourselves that the aerodynamics are as per the design requirements we can advance to the checking of the structural integrity of the airframe, fittings, operation of the radio equipment and linkages and preparation for the flying field. Start at the front of the aircraft and work logically towards the rear end. The spinner should be firmly

attached and in balance, the propeller should also be balanced and free from defects – use a spare unpainted propeller for test flying. Check engine bolts for security and the fixings for the cowl; more than one World Scale competition flight has been nullified through a cowling or hatch coming adrift during flight. Inspect the whole of the fuel system, flush fuel through the carburettor and engine, check the compression to ensure that the ring is seating, operate the throttle barrel, clean out the filter and check for leaks in the tank and pipes and that the fuel feed pick-up is free in movement. Wing fixing dowels, plates, anchor nuts and bolts must all be secure and give positive seating for the wing/s. Pull on the control surfaces to test their security. If they are likely to come adrift it is safer for them to do so now – give a good strong pull, not a tentative tug. Are all the control horns fixed firmly, and the connectors moving freely but with no risk of them accidentally breaking free, are the hinges free in operation? Check all the radio installation for security and

A good smooth runway and a tricycle undercarriage such as on this Tipsy Nipper are big helps for early flights.

protection – you may have done it a number of times previously but you are coming up to the real test – the first flight – and it will give you peace of mind to go through it one more time. Are the servos firmly screwed to the bearers or their mounting plates; most important of all, are the output arm and disc screws thoroughly tightened? (Most servos are mounted inverted in scale models and many a model has been lost through the screw vibrating loose and the output arm falling free of the servo.) Where 'snap-on' type connectors are used in conjunction with a servo output, check that there is complete freedom of movement at the extremes of the travels of the servo – including the operation of the transmitter trims. Binding at the limits of the servo movement can cause the 'snap-on' connector to 'snap-off'. Finally, if you have fitted it, check that the ballast weight is securely fixed; although lead is commonly used as ballast, steel bar stock is easier to fix to bulkheads and engine bearers and it is less likely to allow the fitting nuts to loosen. Give a last check on the operation of the radio equipment – the ailerons are working in the right direction, aren't they?

Preparing your field box for flying should be a routine matter but do not forget the obvious things such as charging up all the batteries, making sure the glowplug lead is sound and has a suitable connector fitted to it, the starter and fuel pump are working and that the fuel is fresh and well filtered. Apart from the normal complement of tools you may require a few spares such as alternative type glowplugs, spare propellers, spare prop-nut, fuel tubing, threaded clevises of various lengths in case major adjustments are required to the control surfaces, some clean rag and for 'Dutch courage' a bottle of your favourite beverage. Recycle and charge your transmitter and flight pack batteries, go to bed and pray for a fine day on the morrow.

Whether you test fly your own scale model or rely on the services of an experienced colleague is a matter for personal decision. It will pay to be honest with yourself, if your flying abilities are limited or if you tend to be of a nervous disposition, swallow your pride and ask for the assistance of a fellow modeller. Just two words of warning before you hand the transmitter over, do be sure that the test pilot is really qualified and not one that just happens to have a good opinion of himself, and do check that he is used to flying on the same mode transmitter that you are. Brief him thoroughly on all aspects of the model, warning him of any peculiarities that you suspect the model may exhibit. Try to pick a time for the initial flight when there are not too many enthusiasts about; they will undoubtedly want to watch the test flight, and inspect the model at close quarters, but this is the one time when you will need quiet concentration and not a lot of questions being fired at you – even if they are all well meant. If you are lucky enough to have the choice of flying from a grass strip or a hard runway, which should you choose? A *large* smooth short cropped grass flying patch is probably impossible to beat for any reasonable size scale model, i.e. a sports field or well tended airfield. These areas do not abound and a very close second comes an asphalt runway; some may prefer this surface to grass for faster flying models. Test flying from a rough patch of grass, or a rough surface runway, is to be avoided if at all possible, much better to delay the test flight until you have permission to fly from a more suitable area. One of the chief aims of a test flight, or any flight for that matter, is the elimination of as many unknown factors and undesirable elements as possible. If we are sure that the model is sound, radio equipment is 100% O.K., that the engine will not give trouble, that the wind is not strong and that the flying area is ideal, we are free to apply our total concentration on the pure flying of the model. So, after an extended range check of the radio – it helps to soothe the nerves – and a final check of the engine performance (remember to hold the model vertically to test the fuel feed in a simulated climb) through the full range of throttle limits, we are ready for the momentous occasion.

Take a look around the area before you start up for the flight to make sure there are no obstacles in the way (on the ground or on the landing approach) and that there are no other models airborne. Work out the alternative positions for landing in case you have to put the model down in a hurry, particularly straight ahead, observe all the normal safety and etiquette rules such as frequencies, keeping your vehicle and boxes well clear of the landing area and warning people of the intending flight. Make sure that you have got your sunglasses on (if you are lucky enough to have sun) your neck strap for the transmitter and that you know the direction of the wind – a gentle breeze is an advantage but a strong gusty wind is grounds for postponement. Taxi trials are always worth attempting, they will give you an indication of the tracking of the model, the likely torque effect with some models and a chance to get the feel of the controls before committing yourself. Models equipped with tricycle undercarriages allow extended taxi trials at speeds near to the take-off speed; keep some down elevator trim on the

transmitter to avoid a premature lift off, terminating the taxi if the nose wheel starts to lift. 'Tail-draggers' have to be treated with more caution in taxi trials as there is always the risk of getting the tail up and the model, perhaps with the assistance of a slight increase of wind strength, lifting off before you are prepared. With some scale designs, more particularly with some of the early prototypes having the C of G rearwards on the wing chord, the wheels are only marginally in front of the C of G and the risk of the model tipping on to its nose is increased. Taxying will not give very much useful information with this type of model but it may give an indication of a bias in tracking direction. Any veering of the model during a taxi run must be investigated and corrected before flying is attempted – it may be a sticking wheel, wheels out of alignment or the rudder out of trim.

Our aim for the first take-off is to get the model safely airborne and to a reasonable height as soon as possible; that does *not* mean that we must rush the take-off, haul the model into the air before it has reached flying speed, or climb away steeply. Quite the reverse is true: the engine should be opened up progressively, starting with the model pointing direct into wind, the model held on to the ground by judicious use of down elevator to keep the wheels in contact with the runway, and a little up elevator introduced when it is obvious that the model has reached flying speed, plus a little for safety. With a tricycle undercarriage model there is no difficulty in keeping the model on the ground, hold the elevator stick with a touch of down during the acceleration period, slowly easing off as the model reaches the required speed and adjusting the direction with the steerable nose wheel and/

Gordon Whitehead, a well-known scale expert, checks rudder and ailerons on his Gloster Gamecock.

or rudder. Quite likely the model will become airborne when the elevator reaches the neutral position, due to the slight excess of speed, but if it does not lift off with a moderate application of elevator, i.e. not more than 15 degrees of the total up elevator movement, abort the take-off and check the model out. Perhaps the model is sitting on the ground with the angle of attack of the wing at an excessive negative angle — although lift is still produced at minor negative angles – or the main wheels are too far behind the C of G to allow rotation of the model for take-off. There had to be some sensible reason for the model failing to lift off when obvious flying speed has been reached and to persevere with the attempt by applying further up elevator may result in the model suddenly 'leaping off' and adopting a severe nose-up attitude. Not an occurrence that bodes well for the next part of the flight! Two wheel undercarriage equipped models need a different approach as the tail must be lifted by the application of slight down elevator once the airflow over the tail surface has increased during the take-off run. From this point on, usually about half way through the take-off run, the attitude of the model should be slightly nose down until the lift-off is required. Release of the down elevator, or slight up, should be sufficient to get the model into the air. Once airborne the model, irrespective of type, period, number of engines or any other factor, should be controlled into a shallow climb-out, allowing the reserve of speed above the stalling speed to build up rapidly. The only time that the action should be countermanded is with a model that is obviously way out of trim or the engine is faltering or stops; in these cases the model is landed straight ahead with as much finesse as you can manage. Once you have reached a height of fifty feet or so, carry out a shallow, steady left turn until you have reached a height of a few hundred feet. The reason for turning is that we do not want the model to fly too far away from us.

Throttle back to about half throttle, try to release the tensions that have inevitably built up in you and trim the model out. Even when you are totally familiar with the transmitter it is none too easy to find the trim levers and adjust them during the apprehensions of the first flight, for if the trims are some way out there is a natural tendency to want to keep your hands on the sticks. Have a colleague standing by and give him instructions on the trim changes you require, taking them just a little at a time. Providing you are reasonably happy with the way the model is flying – you must not expect to be totally relaxed on the first flight – it is advisable to gain more height and try a stall. Knowledge of the behaviour of the model in the stall, and the approximate speed at which it occurs, is all-important as it will give us the warnings of what to expect if we ever get into a dangerously low height, low speed, flying condition. Scale models that are equipped with flaps and retracting undercarriages should be flown in their basic form, i.e. undercarriage permanently down and no flap extension, for the first flight; there is sufficient challenge to keep us busy without having to worry about the 'extras'. Fly around until you have used up about half the fuel – you will probably err on the cautious side – and then practise a circuit and landing approach. Do not aim to land off this circuit, use it to work out the heights and speeds you need for the circuit and carry out the overshoot in good time, with a sensible reserve of height. Keep the circuit fairly wide and line up the model for the landing approach in plenty of time, leaving as few directional changes as possible. Remember the basic rule for controlling the descent, elevator is used for speed corrections and the engine is used for attitude adjustment. For the actual landing, come in with a slight reserve of speed (5 knots for the wife and 1 knot for each child!) aiming to let the speed drop off with the model held a foot or so above the runway. Be firm with the setting down of the model, easier with a tricycle undercarriage where the model can be flown on and down elevator applied to keep it on the ground. At all times near the ground we are trying to keep clear of the dreaded stall conditions. When the model is safely on the ground, you have stopped the engine, switched off the radio and returned to the pits area, it is time to stop and think. Analyse the flight, what went wrong, what was satisfactory? Adjust the control surface settings so that the transmitter trims can be returned to neutral and take a breather. When you have recovered your composure check the model over for any damage or loosening of fixing and prepare it for the second flight. During this flight the model should be tested at all power settings and in various attitudes, noting the trim changes required at the various power settings and the effectiveness of the controls at the various speeds. Do the control surface movements need changing or, with a transmitter with dual rate controls, what is the effect in low rate? Remain cautious during the take-off and landing stages, there will be plenty of time later to bring these up to scale standards. For the third flight you can experiment with flaps, retracting undercarriage and any other aerodynamic devices you have fitted to the model. Try to be methodical in the testing of the flaps, starting with a 10° setting and increasing by 10° increments to the full flap setting, using the same heading and throttle setting for each occasion. You must give yourself time to observe the effects of the flap setting, there is no point in simply applying the flap and then turning off, you will gain no positive information this way. Three flights are ample for the first day's flying, any more and you are likely to become over-confident and undemanding. From this point on it is a matter of getting into a routine of checking, preparation and building up one's confidence in flying the model to the stage where you have explored the full capability of the model. Until you have got the model into every conceivable attitude at the full speed range – at a safe height of course – and recovered to straight and level flight, you cannot consider yourself a fully competent pilot of that aircraft. Once you have mastered the complete range of the flying potential of the model you will be far more confident of recovering from the nasty moments that happen occasionally, even to the best of pilots.

Before leaving the chapter on preparation of the model and test flying, there are two aspects of flight that warrant further examination, one, stalling, because it is the basic enemy of flight and the other, coping with crosswinds, because we may find ourselves having to take this into consideration during many flights.

STALLING

The irreversible laws of physics confirm that for a conventional aircraft, stalling is inevitable when certain critical conditions are exceeded. These conditions relate to the speed and attitude of the aircraft (it is possible to stall an aircraft at *any* speed) but there are many factors that relate to the stalling speed. To give an indication of the complexity of the problems involved. Wing planform,

aspect ratio, wing section, wing loading, dihedral, aileron types, flaps, surface finish of wings, wing and tail positions relative to the fuselage, balance position, air speed, angle of attack, rate of turn, attitude, power setting and air density. This may seem to be a formidable array of factors to deal with in a model but it does emphasise the importance of the subject and that we must accept it, understand it and learn to live – and fly – with it. Full-size pilots are in a better position to cope with the conditions of stalling, as they have constant reference to instruments, e.g. air speed indicator and rate of turn indicator, and are frequently able to feel the onset of a stall by feedback from the control surfaces to the control column. As the airflow starts to break away from the wing section at the inception of the stall, it becomes turbulent and this turbulence is transmitted via the tail control surface to the control column or wheel in the form of buffeting. We have no such pre-warning of forthcoming disasters, nor do we have the audible stall warning devices fitted to so many light aircraft – although there would seem to be no reason why one should not be fitted to a model, it could be good for gaining points in the special ingenuity classification. Our only way of estimating the approach of the stall of the model is by *observing* the speed and attitude of the model from our ground-based position. Estimating the speed of the model is aggravated by the fact that we are actually observing the *ground* speed of the model (true air speed plus or minus the wind speed) – hence the reason for only carrying out test flights when the wind conditions are favourable. In a twenty knot wind the model may appear to be flying very fast when it is travelling downwind but may, in fact, be only a few knots above the stalling speed – a fact that we may only realise when we come to make our next turn. We must learn to estimate the air speed of the model in varying wind conditions if we are to fly our models safely.

Angle of attack is another vital factor in the stalling syndrome – it should not be confused with angle of incidence of the wings, it is the angle of the wings relative to the *airflow.* Let us consider one of the most common causes for stalling on the approach to landing. The model is lined up with the runway but is too low and the pilot, mistakenly, pulls in the up elevator to gain height. As the model then slows the angle of attack of the wing must be increased even further to achieve sufficient lift to keep the model airborne at that altitude. When the wing reaches an angle of attack of 15° or thereabouts, the inevitable happens, the airflow no longer follows the aerofoil section of the wing, lift disappears and the stall occurs. Angle of bank also increases the stalling speed, since part of the lift component is being used in the turning of the aircraft instead of simply keeping it in the air. Up to 45° bank does not have a vast effect but over this figure there is a rapid progressive deterioration. Load factors increase with the increase of the rate of turn and we know that increased wing loadings result in higher stalling speeds, so if we want to avoid stalling on the approach to landings, we must avoid tight turns and low speeds near to the ground! Make the final approach turn nice and gentle, which will only be possible if converging towards the runway during the downwind portion of the circuit is avoided. Stalling is also a problem during the take-off stage when the model lifts off before a safe flying speed has been reached; what normally happens then is that the model stalls, one wing drops and the petrified pilot tries to pick up the low wing by use of opposite aileron. This normally has the reverse effect of that desired, more drag on the stalled wing, and in this instance, the application of opposite rudder is more useful as this has the effect of yawing the model away from the stalled wing (giving more lift to it) and decreasing the angle of attack of the stalled wing. Our principal aims in recovering from, or avoiding, a stall must be to increase speed and reduce the angle of attack.

Parallel chord wings are amongst the most suitable planforms when it comes

Smooth, mown grass is the ideal flying surface, especially for large models such as this Beechcraft 17A Staggerwing

to stalling characteristics, the stall commences at the root and progresses to the tips giving a straightforward stall, and the chance of retention of some aileron control into the bargain. Taper planform wings, especially highly tapered wings, will often stall first at the tip, resulting from the airflow spilling from the high pressure lower wing area to the low pressure on the top surface. A stall associated with these conditions will result in a sudden wing drop and to avoid such nasty habits wings of this planform are usually given some wash-out, i.e. reduced incidence *progressively* towards the tips. In selecting our proto-type we are automatically bound by the planform of the aircraft, so if we are look-ing to select a prototype to give good stalling characteristics in the model, we should choose a lightly loaded design with parallel chord wings with an aspect ratio of around five or six to one. To achieve the equivalent effects in the model we must build light, accurately, and ensure that the C of G location is correct.

CROSSWINDS

We may be in the unfortunate position of having a runway that is out of wind on the day we wish to fly, and is not wide enough to use the width for take-offs and landings. Although it is not suggested that initial flights are considered in any conditions of strong crosswinds it is important to know how to cope with a moderate crosswind component. Let us assume that we have a crosswind blow-ing from the right hand side of the runway – viewed from the direction of landing and take-off. During the take-off we have two effects to consider, the first being the additional lift experienced on the right hand wing panel (the left hand panel is likely to be blanketed by the fuselage). To prevent the right hand wing from lifting first, as the model accelerates to the take-off speed, right hand aileron must be held on to keep the right wing down. Aileron control can be held on from the commencement of the take-off run, and as the speed increases and the effect of the ailerons is more pronounced, the amount of aileron deflection is reduced. The second effect is that of the wind on the rear end of the model, in particular the fin and rudder. Air striking the right hand side of the aircraft (the area side surfaces are greater behind the wheel positions than in front) will cause it to 'weathercock', i.e. turn into wind. How much correction will have to be given to the rudder will depend on the additional factors relating to the swing during take-off, but in reasonably windy conditions the weathervane effect will probably be the major effect. To land in our right hand crosswind we must make our approach aiming the aircraft to the right to take care of drift and, therefore, track straight on the approach. When we reach the point of landing the model is aiming in a different direction to its forward move-ment and left rudder should be applied just before the touch down to 'kick' the model straight. It requires fine judge-ment to get the rudder on at precisely the correct moment, i.e. just before the stall for a genuine three point landing. We must also consider the unequal lift effect from the crosswind and, as the model touches the ground, apply right aileron to prevent the right wing from lifting again. Precision of landings in difficult crosswind conditions can be all-important, and obvious to the judges, in serious competition flights.

Chapter 21

Competitions

Not all scale modellers are, by natural instinct, competition minded; some will never bother to enter a competition throughout their modelling career, and yet they may produce some fine scale models and be competent flyers. There is no doubt though that competitive events have the effect of 'improving the breed' and the standards of scale R/C models would not have reached their present degree of excellence without the elements of competition and rivalry. If you seriously desire to become a successful scale R/C competitor you must be totally dedicated, almost to the exclusion of all other forms of R/C flying. Look through the lists of winners of international and important national events and you will find proof there of the single-mindedness that is essential to achieve results. Those who do well in these competitions are not the type of modeller who tries his hand at most aspects of R/C modelling. Motivation must be there, you must have the will to build a superior model and to fly it better than your fellow competitors; that involves many hundreds of hours of study, building and still more hours of flying practice. Only the highest standards will suffice and there must be a constant striving to improve your own efforts, aiming for that elusive goal of perfection. There is often the misunderstanding that FAI, or Super Scale, is for

the serious modeller and that Stand-Off, or Class 2 Scale, is for the less dedicated individual who does not wish to compete aggressively. This may have been true initially but the standards of Stand-Off Scale models, and particularly the flying of them, are now so high that the two competitions should be considered as different in style rather than different in overall standards. Of course, all competitions are serious affairs at the highest levels, but there are the 'fly-ins', scale 'jamborees' and events all the way down to club level where standards will definitely be in the 'Sports Scale' category – and the enjoyment no less for that. You must decide which particular slot you wish to fit into, and many factors will influence your decision, but the following comments are intended for those dedicated souls who are prepared to work towards the highest peaks of R/C modelling ambitions – and it is rather like climbing mountains, there is always another waiting to be conquered more challenging than the previous one.

To excel in competitive events you must study the competition rules, the competition organisation, the methods of judging (and mentality of the judges) and understand and apply this information to your selection, construction and flying of your scale R/C model. Just to choose a model, build it, prepare the documentation and fly the model in competitions will not obtain the results you are looking for – there is such a thing as Competition Philosophy. First we must thoroughly study the rules governing the specific competition class we wish to enter as this will affect our choice of prototype. Most scale modellers choose a prototype to model because they happen to like that particular aircraft and have always had the desire to model it. For serious competition we must be more selective and choose according to the bonus factors (complexity) that apply to particular aircraft, how well it is likely to perform, in model terms, and how much useful detail can be applied to the model. Rules governing scale R/C competition classes are changed periodically, in an attempt to keep a balance of opportunity for all prototypes, and it is essential to make use of these changes to keep one step ahead of your adversaries. Observe at the competitions why the winner was successful, how his score could have been improved even further and why the other competitors did not do so well. Analyse the judges' marks and learn from them. Sometimes it seems that any further improvement is impossible, and the ultimate in skills has been achieved; this is never the case and improvements are made from year to year, perhaps only in small ways, e.g. a more realistic engine sound or better flight positioning before the judges, but there is always room for that little extra professionalism to be shown. No-one has yet achieved perfect static and flying scores.

SELECTION OF PROTOTYPE

Different approaches are required to the choice of prototype for the Super Scale and Stand-Off Scale events because of the dissimilar rules applied to the static

judging methods of the two classes. With the rules at present relating to Super Scale there is possibly a bias in favour of modelling light aircraft of small overall dimensions with limited complexity, so that all of the items may be accurately detailed. For good competition results it is not always a matter of what is included but that the items that are incorporated should be right in every detail. For example, if there were a full size aircraft with a simple slab wing, basic square sectioned fuselage without any visible engine parts and little external detail, it would be extremely difficult for the judges to down-mark an accurate, well finished, model of the prototype. This may not result in the most exciting scale model ever, but to be successful it is important not to be over-ambitious with the selection of the prototype – some international scale R/C models are hardly the most interesting of aircraft! It is not suggested that you go to these absolute limits, and there should be a sensible compromise between the complex model (giving the judges the opportunity for 'nit-picking' in many areas) and the ultra simple. Judges are human and they may be influenced to some degree by an unusual and interesting prototype. Although there are exceptions to this rule of relative simplicity, e.g. David Vaughan's P-51 *Mustang,* the more complex the prototype, the more careful you must be to ensure the accuracy of every aspect of the model. Having the actual prototype aircraft to examine, measure, photograph and, if possible, observe flying may not be mandatory but it is certainly a tremendous help. Research of the aircraft is immediately made easier and no matter how many photographs one may have of a prototype there are invariably areas where the construction or detailing is not

Hand-launch, as with this little Nieuport 17, often has to be used for club competitions.

sufficiently clear. To be in a position where you can immediately check on any doubtful area of detailing and finish of the prototype makes life so much easier during all phases of design and construction.

Study the complexity factors relating to the choice of subject and use them to your advantage. Beware, however, of going to extremes. To choose, for example, a Sikorsky Type B bomber (a pre 1914, four engined biplane with fixed conventional undercarriage) may give you a 45% bonus factor but imagine trying to build a model of this 100 foot wing span monster and flying it to a scale speed of 60 m.p.h. On the other hand, a model of an Avro 504 (also pre 1914 design double bay biplane) which happens to have good model flying characteristics and will earn you a 25% bonus, may be worthy of consideration. It could certainly figure well in contests where the weather conditions were suitable. From the flying aspect of Super

Scale competitions the ideal aircraft will probably have at least a limited aerobatic potential with a minimum of one special function, e.g. bomb dropping. If you have a non-aerobatic model, without special functions, you are confined in flying to perform – in addition to the mandatory take-off, procedure turn, figure of eight, circuit and landing, etc. – a series of similar 'flat' manoeuvres that are rather dull and easy to down-point by the judges. You will be in particular trouble in windy conditions, when it becomes very difficult to maintain constant ground speeds in these flat manoeuvres. Choosing optimal special functions can give high marking providing they are carried out authentically and the dropping of a bomb, operation of display smoke, crop spraying etc., is less likely to obtain low marks than some of the other 'chancy' manoeuvres. Select in advance a short list of manoeuvres you consider to be the most likely to score high marks and work towards these targets.

Stand-Off-Scale class models must be even more carefully selected for advantageous complexity bonuses. Static judging, carried out from a distance and not check measured, gives fewer chances of picking up extra points for accurate model detailing, and no marks are given for cockpit detail! – often the area where the enthusiasm of the modeller is completely carried away. Judging the model on the ground in this way is bound to become a little more arbitrary as the judges have no immediate means of checking the accuracy of the model and the decisions are more subjective. Flying becomes a major factor for obtaining high marks, and the application of bonus percentages more critical. For these reasons you are more likely to see models of twin engined aircraft with retracting undercarriages taking part in Stand-Off-Scale contests and the entries will reflect a more ambitious choice of prototypes. It is probably true to say that this class is more of a 'flying man's' contest although, having said that, the model must still be built to the highest standards. Judging from a distance is all very well in theory – it is possible to obtain a good cosmetic effect over indifferent construction, when viewed from three metres or more – but judges are more than likely to have seen the model from closer quarters at some time. They would be less than human if they were not affected by the high standard, or otherwise, of construction and finish of a model that has been examined more closely. There are strong feelings from some competitors that models previously entered in the Super Scale class should not be permitted to enter the Stand-Off-Scale classes later; the judges will probably be aware of the accuracy and detailing of the model and may be unduly biased by that knowledge. Check on the sub-division of the total marks attributed to the static judging and concentrate your efforts where they will be most rewarded.

STATIC JUDGING

Because the judging of the Super Scale class is the more critical we will concentrate on the methods used for this form of competition. 'K' factors are allocated to the various parts of the aircraft, totalling 65, and the marks are awarded with a maximum of ten, i.e. the maximum static points are 650. The headings for the markings and their relative 'K' factors

(to the present FA1 Schedule) are as follows:-

		'K' Factor
1.	Fuselage	10
2.	Wings	10
3.	Tail surface	9
4.	Landing gear	9
5.	Propulsion unit	8
6.	Cockpit or Cabin detail	4
7.	Finish, colour and marking	11
8.	Special ingenuity	4

Judging is carried out with the combined elements of scale fidelity and craftsmanship as it is considered to be virtually impossible to separate the two. To have poor construction would, of necessity, result in similarly poor scale fidelity and be an inferior representation of the prototype. Before looking at individual items the judges will probably make a general inspection of the model, checking it with prototype photographs and viewed from equivalent angles. From this initial inspection they will reasonably be able to assess the accuracy of outlines and the correct relative positions of the airframe components and the comparative areas of the surfaces. It is surprising how even small errors will show up in an investigation of this type, before a measurement or reference to the three-view drawing is made. The judges will then proceed to make detail checks under the headings above, referring to the three-view drawings and the photographs and text supplied by the contestant. Main dimensions of all parts of the airframe are checked with the scale rule and there is no excuse for any divergence of these from the scale drawings used by the competitor for the basis of design. In the previous chapters we have considered all of the aspects of construction and finishes and, naturally, we will have attempted to produce the most scale-like representation of the full-size in all respects. It would be superfluous to go through all of the items again but here are a few samples of what the judges may be looking for under the various headings:-

1. Fuselage Cross sectional areas are difficult for judges to check against the three-view drawing and it will assist them if a couple of templates are supplied, they can use these for checking against the model and the scale drawing. Position of surface detail, i.e. footholds, hand grab rails, hatches, navigation lights, must correspond to the photographs and drawings.

2. Wings Fixing methods for the wings on the prototype are often poorly simulated. Whatever method of attachment you use, i.e. single piece wing, plug in wing panels, etc., the true method of attachment must be represented from the outside and made quite obvious. Wing sections that are not scale will obviously be downgraded and this includes the incorporation, or lack of, washout. Templates, if they are a practical proposition, should assist the judge in determining whether the aerofoil section is correct. Incidences, dihedral, sweep back, and in the case of multi-wing aircraft, the gap and stagger of the wings are checked. In the latter case the method of attachment of rigging wires, the section of the wires and the detailing of the fitments will be part of the total consideration. Badly shaped or sectioned wing tips are a certain 'give-away' and flaps and ailerons should be related to the types and methods of operation of the full-size aircraft.

3. Tail Surfaces Cheating, by increasing the areas in the hope of obtaining better flying characteristics, will lead to serious reductions of marks. Where two forms of construction and covering are used for the prototype, e.g. metal covered fin and tailplane and fabric covered control surfaces, these should be duplicated in model form by sensible use of covering and finishes. Removable fairings are not easy to simulate but they must give the appearance of being removable. Control horns, if functional on the model, must be of the correct size and positioned accurately.

4. Landing gear Apart from dimensional accuracy, the judges will be looking for simulation of the attachment points of the legs, springing or shock absorbing methods, cables, brakes, tubing and wheel retention method. The tyres should represent the full-size in contour and tread patterns and the hub cover, if any, must be of the same type and style. With light aircraft wheel types are often substituted during the life span of the aircraft and when this has happened the facts should clearly be stated on the scale drawing and the text. Retracting undercarriages should be accurate in detail and representation of the method of operation of the full-size, wheel well interiors, and the wheel well covers, must be detailed. Tail skids and wheels should be sprung, castoring, retracting or fixed as for the full-size aircraft.

5. Propulsion unit The relatively high 'K' factor for this item is understandable when an exposed engine, or partly exposed, is a feature of the original. When an in-line engine, with no parts visible externally, is reproduced it is vital to take care with the shaping of the cowl, air inlets, fixing methods, propeller and spinner, as these are the only items that the judge can use as a basis for his marking. Totally hiding the operating model engine is essential and thought must be given to the dispersal of the engine exhaust; ideally it should be routed to the scale exhaust position.

6. Cockpit or Cabin detail

No high 'K' factor here, presumably because it is difficult to judge for small scale models of large aircraft and of obsolete aircraft with little data to work on. Although a dummy pilot is not mandatory it undoubtedly increases the realism of the cockpit (open types in particular) and should be included. Radio control equipment should not be visible within the cockpit area and floors and wall coverings should be at the scale heights and thicknesses. To achieve maximum marks the instruments must be well simulated, but not necessarily working, and the associated equipment accurately detailed. The cockpit area inevitably is subject to wear and tear from the pilot climbing in and out, and from servicing, so to add the scuff marks and wearing of the paintwork in certain areas will add to the authenticity.

7. Finish, colour and markings

Carrying the highest 'K' factor, it is all-important that the finishes, colour and markings relate absolutely to the prototype and to the documentation prepared by you. Colour represents the biggest problem, due to the inaccuracies of colour photographs and colour printing and explanations should be documented if there seems to be any deviation between the model and the photographs and colour printing. Actual paint samples would be valuable and many of the military colours are well documented – although fading of these colours may take place when the prototype had been in active service for a lengthy period. A full gloss paint, even if it is used on the prototype and the intention is to represent a 'factory fresh' aircraft, will almost certainly look too glossy and artificial. You must use your judgement to determine the degree of 'matting-down' that is necessary.

8. Special ingenuity

Although it only has a 'K' factor of 4 you will lose all of

Schneider Trophy and other seaplane/flying boat events are increasing. This is a Short Crusader.

these marks unless you incorporate some device/s to be able to inform the judges of the special ingenuity items. They can take the form of simulated machine gun firing noises, scale fuel filling points, oil coolers operating as engine cooling vents, audible stall warning devices, scale exhaust systems, animated figures and many other 'novelty' devices that have been designed and constructed by the competitor. Do not fail to utilise this section, it also gives a chance to introduce a bit of fun into the otherwise serious proceedings – why not a flushing 'loo' in a small airliner!

9. Documentation Top category international competitors have been known to be disqualified from competitions, or lose valuable marks, through having insufficient documentation for their model. Specific minimum requirements of documentation are laid down for the FAI classes, and are notified to entrants for other events, so there is no excuse for failing to have all of the information that is needed. It is a minimum list and can be expanded where the competitor considers it to be justified, but bear in mind that the judges have a very considerable task when they have a large entry to check. Where amplification of aspects of the model are included keep them to the salient points, the ones that will remove any ambiguity or clarify any specific quality of the aircraft. Filling your dossier with irrelevant information will not assist the judges in their deliberations, and taken to verbose limits, will frustrate to the extent that they are less likely to look favourably on your creation. Presentation of the required proofs of scale is almost as important as the presentation of the model; the information should be neatly documented and collated in a folio with the type of aircraft and your name printed on the outside. A loose-leaf binder, with a soft plastic casing, is ideal as this can be updated and changed whenever it becomes necessary. An alternative would be to use a folder containing clear plastic envelope inserts, but do be sure that the plastic is crystal clear or it may alter the colour renderings of the photographs and colour plates. Providing an index is a nice touch, especially if you have rather more than the minimum of information; the sections should refer to the eight items listed previously. Whether you include an additional section on flying characteristics of the aircraft is at your discretion but it should do no harm – providing that it is a distinct and separate section – they have the option of reading it or leaving it, as they wish.

The list of required proofs of scale (FAI Super Scale) is:-

1. A three-view of the prototype of a scale not smaller than $1/50$th. Obviously, a larger scale drawing, e.g. $1/36$th or $1/24$th, is going to be easier for the judges to work with; however, the important factor is that the drawing is clear and accurate. Line drawings, as opposed to tone or coloured plates, are required and they should contain the basic constructional information in addition to the outline. How much additional information to the outline is shown will vary according to the prototype selected; a fabric covered aircraft would normally have all the rib stations, spars, tail surfaces and fuselage construction included. Sheet metal covered aircraft may only indicate the main panel lines and surface features such as radiators, wheel wells, exhaust stubs etc. As previously mentioned, any divergence between the three-views and

the photographs – and the model – should be clearly marked on the drawing and the reasons for the variation noted in the folio. Cross check between the drawings, photographs and model that all are in accordance with one another.

2. The precise scale of the model, the basic dimensions of the full-size aircraft and the sources of this information. Obtain the most reputable sources for the dimensional information, i.e. manufacturers, museums, accepted reference books, and if there are conflicting measurements, keep searching until you can find some degree of agreement. Naturally, the measurements quoted here should be in accordance with the scaled dimensions on the three-view drawing.

3. A scale ruler. Judges must check the model dimensions on the model against the measurements on the three-view drawing and two scale rulers, or one combined ruler, are needed for them to do this. Make the ruler long enough to cover the full fuselage length or half wingspan; it makes sense to mark the ruler to the precise overall length of the fuselage and to denote this clearly. The graduation marks should be clearly made in ink on white card or plastic. This should be glued to a thin wood or plastic base so that there is no risk of expansion or contraction due to changes of atmospheric conditions.

4. Three general view photographs, one of which must be the actual aircraft modelled. Select the photographs to illustrate the basic character of the aircraft and not to hide it. One of the photographs should be a static side view to show the general outline of the aircraft, the other two should also include the whole of the aircraft and can be in frame flying shots if of good quality.

5. Detailed photographs covering the static schedule items (1 to 8) are advisable, but not mandatory, and will assist the judges in marking the more detailed areas of the model. Glossy original photographs are the best for this purpose, as matt prints or half tone reproductions will not show the detail to the same extent.

6. Builder of the model declaration. Under the governing rules of the FAI, and in most other serious competitions, the contestant is obliged to be the builder of the model.

7. A list of components and parts not made by the contestant. Items such as the radio control equipment, operative engine, fuel tank and engine mount will *not* lose the competitor marks if he has purchased them commercially, other items may well do so. Commercially produced wheels, retract systems, canopy covers, transfers and decals, guns, bombs, spinners, may lose the contestant marks on a negative craftsmanship basis.

8. List of items for consideration under 'special ingenuity'. This is your chance to explain how the wind driven generator actually works, or the reason the co-pilot ejects after the canopy has been released! Try to make the reason for including the 'special ingenuity' items convincing, as the more they relate to the construction or operation of the prototype the more sensible they will sound.

Remember that static judging does entail personal opinions – from persons that are well qualified in judging but with differing views and emphasis. Elimination of equivocal areas regarding the prototype and the model will reduce the possibility of downgrading through misunderstandings. Positive facts cannot be denied but uncertain areas are open to speculation and personal points of view; they are to be watched.

Finally, do put your name and address in the documentation folio. It is, from your point of view, an important reference book and without it your model could be worthless as far as competitions are concerned.

FLYING

Competition flying is quite different from any other form of scale flying due to one factor – pressure. Modellers are affected in many different ways when it comes to standing out in front of the judges to carry out their competition flight. For some the mixture of adrenalin and heightened perception brings out the best in their flying but for others, and probably the majority, nerves start to take a hold and the standards of flying are well below the normal. Judges cannot allow any percentage factors for nerves; they are not to know whether the competitor's flight is better, the same or below average and they can only mark on what they see. For those of us that are of a nervous disposition, where the contest flight is something to be viewed with the utmost apprehension rather than enjoyment, we must do everything in our power to reduce the tensions that result in mistakes. Perhaps a quick nip of whiskey, or even a tranquilliser, is the answer for some contestants but for most it is the act of trying to remain calm and cool that is the most important. There are many ways that we can help ourselves in this respect and one of the most vital is the routine practice of flying the model through the scale schedule. The more times we fly the model and practice the various manoeuvres in the schedule, the less likely we are to become flustered when we are flying in the competition. Familiarity is supposed to breed contempt but in our case we hope that it just breeds acquaintance.

Before the flying commences there are a number of ways that we can help to keep the temperature down and improve our chances of a 'normal' flight. Arrive at the contest in good time and find out as

For scale aerobatic events the Zlin and Super Chipmunk designs are popular. They are designed for this type of flying.

soon as you can when you are due to fly. Be prepared for the flight in very good time, check that you have all of the ground equipment that you need and that the model is in full working order. By the time you have made all of these checks there will probably still be twenty minutes or so before your flight time so take a little walk away from the hustle and bustle of the competition flyers and have a look for mushrooms – no matter if you do not find any, it is more of a problem to know what to do with them if you do pick some. Know the weather conditions and the surrounding flying area. Prepare your flying schedule according to the prevailing weather conditions and write out the caller's list. Your caller is a valuable part of the team, and preferably he should be quiet, unflappable but able to give clear, concise instructions to both you and the judges. Some modellers prefer the caller to simply be an 'aide mémoire' and just remind them of the sequence of manoeuvres, but a good caller, and pit assistant, can be far more than that and help you around the schedule with advice and encouragement. Both you and your caller should be smartly attired; you do not have to wear suits but a neat appearance helps to give an air of authority and competence. Do not be afraid of talking to the judges and asking them about any points that you may be unsure about, they will not eat you or turn you into a block of salt. If you intend to carry out some special manoeuvre that is unusual, explain it to them in advance. If, for instance, your 'pièce de résistance' is to fly straight and level at twenty feet altitude followed by blowing up the model in mid-air, tell them about it or they are likely to be terrified. Dropping bombs is another instance; have the courage to tell the judges the area you are aiming to hit –

providing it comes off the effect will be far more convincing. Should there be any reason why you are not entirely happy with the behaviour of the model on the ground before flying, e.g. radio control equipment 'twitching' or engine being temperamental, call an 'attempt' and do not be tempted to risk the flight. Similarly, if you have cause for concern during a flight, usually through radio interference, abort the flight and inform the judges of your reasons. Where suspected radio interference is proved the chances are that you will be offered another flight. Safety is all the more important at a contest as there may be a large crowd of spectators, and with the pressures on, we do not always react in a logical manner. Avoid letting a potentially dangerous situation escalate; if a manoeuvre starts to go wrong, terminate it rather than run the risk of a complete disaster. There is always tomorrow and we only have a bit of pride to swallow if we take the safe way out of a nasty looking situation – the other way and we might lose the model as well.

Simulation of the flight characteristics of the prototype is every bit as important as reproducing the physical qualities of the aircraft. Our model must fly with the same attitude as the prototype, perform turns and manoeuvres in the same style and fly at a scale speed. It is in the area of scale flying speed that there is likely to be some dissension amongst the judges. Is a scale speed a direct relationship with the scale of the model? Many would argue that this is precisely the analogy of model speed to the speed of the prototype, others argue that it should be based on the square of the speed and some prefer to take an empirical view and satisfy themselves that if it looks right it must be right. In truth, it is very difficult to achieve a direct scale-proportion flying speed with many of the models selected. Consider some of the slower flying aircraft of the W.W.1 era; a Sopwith *Pup* to one fifth scale (about the limits of size to be practical in diverse weather conditions) would have to fly at a scale speed of about sixteen miles per hour – just about stalling speed. The problems are compounded when flying through procedure turns, figures of eight and circuits because then we have to fly to an equal groundspeed and not airspeed. We find ourselves in the invidious position of having to fly downwind, with, say, a twelve m.p.h. wind, at a theoretical airspeed of six m.p.h. – not even within the realms of possibility. Except for the large scale models of relatively small fast prototypes (e.g. a quarter scale *Cosmic Wind*) is there any hope of getting anywhere near to the theoretical scale speeds and, even then, are we likely to exceed the scale speed limitations on some occasions? Ironically, when this type of aircraft is modelled, say a Pitts *Special,* the power to weight ratio of the model is rarely sufficient to allow it to perform all of the manoeuvres of the prototype; near continuous vertical rolls are more likely to end up as a one and a quarter vertical roll and falling off the top. Scale speed is a subject that could be debated at very great length, but it may be sufficient to say that we must work out the best compromise possible. Choosing the right prototype and scale will help but from there on we must attempt to convince the judges that the model is flying at an equivalent speed to the full size aircraft. This can be achieved in more than one way. A model of a Bleriot with the engine turning at 15,000 r.p.m. is hardly likely to give the impression of a slow flying speed, even if it is flying very slowly.

Scale speed is only part of the total aim for flying realism and the remainder should be less contentious. Should be, but judges' views remain subjective and no two persons may be in agreement on how a specific prototype flew. This may be a further argument in favour of selecting a contemporary light aircraft as your scale subject, at least the judges are all likely to have seen a similar type of aircraft flying. When it comes to historic aircraft there may be none of the prototypes left in existence and we can only refer to documentation for descriptions of the flight characteristics. Most of us know what *we* think is scale flying of a particular subject but will the judges agree? Authentic scale flying can be taken too far and we must be prepared to stick to the rule book on occasions when the rules are specific, even when they are in opposition to the natural flight procedures of the prototype. Landing circuits are a typical example of this situation. Early aircraft would never have performed a full circuit for landing, theirs would have been a straight-in approach; many light aircraft will do an abbreviated circuit and aircraft such as the *Spitfire* would carry out a curved, banking approach all the way down to the runway – if they didn't, the pilot would never have seen the runway! Despite these undisputed facts the schedule calls for a regular rectangular circuit and anything less will result in degrading of the marks for that manoeuvre. A further example is apparent in the stall turn manoeuvre. Certain prototypes require engine power to be maintained during the yawing phase at the top of the turn, throttling back when the nose of the aircraft drops. Where the rule dictates that the engine of the model must be throttled back as the stall is reached, in the vertically upwards direction, this is exactly what we must do. Competition flying is, then, a compromise of scale speed (slow the model down excessively and it may be impossible to fly the manoeuvres accurately) and scale realism. Do not be too disheartened if the judges do not appear to agree with your interpretation of scale flying realism, the next set of judges may be right on your wavelength.

The flight schedule of FAI competitions has been drawn up with the aim of catering for all of the manoeuvres that any prototype aircraft could perform *and* to give an equal competitive chance to any prototype selected. It would be unreal to expect this aim to be totally fulfilled but the authorities are continually reviewing and adapting the system in their quest to achieve perfection. One typical failing during competition flying, and one misunderstanding should be dispensed with before we consider the individual manoeuvres. Correct positioning of the model before the judges is essential for high marks, as if the model cannot be properly seen by them – because it is behind them, in the sun or too far away – they cannot award any marks for that particular manoeuvre. Ensure that you are in the correct location to commence the manoeuvre before your caller announces it. All manoeuvres commence and finish in straight and level flight (with the appropriate call to the judges) but that does not mean that a loop, a stall turn or a roll is commenced *immediately* from the straight and level. Light aircraft in particular have to be dived to build up sufficient speed to perform these manoeuvres and this must be equally represented by the model. Any elaboration of methods of gaining speed for a manoeuvre, e.g. a reversal to build up speed for a vertical roll, should be preceded by a warning to the judges.

Inspection of the FAI flight schedule will show that there are five mandatory manoeuvres (total 'K' factor of 29) and a choice of five optional manoeuvres with 'K' factor of 4 each. The take-off, circuit and landing alone are worth more in 'K' factor terms than the five optional manoeuvres which immediately suggests that this part of the schedule must be practised assiduously.

Taxi Optional 'K' factor 4. Models equipped with two wheel undercarriage and steerable tail wheels must taxi for fifteen metres, executing 'S' type turns, come to a near stop, or complete stop if brakes were fitted to the prototype. For prototypes fitted with a tailskid the model only has to taxi forward for 15m and come to a near stop. Tricycle undercarriage equipped aircraft are expected to taxi down wind for fifteen metres, stop, turn into wind through a minimum of 120 degrees and take off. The taxi must be commenced from an unassisted 'stand still' start and resemble the full-size aircraft performance, i.e. slow and smooth. Models of prototypes fitted with rotary engines might be advised to opt out of the taxi as the original engine was not fitted with a throttle, only a method of cutting the engine out or fully on. Simulating this, with the model on asphalt runways, may make the model difficult to control on the ground.

Take-off 'K' factor 10. Except where conditions dictate otherwise, the model should take off into wind and after a straight run of appropriate length, lift steadily off the ground and climb straight ahead at a constant climb rate consistent with the prototype aircraft. Flaps should be used where appropriate and retracting undercarriages, where fitted, should be retracted during the straight climb-out. At an altitude reasonable for scale requirements the model is levelled off and the engine/s throttled back. Obvious faults during take-off include allowing the model to swing (and probably over-correcting), lifting off too soon, excessive climb rate and not keeping the heading for sufficient time. Observation of the full-size light aircraft, some of the lower powered versions, shows what a relatively long, slowly accelerating take-off run they have; some of the best simulations with models have occurred when the engine has not been giving full power.

Straight Flight 'K' factor 3. Performed upwind for a minimum of ten seconds, must be straight and level. Make sure the model is trimmed out before commencing and keep the model down to a reasonable speed – there is a tendency at this stage to try to get the flight over with as quickly as possible!

Procedure Turn 'K' factor 3. Can be flown immediately on completion of the straight flight, but if you have ample time for your schedule, is better taken as a separate manoeuvre. Keep the manoeuvre to a fairly tight radius but not overbanked and maintain a constant radius turn with no changes of altitude. To achieve a flatter turn, more akin to full size, use should be made of inside, or bottom, rudder. As the aileron and up elevator are applied feed in a touch of rudder, in the same direction as the aileron; as the nose starts to drop, ease off the aileron and adjust the elevator to suit the rate of turn. As with all manoeuvres it is a matter of co-ordination

between the four principal functions and we must use them to create the best possible scale effect.

Figure of Eight 'K' factor 4. For slower models, in windy conditions, this can be a most difficult manoeuvre to fly accurately and it is under-valued at a 'K' factor of 4. Constant use of throttle is essential if the circles are to be of equal diameter and the intersection is to be directly in line with the landing circle and judges. Add to this the problems of keeping a consistent ground speed and constant altitude and you have one of the most difficult compulsory manoeuvres to perform accurately. Without taking it to extremes, the diameters of the circles flown should be quite small; the 100 metres maximum diameter is far too great for slower models of large scale. Methods of attaining a flat turn, as mentioned in the Procedure Turn, can be employed, but in strong winds the opposite rudder control may have to be introduced as the model turns into wind, i.e. by slipping the aircraft to allow for drift. As the method of flying a Figure of Eight will depend on the type of model and the strength and direction of the wind it is a manoeuvre that you must constantly practise in varying wind conditions.

Rectangular circuit and approach 'K' factor 4. Full size aircraft normally operate on a left-hand circuit (unless there are local reasons for doing otherwise) and perhaps this is the reason that the vast majority of modellers also perform left-hand circuits – almost to the exclusion of right-hand patterns. There is no certainty that a left-hand circuit will apply on the day/s of the competition, since it will depend on the wind direction and the siting of the judges and spectators, and you must be prepared to execute the landing circuit and approach in either direction. Good circuit discipline is all about planning. You must estimate the wind strength and direction and be prepared to adjust the attitude and speed of the model to suit. There are a number of common failings in flying the landing circuit including:-

1. Failing to enter at the correct height and straight and level. Circuit heights do vary from airfield to airfield but 300 metres is generally taken to be circuit height. For a one sixth scale model the circuit height would therefore be 50 metres:

2. Performing ill-defined crosswind legs. The turns into and out of the crosswind legs should be positive and the turns from the up and downwind legs should not be a gentle arc:

3. Failure to allow for drift on the crosswind legs:

4. Converging on the runway during the downwind leg, i.e. not flying parallel to the runway but 'crabbing' in towards it. This very common fault results in the two final turns on to the approach merging into one:

5. Allowing the model to go too far downwind before making the final crosswind turn, more frequently happening on windy days and compounded by failing to allow for drift on the crosswind leg. It is a fairly rare occurrence for a model in competition flying to overshoot the landing circle, the model is more often struggling to make the circle and liberal amounts of engine power are being applied. The aim of the last part of the circuit is to throttle back as you commence the final crosswind leg and to combine the circuit and approach with minimum use of throttle:

6. Failing to appreciate the problems mentioned in (5.) above and having to climb on the final approach. If you have misjudged your downwind turn it is better to keep the throttle open during the crosswind leg and first part of the approach, rather than letting the model get too low, requiring excessive power settings and a climb to get into the correct landing approach position.

Where flaps and retracting undercarriage are fitted these must be operated at the respective scale positions, i.e. undercarriage at the latter end of the downwind leg and flaps commencing at the start of the final crosswind leg. Flap control can be useful for adjusting the rate of descent on the final approach, ensuring a relatively high safe approach without the risk of overshooting, but you must be fully aware of the trim changes that take place at the different flap settings.

Landing 'K' factor 9. With the high 'K' factor allocated to the actual landing every effort must be made to touch down smoothly in the prescribed area, to keep the model straight and to roll to a stop without tipping up. Tricycle undercarriage equipped models are probably favoured for the landing, but they must touch down main wheels first and the nosewheel gradually lowered onto the ground. Accurate three-point landings with slow flying, lightly loaded models are notoriously demanding in any conditions above a light breeze but it should be remembered that the prototypes in equivalent high wind strengths would probably settle for a 'wheeler' landing. When opting for this more positive form of landing, forewarn the judges of your intentions and reasons. There is a risk of being so relieved after touching down the model after the competition flight that you relax your concentration and forget about the landing roll. The competition schedule is not complete until the model is at rest at the end of the landing!

OPTIONAL MANOEUVRES

A choice of five optional manoeuvres from twenty (numbers 17, 18 and 19 are for non-aerobatic aircraft only) gives adequate variety for all types of aircraft. Select the ones that are the most effective in terms of the prototype aircraft but are not likely to result in low scores, i.e. manoeuvres where it is possible to make a complete 'hash' of the attempt. All options carry a 'K' factor of 4. Some of the more advanced aerobatic manoevures are described in greater detail as it would seem likely that in future there will be scale R/C competitions designed with aerobatics more in mind.

1. Multi-engined models It is obligatory that all the engines shall be running from the take-off to the completion of the figure of eight manoeuvres but it is doubtful whether a high number of marks would be scored if one or more engines failed during the flight schedule. Circuit flying with one engine dead is not to be recommended and the prudent modeller would terminate his flight in these circumstances.

2. Retracting landing gear. Apart from operating the retracting undercarriage at the normal stages, i.e. after take-off and before landing, an upward run could be included to give the judges a closer view

of the scale operation of the undercarriage – unless the action is less than life-like in which case it is preferable to limit the operation to the standard situations.

3. Retract and extend flaps. Flaps should be operated for take-off and landing where the prototype would be expected to use them. Because of the distances involved from the judges to the model during the raising and lowering of the flaps on the take-off and landing phases of the flying, a separate upwind run should be included to demonstrate their operation. A hint of the trim changes involved is not unreasonable but corrective control must be applied to the elevator and throttle to prevent this becoming too obvious.

4. Dropping bombs or external fuel tanks. Perform these actions in a like manner to the prototype. If a scale model of heavy bomber is being demonstrated the bomb doors must be opened on the approach, upwind, followed by the dropping of the bombs. Dive bombers must make the characteristic steep dive, with dive brakes out, release the bomb in the final stages of the dive and make a low level recovery. The bombs themselves must be sufficiently heavy to take up a steady trajectory and if they are designed to 'explode' on impact, aim to drop them near to the judges – but not near enough to scare them. Releasing external fuel tanks does not present too many problems but make a positive approach, throttle back and release directly in front of the judges.

5. Stall turn. There are two sensible alternative positionings for the stall turn, down wind or directly in front of the

A large-scale Eindekker flares out for landing. Absence of pilot detracts from overall effect.

judges. The latter positioning gives the opportunity for the judges to observe the vertical portion of flight and the yawing through 180°; it also gives them the chance to see the effects of drift in strong wind conditions. Down wind stall turns are preferable in all but light wind conditions as there is no obvious drift factor. Most models will stall turn better in the opposite direction to the rotation of the propeller; make use of this aid. Most common faults in performing the stall turn are failure to get the model truly vertical and applying rudder too early, thus changing the stall turn into a wing-over.

6. Immelman Turn. During W.W.1 the German ace, Max Immelman, perfected this manoeuvre as a means of changing direction through 180° and to gain an advantage over his adversary. It should not be confused with a wing-over, it *is* a half loop followed by a half roll. Early aircraft and light aircraft would have to enter the Immelman turn after a dive to increase speed; with the model this may entail the application of rudder to counteract the effects of torque. Entry speed for the turn should be similar, or a little higher, than that of a loop and the

wings must be level at the entry. Undoubtedly the biggest failing in performing the manoeuvre is in commencing the half roll too soon, it should not be started until the nose has dropped beyond the level position. In fighting tactics it was not devised as a height-gaining manoeuvre, the intention was to execute the turn and be in a position to attack the oncoming aircraft. Commencing the roll too soon, with a low air speed – and falling lower still in the roll – will almost certainly result in the model 'wallowing' out of the roll and possibly stalling.

7. Loop. Not many aircraft perform a true, fully circular loop, the result is more of an ellipse and this is acceptable for R/C scale contests providing it is not too elongated. Entry and exit positions should be coincidental (adjustments made for wind conditions) the wings must be level throughout and the throttle reduced as the model comes over the top of the loop. Positioning in front of the judges is obviously important, they will not be able to assess the loop if it is performed end on or at an angle to them. The radius of the loop should be appropriate to the prototype; fast, heavy air-

Aerobatic biplanes such as this ⅓ size Pitts, the Jungmeister/Jungmann, Stampe etc. are equally agile in model form.

craft use up a lot of sky in performing looping manoeuvres.

8. Reversal – or 'Split-S'. Again, there should be a different approach for light aircraft and faster, more aerobatic types. The standard entry for a reversal with a light aircraft would be to dive to gain speed; raise the nose about 10° above the horizon and then commence the half roll. Too frequently the scale model is rolled directly from the straight and level position, but the only reason for rolling from this position would be as a diversionary tactic by the prototype; it is a legitimate manoeuvre to lose height.

9. Cuban Eight. This may be considered as the combination of two Immelmans with the half rolls delayed until the aircraft is at an angle of 45° to the horizon. There should be a momentary checking before the half roll is commenced, the loops should be of equal radius and the intersection central.

10. Spin. The knowledge of why a model spins, and how you can enter and recover from a spin, is one of the prime essentials for safe scale flying. Maybe we do not intend to include spins in our aerobatic schedule but we may, inadvertently, let the model reach an attitude where a spin is imminent. Quite simply, an aircraft cannot be recovered from the spin until it is unstalled. Even so, a spin will not occur unless there is a yaw component present during the stall and, for deliberate purposes, this is introduced with rudder deflection. It should be appreciated that yaw may be introduced by the application of ailerons (sometimes in the opposite direction to the natural banking direction) and by the aircraft 'slipping' in a steep turn. These conditions, plus an increased angle of attack introduced by up-elevator, may be produced during the turn on to final approach for landing!

Some models are too stable to spin and some prototypes are prohibited from spinning because of their inability to recover from it; in both cases it would be foolish to include spinning in your competition schedule. Entry to the spin should be at a safe height, with the nose held high, motor throttled back (although this is not necessarily full-size practice) and at the point of the stall, *full* elevator and full rudder applied simultaneously. Most models enter a spin more readily in one direction compared with the opposite rotation, and it may assist to introduce some sympathetic aileron – it may also have the opposite effect. With the spin well established the model is normally at a marked nose down attitude and auto-rotating positively. Models that have a tendency to develop into a flat spin, i.e. nearly horizontal, should not be intentionally spun as recovery may be impossible, difficult or, at the very best, non-positive in recovery. A normally established spin will continue as long as full rudder and elevator are maintained and many models will automatically recover when the controls are centralised. For competition work, however, we require the model to be precise in the recovery and to complete the three-turn spin on the same heading as that entered. Recovery action for full-size aircraft is to first centralise the rudder for up to one turn of the spin, and then centralise the elevator – perhaps applying slight down elevator. The reasoning behind this action is that if the elevator is centralised at the same time as the rudder, there may be an excessive build-up of speed and a potentially dangerous spiral dive result. This method may or may not be applicable to scale R/C models – it is not unknown for a model to transfer from a spin in one direction to a spin of the opposite rotation when full elevator has been maintained and slight opposite rudder applied – always a risk when intending to centralise rudder. No two scale models will react to spin entry and recovery in exactly the same way (even with supposedly identical models) so you must practise spinning until you understand the characteristics of your model completely. Providing you keep

the nose high, wait for the model to genuinely stall and immediately apply *full* elevator and rudder movements there is little risk of the model only entering a spiral dive – obvious by the increased rate of descent and lack of auto-rotation.

11. Roll. Here you have a choice of Slow Roll, Barrel Roll, Hesitation Roll or Flick Roll and the type must be nominated before commencement of the manoeuvre. Rolling manoeuvres, with the exception of the Flick Roll, are best performed downwind where the roll is given the impression of being extended, and the errors less noticeable.

Slow Roll Arguably the *most* difficult manoeuvre to achieve accurately with anything but an advanced scale aerobatic design. Ignore the competition aerobatic model's three slow rolls, these are more akin to the aileron rolls performed by fast jets – although a certain degree of top rudder may be used in the process. Generally speaking, the faster you enter a slow roll the easier it is to perform; maximum skills are required when the entry speed is towards the minimum possible and with a slow, bulky scale model. This applies equally to full-size and R/C models but the latter will not receive high marks if the manoeuvre is taken at an unrealistically high speed. Even bigger problems arise when you are flying a model of a prototype that does not have an inverted fuel system fitted, e.g. *Tiger Moth* or Curtis *Jenny*. As the model slows and the engine is throttled back at the inverted position, the control surface movements have to be increased or the roll rate will reduce, perhaps stop altogether. Even more drag is now being produced by the large control surface movements and there is every chance that the model will 'fall out' of the last quarter of the roll. The aim of the slow roll is to rotate the aircraft with the nose 'fixed' on an imaginary point on the horizon ahead – difficult enough to achieve with a full-size aircraft and even more difficult with an R/C model where you are not relative to the aircraft. To co-ordinate a slow roll it is necessary to use a combination of aileron and rudder (plus elevator) sometimes in the same direction and on other occasions with crossed controls, i.e. rudder opposite to aileron direction. The latter occurs during the second and fourth segments of the roll (imagine the roll divided into four quarters, viewed from the end) to prevent the nose of the aircraft from dropping. Rudder movements are in fact progressive throughout the slow roll and must be used as required by the particular model you are flying. For some models of prototypes capable of performing acceptable slow rolls, e.g. Cessna *Aerobat,* it may be impossible to obtain consistent results without reaching scale speeds that are unrealistic. In these circumstances it would be wise to delete the slow roll from your competition repertoire.

Barrel Roll The barrel roll can be thought of as a 'corkscrew' loop and at no stage should down elevator be applied; the ideal barrel roll should maintain not less than 1g throughout the manoeuvre. Correct entry of the barrel roll is important; dive the model to build up speed, bank the aircraft in the desired direction and feed in up elevator, adjusting the degree of bank and tightness of the roll with elevator. Once mastered it is not a difficult manoeuvre to perform, and with

positive g all the way through, it is not necessary to reduce the throttle until the model is over the top. Avoid letting the model wander off course or pulling in too much elevator at the top and thereby losing altitude.

Hesitation Roll Takes the form of a slow roll divided into four positive sections with a distinct break in between. Powerful ailerons are essential for the hesitation roll and the movements on the transmitter must be positive and rapid – it is not a manoeuvre for 'feeling your way through', the positions on the transmitter are predetermined and must be precisely attained. Count your way through the hesitation portions of the roll, i.e. roll to vertical, one-two, roll to inverted, one-two, roll to vertical etc., etc. Only models of prototypes with full aerobatic potential should include the hesitation roll or the:-

Flick Roll (sometimes known as the Snap Roll). Flick rolls can be best described as high speed horizontal spins with power applied. High speed describes both the entry speed, which should be quite a few knots above the standard stalling speed, and the rate of rotation, which can be very rapid indeed. Flick rolls are not difficult to perform, but the art comes in being able to stop the rotation precisely, to finish at a given attitude and heading. The full size Bucker *Jungmeister* is capable of performing excellent flick rolls and to watch one of these aircraft go from knife edge flight on one wing tip through one and a half flick rolls to knife edge on the other wing tip is one of the most exciting manoeuvres it is possible to see. Flying of this calibre needs supreme concentration and co-ordination. Entry to the flick roll is gained by raising the nose of the model, allowing the speed to reduce (experience will tell you the best entry speed) and applying full up elevator and rudder – normally in the opposite direction to the propeller rotation. Recovery is by giving full opposite rudder and centralising the elevator, or slight down elevator, practice will determine the moment that this action must be initiated to 'stop' the model at the required attitude. As with the standard spin, the lesson to be learned from the description of this manoeuvre is that excessive elevator and top rudder (to eliminate side slipping) on a steeply banked approach for landing, can produce similar results.

12. Parachute drop. Any old Woolworth's parachute will not do for this option. The parachute must be realistic and must drop from a scale location, i.e. bomb bay or hatch for cargo parachutes or side or rear doors for personnel. For open cockpit aircraft the parachutist may be ejected by inverting the model, this is a chancy business as there is always the risk of fouling the parachute by parts of the airframe. Parachutists are not dropped with the aircraft travelling at high speeds and the model should be slowed to a sensible degree before discharging; directional changes are normally made with rudder during the run in for the jump but beware of the dreaded spin!

13. Touch and go. Touch and goes are performed in full-size aircraft as practices for landing without having to incur the delay of coming to a halt, back taxying, and taking-off again. For the exercise to be worthwhile the model should be genuinely landed, run along the ground and only then the throttle is opened up to go round again. The model must follow this pattern and a touching of the wheels on the ground, bouncing back into the air and opening up the throttle, does not constitute a touch and go. Three metres is the minimum distance specified for the wheels to be in contact with the runway, but the manoeuvre will be more convincing if the distance is considerably

Tony Briddle positions a ¹/₃ Quadra-powered Sopwith Swallow for a slow flypast at Old Warden.

longer, with the model decelerating before commencing the go round.

14. Overshoot. If an aircraft is too high on the landing approach the pilot will make a decision to abort the landing and carry out another circuit. Where that decision is made will depend on the degree of misjudgement the pilot has made; from the model schedule aspect that point is three metres above the landing circle. Make a standard approach, but higher than normal, throttle back, use flaps if they are fitted and aim the model for the three metres above the landing spot. A little excess speed in the descending approach is permissible, simulating the full size 'hope' of getting the aircraft down, the throttle should be opened up immediately above the landing circle and the model climbed ahead. Make the approach obviously high, it would be feasible to land from a shallow approach for competition purposes. It is *not* the intention that the overshoot has been caused by an obstruction on the runway, or instructions from the tower to go round again.

15. Side-slip to left and right. Not recommended as a manoeuvre to be performed on the landing approach, for safety reasons mentioned before. The model must maintain the same heading whilst dropping first one wing and then the other, with a yaw of at least 20° in each direction.

16. Flight function performed by prototype aircraft. This covers a whole multitude of possibilities from aerobatic manoeuvres to specialised items such as smoke generators, crop spraying, message snatching and any function that the prototype was capable of. Proof must be given to the judges of the authenticity of this function by the subject aircraft.

17. Flight in triangular circuit.

18. Flight in rectangular circuit.

19. Flight in straight line at constant height.
The above three options are intended as alternatives for non-aerobatic models without any other special features. They can only be described as dull options but, with a 'K' factor of 4, it is difficult to rule out the straight line flight as a points gatherer!

20. Flight in straight line with one motor throttled. With the above option (19) being available it is difficult to see why anyone should choose to select this manoeuvre. There are few multi-engined aircraft that are entirely happy flying with one engine throttled back, the problems are certainly not made any easier with a model in this condition.

So, "you pays your money and you takes your choice". It is unfortunate that, as with selection of prototypes, it does not seem to be prudent to be too ambitious in the selection of flight manoeuvres. Results tend to suggest that the winners opt for the most 'foolproof' alternatives and that, for competition work, is the way to do it — use every rule to the best of your advantage.

Chapter 22

Conclusions

Once you have been bitten by the scale R/C aircraft bug, and have built and flown your first couple of scale models, there comes the time when your horizons widen and you begin to search for greater challenges. At first glance it may seem that 'it has all been done before' and that all the exciting and interesting prototypes have been modelled before. You may also think that the standards of modelling excellence must have reached zenith and that no further improvements can be made. There used to be a joke about the contestant in a scale competition who lost points because he had fitted his model 'Richthofen' pilot with the wrong coloured socks – it is now becoming less of a joke. On both counts,

of prototype selection and modelling standards, you would be wrong if you thought we had reached the ultimate. Perfection is a dream and although we must constantly strive for it, it can never be attained. For any model that we build, however much it is praised by fellow modellers, we know that there are parts of the model that are unsatisfactory and could be improved upon. Some modellers get near to the topmost peak of scale R/C modelling and some will go to extraordinary lengths to duplicate all aspects of the prototypes. Some years ago a modeller par excellence took as his subject a De Havilland *Tiger Moth* biplane as used in the Barnstormers Flying Circus – a group of itinerant

The shape of things to come? This twin impeller A10 shown at Dortmund spans 2.32m – 91½ ins!

aviators organising Air Displays throughout Britain. He not only built a superb replica of this aircraft but he used to regularly visit the displays to see whether any modifications had been made to the 'Tiger' or if there were any new scratches or marks. These would be faithfully reproduced on the model, including simulation of a wallpaper patch on an aileron which, on the prototype, had to be fitted as a hasty repair when the linen covering had been torn by some barbed wire. On a ferry flight from Ireland to England, following an Air Display, the weather deteriorated very rapidly and the aircraft in the travelling circus had to divert to an alternative airfield. Unfortuantely, due to the very poor visibility conditions, the pilot of the 'Tiger' found himself on the inside of a group turn and banking fairly steeply. A mixture of lack of visible horizon, vertigo, steep turn and pulling in too much up elevator caused the aircraft to flick into a spin (have we read of this problem before?). Thanks to some splendid work by the R.A.F. Air Sea Rescue service the pilot and his passenger were hauled out of the water and into the helicopter within six minutes of crashing into the sea – the 'Tiger' sank irretrievably to the bottom in less than this time. This put our scale modelling fanatic in a real quandary; should he go to the nearest cliff, fly the model over the sea, put it in a spin and watch it sink below the waves? In the end he settled for a less painful compromise and superimposed a photograph of the model on to a sea-scape with the model descending into the waves and the pilot standing up saluting. Incidentally, the pilot of the full size *Tiger Moth* was British National R/C Scale champion and he also has constructed an excellent scale model of this fated subject.

Regarding prototype selection, there is nothing to fear from a shortage of subjects, as a glance through any reference books on aircraft will quickly show. For example, this book has failed to cover the ever-growing interest in Helicopters, Autogiros and Seaplanes, not because of any lack of interest in these subjects but simply through a lack of space. Helicopters have now come of age and scale R/C models must now outnumber the sports variety, twin rotor models have been successfully flown and there are few prototypes that can now be classified as 'impossible'. Autogiros, although a much more limited field, are also becoming a practical proposition, but only after many years of research.

Considering that very many modellers live within reasonable distances of fresh water or sea water areas, we make very poor use of the water facilities available for our radio controlled model aircraft. All too few flying boats and seaplane prototypes are modelled and the numbers of events and contests organised for these classes of models are very limited. Modellers who have taken the trouble to experiment with water-based models know of the delights of this form of flying and are invariably enthusiastic about their experiences. Taking off from, and landing back on, water adds another dimension to your flying and the sight of a model accelerating across the water, rising onto the step of the hull or floats and lifting majestically off the waves, is stirring – and not something that can be experienced with land-based aircraft. Certainly there may be a greater challenge in the design, construction and operation of a flying boat or seaplane – the rewards more than compensate for the extra effort expended. Once again, there can be no excuses tendered for the lack of scale subjects, there are a wealth of prototypes just crying out to be modelled. The range is vast and varies from the earliest 'sticks and string' examples such as the *Voisin* of the first decade of the century to the imposing and stately *Clipper* and *Empire* flying boats of the pre W.W.2 era. Plenty of small flying boats and floatplanes are still in existence and suitable prototype subjects have abounded throughout the history of aviation. Floatplanes come in a diverse selection of shapes and sizes, the Americans had their Curtises, Sikorskys and Grummans, the British aircraft such as the Sopwith *Baby,* the *Swordfish* and the superb Schneider Trophy racers. The Germans have always been seaplane minded with Rumplers in W.W.1 and Arados and Dorniers in later years; during the W.W.2 period the Japanese had a great range of floatplane types. A surprising number of conventional land-planes have been fitted with floats and the selection of prototypes converted to aquatic activity was quite amazing. *Tiger Moths, Spitfires, Dakotas,* not to mention a large number of light aircraft, have all been fitted with floats and there were even plans to fit them to *Lancasters.* Literally, there is a choice of hundreds of prototypes that operated from water, but experience shows that you are not necessarily limited to flying these designs from water, since they can be operated by utilising a take-off dolly and landing back on the grass. Or you can select one of the amphibious designs and have the best of both worlds.

Large scale models are here to stay, as described in a previous chapter, and who is to deny the awesome grandeur of a twenty-two foot wing span *Lancaster*? At the opposite end of the scale there is much development work to be done on indoor R/C scale models. With radio equipment becoming available in the 'flea-weight' class, ultra-light scale models, powered by electric motors or CO_2 motors, are eminently practical. The CO_2 engine in particular, now they have developed more efficient storage tanks, offers a real potential for indoor scale models and it would be surprising if this aspect of R/C modelling did not become more popular in the future. One can envisage national competitions being held in the large conference centres that offer ample indoor areas for such events – or some of the excellent sports stadia now in existence. No doubt a class of 'Peanut' R/C scale models would start at a relatively simple and basic level and develop quite rapidly to a high standard scale event.

Ducted fan units have given the chance to model some of the jet propelled proto-types of the last thirty-five years or so. Efficiencies of these units are improving and designers are becoming more aware of the aerodynamic requirements for models using this motive force, but what we are looking for is a true gas turbine engine that works on the same principle as the full size jets. Experiments have been made in this field with, recently, great success; when some entrepreneur can see a commercial outlet for them the development will move ahead more rapidly. Costs of such engines would be extremely high, the amount of research and engineering would make this inevit-able; there would, however, be quite a few enthusiasts prepared to purchase such an engine for the kudos of flying a true scale R/C jet model. What may seem impossible today often becomes the commonplace tomorrow and our modelling children are likely to be build-ing and flying more jet type models than propeller driven types.

Within the ranks of the existingly feasible projects there is plenty of scope for more formalised use of scale model aircraft. Modellers tend often to be 'loners' but there has been a steady increase in the participation of R/C models at public events and the many displays organised purely for the public entertainment by clubs and groups. Good as some of these displays are, there is a lot still to be done to realise the full potential of the R/C models. Scale setpieces could be devised, re-enacting an episode from our aviation past, air battles, attacks on shipping, famous solo flights, air display simulations, etc. etc. Formation work with R/C models calls for a lot of practice and understanding but it is possible, can be very thrilling to watch – and nerve-racking to perform. Presenting R/C scale modelling to the general public in an entertaining and responsible way can only benefit the hobby. It will prove to them that it is an adult hobby with all the virtues of which we are already fully aware, and a closer understanding of our problems relative to flying fields – and noise – will certainly do no harm. By taking our hobby to the people we may get more converts and anyone who is engrossed in a satisfying hobby or sport wil want to spread the 'gospel'.

I have had the good fortune in my modelling career to have had the opportunity to design, build and fly R/C scale model aircraft for films and television programmes. It has been a fascinating, rewarding and on occasions, fraught and frustrating experience and one that I accept as a tremendous bonus to my modelling activities. To be able to pursue a | hobby that is satisfying is good, to be asked to do it and to be paid for the privilege of doing it is doubly good. Nearly twenty years ago my brother and I realised the potential of using R/C scale models for film work –

he was a film stunt pilot and we had both been involved in organising and flying in full-size air displays. Some of our first experiments involved flying R/C models from a helicopter (piloted by Gilbert Chomat who was responsible for the superb camera helicopter flying in the 'Sound of Music' and 'Blue Max' films) and the results of these experiences confirmed our views. Knowing that something is possible, and persuading the authorities that it should be done are two different matters and the initial lack of enthusiasm from the film companies was not encouraging. Unfortunately, too, the rare occasions that R/C models were used in films did not meet with unqualified success. Film agents tended to select individuals that were supposedly at the top of their modelling tree (and some of them turned out to be 'prima donnas') instead of choosing a team. Eventually, however, some television work came along in the form of building and flying a number of W.W.1 British and German R/C model aircraft for a series for the BBC called 'Wings'. As this was the first drama series to include R/C model aircraft as a major part of the production it was essential that it was successful. Quite simply, if the model sequences were not effective they did not have a drama series – between 10 and 12% of the viewing time concerned the flying of aircraft and 95% of that involved the models. As soon as the Directors accepted that an R/C model could be 'stage directed' in the same way that they directed actors and actresses, we were in business. Much was learned in that first thirteen episodes of 'Wings', both from the film production side and from the point of view of finishing and the flying of the models. If competition flying is tension making, flying for film work can be positively fraught with

Two of the author's 11ft. DC3 Dakotas built for the TV series "Airline"

anxiety. You are flying before the most critical of all judges – the camera lens – and every flight is to simulate specific action. Sometimes you would have to perform a particular sequence many, many times until all the factors of filming were correct, i.e. the model entered frame at the right height and attitude, performed the manoeuvres correctly, flew out of frame at the right position, there was no camera wobble, the model was in focus, the light was correct, no birds flew into the foreground, no out of period background came into view, etc. etc. When the particular sequence happened to be an approach and landing (on a spot) complete with crosswind as well, with a closely defined roll out route,

you can imagine that concentration was at a premium. Some days we (two pilots with an occasional third) got through the best part of five gallons of fuel and that represents enough scale flying for anyone in one day. The programmes were sufficiently successful to warrant a second series of 'Wings' being produced and altogether we built three Avro 504K, three Albatros C1, six BE2C, three Fokker *Eindekker* and one Sopwith *Pup* models. All the models were to one sixth scale, built to approximately Stand-Off Scale standards and had to be strong enough to withstand the fairly rugged operating conditions that frequently prevailed. Some models clocked up over 250 flights – not bad for a scale model – and only

Another eleven-footer, a D.H.88 Comet for a TV programme not started as this book was published.

No project need be too ambitious. Although this 747/Space Shuttle uses airscrews (removed for display) gas turbines could be available by the middle 1980s.

one could be considered as a total write-off; we *did* learn a lot about repairing models, though. In the second series, where a considerable amount of three and four up 'dog fights' were scripted, we had six mid-air collisons in one week and a Fokker *Eindekker* that was involved in five of the collisons is still flying! Just imagine going down to your local flying field and participating in a 'no-holds-barred' dog fight *and* being paid for it – even if we were responsible for repairing the models!

Since then I have been involved in the aircraft sequences for the 'Flambards' drama series (Bleriots, Blackburn *Monoplanes* and similar early flying machines) and a number of other television and film projects. It represents a different facet of scale R/C model aircraft building and flying, an exciting and challenging one but, more importantly, one that could help to bring the hobby into good repute and have the respect of the public. Not everyone can be lucky enough to make a profit out of their hobby – and I do consider myself to have been very lucky in that respect – but anyone can profit from the enjoyment and satisfaction that R/C scale modelling can bring.

I hope that this book has opened up a few new modelling vistas, has increased your awareness of, and enthusiasm for, designing, constructing and flying radio controlled scale model aircraft. If, on the other hand, you believe that you *have* done it all before – now is the time to go fishing. Or, to misquote Dr. Johnson, ''If you are tired of modelling, you are tired of life''.